Unvanquished

Unvanquished

A U.S.–U.N. SAGA

Boutros Boutros-Ghali

RANDOM HOUSE

NEW YORK

Grateful acknowledgment is made to the following for permission to reprint previously published material:

The Economist: Excerpts from "Boutros Boutros and the Weight of the World" (*The Economist*, 5/23/92, pg. 43). Copyright © 1992 by The Economist Newspaper Group, Inc. Reprinted by permission. Further reproduction prohibited. www.economist.com.

MICHAEL IGNATIEFF: Excerpts from "The Seductiveness of Moral Disgust" by Michael Ignatieff. Originally published in *The New Yorker*. This essay also appeared in *The Warrior's Honor: Ethnic War and the Modern Conscience* (New York: Metropolitan Books, Henry Holt and Company, Inc., 1997). Reprinted by permission of Michael Ignatieff.

The New York Times: Excerpt from "The New World Cops" (editorial) from June 28, 1992, and "Conflict in the Balkans . . ." by R. Cohen from August 31, 1995. Copyright © 1992, 1995 by The New York Times Company. Reprinted by permission of *The New York Times*.

TIME, INC.: Excerpt from "Under Fire" from the January 18, 1993, issue of *Time* magazine. Copyright © 1993 Time, Inc. Reprinted by permission.

The Washington Post: Excerpt from the editorial "279 Security Council Vetoes Later" (June 21, 1992). Copyright © 1992 by The Washington Post. Reprinted by permission.

Library of Congress Cataloging-in-Publication Data
Boutros-Ghali, Boutros
Unvanquished : a U.S.-U.N. saga/by Boutros Boutros-Ghali.
p.   cm.
Includes index.
ISBN 0-375-50050-2
1. United Nations—United States.   2. United Nations.
Secretary General.   3. Boutros-Ghali, Boutros, 1922–
I. Title.   II. Title: Unvanquished, a United States-United Nations saga.
JZ4997.5.U55B68   1999   341.23'73—dc21   98-44866

Random House website address: www.atrandom.com
Printed in the United States of America on acid-free paper
2 4 6 8 9 7 5 3
First Edition

I dedicate this book to the men and women of the United Nations,
civilians and soldiers together, who have given their labor,
talents, learning, and on many occasions their lives, to the cause of
peace, development, and democracy for all peoples.

A Note on the Text

The patience of the reader and the common sense of the author require that only part of my years as secretary-general of the United Nations be covered here. I do not go into the remarkable success story of El Salvador or other undoubted UN achievements, such as its crucial role in helping to end apartheid or to facilitate Mozambique's transition from a closed to an open society. Nor have I taken up certain problems that, despite many years of time and effort, continue to occupy the United Nations, such as Cyprus and Western Sahara. My emphasis in this book is on the United Nations' most controversial, difficult, and portentous problems.

After the U.S. veto of my reelection as secretary-general, there came a widespread perception that I must have been in an adversarial position with the United States from the start and that my alienation must have deepened as a result of being the only UN secretary-general to be denied a second term. This book tells of many difficult encounters. Whatever criticism you may encounter in these pages is the result of disappointment, for my admiration for the United States has never diminished. My hope is that the United States, which created the United Nations in 1945, will eventually allow the organization to fulfill its original promise.

Acknowledgments

I greatly appreciate the support provided for this project by the director of the Hoover Institution, Dr. John Raisian; Deputy Director Charles Palm; and Archivist Elena Danielson. Editor Romayne Ponleithner's incisive contributions were indispensable to the completion of this volume.

Many colleagues and friends have helped me in preparing this book. I will not list them, as many have asked not to be mentioned, but they all have my deepest thanks.

Contents

Unvanquished

American Support:
Loss After Gain

(1991–1992)

As the end of my five-year term as UN secretary-general approached, some friends, colleagues, and UN member states asked me to seek a second term. In their view I had strengthened the independence of the secretary-general's job and performed it well. All previous secretaries-general had served two consecutive terms; if I did not do so, it would be a slight to my country, Egypt, and to my continent, Africa. I agreed. And to be honest, my own pride and sense of achievement drove me to want a second term. There was a risk, however: 1996 was an American presidential election year. Only once every two decades did a UN and a U.S. presidential election fall in the same year. I knew that the UN decision might get caught in American politics. It did.

In January 1996 I was invited to give a lecture at Oxford University. Two of my predecessors had lectured there, Dag Hammarskjold in 1961 and Javier Pérez de Cuéllar in 1986. Both had spoken about the role of the secretary-general. So did I, though my world had changed dramatically from theirs. My lecture stressed the importance of an independent secretary-general, as envisioned by the UN Charter, and the urgent need to find new ways to finance UN operations, since the United States refused to pay its contribution.

My words angered the White House and Congress. Staff aides and spokesmen for both parties noted that I had been far too independent over the past five years. My suggestion that a modest levy on international airfares might be used to finance UN expenses was denounced in the Senate as an attempt to impose taxes on American citizens in defiance of the U.S. Constitution. Although I was merely repeating an idea first put forward by Pérez de Cuéllar and backed by me five years before, the UN Information Office in Washington used the word "firestorm" in describing Washington's reaction to my Oxford lecture. Forty-some members of Congress from both sides of the aisle signed a letter criticizing me.

In mid-February 1996, at a reception I was giving at the secretary-general's residence on Sutton Place in New York City, I asked to have a word with two friends, former Secretary of State Cyrus Vance and David Hamburg, president of the Carnegie Corporation. I wanted their advice. Should I say publicly that I would be a candidate for a second term as secretary-general? Or should I avoid the issue and be "undecided" during the American presidential campaign?

Cy replied that the two events—the U.S. and UN elections—should be kept as separate as possible in the minds of the public. I was then being regularly derided and attacked by Senator Bob Dole, the leading Republican candidate for president. His mocking pronunciation of my name—Boo-trus, Boo-trus—sounded like a jeering crowd, and his claim that American troops served under my "command" invariably aroused his audiences. Candidates on the right were telling Americans that the United Nations was a global conspiracy to rob them of their sovereignty and that "black helicopters" belonging to the United Nations had been overflying the Rocky Mountain states in preparation for a UN takeover of the country. So, Cy said, perhaps I should declare my candidacy now, early in 1996, well before the American political conventions of midsummer. I was not so sure. I was afraid that an announcement would only stimulate U.S. opposition to my reelection. I asked Cy and David to inquire quietly on my behalf.

Soon afterwards the quarterly journal *Foreign Affairs* carried a version of my Oxford lecture, in which I stressed that an independent secretary-general was essential to the United Nations' credibility. Editorials interpreted my publication of this article as a deliberate provocation of the United States. My article was said to be a thinly veiled declaration of my intention to stand for a second term.

Not in Favor

Then at 8:00 on Sunday evening, April 14, Vance and Hamburg came to see me. Cy appeared deeply embarrassed and uncertain how to begin. He took a small piece of paper out of his pocket and read a message to me from Secretary of State Warren Christopher: "The administration has decided not in favor of your reelection."

I told Cy and David that I was surprised by this message, but I would not change my mind even if the United States vetoed me. "I have strong expressions of support from Africa, Latin America, Russia, France, and China," I said. I asked Vance and Hamburg to keep Christopher's awkwardly worded message and my reaction in confidence, for if it got out, I would not be able to work normally at the United Nations, and there was a lot to do in the months ahead. I asked Cy and David to tell Christopher that I intended to remain quietly "undecided" about my future throughout the American presidential campaign. Although I would declare myself after November 5 for a full five-year second term, I wanted to assure the administration that I would step down before the end of the second term, when my work, primarily reform of the UN Secretariat, was placed on a solid footing.

Eight days later Christopher telephoned me from Jerusalem. I was surprised that he regarded the issue of my reelection as important enough to interrupt his Middle East schedule to call me. He spoke circuitously, apparently concerned that his call might be monitored. Nonetheless, I understood him to confirm that the Clinton administration had decided "not in favor" of me. I replied so that anyone who happened to be listening would understand: "I am a candidate for reelection, despite the opposition of the U.S." On May 3, 1996, *The Wall Street Journal* carried a one-paragraph item entitled "Bye-Bye Boutros," stating that the administration had decided to get rid of me as secretary-general, no doubt an official leak. The United States had already gone into action. Jean Daniel, editor of *Le Nouvel Observateur,* told me that the United States had asked Spain's prime minister, Felipe González, to become a candidate. "No," González had replied, "there is a good secretary-general now."

Early in the morning of Monday, May 13, Warren Christopher came, at his request, to see me. We sat in the Great Room, which ran the length of the secretary-general's residence in New York City. There was a fireplace at each end, one carved with the heads of George Washington and Benjamin Franklin, and the other, where we sat, displaying the likenesses of Thomas Paine and Alexander Hamilton. As always, I was impressed with Christopher's impeccable tailoring and recalled that, at the UN fiftieth anniversary gathering in San Francisco, my wife, Leia, had asked him where he had his suits made. Christopher had named a Savile Row tailor, Chester Barrie. The majordomo brought pastries and coffee in the Middle Eastern style. My guest ate heartily but seemed abashed and defensive. He said he had come to confirm what he had said on the telephone from Jerusalem, that the Clinton administration had decided that I should not continue as secretary-general. "Why?" I asked.

Christopher said he could not answer my question, "because of our friendship." I said, "Come on, Chris, as a friend you owe me an answer. It's important for me," I continued, "to understand what mistakes I have made and what I have done to provoke this." The first priority of a secretary-general, I said, has to be the relationship between the United States and the United Nations. "America is the only superpower," I said, "and this means that the U.S. dislikes the very idea of multilateralism." There always are strains and differences between the United States and the United Nations. "That is just normal," I said, "so what I have done to cause this abnormal U.S. decision?"

Christopher repeated that he could not tell me the reason. "You are an outstanding lawyer," I said. "Why not defend my case to President Clinton?" Christopher attempted a smile. "I am the president's lawyer," he said, "not your lawyer." I mentioned the many Americans I had appointed to UN jobs at Washington's request over the objections of other UN member states. I had done so, I said, because I wanted American support to succeed in my job. Christopher made no reply.

As he was leaving, I asked him to step into the library, which overlooked a lawn and the East River with its morning traffic of barges and tugboats. I gave him a book, *The Portraits of Fayoum: Faces from Ancient Egypt*. At the end of the pharaonic period in ancient Egypt the covers of sarcophagi were painted with the portraits in life of the persons mummified inside. A "portrait of Fayoum" had been discovered at an oasis near Cairo, marvelously preserved. I had wanted to possess one of these beautiful artifacts, I told Christopher, but because of the expense, I could only prize them through books, such as the one I wished to present to the secretary of state on this occasion. Christopher seemed pleased and interested in the book. Then, turning serious once more, he insisted that our talk be kept confidential and asked me not to reveal my intention to stand for reelection. I readily agreed, for publicity would damage my effectiveness in office. Because the press would be aware of our meeting, we agreed on parting to say that we had discussed the UN financial crisis.

Though Christopher refused to tell me why the United States had decided that I must go, I knew that the reason was to be found in the political dynamics of the 1996 American presidential campaign combined with the remarkable events of the previous five years.

The Politics of an International Election

My UN adventure had begun almost five years earlier, when a moment's conversation changed my life. In May 1991, as we flew over the Mediterranean from Cairo to Paris, Egyptian President Hosni Mubarak told me he was going to promote me to vice–prime minister for foreign affairs. "And, Boutros, since you love to work, I will also give you the post of minister of emigration, a ministry which needs to be gotten under control." The ministry for emigration was responsible for more than 3 million Egyptian émigrés in the Arab world, Europe, Australia, Canada, and the United States.

As Mubarak's new vice–prime minister, I was entrusted with special diplomatic missions. While representing him at the June 1991 summit of the Organization of African Unity (OAU) in Abuja, Nigeria, the post of UN secretary-general was raised in a closed meeting of leaders, for it was "Africa's turn" to select someone for the job. Candidates from Cameroon, Ghana, Nigeria, Sierra Leone, and Zimbabwe were mentioned.

"There is not a single French speaker on this list," President Omar Bongo of Gabon said. Someone else added, "They all come from West Africa." Then President Bongo confronted me: "Boutros, why don't you present yourself? You speak Arabic, French, and English; you would be an excellent secretary-general of the United Nations." I had known these leaders for fifteen years or more. I had created a special fund for cooperation in Africa with a budget of millions of Egyptian pounds under my direction, which enabled me to send hundreds of Egyptian experts to African countries each year and bring hundreds of Africans to Egypt for training. Despite the relatively modest fund, it was popular and helped explain the sudden decision of African leaders to think of me for the top UN position.

I had written the first book about the United Nations to appear in Arabic. When I was a young visiting professor at Columbia University in 1954, I had wanted to work at the United Nations. At one time I had hoped to head UNESCO in Paris. And in recent years I had thought about the post of UN secretary-general. I had had no such desire during the cold war, when the United Nations had been pushed aside by the superpowers. But now there was a real role to play and a chance to put into effect ideas I had been working on for years.

I told President Ibrahim Babangida of Nigeria, the president of the summit, that I was honored but that President Mubarak would have to agree. The African presidents replied almost in unison that they would get Mubarak's approval.

When I told President Mubarak what had happened at Abuja and that I was interested, he was not enthusiastic. "If you fail, it will be a defeat for Egypt," he said.

"Mr. President," I said, "there are elections. One may be elected, just as one may not be elected. When I stood for election to Parliament, though a member of your cabinet, I took a risk; I might have failed." I had already discussed my chances with Egypt's new minister of foreign affairs and with the president's advisers. They all said that my election would be marvelous for Egypt, but that it would not be easy. President Mubarak remained reluctant; he had just promoted me, and now I wanted to leave. But on June 16, 1991, he finally agreed. In one short month my career had taken a radical and unexpected turn.

Electing a UN secretary-general had often been an agonizing and embittering experience. And recently commentators on the United Nations have deplored the lack of a specific set of standards for choosing a secretary-general. It is ridiculous, even disgraceful, they say, to select "the world's top diplomat" for "the world's most impossible job" in such an unstructured, chaotic manner. Instead, they have proposed drawing up criteria for candidates, who would then be screened by committee, rather like choosing a Rhodes scholar or a college president. Aristotle, in his *Politics,* supports this position, saying that "it is improper that the person to be elected should canvass for the office; the worthiest should be appointed, whether he chooses or not."

But this would make the United Nations into just another international bureaucracy. The drafters of the UN Charter left the matter to be shaped largely by changing international needs, stipulating only that "the secretary-general shall be appointed by the General Assembly upon the recommendation of the Security Council." The rest is left to the messy business of politics.

The office of secretary-general is, by design, weak yet pivotal. The incumbent has no financial base and no substantial say over what goes on throughout most of the UN system. Yet in a world organization whose member states differ vastly in wealth, power, and size, the secretary-general often serves as the fulcrum for cooperative progress. But all comes down to politics, again and again.

I looked forward to campaigning for the job as a wonderful adventure. I cited Aristotle against himself. He did not say "Man is the appointed animal"; he said, "Man is the political animal." And I recognized that political animal in myself. In planning my campaign, I recognized three necessities: the backing of my own country, acceptability as the representative of my region or continent, and familiarity with the problems and leaders of every part of the world. I would have to make my case politically to gain the support of key countries, regions, groups, and international networks, not only to win office but also to be effective in the job.

France's backing would be necessary. Paris was determined that the United Nations continue to give French its proper role as the traditional language of diplomacy. I had gained Egypt's entrance into Francophonie, the worldwide association of nations sharing French language and culture, and I had personal ties to President François Mitterrand. Beyond France, I needed support from the other permanent members of the Security Council: Britain, China, Russia, and, most important, the United States.

I asked Ambassador Joseph Verner Reed, the elegant, extravagantly gracious, and talented former State Department chief of protocol, whose ironical view of the world I had long enjoyed, to speak to President Bush on my behalf. In Cairo in July I met Secretary of State James Baker and found him friendly but focused on non-African candidates. In addition to these rivals, there was another African competitor for the UN job besides me. This was Bernard Chidzero, Zimbabwe's senior economic minister, who had experience in the UN system and who was backed by the Commonwealth and Great Britain. Chidzero addressed me in French to show that he too spoke the language of Molière. I knew him well enough to tease him: "If you want the approval of France, you must not only speak French, but speak English with a French accent."

George Bush Drops In

Back in Cairo, President Mubarak handed me a letter that I was to hand-deliver to President George Bush. But in Paris on September 10 at the Quai d'Orsay, I was told in confidence that the U.S. State Department opposed my candidacy.

On September 13 I went to the White House to see National Security Adviser General Brent Scowcroft. By prearrangement, President Bush stopped in to say hello. If I had gone to the Oval Office, Bush would also have had to receive other candidates there publicly, Scowcroft said. Tall and strong-looking, Bush was impressive, a far more imposing figure in person than he seemed on television or in newspaper photographs. He was far more interested in the situation in the Middle East—Muammar Qaddafi, Saddam Hussein—than in Mubarak's letter about my candidacy.

On Capitol Hill the chairman of the Senate Foreign Relations Committee, Claiborne Pell, told me he favored the candidacy of Prince Sadruddin Aga Khan, a son of the spiritual leader of the Ismaili Muslims and a former UN high commissioner for refugees. The writer Arnaud de Borchgrave, an old friend, told me, "The White House has already decided on Sadruddin Aga Khan." Outside the developing world, few seemed to know that it was "Africa's turn."

After this brief American visit, I went to Canada as minister of emigration, a role I had almost forgotten, to meet members of the Egyptian diaspora. In Ottawa I called on Prime Minister Brian Mulroney, who listened to me talk about my UN hopes without comment.

I soon learned why. Mulroney had been President Bush's first choice to become UN secretary-general, but the White House had learned that support for Mulroney would offend Africa and the third world, which did not want anyone from the wealthy, industrialized "North." Bush had then shifted to Sadruddin Aga Khan, who he thought would be acceptable to the developing countries.

On the same trip I visited the editor of *The New York Times*, A. M. Rosenthal, who asked bluntly, "Do you want to be secretary-general?" "Of course," I replied, "that's why I have come to see you." "At last!" Rosenthal exclaimed. "Someone who is honest about what he wants!"

In late September 1991, I accompanied President Mubarak on an official visit to Moscow, which was in turmoil following the August collapse of the Soviet Union. Mubarak told me that when he met Mikhail Gorbachev tête-à-tête, it was the Soviet leader who mentioned my name first and said that he would firmly support me. I had a long-established relationship with Moscow and had worked to restore Egyptian-Soviet ties after President Anwar Sadat broke with the USSR in 1979. I was president of the Egypt-USSR Friendship Society, a position I had sought precisely because I was pro-American and did not want the job to go to someone who might undermine U.S. policy in the Middle East. Gorbachev later told me that after we left Moscow, Prime Minister John Major of Great Britain called to propose Gro Harlem Brundtland, the Norwegian prime minister, for the UN job. "We have already committed ourselves to Egypt," Gorbachev replied.

A Letter from Friends

Back in Cairo, I telephoned the American ambassador, Frank Wisner, to tell him of Moscow's support so that he could pass the word to the State Department. I was picking up commitments, but I did not know how to deal with Washington. Ambassador Roy Atherton organized Ambassadors Lucius Battle, Hermann Eilts, and Nicholas Veliotes—all of whom had served in Cairo—to write a letter to President Bush. Wisner too would have signed had he not been barred from doing so as an active member of the U.S. administration, Atherton told me. "In our judgment," the four ambassadors wrote, "Dr. Boutros-Ghali has the stature, breadth of experience, international respect and recognition, intellectual vigor and creativity, and diplomatic skills required to lead the institutions of the United Nations in the years ahead." Reed delivered the letter to Bush by hand. Reed told me later that Bush's favorable opinion of Sadruddin Aga Khan was not shared by Baker, who had not liked Sadruddin's handling of the UN humanitarian program for Iraq and Kuwait at the time of the Gulf War. Baker supported Hans van den Broek, the former Dutch foreign minister. In October at the General Assembly session in New York, Reed had a sharp discussion with Baker when Reed told him that the next secretary-general would have to come from Africa. By this time, Bernard Chidzero and I were running neck and neck; all other African candidates had been effectively eliminated.

On Thursday morning, November 20, at the Hôtel Crillon in Paris, I met the American assistant secretary for international organizations, John Bolton. He was "at odds," I had been told, with Secretary-General Javier Pérez de Cuéllar, apparently feeling that Pérez de Cuéllar had been insufficiently attentive to American interests. I assured Bolton of my own serious regard for U.S. policy. "Without American support," I said, "the United Nations would be paralyzed." Not long after our meeting Bolton made a strong statement before the Congress, declaring that "UN peacekeeping remains one of the best bargains there is with respect to the maintenance of world peace." Obviously, Bolton told the Congress, "the amounts which the world spends on UN peacekeeping are only the minutest fraction of what the world spends on armaments."

Later that day, still in Paris, Abdel Raouf Al-Ridy, Egypt's ambassador to Washington, told me that Baker was ready to support me. Could this be true?

I had flown to Bonn to ask German Foreign Minister Hans-Dietrich Genscher to help me get U.S. backing. The decisive vote might be taken at the United Nations in New York that same evening, but I was exhausted and fell asleep. At midnight, I was awakened by a noise at the door and a victory cry: "We won! We won!"

The next morning I telephoned my wife, Leia, and President Mubarak. Cairo was jubilant, they said. Crowds of people were in the streets congratulating one another. Klaxons were blowing all over the city, as if Egypt had won the World Cup in soccer. For the first time an Arab had been elected to a major international office! I telephoned President Mitterrand to thank him and called on Foreign Minister Genscher. "I knew that you would win," he said. "I always bet the winning horse." That afternoon in Germany I received President Bush's congratulations. Later I was told that Bush and Baker had failed to agree on a candidate and so had given the U.S. ambassador to the United Nations, Thomas Pickering, no definite instructions. The United States had abstained in the vote that elected me the sixth secretary-general of the United Nations.

My investiture took place in New York on December 3. I took my oath in Arabic and gave my speech in three languages, Arabic, English, and French. I cited the medieval Islamic philosopher al-Farabi, who had dreamed of "the virtuous city." The greatest dream of all, I said, would be a virtuous association of nations, and I hoped the United Nations would fulfill this vision. I set out themes that would characterize my five years in office: peace and the need for diplomacy to prevent conflict; development to narrow the gap between North and South; reform to prepare the United Nations for the post–cold war world; and democratization not only within states but also among the states of the international system.

By chance President Nelson Mandela of South Africa was in New York, and his presence gave a special symbolic value to the inauguration of the first secretary-general from Africa.

On Tuesday, December 5, in Washington, I had warm meetings with Baker, Scowcroft, Lawrence Eagleburger, and Bolton, all of whom were far more familiar than I with the intricate mechanisms of the United Nations. President Bush received me in the Oval Office, where I stressed my commitment to reforming the UN Secretariat. Emerging from the White House, I avoided the press corps and went to a hospital to see Moussa Sabry, an Egyptian editorialist and former confidant of President Sadat. With his usual lively expression and curious intelligence, Moussa Sabry wanted to know every detail of what had happened. Together we had gone through many difficult times. He was dying of cancer, and I knew I was losing a colleague and dear friend.

Returning to Egypt, I submitted my resignation as vice-premier and minister, as member of Parliament and the National Democratic Party, as president of the Society of African Studies, as president of the Egypt-USSR Friendship Society, and as editor in chief of *Siassa Dawlya* (International Politics), a review I had founded years before.

In my last parliamentary meeting, the president of the Chamber of Deputies, Fathi Sorour, declared, "Your nomination is an honor for each Egyptian, each Arab, each African . . . the selection of a scholar, of a minister, of a parliamentarian like you to occupy this post during this time in history, is a tribute to Egyptian diplomacy." His remarks were interrupted again and again by applause. Praise is a heady wine, and it is easy to acquire a taste for it. But the applause was for the nation and people of Egypt, and all of us in the Chamber were filled with pride at this international tribute to our country.

On December 18, 1991, Hosni Mubarak gave me a ceremonial embrace and awarded me the Grand Cordon of the Nile. As he pinned the decoration on me, he whispered, "I am going to ruin your suit, but you can get a new one in New York." Mubarak and I shared a love of fine suits. Much later I could only smile when a critic called me "The Suit in History." Thus I began a new career at age sixty-nine.

The House on Sutton Place

The four-story Georgian town house at 3–5 Sutton Place had been built during the 1930s for a daughter of J. P. Morgan and later bought by Arthur Houghton of Corning Glass, who had offered it to the U.S. government as a residence for the American ambassador to the United Nations. When his offer was rejected in 1972, he gave it to the United Nations Association of the USA when that private organization was seeking a suitable residence for the UN secretary-general.

But I could not move in, I was told, because the building was about to undergo extensive maintenance and remodeling. A $2 million to $3 million budget had been approved by my predecessor. A new roof was needed, and all the windows would be bullet-proofed. The whole house would be air-conditioned. A Jacuzzi would be installed. While the work proceeded I would live at the Waldorf-Astoria at a cost of about $40,000 a month, an unthinkable sum. How could I live at the Waldorf at such a cost? To me, the house looked fine. I saw no need for bullet-proof windows. I had the roof inspected and after minor repairs, it was pronounced "okay." I did not want the bureaucrats to treat me like an Arab sheikh, which they seemed to want to do. I decided to move into Sutton Place after a few weeks of basic maintenance work.

In Egypt the sunrise means life, which is why the tombs of the pharaohs are all on the west side of the Nile. Our house in Cairo had a magnificent view of sunrise over the Nile, and Leia and I were delighted that the house on Sutton Place overlooked the East River. We tried to make the rooms reminiscent of our Cairo life. I installed my large collection of bronze birds, some of enormous size, which I had acquired from China, Egypt, India, Iran, Japan, and Syria. In the library I arrayed my collection of Ottoman pen cases, a kind of scabbard used by the official scribes and high secretaries of the empire. I had begun the collection as a student, when my mother had given me the pen case of my grandfather, a historian, saying, "This is for you because you are now the scholar of the family." Our friends at the Metropolitan Museum of Art lent us paintings by French artists whose work we had loved when we had lived in Paris: two works of Matisse's Moroccan period for the library, a Dufy for one end of the Great Room, and a Utrillo for the other. In the small study we hung a Léger. In the dining room we placed a painting by Kandinsky and a sculpture by Archipenko and called it the Russian Room. I had sent from Egypt two Coptic sculptures from the fifth and sixth centuries and placed them in juxtaposition with a contemporary stone mask from Zimbabwe, with striking effect.

I spent long hours in the early weekends of the year arranging the art and books and antiques. I tried something similar, on a small scale, in my UN office, putting up a painting by Kees van Dongen lent by the Museum of Modern Art. Later, when Mrs. "Happy" Rockefeller came to the thirty-eighth floor, she exclaimed, "That's *my* van Dongen!" She had lent it to the Museum of Modern Art and had hung a copy in her home.

First Order of Business: Reform

Only a week or two after moving onto the thirty-eighth floor of the UN Secretariat building, I began to realize that the United Nations was far from ready for center stage in international affairs. Its performance was not up to that of the major foreign ministries of the world. In 1992 the United Nations had barely begun to acquire the information technology that by then was taken for granted by government agencies, businesses, and academic institutions involved in world affairs. The staff, which included many dedicated, intelligent, and well-educated people, was nevertheless bloated, slack, and out of touch, partly because the United Nations had been marginalized by the superpowers during the cold war. Some UN officials owed their jobs, and a good part of their income, to their national governments, and they often considered the implications for their relations with their home countries instead of attending to the job at hand. The international civil service as a whole lacked the intensity and independence intended under the Charter.

As secretary-general, I had no authority to transform the system on my own, but I at once took action to launch some drastic reforms. In the first briefing book I received, I learned that the Secretariat was organized into "some 35 departments," as if the exact number were not known. I set myself a sixty-day deadline for streamlining the Secretariat and quickly went about reorganizing the thirty-eighth floor, the "command post" of UN headquarters. My office was on the north end of the floor, overlooking the East River. I soon discovered with delight that some tiny birds were conducting their affairs outside my windows, apparently trying to nest there. They were house finches, I was told. I marveled at how such small creatures could function in the strong winds so far above the ground. I wondered whether I could do as well.

"If you can abolish one or two positions, you will be doing much," Secretary-General Pérez de Cuéllar had said to me as he handed over the office. I wanted to go far beyond that. In February 1992 I announced the first changes to consolidate UN functions into well-defined categories. For example, I created a Department of Political Affairs that incorporated six former departments: Security Council Affairs, Special Political Questions (which had dealt primarily with decolonization), the Center Against Apartheid, General Assembly Affairs, Disarmament, and Research. I then abolished eighteen high-level posts, such as the director-general for development, the under secretary-general for law of the sea, and the under secretary-general for conference services. These cuts saved some $4 million. In addition, I delegated and decentralized the system by stopping the practice of having dozens of top officials report directly to me. Other reforms aimed to reduce budgetary and staff levels.

I was determined to reduce inefficiency and overlap sharply, but almost every staff member I transferred, demoted, or removed turned to his or her national government for help, and I was besieged by ambassadors demanding to know why I was taking punitive measures against their nations. I antagonized the staff by my public comments about the UN bureaucracy being even worse than that of my own national government, in which I had served for more than forty years.

Most alarming was the revelation that the United Nations, now about to be entrusted with new and unprecedented responsibilities, was on the brink of insolvency. Pérez de Cuéllar, in his farewell address to the General Assembly, said that despite valiant efforts to solve the United Nations' financial crisis, he was compelled to report that he had failed. Because the United States refused to honor its legal obligation to pay its dues (formally, its "assessed contribution") in full and on time, many other countries felt free to ignore their own obligations, claiming that they would only be paying what the Americans owed.

As I came onto the job, unpaid assessments were close to $1 billion, about half relating to the regular budget and half to peacekeeping operations. Only 67 of 159 member states had paid their regular assessments in full. The United Nations had been drawing on cash reserves to pay its current operating expenses, but by August 1991 the reserves were exhausted. There was no choice but to borrow from the few solvent peacekeeping operations to keep the organization going. I was informed as I first walked into my office that "the Secretary-General's capacity to resort to ad hoc arrangements and stopgap measures has been virtually exhausted." Pérez de Cuéllar had bequeathed to me a set of proposals aimed at ending the crisis, such as commercial borrowing or charging interest on assessments not paid on time. I was grateful for his ingenuity, but I did not see how these proposals would ever win support.

I knew that I must make immediate, even shocking, decisions to try to bring real reform to the organization. In May 1992 I suggested, but did not specifically recommend, a list of ways to pay for the new demands by member states for more UN peacekeeping operations. Some of these ideas had come from my predecessor; some were new. I asked the member states for an emergency peacekeeping fund of $50 million and an endowment fund of $1 billion. I suggested that the United Nations' perpetual financial crisis might be solved by such measures as a tiny tax on international air tickets, a levy on arms transfers, interest charges on unpaid UN assessments, and payment of UN peacekeeping assessments out of national defense budgets, which would illustrate how small were the costs of UN peacekeeping in comparison with the huge military outlays of the major powers. But with a fourfold increase in the demands being made on the United Nations at a time when it verged on bankruptcy, I had to generate new ideas to raise money.

The Volcker-Ogata Report

I asked Paul Volcker, the former chairman of the U.S. Federal Reserve Bank, and Shujiro Ogata, former deputy governor of the Bank of Japan, to convene an independent international advisory group to consider the United Nations' financial crisis. Their report, submitted twelve months later, stressed "the contrast between the demands placed on the United Nations and the smallness and precariousness of its financial base."

The United Nations, Volcker and Ogata said, provides "the only existing framework for building the institutions of a global society. While practicing all the requisite managerial rigor and financial economy, it must have the resources—a pittance by comparison with our society's expenditures on arms—to serve the great objectives that are set forth in its Charter."

The report's key recommendations stated that all countries must pay their UN dues on time and in full; that the United Nations should be authorized to charge interest on late payments; that governments should include payments for UN peacekeeping in their national defense budgets; and that a $400 million revolving reserve fund be created for peacekeeping, financed by three annual assessments.

The great merit of the report was its clear and simple message: The United Nations is vital, and its member states should pay their dues. Many readers viewed the report as directed specifically at the United States. I personally gave the Volcker-Ogata report to President Bush and provided copies to all UN member states. I then transmitted it to the General Assembly, but it took no action.

President Bush asked me what I wanted in an American on my staff. "You are interested in reform," I said, "so let me have a good administrator, someone who will demonstrate that the U.S. is strongly in favor of change." Bush proposed former governor of Pennsylvania and attorney general of the United States Richard Thornburgh, whom I named under secretary-general for administration and management. Thornburgh was deeply interested in humanitarian problems, especially those of the disabled, and invited me to a reception he had organized at the United Nations. When I was introduced to one of the delegates, I automatically extended my arm to shake hands, but he had no right hand. I turned toward his left hand, but he had no left hand. He smiled at me and said, "Put your hands on my shoulders." I did but was so moved by his courage that I could not speak. I put Thornburgh in charge of reform issues and said I would support whatever he recommended. Because I believed that the focus of the United Nations must be in "the field," where economic, social, and political decisions take effect, a unified UN presence at the country level would enhance the impact of the United Nations' various efforts. The United States agreed and recommended that I appoint UN resident coordinators. I insisted that every UN program in a capital city be located in a single building or complex so that support systems could be consolidated and costs cut drastically.

On one of my first trips as secretary-general, I was shown a UN field operation in Accra, Ghana, where different UN agency operations were physically separated by a wall and each side had its own administrative organization. In an explosive show of temper, as the officials on the scene gaped in astonishment, I demanded that the wall be torn down at once.

When attending diplomatic receptions in one national capital after another, I had been struck by the absurd sight of half a dozen or more vehicles parked outside the host embassy, all sporting the blue UN flag. Now that I was secretary-general, I would consolidate UN representation in the capitals of member states and ensure that there was just one "UN representative," without impairing the ability of the agencies to carry out their various individual tasks.

Fortunately, I also had an opportunity to innovate. The United Nations was establishing itself in the capitals of the newly independent republics of the Soviet Union. During the winter of 1992–1993 I succeeded in opening UN "interim offices" in seven of these capitals. What was new was that these offices were in common premises, their heads bore the title of UN representative, and they were responsible for coordinating not only the United Nations' developmental and humanitarian programs but also its peacemaking and other political activities, including public information. In the three capitals where the UN representative was from the Secretariat in New York and not from one of the agencies, there were ominous institutional and personality problems. But, encouraged by my small success, I set up a task force to prepare a scheme for wider application.

After several months of hard interagency negotiation, the task force recommended that I submit to the General Assembly proposals to consolidate what had been achieved and to apply the same arrangement to other states that were newly independent, such as Eritrea, or were emerging from a long civil conflict, such as Cambodia. The offices would be renamed "integrated offices." My intention was to make this arrangement standard throughout the world.

But even these modest proposals were defeated in the General Assembly. The opposition was led by my erstwhile colleagues in the nonaligned movement, who variously accused me of aspiring to sovereign powers by appointing "UN ambassadors," of wanting to gather intelligence, and of diverting to political purposes money that had been contributed for development and humanitarian relief. This last point rang a bell with some of the donors. And I was told that the agencies were active in the corridors. I tried to save the day, but my proposals foundered. I was quickly learning how difficult it was to reform the United Nations.

The UN bureaucracy was further shocked when I ordered that no under secretary-general could travel without my approval and directed that all other high official travel had to be personally approved by an appropriate supervisor. I decided to do this soon after I took office and found the members of the "inner cabinet" that I had created were frequently abroad and I was the last one to learn of their travels. Money was being wasted on unnecessary "special missions." I also upset the bureaucracy by putting all high political appointees on one-year contracts, instead of the traditional three- or five-year contracts; if they performed well, the longer term would be approved. This seemed only rational to me, but a journalist in the UN press corps described me as hanging a "sword of Damocles" over the heads of my colleagues.

The UN staff complained that these reforms made them feel even more overworked, underappreciated, and underpaid, and I was denounced by member states whenever the sinecures of their own citizens were threatened. A *New York Times* review of my first reforms was headlined RED TAPE CUT, FEATHERS RUFFLED, FUNDS EXHAUSTED. The first two of these phrases were owing to me; the third resulted from the failure of the United States to pay its dues.

The U.S. arrears compelled me to focus almost entirely on financial expedients, such as shifting funds out of peacekeeping accounts to cover regular budget expenses. The United Nations was living hand to mouth. By midsummer 1992 I had to take the unprecedented step of notifying the member states that the United Nations might not have enough money to operate beyond the end of summer. UN monthly operating costs were $310 million, and our total cash reserves were $380 million. Meanwhile, UN members owed $848 million to the regular UN budget and $1.2 billion for peacekeeping operations. "Unless the United Nations receives substantial payments of outstanding assessed contributions within the next month . . . it will not be possible to finance new missions, and even existing operations will be in jeopardy," I wrote in a series of personal letters to the leaders of countries in arrears. The United States was the worst offender, with arrears of $517 million of the $848 million owing to the regular account.

I announced drastic cost-cutting measures. I ordered the Secretariat to curtail services, such as translation for conferences and working groups. I sharply reduced official travel and eliminated weekend meetings. I decided to reduce by more than 20 percent the number of temporary staff normally engaged for the General Assembly's session. Most controversially, considering the daily work schedule at the United Nations, I declared that meetings of the General Assembly would not be provided with staff services beyond 6:00 P.M. These steps would create a new working culture at the United Nations.

Reform Brings Opposition

United Nations Staff Day would not be much of a celebration this autumn, I was told, because of the "wild rumors about impending staff cuts and changes." So I tried to convey to the UN staff my awareness of the fact that, though unappreciated and underpaid, they were over-burdened. I knew that their families felt the pressure, and in peace-keeping duties many of them were risking their lives. I said that a Secretariat with a streamlined structure, clearly delineated responsi-bilities, and managerial accountability would not only serve the member states better but also mean greater job satisfaction for the UN staff.

Alexis de Tocqueville noted that revolutions erupt not when things are at their worst but when reforms are making them better. This seemed to be happening to me. As I focused on reform, longtime critics of the United Nations—primarily in the U.S. Congress and press—demanded ever more, to an extent impossible to satisfy without decisions that mem-ber governments showed no inclination to make.

The attacks on me over reform were shaped by a four-part series of articles in *The Washington Post* in September 1992 written by William Branigan under the headline AS UN EXPANDS, SO DO ITS PROBLEMS: CRITICS CITE MANAGEMENT, WASTE. The series chronicled decades of bureaucratic expansion and administrative shortcomings, none of it my fault. Indeed, the series approved my investigation of the costs of peacekeeping opera-tions. Nevertheless, a variety of editorialists and politicians began to blame me personally for decades of UN mismanagement and expected me to clean it up immediately and completely. This I was ready to at-tempt, but I could accomplish only so much with my limited powers. Most of the excesses Branigan cited resulted from the demands of the member states, not from the UN organization itself. The main problem, as the *Washington Post* series correctly pointed out, was the North-South split. To the rich nations, reform meant cutting costs, eliminating waste, and generally scaling back. To the poor, reform seemed designed to deemphasize the organization that best served and represented their interests—the United Nations. With each reform, affected bureaucracies appealed to their home governments for support, which they generally got—even when their governments had demanded UN reform in the first place.

For example, I proposed merging the ineffective Santo Domingo–based headquarters of the International Research and Training Institute for the Advancement of Women (INSTRAW) with the New York–based UN Development Fund for Women (UNIFEM) to form a stronger and more unified program for women. Prepared for a political battle, I ensured that my proposal was backed by an eight-member task force that included representatives from INSTRAW and UNIFEM, as well as from the UN Development Program (UNDP), the UN Population Fund, and the Secretariat.

No, said the Advisory Committee on Administrative and Budgetary Questions (ACABQ), an active and powerful panel composed of individual experts chosen from the UN member states, including at that time the United States. Although supposedly independent, the panel was highly politicized. It concluded that my plan to eliminate nineteen jobs at INSTRAW, relocate nine jobs to New York, and save more than $600,000 might adversely affect research and training. My proposal was also vigorously resisted by the Dominican Republic, the host country for INSTRAW. In November 1993, when I defended my merger idea in a report to the General Assembly's Third Committee, I was accused of presenting a fait accompli, preempting a decision that belonged to the General Assembly. My failure to address the concerns of the Dominican Republic was described as "condescending and arrogant."

I looked for support to the major states clamoring for reform, but most of them, including the United States, remained silent for fear of attacks by angry third-world countries, and, above all, they did not want to offend China. Bureaucratic opponents of my proposed reform warned that disruption caused by my move might adversely affect preparations for the 1995 Beijing Women's Conference. The end came when the General Assembly's Third Committee unanimously adopted a resolution postponing the issue and giving it to the ACABQ for "in-depth analysis." This powerful body advises the General Assembly on all UN budget and administrative matters. Its members are supposed to be experts serving in an individual capacity. But in reality they speak for their governments. To resist my initiative, the ACABQ resorted to concocted arguments: reform might not be in the interest of one or another member state; it might undermine staff morale; or it should be postponed until it could be considered as part of a major overall transformation of the entire UN system at some point in the future.

A Unique Summit

Only four weeks after I took office, an event unique in UN history would take place: the first meeting of the Security Council at the level of heads of state or government. Instead of ambassadors sitting around the Security Council table, the countries would be represented by their highest political authorities, presidents and prime ministers, with their foreign minister or secretary of state seated behind them as staff. As this event drew near, I felt like the new boy in school who would have to sit for an examination before fifteen world leaders. This would be an unprecedented moment of solidarity in world affairs. It would be the first *conceptual* gathering after the cold war. As the moment approached, I grew anxious.

John Major would be in the chair, as it was Britain's turn to preside over the Security Council in January. It was rumored that Major had called the summit to strengthen his image for the next parliamentary elections. The French delegation, however, said that the summit had been Mitterrand's idea and that the British had agreed. Whoever proposed the meeting first, I wanted it to result in a more effective role for the UN secretary-general.

By the eve of the Security Council summit, a draft had been prepared announcing the main objective: to ask the UN secretary-general to produce a new approach to international stability and security for a new era. I had been shown the draft in advance and commented on it favorably. On January 31, 1992, the big day, I stood at the entrance of the United Nations to receive the heads of state or government.

John Major appeared, smiling and amiable. King Hassan II of Morocco was dressed all in white with a Capuchin hood over his head and white babouches on his feet. George Bush seemed happy to be back at the United Nations, where he had served as U.S. permanent representative. I was fascinated by the demeanor of François Mitterrand. His eyes sparkled with joy; he seemed to feel a personal victory in my election.

There were also Narasimha Rao, prime minister of India, who embraced me in tribute to our work for the nonaligned movement; Carlos

Andrés Pérez, the president of Venezuela, a friend and fellow worker in the Socialist International and the Group of Four (Egypt, India, Senegal, and Venezuela), created in Paris in 1989; and Chancellor Franz Vranitzky of Austria, another colleague from the Socialist International. Representing President Robert Mugabe of Zimbabwe was Nathan Shamuyarira, minister of foreign affairs, whom I had known in 1969 as a young professor at the University of Dar es Salaam and a militant for the independence of his country, then known as Rhodesia. I renewed my acquaintance with Kiichi Miyazawa, prime minister of Japan; Wilfried Martens, prime minister of Belgium; and Li Peng, prime minister of China. It was my first meeting with Boris Yeltsin, whose bluff, genial greeting I found striking.

We were seated around the Security Council table. John Major presided; I was at his right. On my right was Boris Yeltsin. Bush frequently exchanged remarks with Baker with an air of amused complicity. John Major opened the meeting: "Our presence here today marks a turning point in the world and at the United Nations."

François Mitterrand took the floor first. He announced that France was "ready to put at the disposal of the secretary-general of the United Nations at any moment, within a space of forty-eight hours, a contingent of one thousand men for peacekeeping operations—a number that could be doubled within a week." I was gratified to hear Mitterrand reiterate a call I had written for a speech given by Mubarak in 1990: the end of the cold war confrontation between East and West must not be replaced by an iron curtain between North and South.

Then Boris Yeltsin's voice resonated throughout the room: "Perhaps for the first time ever there is now a real chance to put an end to despotism and to dismantle the totalitarian order, whatever shape it may take." He then announced that the last ten political prisoners in Russia had been pardoned: "There are no longer any prisoners of conscience in free Russia." Everyone felt the dramatic import of those words.

President Bush was specific. He made two demands: No normalization with Iraq was possible as long as Saddam Hussein remained in power. And Libya must comply fully with the positions of the United States, Britain, and France concerning Pan Am Flight 103 and UTA Flight 772, the aircraft destroyed by terrorist bombs. Bush stressed that the Security Council had unanimously called upon Libya to comply with Resolution 731 of 1992.

The American president's demands worried me, because Iraq and Libya would expect me, as an Arab, to understand their point of view, while the United States would expect me to follow its lead in pressuring these "pariah" states. I was determined to follow one rule: to support and seek to fulfill all resolutions of the United Nations.

I offered lunch for the leaders at small tables. George Bush was seated on my right and Boris Yeltsin on my left. I tapped my glass and rose to say, "Today is the first time that we have had the pleasure of being gathered around a table in this way and that we have shared, as the Arab saying goes, bread and salt." But I sat down having forgotten to raise my glass to the health of my honored guests. Embarrassed, I apologized to Boris Yeltsin. "It's not serious," he told me. "What counts is the friendly atmosphere surrounding this table."

———

At the conclusion of the meeting Prime Minister John Major read out the summit's declaration that I should come up with "recommendations on ways of strengthening and making more efficient the capacity of the United Nations for preventive diplomacy, for peacemaking and for peacekeeping" and of making greater use of the good offices and other functions of the secretary-general under the UN Charter. Major added, "Our new secretary-general is a lucky man. He is the first secretary-general in many years to inherit a United Nations that is confident in its own ability to solve problems while still being conscious of the magnitude of its task."

After the final session in the afternoon of January 31, 1992, I met with Premier Li Peng of China, who politely told me to learn to distinguish between international wars and civil wars. He meant that the United Nations' role applied to war in its classic sense: when one country attacks another across internationally recognized boundaries. When it came to internal conflict, China insisted, any UN involvement would encroach on the sovereignty of the state involved. Li was undoubtedly thinking primarily about Taiwan and Tibet, but China would stand for the principle of strict nonintervention in internal affairs wherever the issue arose.

The larger problem was, as I reflected on Li's words, that although most current conflicts were in fact *within* the borders of a single state, many of them could legitimately be said to threaten wider interests of international peace and security.

Making "Greater Use" of the Secretary-General

At this first summit of the Security Council I had been asked to assume more responsibility than any of my predecessors. To be true to this mandate, I would have to defend the independence of my office and confront any member state, large or small, that opposed my exercise of the responsibilities the member states as a whole had given me. I had no illusions about the difficulties this would entail. I had won my post through politics, and now I was being asked to become a political leader. But in order to be a political leader, I would have to assert the independence of my office, and this could destroy me politically.

I had no time to dwell on these concerns. I was eager to draw up the report the Security Council had requested. I knew that policy was made by the written word, that texts made things happen in the realm of high diplomacy and statecraft. Writing forces concepts into life. Before I became secretary-general, I would write almost every day, whenever I could, for eight hours—from late afternoon until about 2:00 A.M. I prepared myself with exercise and diet and even with the right clothes—comfortable but not casual—for the task. By sleeping in the afternoon before starting to write, I could, in effect, turn one day into two. It seemed quite natural to me. My temptation was always to continue writing when the eight hours were up, but I knew I had to stop or I would not be fit to write the following day. Leia said my writing was exhausting and repeatedly urged me to relax. But writing was relaxation for me.

In my new job I would not be able to keep to this writing schedule. I was at the center of a political effort at consensus building, with a mandate that had no precedent in UN history. In asking the secretary-general to propose a new agenda for peace, the Security Council had delegated a responsibility that hitherto had belonged to the Security Council itself. A Canadian report later declared, "Implicit in this approach was encouragement to the new Secretary-General to assert his authority as the leader of the United Nations, and as an influential international political figure. Boutros-Ghali . . . was more than willing to seize this early and challenging invitation to assert a high political profile."

As the weeks went by, I worried over each draft of my report. After twelve or thirteen versions, I stopped counting. Although the Security Council had given me a deadline of July 1992, by mid-May I felt that the text was ready to be released. Becasue the Security Council had asked me to circulate the document "to the members of the United Nations," I issued it as a report to the General Assembly in the United Nations' normal drab typescript. But I also decided to call it *An Agenda for Peace* and to publish it in a UN-blue bound booklet for the public.

An Agenda for Peace

The media and member governments paid particular attention to points that I raised in *An Agenda for Peace*. First, I argued for preventive deployment of UN peacekeeping missions in some situations where previously the United Nations had not been able to act quickly. In the past, UN forces had been sent only after a conflict had occurred and a cease-fire had been agreed on. Preventive deployment meant that UN forces could be dispatched quickly, at the earliest warning of serious trouble.

The other concept I proposed was "peace enforcement," a rapid-reaction capability. Combat-ready units provided by member states would fill the gap between traditional UN peacekeeping units—which were lightly armed, had the consent of all parties, and were not expected to fight—and large-scale operations, such as that authorized by the United Nations during the Korean War, to maintain international peace and security. "Such units from Member States would be available on call and would consist of volunteers. These troops would have to be more heavily armed than peace-keeping forces and would need to undergo extensive preparatory training within their national forces." My idea at first sparked great interest, but soon it was igmored or declared to be politically impossible.

I called for as many countries as possible to make available up to one thousand troops each on a standby basis, so that operations could get under way in a few days rather than the two to three months that it now took. This readiness to act would itself be a form of deterrence or preventive diplomacy. This was not a radical call for a UN standing army but came from Article 43 of the Charter, under which all members of the United Nations "undertake to make available to the Security Council, on its call and in accordance with a special agreement . . . armed forces, assistance, and facilities, including rights of passage, necessary for the purpose of maintaining international peace and security."

The American press approved. *The New York Times* summed up the key message of my report as:

WANTED: Small, highly mobile army, able to respond overnight to civil disorder. Must be able to enforce cease-fires, cope with natural disasters, facilitate relief and deal impartially with all belligerents. Reply to United Nations, N.Y.

That in essence is the notice United Nations Secretary General Boutros Boutros-Ghali has now posted in a remarkable report to the Security Council. He speaks for a world that, if it is to have peace, must also have peace officers. . . . By advancing these ideas, Mr. Boutros-Ghali provides a coherent starting point for a permanent mechanism, transcending crisis-by-crisis response. He offers President Bush and other heads of state a forthright example of the new leadership needed in this new era.

The Washington Post, in its lead editorial, wrote:

Mr. Boutros-Ghali is committed to an expansive internationalist vision of the United Nations: He would have member states yield some sovereign prerogatives to larger, common political associations. His view of the U.N.'s actual functioning rests heavily on the role of its bureaucracy. But you would expect no less from the secretary general. He is in a good position to set the large scene. His insistence that the U.N. can mobilize the requisite resources, experience and skills to soften the strains of international life seems to us unanswerable.

An Agenda for Peace, the newspaper said, "responded to the can-do spirit of the day." I had given my "bosses in the Security Council the report they ordered up in January." I had "breathed new life into the U.N." The European and Arab press was even more enthusiastic. I could not have asked for a more positive start in my job.

The Forty-seventh General Assembly convened in September 1992. In the general debate in September and October, virtually every national leader who spoke either endorsed my idea to make armed forces available to UN peacekeeping on an on-call basis or urged that it be given serious study.

The U.S. Department of State seemed to favor designating U.S. military units for UN peacekeeping, but the Department of Defense did not want U.S. troops under command of foreign officers and feared getting bogged down in protracted conflicts where U.S. soldiers could become special targets. Bill Clinton, running for the presidency, declared that "the key is to give the UN the tools to move in quickly to defuse tensions before they escalate. We should explore the possibility of creating a standby, voluntary UN rapid deployment force to deter aggression against small states and to protect humanitarian relief shipments." But on the margins of the debate could be heard extremist voices asserting that *An Agenda for Peace* was an attempt to create a standing UN army under my command.

By the end of my first six months in office, I had selected my close advisers: Marrack I. Goulding, an erudite Briton with a powerful yet comforting personality; Jean-Claude Aimé, a Haitian with long experience in UN affairs and a diplomat of Renaissance subtlety; Fayza Abulnaga, once my student and now a brilliant young Egyptian diplomat; Alvaro de Soto, a truly cosmopolitan figure from Peru, deeply informed about key issues in Latin America; and Charlie Hill, a quiet American with a profound grasp of the theory and practice of foreign affairs. Later I sought the assistance of Ismat Kittani, a Kurd from Iraq, Chinmaya Gharekhan of India, and Rosario Green of Mexico. As my senior political advisers, they brought experience, wisdom, and creativity to the task.

CHAPTER 2

Encountering New Conflicts

(1992)

As I started out, the United Nations was beginning an unprecedented operation in Cambodia, taking that ravaged country into receivership until it could regain governmental legitimacy and international acceptance by way of a UN-conducted election. Cambodia would be the first—and still only—place where the United Nations would actually run the election, in contrast to monitoring an election organized by others.

On the eve of taking office I met with Yasushi Akashi, a Japanese who had risen through the ranks of the United Nations to become under secretary-general for disarmament. Intelligent, quick, and with staccato speech, Akashi knew the workings of the Secretariat. I asked him to give up his UN post in New York and take charge of the Cambodian operation. Akashi did not hesitate. "I am a samurai," he said. "Accordingly, I must accept this challenge."

Part of my plan to restructure the Secretariat was to put the disarmament office into the Department of Political Affairs and thereby abolish Akashi's post. But I wanted him to direct UN peacekeeping in Cambodia, because I wanted greater Japanese participation in UN activities. Akashi would be the first Japanese to serve as special representative of the secretary-general in a peacekeeping operation, and Cambodia would be bigger than any previous UN peace operation.

When the rumor spread that Akashi would go to Cambodia, I was criticized for sending a Japanese on such a mission. Asia was still trauma-tized by the Second World War, I was told. "You may understand the Arab and African world, but obviously you are ignorant when it comes to Asian sensibilities." Claude Cheysson, the former French foreign minister, wrote to tell me he was shocked by my choice. I asked Akashi to say noth-ing about his nomination until I had the approval of Prince Sihanouk.

Engaging Prince Sihanouk

I knew Prince Norodom Sihanouk from having established diplomatic relations between Egypt and Cambodia. When I telephoned the prince, he graciously accepted Akashi's nomination and announced it at once, putting me in a delicate position with the Security Council, which had not yet approved my choice. But on January 9, 1992, I was able to make the official announcement.

Prince Sihanouk was the pillar of all hopes for Cambodia. Intelligent and cultured in the arts, music, cinema, and literature, he had lived with the troubled history of his country since his youth. Perhaps because of his cancer, which he faced with courage, he was volatile and easily dis-couraged. Often he would speak of resigning or of his need to return to Beijing for medical treatment. Trying to offset this, I engaged in a long and very personal correspondence with him, entreating him to continue his role as unifier of the Cambodian people.

Letters to Sihanouk had to be written with the greatest care. I would produce several drafts before settling on the proper tone of admiration and praise, which he received automatically from the Cambodian people but insufficiently from the outside world. Sihanouk loved to receive let-ters written in sophisticated and literary French. I tried to please him, hoping to sustain his attention and support. Hours of effort were needed to win Sihanouk over; an instant's slip might be perceived as a slight, and he would be gone.

Battered by the cold war struggle for Southeast Asia and ravaged by the genocidal Khmer Rouge, then occupied by the Vietnamese Army in 1978 and ruled by a regime installed by Hanoi in 1979, Cambodia for over a decade had been the battleground of a civil war between government forces backed by Vietnam and the Soviet Union, and the Khmer Rouge, which was supported by China and Thailand.

The end of the cold war provided an opportunity to create a new, legitimate Cambodia. An international agreement had been signed in Paris in 1991 by nineteen states, including those of the Association of Southeast Asian Nations, the five permanent members of the UN Security Council, and all four Cambodian factions: the government of Hun Sen, the Khmer Rouge, the United Front for an Independent, Neutral, Peaceful, and Cooperative Cambodia (FUNCINPEC), and the Khmer People's National Liberation Front.

Under the Paris Agreement, the United Nations was to exercise direct control over the main departments of the administrations run by the factions; conduct elections; coordinate the repatriation of refugees; supervise the withdrawal of foreign forces, the cease-fire, and the demobilization of the factions; and with the International Committee of the Red Cross coordinate the release of prisoners of war. On February 19, 1992, I proposed a UN force of twelve infantry battalions, amounting to some 16,000 troops, 3,600 police, and 1,000 international staff, estimated to cost more than $1.7 billion, a far larger undertaking than any previous UN operation, and far beyond the concept of traditional UN peacekeeping. The UN was not prepared for it; deployment would be agonizingly slow, and many mistakes marked the effort to get the operation under way.

With these worries I decided to go to Phnom Penh a few months after taking office. The Khmer Rouge, who under the Paris Agreement could join the political process, were turning against it, accusing the UN of favoring Hun Sen's Vietnam-installed regime. Most observers predicted that UN-run elections would simply legitimize Hun Sen's rule.

On April 18, 1992, I was greeted at the airfield by Prince Sihanouk. As we rode toward the capital, which reminded me of a provincial French town, thousands of children along the way waved the light blue UN flag. The prince smiled at me, repeatedly bowing as he sat in the car, his palms pressed together in the gesture of respect: "You see how much the Cambodian people love you, how much they recognize and appreciate what you've done for Cambodia." I was surprised that the center of Phnom Penh showed few signs of wartime devastation, nor was there evident poverty.

We arrived at Khemerin Palace, the royal residence, where Prince Sihanouk decided I should stay. Princess Monique, his wife, had put the prince's study at my disposal. I was dazzled by their hospitality, kindness, and exquisite courtesy. At a meeting with the prince and his colleagues, Sihanouk spoke of his country's two most prominent neighbors—Thailand to the northwest and Vietnam to the southeast—as perennially having sought to dominate Cambodia. "Vietnamese troops have left our territory for theirs," he said, "although the Khmer Rouge pretends to the contrary." The prince insisted that a UN presence continue for three months after the elections, which were to take place the following year, but already I was feeling pressure from the United States and other major countries to ensure that the UN effort would cease as soon as the election was over.

The very name of our operation, UNTAC—United Nations Transitional Authority in Cambodia—revealed its intended scope. While the Supreme National Council was the repository of Cambodian sovereignty during the transitional period, my special representative was obliged to heed its advice only if there was consensus in the Council. If there was no consensus, which was often the case, he had the right to take the final decision. In theory this gave him great powers, almost powers of trusteeship. Unfortunately, however, UNTAC failed to take control of the core ministries and functions—admittedly a difficult task—and the United Nations was never able to exercise the authority that the Paris Conference had intended it to have. It pursued its mandate of helping the Cambodian people elect a government of recognized legitimacy to rebuild a land devastated by the Khmer Rouge's genocidal holocaust. But the Khmer Rouge was still at large, menacing the country from its remote forest bases. Yet it, too, would somehow have to be integrated into the new Cambodian polity.

Sihanouk had obtained foreign aid to repair the Buddhist temples of the capital, and palatial edifices and art objects of antiquity were being restored. He was proud of the glories of Cambodian culture and trembled with delight when pointing out to me the elegance of his gold-appointed throne room. Sihanouk's sophisticated court combined Parisian elegance with the ancient stateliness of Asian royalty. Servants were everywhere, reverently bowing to Sihanouk's feet and retreating awestruck from his presence. To them, he was not only a king but a god.

The Land-Mine Crisis

Beyond the city I found hideous carnage in a countryside littered with land mines and fearful of the Khmer Rouge. I was stunned to see the horrors that land mines had created. Years before, as Egypt's minister for foreign affairs, I had gone to a hospital on the Thai-Cambodian border where hundreds of children were being treated for lost limbs and wounds caused by mines. Here, inside Cambodia, I saw that, faced with the need to cultivate their fields, fetch water, or let their children play, thousands of people were using land that might explode any moment. Every day children, farmers, aid workers, and travelers were killed or maimed.

A common sight was the legless, blinded, ravaged bodies of the living, often children, condemned to a marginal future and placing a tragic burden on a nation striving for development. As the maimed children grew, their prosthetic devices had to be changed. The costs were staggering. Red signs warning of mines were posted only a few feet from the heavily traveled road to the treasured cultural site of Angkor Wat. Mines were planted around electric plants, power lines, and water treatment plants and along key roads, in market centers, and in storage and harbor installations. Vast tracts of potentially productive land had been abandoned, posing a virtually insuperable obstacle to postconflict economic recovery.

Mines would lurk in the land for generations. In Egypt's western desert we were still trying to clear land mines laid by the British and German armies in the Second World War. The United Nations estimated that more than 100 million mines designed to cripple, not to kill, were deployed in sixty-two countries, mostly in civilian and commercial locations, bringing everyday terror to large populations. Here in Cambodia I determined to campaign for a worldwide ban on land mines.

Betrayal by the Khmer Rouge

Phnom Penh's only respectable restaurant was named, in English, "No Problem." Akashi said the name reflected the high spirits of soldiers setting out on a new mission. A colleague claimed that the name indicated that France's traditional cultural influence had been replaced by that of "the Anglo-Saxons." Others saw it as a symbol of the distortion of the local culture by the arrival of a huge foreign presence with resultant prostitution and other corrupting influences. Regrettably, this was true, despite our efforts to contain it. The situation was worsened because land mines made it impossible for many rural people to return to their farms and villages. They had nowhere to go but to the city and no way to survive but by selling their bodies and living by their wits.

Prince Sihanouk was supposed to chair Supreme National Council sessions, but most of the time he was in North Korea, where Kim Il Sung welcomed him, or in Beijing for cancer treatment. The Hun Sen regime was using its political network to try to intimidate its chief competitor, Prince Ranariddh, Sihanouk's son, and his party, FUNCINPEC, to withdraw. Ranariddh refused to quit, but his party seemed listless. The Khmer People's National Liberation Front seemed hopelessly split, while the fourth of the Cambodian factions, the Khmer Rouge, was moving deeper into violent opposition. The Khmer Rouge violated the cease-fire, refused to demobilize, and obstructed the deployment of "Blue Helmets" to the countryside, all clear violations of the accord it had signed in Paris. When Akashi and Lieutenant General John Sanderson, the Australian commander of UNTAC, approached the Khmer Rouge guerrilla headquarters at Pailin, on the Thai-Cambodian border, their entry was barred by a single bamboo pole across the road. It was a key moment. UNTAC's mandate did not permit armed confrontation with the Khmer Rouge.

By midsummer 1992 UNTAC was excluded from all Khmer Rouge–occupied parts of the country. When the Khmer Rouge refused to move into cantonments to lay down their weapons, the other three Cambodian parties began to resist demobilization and disarming, and the Blue Helmets had no Security Council authorization to compel any of them to abide by the Paris Agreement. We had planned to complete the assembly of the factional armies by July 1992, but by that time only 13,500 fighters had come into cantonment, less than 7 percent of the estimated total in the country. On July 14, 1992, I told the Security Council that every available means should be used to persuade the Khmer Rouge to cooperate with the United Nations.

Two weeks later I received a letter from Akashi expressing deep anxiety: "Insecurity grows in the country proportionately to the acts of gangsterism, and the murder of peasants and resident Vietnamese. The economic situation is precarious."

Despite intensive diplomatic efforts by Japan, Thailand, France, and Indonesia, the Khmer Rouge only hardened its stance, claiming that a neutral environment for the electoral process had not been created. The Khmer Rouge began to attack UN helicopters and seize UN personnel in a campaign of brutal intimidation. Perhaps, I thought, the Khmer Rouge sees no alternative to violent opposition. I instructed Under Secretary-General Marrack Goulding to try to open a back channel with them, but to no avail. Would we have to pursue the peace process without the Khmer Rouge? If so, we would have to keep it isolated and unable to use fear as a weapon to wreck the electoral process.

The complicated provisions of the Paris Agreement really came down to a single objective: to create a new Cambodian government with international legitimacy. The national election would be the ultimate test. But the hold of the Hun Sen government was so pervasive that it seemed impossible to conduct an election that would not simply ratify its rule, just as the Khmer Rouge asserted would happen.

Nonetheless, UNTAC began to affect Cambodian society. The UN human rights team obtained the release of political prisoners. The civic education program helped real political parties emerge. Radio UNTAC provided the people with their first-ever reliable source of news, as well as instruction on democratic political behavior. The UN high commissioner for refugees was resettling hundreds of thousands of refugees from camps along the Thai border.

Despite bureaucratic inertia, long-delayed prefabricated housing, office supplies, and communications material arrived. By mid-July 1992 the UN military force in Cambodia reached 14,300 men. The delays were attributable partly to the United Nations' complex rules for administrative and financial management, but more directly to the fact that the Security Council was beginning to mandate other massive UN operations.

It was difficult to believe that we could create conditions for a free and fair election in this ravaged land. But as Prince Sihanouk, bowing as before, escorted me to the airport, I promised him that I would return in twelve months, before the major event, the May 1993 election.

Into the Balkan Cauldron

At the Security Council summit, Li Peng had told me to learn the difference between an internal and an international conflict. It was good advice, for the distinction was a fundamental part of the UN Charter. But the upheaval in the Balkans was both internal and international, and the overlap was hard to deal with.

Serious fighting within Yugoslavia began in 1991. With the cold war ended, the Socialist Federal Republic of Yugoslavia, like the Union of Soviet Socialist Republics (USSR), began to come apart. Serbia refused to recognize federal authority, essentially seceding from Yugoslavia. Then the Croatian and Slovenian parts of Yugoslavia declared themselves independent, arousing the opposition, with Yugoslav People's Army support, of Serbs living in Croatia. Efforts by the European Community to stop the hostilities were unsuccessful.

Secretary-General Pérez de Cuéllar appointed Cyrus Vance, the former U.S. secretary of state, to work with the European Community's envoy, Lord Carrington, to seek a diplomatic solution. As one of his last acts in office, Pérez de Cuéllar wrote in the strongest terms to urge Germany not to give diplomatic recognition to Croatia, a land with historic ties to Germany. If Croatia's independence were accepted internationally, other parts of Yugoslavia would declare independence as well, and a drastic struggle for territory could break out.

Pérez de Cuéllar's plea was ignored. On December 16, 1991, the European Community agreed to recognize Croatia and Slovenia within thirty days. Four days later the Republic of Bosnia and Herzegovina declared its desire for recognition as an independent state. Bosnia was a multiethnic society whose long history displayed periods both of mutual amity and of hate-spawned violence. The cataclysm that subsequently engulfed Bosnia cannot be attributed solely to foolish acts of diplomatic recognition, but recognition undoubtedly triggered the explosion, and strife erupted between those who wanted independence (the Muslims), those who opposed it (the Serbs), and those who took advantage of the Muslim-Serb fight to consolidate their hold over their own areas (the Croats). Only later, when it became clear that the West and the nonaligned would insist on independence, did the groups start fighting about who would prevail in the new Bosnian state.

As I took office on January 1, 1992, the war in the Persian Gulf had recently ended; it had been an international war of one state, Iraq, against another, Kuwait. Some saw the UN Security Council–authorized coalition, led by the United States, as a model for meeting future security challenges. But wars across state borders, like that which led to Desert Storm, were not likely to become the main threat to peace in the post–cold war world. Ethnic, religious, and cultural conflicts were erupting *inside* the borders of states. Article 2(7) of the UN Charter prohibited intervention in the affairs of member states. At the same time, the UN Charter obligated the UN Security Council to act "to maintain international peace and security." The founders of the United Nations, and the basic principles of international order in the modern era, had not foreseen or offered a way to deal with conflict within states, conflicts that might not obviously or immediately be understood to threaten international peace and security. The conflict boiling up in the former Yugoslavia was complicated, the dangers of getting trapped were evident, and the precedents—historical, cultural, and legal—were difficult to grasp. Faced with this perplexing and volatile war, the United States chose not to assume a leadership role, nor did the Europeans; instead, the United Nations was pushed to the forefront.

UN involvement in the former Yugoslavia began in the classic tradition of peacemaking and peacekeeping. In January 1992, on my second day in office as secretary-general, Cyrus Vance brought about a cease-fire between Croatia and the Yugoslav People's Army. Vance came to my thirty-eighth-floor office to urge me to send UN peacekeepers to maintain the cease-fire. It was intended to be peacekeeping according to well-established principles, but the bitter violence in the Balkans as Yugoslavia broke up had everyone worried and reluctant to get involved. Marrack Goulding, under secretary-general for peacekeeping operations, argued against Vance. "The peacekeepers will come back in body bags," he warned.

I shared his fear; I was afraid that what the Congo operation had done to the United Nations under Dag Hammarskjold in 1960, the conflicts of the former Yugoslavia would do to the United Nations under me in 1992. But I did not need time to think it over. "I must go with the counsel of my old friend Cy," I said. My friendship with Cyrus Vance went back to a London meeting on the Middle East in the 1960s. When we had worked on the Arab-Israeli peace process in 1978–1979 during his time as secretary of state, Cy had won the trust and admiration of both Prime Minister Menachem Begin and President Anwar Sadat, not an easy thing to do. He was honest, objective, and wise.

So in my first substantive act in office, with the Security Council's authorization, I sent the first UN Blue Helmets into the former Yugoslavia as the United Nations Protection Force (UNPROFOR). They were deployed in three areas of Croatia where Serbs made up a substantial part of the population and where ethnic tensions had led to armed conflict: eastern Slavonia, western Slavonia, and the Krajina. The United Nations' mandate was to ensure that these three areas of Croatia were demilitarized and policed and that the Yugoslav People's Army withdrew from Croatia. In the months to come, there would be several enlargements of the UN mandate in Croatia.

The original UN mandate related only to Croatia, but the situation in Bosnia worsened rapidly after the independence referendum there on March 3. "The deteriorating humanitarian situation in Bosnia-Herzegovina is of great concern to me," I said to the press. "The fighting makes it difficult, if not impossible, to provide for the most basic human needs of the innocent victims of this tragic conflict."

I was encouraged by U.S. Assistant Secretary of State John Bolton's statement to Congress on March 25. The deployment of UN peacekeepers to the former Yugoslavia, Bolton said, was specifically tied to the European Community's attempts to negotiate a resolution of the conflict. If those talks did not succeed, Bolton said, "and if the parties abandon good-faith efforts to resolve their differences, the Security Council will have to reexamine the mandate of that mission." Bolton's words were clear and firm and paralleled my position exactly: "We do not view UN peacekeeping as the savior of lost causes, to be thrown into a crisis willy-nilly when all else fails."

At this time the United Nations had established its headquarters in Sarajevo (because it was more neutral, in relation to the Croatian conflict, than Belgrade or Zagreb), but the force had few other responsibilities in Bosnia. In the Security Council, however, there was talk of enlarging its mandate there. At the end of April I sent Marrack Goulding to look into the feasibility of doing this and, as a token of my concern, brought forward the already planned deployment of forty military observers in Bosnia.

Goulding came back with a grim report. As I reported to the Security Council on May 12, 1992, Sarajevo was suffering heavy shelling and sniper fire nightly: "All international observers agree that what is happening is a concerted effort by the Serbs of Bosnia-Herzegovina, with the acquiescence of, and at least some support from, the Yugoslavian national army, to create 'ethnically pure' regions. . . . The techniques used are the seizure of territory by military force and intimidation of the non-Serb population. The conclusion of a partial cease-fire agreement between Croat and Serb leaders on 6 May 1992 has revived suspicions of a Croat-Serb carve-up of Bosnia-Herzegovina, leaving minimal territory to the Muslim community, which accounts for a plurality (44 per cent) of the population . . . the situation in Bosnia-Herzegovina is tragic, dangerous, violent and confused."

In mid-May 1992, as I was finishing *An Agenda for Peace,* I gave the Security Council my views on establishing a UN peacekeeping operation in Bosnia. I had agreed to put the United Nations into Croatia because Vance had achieved a cease-fire there, but in Bosnia a war was raging.

President Alija Izetbegović had pressed for a peacekeeping operation, although he acknowledged that no agreement existed between the parties on which its mandate could be based. UNPROFOR was needed to escort refugee convoys. But the Bosnian Serbs had opposed any increase in the UN presence in Bosnia and had decried the usefulness of the few military observers who were already there.

I advised the Security Council that "in its present phase the conflict is [not] susceptible to the United Nations peacekeeping treatment." There was no basis for a workable mandate. If the EC's current negotiations led to agreements, it might turn out to be more appropriate for it, rather than the United Nations, to undertake the peacekeeping that would then become possible. Moreover, I said, "a successful peacekeeping operation requires the parties to respect the United Nations, its personnel and its mandate." None of the three Bosnian parties was doing so. To provide armed escorts for humanitarian convoys would risk involving the United Nations in hostile encounters with those whose cooperation it needed if it was to succeed in its tasks in Croatia.

The Security Council chose not to heed this recommendation against any enlargement of the United Nations' mandate in Bosnia. Its Resolution 752 of May 15 required UNPROFOR to provide armed escorts for humanitarian convoys, demanded that "all irregular forces . . . be disbanded and disarmed," and called on all parties to cooperate with the United Nations to achieve this. This was the beginning of the unrealistic "mission creep" that was to lead the United Nations into its disaster in Bosnia.

Under the title "Boutros Boutros and the Weight of the World," *The Economist* reported on May 23, 1992:

> Mr. Boutros Boutros-Ghali told the Security Council that it was impractical to send UN peacekeepers to Bosnia while the war there was still pursued with such ferocity. If the Council members wanted to intervene, they should not try to do so on the cheap; they would have to consider sending in tens of thousands of troops equipped with offensive capability. Even if they opted, at this stage, only for armed escorts to protect the relief convoys, they would have to think along similarly expensive lines; a convoy led by the UN had been brutally ambushed by Muslim militiamen. But the Council, ignoring his warning, voted two

days later for the provision of armed escorts without going into their military needs.

The article went on:

The new Secretary-General, who for many years was the *eminence grise* of Egyptian foreign policy, is not a table-thumper, a politician, or even a good speaker. But he is beginning to show a sure touch and may be less worried than his predecessor about making enemies. One sign of this is his readiness to accuse the Council of telling him to find people to do difficult and dangerous things without giving him the wherewithal to do it.

A few days later, as the war intensified, I had to order most UN personnel to leave Bosnia because their lives were in danger. About one hundred UN officials would remain at UN headquarters in Sarajevo to try to reestablish the cease-fire and carry out humanitarian assistance. The European Community withdrew its observers at this time, and the United States recalled its ambassador, Warren Zimmerman, from Belgrade.

On May 30 I had to report back to the Security Council that the disarming and disbanding envisaged in Resolution 752 were likely to be feasible only in the context of an overall political agreement on constitutional arrangements for Bosnia and Herzegovina. The only alternative, I said, although the Security Council resolution did not mention it, "would be for international troops to undertake the immobilization and/or destruction of some or all of the weapons of the disbanded units or elements."

Lord Carrington's Nightmare

I liked and admired Peter Carrington. Years before, he had solved the seemingly impossible set of issues surrounding the transformation of the British colony of Rhodesia into the independent African state of Zimbabwe. I had watched this through the prism of the Organization of African Unity, which had taken the role of a Greek chorus in the liberation of Zimbabwe. But every time I saw Carrington, I recalled the time a decade before, when he had represented the European position on the Arab-Israeli peace process. This had brought him into frequent confrontation with Israeli Prime Minister Begin, who referred to Carrington as "Boutros," the Arab name corresponding to "Peter." In my role as Egypt's minister of state for foreign affairs, Prime Minister Begin had referred to me as "Boutros" whenever he regarded me as cooperative, and as "Peter" when he didn't think so. I believe Carrington was unaware of this strange connection.

I went to London to meet Lord Carrington on July 2, 1992, at the Dorchester Hotel. "For the last few months I have been sleeping with Yugoslavia," I said to Carrington. "I have been having nightmares about it," he replied. For the first time, I said, the United Nations might be involved in a self-contradictory operation: peacekeeping requiring complete impartiality toward the parties and peace enforcement against one party. Public pressure was rising, and the Security Council was anxious for action. The Council, I said, "is becoming like the General Assembly: it is using phrases and making demands that it knows cannot be implemented, in order to please public opinion." The United Nations needs to preserve its credibility for other activities in the world, I said. In Africa, I said, the United Nations is being accused of paying attention to Yugoslavia only because it is in Europe and of ignoring conflicts in places such as Mozambique and Angola.

Carrington said that he would go to Sarajevo to see Izetbegović and Radovan Karadžić. "Should I then go to New York?" he asked, adding, "I don't want to." I urged Carrington to go to the United Nations, because I wanted to stir up interest in an international conference on the former Yugoslavia, perhaps including the Conference on Security and Cooperation in Europe (CSCE), the European Community, and the Security Council. Carrington sighed and said, "Come back, Tito," recalling how Tito had kept Yugoslavia together.

One week later, Carrington and I met on the thirty-eighth floor of the United Nations. "If I may update you on Bosnia-Herzegovina," he said, "most people see it as poor Muslims being put upon, wicked Serbs, and neutral Croats. In fact, the Serbs *are* wicked, but so are the others." I was inclined to agree with him. The West seemed to regard the Serbs as the only wrongdoers, whereas I felt that no party in Bosnia was free of at least some of the blame for the cruel conflict.

On July 17, 1992, in a deal reached in London in Christie's art auction house, of which Carrington was chairman, the Bosnian Serbs, Croats, and Muslims signed a cease-fire and agreed to place under international supervision all heavy weapons, such as combat aircraft, armor, mortars, and rocket launchers. Within twenty-four hours the Security Council welcomed the agreement, called upon the parties to declare the locations and quantities of the heavy weapons to the UN Protection Force immediately, and requested that I report within three days on the implementation of the decision. This was ridiculous. I told Carrington that the agreement he had brokered was not realistic, and he did not disagree. The meager UN presence on the ground could not accomplish such a huge task, even had the warring parties been serious in signing the agreement, which they revealed they were not when the UN commander in Bosnia contacted the three parties but received no cooperation whatever.

I reported to the Security Council on July 21, 1992, that the United Nations had neither the mandate nor the means to carry out its request. Despite the "cease-fire" signed at Christie's, the fighting had not stopped. The parties were not cooperating. In fact, they were relocating their heavy weapons to places where they could not be monitored. Moreover, no peacekeepers were available for the job.

My letter to the president of the Security Council conveyed the tension: "I now find myself in the invidious position of having to advise the Council on the implementation of a mandate behind which the Council has already thrown its political support. Expectations have been raised by the Council's action. I must express my considered opinion that it would have been preferable if the Security Council, as has been the usual practice heretofore, had requested and awaited a technically grounded opinion by UNPROFOR, before taking such a position. In light of the grim news which has come out of Bosnia-Herzegovina for the past weeks, I can understand the Council's desire to seize the opportunity which appears to have arisen out of the London talks. At the same time, I very much hope that it will be possible for the Council and the Secretary-General to work in greater coordination. I am, of course, at the service of the Security Council. At the same time, however, I would hope that my views would be ascertained in areas which are clearly within my competence."

That same day the Security Council held consultations on the matter. The president of the Council noted delicately that my letter "touched on fundamental questions relating to the relationship between the secretary-general and the Security Council, which the Council might wish to bear in mind for the future." Sir David Hannay, the British ambassador to the United Nations, declined to comment on my letter on the principle "Least said, soonest mended." Hannay and I sometimes disagreed, but we were always on good terms. His manner was imperious—not unlike mine, some said—but he was one of the finest ambassadors to the United Nations I knew.

The Toronto *Globe* wrote that "Boutros-Ghali revealed the Council's action for what it was: claptrap, of a typical UN kind." The Security Council had adopted a measure without accepting the obligations involved, to which it had given no thought.

I had not been in office six months, but I was already in trouble with my major constituents. I had annoyed both the U.S. and the European powers by resisting their calls for bigger UN peacekeeping operations in the Balkans, pointing to the fact that there was no will on the part of the Security Council to provide UN forces with the weapons and mandates they would need to operate effectively in the middle of a bitter and bloody war. Even my own homelands were unhappy with me: Africa, because of the attention I was giving to peacekeeping rather than to development in the poorest countries; and the Islamic world, which wanted a UN war against the Serbs on behalf of the Bosnian Muslims.

In mid-July 1992, I criticized Lord Carrington, the European Community's representative for Bosnia, and, by implication, the Europeans in general for their approach to Bosnia. They cared more about this disaster in Europe than about equally great or greater disasters in the non-European world, I said. That was understandable, but they should not expect the United Nations to do the same. The United Nations could not attend to one conflagration and ignore another. If the Europeans wanted more activism on Bosnia, they should do more themselves, not expect the United Nations to divert critical resources to a conflict in Europe at the expense of conflicts in Africa, Asia, and Latin America.

I reported to the Security Council on July 27, 1992, that developments had radically altered the premises on which the UN peacekeeping plan for Bosnia had been formulated. The situation on the ground was drawing the UN forces into functions and conflicts far beyond normal peacekeeping practice. The time had come to put Bolton's statement to Congress into effect: the Security Council should reexamine the United Nations' mandate in the former Yugoslavia.

On August 8, 1992, *The Economist* stated, "The new Secretary-General has risen splendidly to the occasion. But his rise is upsetting those around him." In a world of inflated egos, the magazine wrote, Boutros-Ghali may be going too far. The British press "plainly got under

his too-thin skin. But it was absurd, and unworthy, of him to suggest recently that critics were yapping at him because he was a 'wog.'" Wog was
a derisive term from the days of my youth under British colonialism; it
stood for "westernized oriental gentleman." I recalled an Egyptian story
from World War II: A British soldier in Alexandria says to his commanding officer, "Sir, I saw two wogs walking on the beach." The officer replies
sternly, "That was King Farouk and his security guard." The soldier cor-
rects himself: "Sir, I saw King Farouk walking with another wog." I had
made my "wog" comment with a smile.

"Boutros-Ghali, the first UN Chief from the African continent, has already managed to alienate the African and other Third World diplomats,
the UN staff, most of the press corps, and . . . the untouchable 'Big Five'
members of the Security Council," the daily *Australian* wrote in mid-
August 1992. "Descriptions like 'arrogant' and 'heavy-handed' are now
frequently heard in UN corridors. And the derisive name 'Boo-Boo' has
firmly stuck to the embattled Secretary-General." The confrontation had
even stimulated a whispering campaign that I might be forced out of office before my five-year term expired. None of this caused me second
thoughts.

The reaction of Europe, the West, and the world to the Bosnian horror
had been fragmented and self-deceptive. The United States, NATO, the
CSCE, and the Group of Seven (G-7) each took its own position on
Bosnia, sometimes conciding, often divergent. But all of them were
using the United Nations as a substitute for making their own hard decisions and allocating adequate resources. On the ground, the UN soldiers
were in an increasingly impossible position. They had been sent there to
help those who were providing humanitarian aid, and both the Serb and
Bosnian forces knew that they were not allowed to use force if challenged. A pattern of checkpoints and extortion benefited the fighters and
progressively humiliated the UN troops. For the first time in memory,
Blue Helmet peacekeepers, who formerly had been welcomed, were
threatened and treated with contempt by those they had come to help.
Many lives were saved, and many people rescued, but the United
Nations was not authorized to affect the balance of forces. I believed that
the UN Protection Force was being used by Europe and the United
States to show that "something" was being done about the hell that
Bosnia had become, as well as a scapegoat for the failure to stop the hor-
ror altogether.

Despite my recent sparring with the press, my relations with the Bush administration were good. Although there was growing criticism of my "abrasive" style, "The U.S. Government is basically happy with him," an American official told *The Washington Post.* "We, less than everybody else, are concerned about the niceties. We *wanted* a forceful secretary-general in management, innovation, and rethinking of the United Nations."

President Bush clearly had a large vision for the United Nations in the 1990s. In his policy paper "National Security Strategy of the United States," he had recognized that many conflicts were likely to emerge beyond the scope of traditional security systems. The United Nations would provide a way to organize the international response. Bush also aimed to have what the United States owed the United Nations paid up by 1995, which would be the United Nations' fiftieth anniversary year. Throughout the summer of 1992, I felt that the Bush administration knew that my policy was to prevent the United Nations from being misused as a substitute for the difficult decisions that Europe and the United States would themselves have to take in regard to the Bosnian crisis.

The London Conference

To try to achieve some coherence in the diverse approaches to the Balkan crisis, in midsummer 1992 the EC invited me, as UN secretary-general, to cochair, with Prime Minister John Major of Great Britain, in his capacity as current president of the EC, an "International Conference on the Former Yugoslavia." As the first major collaboration of its kind between the United Nations and a regional organization, this was a remarkable procedural innovation in world affairs.

Prime Minister Major and I convened the London Conference on August 26, 1992. I stressed that the territories of the former Yugoslavia, now at war, had been given diplomatic recognition and admitted to the United Nations. "This makes it," I said, "an international conflict." Not only was the future shape or security of one or more UN member states at risk, but so was their existence.

A division of labor had been agreed upon by the European Community and the United Nations, with the European Community taking the lead in monitoring the cease-fire and negotiating for a peaceful solution, while the UN peacekeepers were to focus on protecting humanitarian work. But as the fighting worsened, the European Community withdrew its personnel from Sarajevo, leaving the United Nations as the only international presence in Bosnia.

I spoke frankly to the London Conference about what its members knew but refused to acknowledge: "The expectations of the international community—which has been shocked by the horror of the conflict in Bosnia and Herzegovina—continue to exceed the resources and capacity of the United Nations Protective Force. . . . That although the Security Council has called for a number of actions by all sides to the conflict . . . the United Nations force has been explicitly authorized and equipped to implement only the 5 June 1992 agreement [to reopen the Sarajevo airport for the purpose of humanitarian relief]. This it has done in most difficult and dangerous conditions."

What had to be realized, I said, was that for the United Nations to succeed in what it had been asked to do, UN personnel had to depend on the cooperation of the irregular fighting forces of the conflicting parties, and all these groups were bitterly hostile toward all attempts to stop the bloodshed and restore peace.

I wanted to force the London Conference to accept reality: "I wish to insist that the UN mission, with its present mandate, cannot by itself bring this crisis to an end or to a durable political solution. More, much more, is urgently required. That is why we are here today in London!" I tried to set out a framework within which everyone could see how, when, and whether intervention should be carried out. I wanted to make two points completely clear.

First, I said, the international community cannot step into every area of violence that erupts around the world. But some disputes compel our attention: those that threaten international peace and security; those that transgress the fundamental moral standards that humanity holds in common; and those that, unless resolved correctly, would tend to undermine the foundations of the international system. Clearly, the crisis in Bosnia met each of these three criteria.

Second, I urged the London Conference to find a formula through which diversity can be respected yet government can serve a common purpose and enjoy a common allegiance. "If every ethnic, religious, or linguistic group claimed statehood, there would be no limit to fragmentation," I warned. This meant that Bosnia deserved to endure as a multiethnic state.

I asked the London Conference members to face a brutal future in Bosnia: that if the peacekeeping function of the UN operation were frustrated and hostilities intensified, the UN force should either be withdrawn or become part of a wider international effort to solve the crisis not only by diplomacy but by military might.

Lord Carrington appeared at the opening of the London Conference but was litle seen at the conference thereafter. Rumors were reported in the media that I had demanded his resignation because he had attempted to place more responsibilities on UN peacekeepers without consulting me or considering the need to match such new responsibilities with new resources. In fact, I never urged Carrington to quit; he had been appointed by the European Community, and I had no authority over him. Sick of the intransigence of Serbs, Bosnians, and Croats alike, Carrington was rarely on the scene of the crisis, preferring to work from London. When the London Conference began, everyone knew that he would soon be replaced by Lord Owen. Trained as a physician, David Owen had been British foreign secretary in the late 1970s. When the Labour Party had lost power, Owen had become a founder of the Social Democratic Party, and when the SDP had disbanded in 1990, Owen had seemed to have no political future. I regarded Owen as elegant, courageous, and refreshingly independent. We had much in common: we were both considered arrogant and abrasive, we both felt that all the parties in the former Yugoslavia shared in the blame, and we were both skeptical about Washington's approach.

The London Conference declared its support for the continued existence of Bosnia-Herzegovina as a state, its refusal to accept the acquisition of territory by force, and its support for the creation of an ongoing, institutionalized negotiation process. The London Conference also created a well-structured system to bring about a coherent international effort. Six working groups were set up: three under the United Nations and three under the European Community; all would report to a steering committee headquartered in Geneva and chaired by Cyrus Vance as the UN envoy and Lord Owen as the new EC envoy. In other words, the London Conference would actively continue through the work of the new negotiating team.

As the London Conference was drawing to a close, I asked the delegates who was going to pay for all this. Silence. I said that the United Nations was in dire financial straits and had no funds. "You must create a special fund," I said to the conference members. Again, silence. Slowly, discussion began about a formula for assessing contributions to such a fund. Would it follow the UN's rate of assessment? Or should EC criteria be used? The Japanese delegate declared that unless a clear set of guide-lines was established, Japan could contribute nothing. More silence. Prime Minister Major was visibly unhappy with this stalemate, angrily asking his staff why they had not briefed him about this obvious problem. Larry Eagleburger raised his hand. "The United States pledges three million dollars," he said. That broke the logjam—at least for the remaining hours of the conference session. Later it took me ten telephone calls to extract that $3 million from the U.S. Department of State. All international conferences are the same: The delegates studiously avoid talking about money because money is always a divisive topic. Let someone else solve it later, they say.

When the Security Council in 1992 affirmed the new statehood of Bosnia, Croatia, and Slovenia, it also concluded that the Federal Republic of Yugoslavia, which comprised the two remaining parts of the old Yugoslavia—Serbia and Montenegro—could not automatically assume the UN membership of the former "Socialist Federal Republic of Yugoslavia" and that the new regime in Belgrade would have to apply for membership. This was important leverage. The Charter required that new states had to be "peace-loving"; hence the Federal Republic of Yugoslavia would have to stop supporting the war in Bosnia if it ever wanted to be a full UN member state. As time passed, however, international willingness to use this pressure evaporated, and the Belgrade government's UN membership ceased to raise questions.

The immense gap between our efforts and the events in Bosnia continued. Lieutenant General Barry McCaffrey testified to the Senate that it could take up to 120,000 troops to secure humanitarian aid. The UN peacekeeping personnel then deployed numbered about 14,000, and none could be considered "troops" capable of enforcing security. In Washington, George Kenney, a U.S. Foreign Service officer, prominently resigned in mid-1992 in protest over the Bush administration's "ineffective and counterproductive" approach to Bosnia.

The Vance-Owen Plan

Meanwhile, Vance and Owen were relentlessly trying to create a UN-EC peace plan. Their concept was to create Swiss-like "cantons," each of which would be identified with one of the three parties: Serb/Orthodox, Croat/Catholic, and Bosnian/Muslim. Each ethnic party would have three cantons, for a total of nine. The tenth entity would be Sarajevo, which would be jointly governed by all three. This was a good way to reflect the realities of different population groupings on the ground while preserving Bosnia-Herzegovina as a multiethnic, multiconfessional state. But the Serbs would have to relinquish 60 percent of the territory they had taken by force.

Vance and Owen realized that this plan was far from ideal. Owen called it "a peace from Hell." But in my opinion it was as much as could be managed.

At the end of the year I reported to the General Assembly that the United Nations and the European Community had done much to identify the form of a future political settlement in Bosnia.

A new and growing concern was Macedonia, where, as Cyrus Vance reported to the Security Council on November 13, 1992, a "festering situation" was raising fears that war might spread to that former Yugoslav republic. So far, the war had been contained within Bosnia's traditional borders. It was important to keep it from engulfing Macedonia, for that could stimulate other outbreaks beyond Bosnia as well. Macedonia, with its large Albanian minority, was of particular concern to Greece and Albania, as well as to Bulgaria; war in Macedonia could add an entirely new dimension to the Balkan crisis.

As a result of a proposal made to the Security Council and the report of an exploratory team, I recommended on December 9, 1992, to the Security Council that "a small UNPROFOR presence be established on the Macedonian side of that republic's borders . . . with an essentially preventive mandate." I asked for an infantry battalion and a group of thirty-five UN observers. The United States offered troops, and the operation was successful as the first example in UN history of "preventive deployment." It gave me satisfaction to see a concept from *An Agenda for Peace* put into effect on the ground.

At the end of 1992, Vance, Owen, and I met with Bosnia's president, Alija Izetbegović, and Foreign Minister Haris Silajdžić at the Palais des Nations in Geneva. The Bosnians declared that the situation was worse than ever: the Serbs were taking more and more land and intensifying their "ethnic cleansing." The United Nations should lift the arms embargo and allow the Muslim population to defend itself, they said.

Under the UN Charter, a state has the right of self-defense unless the Security Council has acted. The Security Council had imposed an arms embargo on the whole of Yugoslavia soon after fighting broke out in

Croatia in the summer of 1991. The Muslim side in Bosnia tried to create the impression that the embargo applied only to itself and argued that it was unfair; the world should either intervene with force or let it acquire arms to defend itself. Although this argument was disingenuous, it did have some force in the beginning: the Muslims did have very few weapons, while the Bosnian Serbs had access to the vast resources of the Yugoslav People's Army and the Bosnian Croats were being armed by Croatia. But by this time I knew that the Bosnian Muslims were already receiving clandestine arms shipments from Muslim countries. And the countries contributing troops for UNPROFOR, including some NATO members, made it clear that if the arms embargo were lifted, they would withdraw their contingents so as to avoid getting caught in the middle of a full-scale, fully armed war.

I told Izetbegović that the international community wanted to continue the peace process, because it believed that a settlement might be reached. "The international community is currently in favor of the Muslim population of Bosnia," I said, "and is sending humanitarian assistance to you." By contrast, I said, "I could give you a list of countries which are receiving nothing and whose problems are considerably more difficult than those being faced by Bosnia." International opinion can change in a matter of hours, I said. I mentioned Angola, where U.S. and South African support for Dr. Jonas Savimbi had been lost in less than a day when fighting had broken out in early November. I warned Izetbegović that if the Muslims received arms and took military action, international support for them would evaporate. "We know that already," Silajdžić said.

New Year's Eve in Sarajevo

On a bitter cold December 31, 1992, Cyrus Vance and I stepped out of an aircraft at Sarajevo, put on flak jackets and blue helmets, and visited the UN troops, including the Egyptian contingent. This was the first time Egyptian soldiers had served in a UN force since the Congo operation more than thirty years before. It had not been easy to obtain this Egyptian army presence in Bosnia. Mubarak, always a cautious leader, did not want to put "his boys" in danger. The Egyptian peacekeepers gave me an extravagant welcome, which lifted my spirits greatly. I then visited the sick and wounded in the hospital. The doctor in charge was a Croat, a fact that was stressed to me as an important symbol of Sarajevo's multi-ethnic character.

In the building housing the Bosnian presidency I spoke to Vice President Ejup Ganić in front of a large group of reporters. "Bosnia is a full-fledged member of the United Nations," I said, "and as such the United Nations must preserve Bosnia's independence and territorial integrity." I assured the Bosnians that the United Nations shared their frustration at all the horrors that had occurred. I condemned the criminals who had wrought these horrors and said I hoped that an international court would condemn them too. I firmly urged all parties to continue to negotiate and to support the Vance-Owen peace plan.

As I emerged from the building, a crowd gathered to shake their fists and call me a "fascist" and a "murderer" and shout insults at the United Nations. I tried to talk to the mob, but an Egyptian general from the Blue Helmet contingent who was accompanying me held me back. "Please don't do it," he said. "Why?" I asked. "Because if anything happens to you, Mubarak will hang me," he said. "So," I replied, "you are afraid for yourself and not me?" "Yes, sir," he said. I took his arm. "Come, let us take the risk together," I said and pulled him over to the crowd, where I explained to them without success the limitations under which the United Nations was ordered to operate. But the discussion calmed the crowd, and we left safely. "*Al Hamdulillah!* [Thanks be to God!]" the Egyptian general exclaimed as we left. "See," I said, "we have the protection of God."

The Egyptian contingent wanted me to join them at lunch. No, said UN headquarters, the secretary-general belongs not only to Egypt but to the entire UN mission. So they compromised. I ate at UN headquarters, but the Egyptian soldiers provided Egyptian food, including my favorite dish, *foul,* or horse beans. The taste made me homesick.

Back at Sarajevo Airport, I met with the deputy of Radovan Karadžić, the Bosnian Serb leader. The Serbs, he declared, considered the Vance-Owen plan a good basis "not only for the present round of negotiations, but also as the basis for future rounds."

As I prepared to leave Sarajevo, reporters asked me whether I felt humiliated by the hostile comments I had heard from the people of the besieged city. "I must accept insults from them," I said, "because they are suffering."

The press had heard me say in public in Sarajevo what I had said in Geneva in private to the Bosnians: that I had admonished the Sarajevans by saying, "You have a situation that is better than ten other places in the world. . . . I can give you a list." This was interpreted as brutal and un-feeling on my part. It was New Year's Eve, and I wanted to give the people of Sarajevo a message of hope. I meant that the Bosnian Muslims were not alone; they had the support and goodwill of the international com-munity and of friends all around the world. There was, therefore, a greater chance that the outside world would press for peace and justice in Bosnia. Regrettably, I said, this was not true of the "orphan conflicts" in Africa, about which few people knew or cared or with which they tried to help. The Europeans expected me to concentrate on Bosnia. Although I was deeply concerned about Bosnia, my job was to be concerned about other crises as well. In fact, the Security Council had required the United Nations to become massively unbalanced in favor of the prob-lems of the former Yugoslavia, and I found myself increasingly thinking about Somalia.

Somalia: Humanitarian Aid Hijacked

Somalia is a desperately poor, dry, hook-shaped country in the Horn of Africa with a recent history rich only in colonialism, hunger, disease, and weapons transferred from abroad as part of the cold war competition be-tween the United States and the USSR. In December 1990 the govern-ment of President Mohammed Siad Barre collapsed. Throughout 1991 Somalia was torn by factional fighting. With no central government, the country fragmented as rival militias fought for food, prestige, and terri-tory. As one of the world's ten poorest countries, Somalia had little to rely on in time of trouble. Schools closed. There was no electricity. Local gov-ernment disappeared.

By 1992 Somalia had become a "failed state." For the past half century, it had been assumed that nations emerging from colonialism and gaining entry into the United Nations would achieve "statehood" as a permanent condition; it was never envisioned that statehood could be lost. But So-malia had reverted to the prestate condition described by Hobbes as "no arts, no letters, no society . . . continual fear, and danger of violent death." In Somalia it was "the war of all against all." Armed bands of ren-egades roamed city streets and country roads in "technicals," light trucks fitted with machine guns—in effect, homemade tanks. The militias and bandits looted the docks and storehouses of agencies sent to help the

Somali people. Humanitarian relief workers were attacked by these gangs, who prevented food from reaching the starving and took it for themselves. Television showed scenes of gunmen feasting while emaciated women and children watched.

Most adult males in Somalia, like those in countries on both the African and Middle Eastern sides of the Gulf of Aden, are addicted to *qat*. Chewing large quantities of the leaves of this plant throughout the day creates at first a state of exhilaration and false courage, followed by dazed lethargy during the hot afternoon and evening. The *qat* plant is cultivated in Ethiopia, Kenya, and Yemen. Controlling the huge daily air shipment of the leaves had become a chief source of income for the warlords of Somalia and a method of payment in kind to the fighters under their command.

In early January 1992 I sent Under Secretary-General for Political Affairs James O. C. Jonah to Mogadishu to meet with the two paramount warlords, Mohammed Farah Aidid and Ali Mahdi, to try to arrange a cease-fire in the capital and access to international relief. Both sides declared support for a UN role in bringing about national reconciliation, though Aidid made no secret of his strong opposition to the deployment of UN forces. After many efforts, a cease-fire pledge was achieved in April 1992, and I asked the Security Council for authorization to dispatch a small military detachment to monitor the cease-fire and provide security for humanitarian aid deliveries to the people of Mogadishu. The Security Council, however, authorized only military observers at that time. As soon as the mission was approved, I appointed Ambassador Mohamed Sahnoun of Algeria, a former assistant secretary-general of the OAU, my special representative for Somalia. I had known Sahnoun for many years and looked forward to working closely with him. I chose him not only for his close knowledge of African affairs but also because I wanted to increase the number of Africans in key UN positions.

But the famine toll continued to rise, and I became more and more convinced that an armed force was needed. The existing UN presence in Somalia was incapable of containing the famine. The towns were swollen with people fleeing violence and searching for food, but all social services had been destroyed. Hundreds of thousands were in camps without access to food, water, sanitation, or health services.

Deaths in Africa are no less significant than deaths in Europe. I tried to goad the Security Council into a sense of urgency. I contrasted their indifference to the horrors of the Horn of Africa with their preoccupation with the "rich man's war" in the former Yugoslavia, where the horrors of what was called "ethnic cleansing" were taking place. I said that this double standard must stop.

In holy books, you are rich if you are surrounded by faithful friends and relatives; they will help you when trouble comes. You are poor if you are orphaned or alone. In this sense, the people in the former Yugoslavia, although horribly afflicted by conflict, were still "rich," because the world cared. But Somalia was an orphan. When I raised a question about the Security Council's attention to Bosnia and inattention to Somalia, Sir David Hannay, the British ambassador to the United Nations, told me, "There is no lack of commitment in the Security Council to implement every plan which the secretary-general proposes. There are, however, major problems in effecting the plan for Somalia," he said, without specifying what they were. I objected that "the situations in Bosnia and Somalia are basically similar—except for the fact that the parties in Somalia are not sophisticated and did not wish the UN to become involved, whereas those in Bosnia are sophisticated, welcome the UN, but violate the agreement the UN helps them to conclude."

But in mid-1992, when the work of photojournalists began to appear widely in the Western media, especially the image of a scrawny, dying Somali baby crawling weakly in the dirt as a vulture watched patiently, the international community was at last shocked into action.

In August 1992 the Security Council finally decided to take firmer action. While the humanitarian agencies prepared an emergency airlift of food and medicine to Mogadishu and some inland locations, the Security Council authorized the deployment of one UN battalion to oversee its distribution. This was called "secure humanitarian assistance," and it was something new for UN peacekeepers, a form of "peace enforcement," as mentioned in *An Agenda for Peace*. No Somali government approval for the mission was obtained, because there was no Somali government.

However, it soon became clear that Aidid regarded the United Nations as simply another target for the depredations of his armed bands. Threats and obstructions were encountered at every turn. By September 1992 we saw that the UN force might be able to guard the Mogadishu docks and airport, but it could not operate in the interior of the country, where the famine was at its worst. Additional UN troops were needed to help establish a cease-fire throughout the country, to protect humanitarian aid deliveries, and to encourage national reconciliation.

Speaking at the United Nations, President Bush acknowledged the need for countries to train soldiers for such duties and have them available to the United Nations for dispatch to places such as Somalia on short notice. He said that he was directing the Pentagon to set up such training. Bush's decisions were hailed by *The New York Times* on September 1, 1992. "But," the *Times* asked, "when will Mr. Bush gather the political courage to say what this specific Somalia operation demonstrates about a larger problem—that the world needs a permanent, multinational cavalry on call for just such emergencies?" This was an idea written into the UN Charter, the newspaper said, and "all but forgotten until a few weeks ago when Secretary-General Boutros Boutros-Ghali proposed such a standing army"—the ready force, that is, that I had called for in *An Agenda for Peace*.

But opposition from the Somali militia leaders prevented such deployment. These leaders were taking an aggressive, threatening stance toward the United Nations and spreading the rumor that the United Nations intended to "invade" the country. The warlords saw the UN Somalia operation as a threat to their own privileged positions at the expense of the Somali people.

American politicians and officials who visited Mogadishu commended the "great job" my special representative for Somalia, Mohamed Sahnoun, was doing, noting that Sahnoun had established a dialogue with every Somali leader. Nevertheless, while Sahnoun's performance was popular with the private, nongovernmental personnel who were in Somalia to deliver aid, I was worried by his efforts to "understand" the militia leaders, Aidid and Mahdi, and establish "warm relations" with them. This did, indeed, make it possible to deliver food and aid, but it perpetuated the criminal establishment that had taken over the country, and lengthy negotiations between the warlords had to be carried out before food could be distributed within the various fiefdoms under their control. As the *Financial Times* described the process, "Each shipment has to be accompanied by scores of ragtag gunmen in macabre 'Mad Max' vehicles employed by aid agencies. But in a starving country where almost everybody, including six year olds, carries machine guns, bazookas and rocket-propelled grenades, food convoys are often diverted or ransacked."

At first 10, then 20, and eventually up to 50 percent of the food went to the warlords, a formula for endless UN involvement and certain failure. In mid-1992 Sahnoun decided to convene a UN meeting to discuss Somalia, which was fine, but he wanted to hold it on the Seychelles Islands. This was unnecessary and expensive. When I asked him why he was holding such a meeting without my approval, he submitted his resignation. Though I asked my chief of staff to send a message to Sahnoun, in effect saying, let's forget it and continue to work together, Sahnoun resigned on October 1, 1992. I was sorry about this, because he was a good diplomat and a respected colleague. In his final report to me, dated October 12, 1992, Sahnoun wrote that he "had established collaborative relationships on an ad hoc basis with some Somali partners. This will involve the so-called 'technicals' for security." These negotiations had resulted in "escalating demands" from the armed groups, who threatened to use force to have their demands met. In order that convoys be allowed to reach the starving population, Sahnoun's UN operation had fallen victim to a Somali protection racket. Wire services reported that "Despite appeals to Boutros Boutros-Ghali from Britain—who described Mr. Sahnoun as 'indispensable'—and other governments and relief agencies . . . Mr. Sahnoun left. Fighting back tears at Mogadishu airport, he spoke to the television camera of 'bitter experiences with the UN' and his disappointment "at the lack of support from the UN system as a whole."

In October 1992 Ismat Kittani replaced Sahnoun. Kittani, a prominent ex-Iraqi diplomat of Kurdish origin, had been under secretary in the Foreign Office in Baghdad. A former president of the UN General Assembly, Kittani knew the United Nations well from twenty years' experience. He was an immensely talented diplomat and gentleman whose carefully worded advice was always valuable. When Kittani arrived in Mogadishu, he reported that Sahnoun's practice of paying protection money had created a highly tense situation. Aidid, apparently seeking further payoffs, demanded that UN troops leave the airport. Kittani refused to withdraw the troops, and the next day the Pakistani UN battalion came under heavy fire. At the same time, Mahdi's faction threatened to shell any ship attempting to dock at Mogadishu, claiming that food cargoes were being diverted to Aidid's faction. Meanwhile, in southwest Somalia, relief workers from UNICEF, the UN world food program, and private aid agencies were trapped in the city of Bardera by factional fighting, and food stocks were being looted.

Bush Takes the African Plunge

In a letter of November 24, 1992, I reported to the Security Council that the amount of aid reaching its intended beneficiaries was often barely a trickle. "Looting and banditry are rife. Amid this chaos, the international aid provided by the United Nations and voluntary agencies has become a major (and in some areas the only) source of income and as such is the target of all the 'authorities,' who may sometimes be no more than two or three bandits with guns. In essence, humanitarian supplies have become the source of an otherwise non-existent Somali economy." The cycle of extortion and blackmail must be broken, I insisted, and security conditions established that will permit the distribution of relief supplies. "I cannot conceal from the Security Council that the situation is not improving and the conditions which have developed . . . make it exceedingly difficult for the United Nations operation to achieve the objectives approved by the Security Council."

The next day I received a visit from Lawrence Eagleburger, who had become acting secretary of state when James Baker resigned to manage President Bush's campaign for reelection. Larry and I had known each other only a short while but had quickly established a friendly, bantering relationship. Within a very few days (on December 8, 1992), Eagleburger was named secretary of state in his own right.

Eagleburger greeted me with his usual charming sarcasm. He was superciliously deferential to me in my new role, calling me "Effendi," a term of respect meaning "learned one" in the Ottoman Empire. I contributed to the joke, insisting, "You must refer to me as Pasha, for that is the title befitting my rank." Eagleburger, never to be denied the last word, said, "Okay, Sultan."

"Look, my friend," Larry said when we were alone, "you need help and we can give it." Then, in the stilted jargon of diplomacy, Eagleburger said that "if the Security Council were to decide to authorize member states to use forceful means to ensure the delivery of relief supplies to the people of Somalia, the United States would be ready to take the lead in organizing and commanding such an operation in which a number of other member states would also participate." This was President Bush's "coalition model," which had been employed in the Persian Gulf War against Saddam Hussein. The United States believed that it could also work against the warlords of Somalia.

I reported this to the Security Council, urging it to make a very early decision to adjust the approach to Somalia. Experience had demonstrated that the chaotic fighting there could not be dealt with by a UN operation based on the accepted principles of peacekeeping. There was no alternative to a Chapter VII operation—in other words, force. "If forceful action is taken," I said, "it should preferably be under United Nations command and control. If this is not feasible, an alternative would be an operation undertaken by member states acting with the authorization of the Security Council."

Thus the Security Council authorized, and the United States agreed to lead, an unprecedented peace operation to provide a secure environment for humanitarian relief. The news that American forces would enter Somalia stunned the fighting factions and threw them off balance. Both Aidid and Mahdi hastened to "welcome" the initiative. On December 4, 1992, President Bush wrote to me stating that the United States' mission was "to create security conditions which will permit the feeding of the starving Somali people and allow the transfer of this security function to the United Nations peace-keeping force." As soon as this had been achieved, Bush wrote, "The coalition force will depart from Somalia, transferring its security function to your United Nations peace keeping force."

The Security Council, by its Resolution 794 of December 3, 1992, decided to intervene militarily in Somalia under Chapter VII. "All necessary means" were to be taken to establish a secure environment for the unimpeded delivery of humanitarian assistance. The Unified Task Force (UNITAF) would be spearheaded by the U.S. armed forces.

Disarm the Gangs?

As the United States prepared to go in, I told the Security Council that "the first condition is that the Unified Task Force should take effective action to ensure that the heavy weapons of the factions are neutralized and brought under international control and that the irregular forces and groups are disarmed before the Unified Task Force sent on 8 December 1992 withdraws." I made the same points in a letter to President Bush, adding that "without this action I do not believe that it will be possible to establish the secure environment called for by the Security Council resolution or to create conditions in which the United Nations' existing efforts to promote national reconciliation can be carried forward and the task of protecting humanitarian activities can safely be transferred to a conventional United Nations peace-keeping operation."

But the Pentagon instantly announced that it had no intention of disarming the factions, and the Bush White House, then in its last days, did nothing to override this military reluctance to do the job right. When U.S. Marines landed on the beach at Mogadishu on December 9, 1992, the multitude of press photographers there to meet them recorded the amusing sight of marines in full combat gear hitting the beach and digging in, automatic weapons at the ready, while groups of bemused sightseers lazily looked on. The marines then took over the airport, meeting no resistance.

But the U.S. forces refused to disarm the Somali militias. Even when they came upon a major cache of weapons, the U.S. commanders of the Unified Task Force were under orders not to seize them. In my opinion, three critical steps were needed: disarming the warring groups; establishing a secure environment; and creating a workable division of labor between the U.S. and UN operations on the ground. The United States did not do any of the three.

Nonetheless, the very presence of the Unified Task Force caused the Somali warlords to lie low. Over the course of five months, the Task Force opened access to more and more remote areas of the country. The delivery of food and medicine was protected, and nongovernmental organizations expanded their relief operations. The result was a dramatic drop in malnutrition and the number of deaths from starvation.

Haiti, Fate, and Freedom

As the United Nations was getting more involved with Bosnia and Somalia in 1992, I was asked to play a role in Haiti. My deep interest in the fate of black Africa had long before led me to an interest in Haiti, an African country located in the New World. I knew something of the belief in *voudou* in West Africa and its Haitian branch. Later, during a meeting in Cotonou, Benin, in West Africa in 1995, I was asked to inaugurate a monument called "the door of no return." On the inside of the doorway, slaves were depicted being led away in chains; on the outside, from the sea looking in toward Africa, were scenes of their souls and the souls of their descendants returning to Mother Africa. Those returned souls could be consulted, it was believed, by the living in Haiti through *voudou*.

A Francophone nation, Haiti was the first independent republic in Latin America and the first independent black republic anywhere. Created by the 1804 revolt of slaves against Napoleon, Haiti's sovereign independence was not given diplomatic recognition because slavery remained legal. Ostracized from the international community and prey to big powers, Haiti depicted its turbulent history on its flag, which bristles with cannons and banners. But although born in a struggle for liberty, Haiti for more than a century was ruled by a sequence of dictators, each profiting from the misery of the people.

From 1843 to 1911, eleven Haitian heads of state were deposed by coups d'état. Between 1911 and 1915, six presidents were assassinated, which prompted the United States, fearful that Germany would use Haiti as a base to threaten the Panama Canal, to occupy Haiti in 1915 with a force of U.S. marines. The United States did not depart until 1934 and remained a political force for years thereafter. In 1957 a ferocious dictator, François Duvalier, known as Papa Doc, took power and ruled through a gang of thugs called Tontons Macoutes, who frightened the entire population, including the army. Upon his death in 1971, Duvalier was succeeded by his son Jean-Claude, "Baby Doc," whose corrupt incompetence led eventually to his fall from power on February 7, 1986, and his flight to refuge in France. As Egyptian minister of state for foreign affairs, I had been asked by the French president whether Egypt would give asylum to the young Duvalier. But President Mubarak had refused and reproached me even for asking him. Egypt has taken too many political refugees already, Mubarak said, and has enough problems with them.

In the twentieth century Haiti became a symbol of the suffering and the struggle of the third world, displaying the worst afflictions of the countries of the South: crushing poverty, brutal dictatorship, outside intervention and exploitation, and deteriorating conditions of health and environment. Because of all these factors, Haiti's destiny is of international significance.

After the departure of Baby Doc, the Haitian people began a long and painful march toward democracy. Following a series of coups d'état, agreement was reached in 1990 among the various political factions to name a provisional president, who, in turn, requested UN help in organizing and observing democratic elections. Father Jean-Bertrand Aristide became the first popularly elected president in Haiti's history. The 1990 election was made possible by the United Nations Observer Group for the Verification of the Elections in Haiti (ONUVEH). The UN mission included security personnel and, in close cooperation with the Organization of American States (OAS), provided a stable environment for the election.

The Haitian request was not met with enthusiasm by Latin American and other third-world states, which were reluctant to set a dangerous precedent. It provoked debate first on the interpretation of Article 2(7) of the Charter, which forbids UN intervention in the internal affairs of a member state, and, second, on the respective jurisdictions of the General Assembly and the Security Council. One compromise solution was that the General Assembly assist with the elections while the Security Council assisted with the security. In the end the General Assembly adopted a resolution entrusting the OAS with the Haitian question. The United Nations would send observers for the electoral process and advisers for the security of electoral operations. They could be drawn from military institutions, but they would not be Blue Helmets.

The elections were greeted as the most democratic in Haiti's history. The victory of Jean-Bertrand Aristide—"Titid," the populist and demagogic priest of the shantytowns—was stunning. He was elected on the first round with about 67 percent of the vote. Having fulfilled its mandate, the United Nations left Haiti, only to be reproached later for its swift departure. A continued UN presence, even a symbolic one, might have prevented the unfortunate events that followed.

President Aristide was installed on February 7, 1990. On September 30 a coup d'état was carried out by Commander Michel François. General Raoul Cedras took charge of the junta running the country. Aristide was given refuge in Venezuela by President Carlos Andrés Pérez, and subsequently in Washington, D.C.

The OAS demanded Aristide's immediate reinstatement and imposed sanctions against Haiti. Although Aristide sought the intervention of the United Nations, the United Nations left the resolution of the crisis to the OAS. This organization, which I had studied closely during my academic career, was directed by João Clemente Baena Soares, a Brazilian. Short, sturdy, and fastidious about matters of protocol, he fiercely—and rightly—defended the independence of his organization. I had met Baena Soares in June 1992 at the Rio "Earth Summit," where I told him of my desire to see regional organizations take a greater world role in cooperation with the United Nations.

At the same time—June 1992—President Aristide sent me a letter complaining that the OAS "did not know how, up until the present—despite their good intentions and their indefatigable efforts—to restore democracy in Haiti. . . . The resolutions of the Council of Ministers of Foreign Affairs of the OAS, intended to lay pressure on the putschists, have not attained the objectives wished for." Aristide seemed determined to remain aloof and difficult. He expected the OAS and the United Nations to restore democracy to Haiti and return him to office while criticizing one to the other and avoiding any engagement with the problems himself. I passed a copy of Aristide's letter to Baena Soares and in reply received a message explaining at length all the actions undertaken by the OAS in favor of Haiti. I was learning how hard it was to engage Haiti, the OAS, and the United Nations in a cooperative effort.

On the afternoon of Tuesday, September 15, 1992, I met with President Aristide, who had come to New York to receive a Press Service Award. We had not previously met. I welcomed him to my office and told him that I would do all I could to keep international attention on Haiti. But if the status quo continued, I said, such interest would gradually fade.

President Aristide, a short, slender man with a slight squint, expressed himself in refined French, with long sentences that sometimes approached alexandrine verse. He had the demeanor of an unctuous prelate. He hoped for Security Council action. I explained that UN involvement was limited because the General Assembly resolution had placed the OAS in charge of the Haitian problem. I advised Aristide to try to gain greater support among the United Nations' member states.

He took my recommendation to heart. Two weeks later, on September 29, 1992—one year after the coup d'état—he spoke during the general debate of the General Assembly. Thousands and thousands of Haitians were gathered at the UN building and in the neighboring streets. Before a packed hall and in an electric atmosphere, Aristide displayed his dazzling talents as a spellbinder. He cited Cicero, Plato, Aristotle, and Archimedes, passing from French to Creole and back to French with Latin tags. The former seminarian had become a poet-orator: "I found Haiti, where the roots of liberty set down by Toussaint L'Ouverture, endured . . . diminished, sometimes battered, but never finished": *"J'ai trouvé Haiti ou les racines de liberté plantées par Toussaint L'Ouverture sont toujours combattues, quelquefois battues, mais jamais abattues."* It was impossible not to have mixed feelings about Aristide. In his political dealings he was exasperatingly obstinate and obtuse, but in public he was a thrilling presence, embodying Haitian hopes for deliverance from the country's misery.

The United Nations and the OAS in Harness

On November 24, 1992, the General Assembly adopted a resolution calling on the secretary-general, with the cooperation of the OAS, to try to resolve the crisis in Haiti. In effect, the United Nations was asked to take charge of the Haitian case. Aristide had won the first round of his fight to relegate the OAS to a lesser role. I named a special envoy for Haiti, Dante Caputo, a former Argentinean minister of foreign affairs who spoke French. Proudly conscious of his Latin identity, Caputo was already the special envoy of the secretary-general of the OAS, so his nomination by me, I thought, would be the key to the problem of UN-OAS cooperation. It was an innovation. I telephoned the current Argentinean minister of foreign affairs to ask for his approval. "We accept your choice, even though Dante Caputo belongs to the opposition," he said only half jokingly.

President Aristide had requested a civil mission to verify respect for human rights and to open dialogue among the Haitian parties in preparation for his return to Haiti. But the U.S. administration was ambivalent about his return. State Department officials seemed to regard the restoration of Aristide as a moral imperative. Defense and intelligence officials seemed to fear that Aristide would suffer a violent end at the hands of the Haitian army or would inflame the people's passions with his demogoguery and further destabilize the country. While official U.S. policy favored a very large mandate, including institution building, creating a new police force, and professionalizing the army, many other nations felt that any such intervention would violate Haiti's sovereignty and exceed the scope of the United Nations' proper role.

CHAPTER 3

Running into Trouble

(1993)

My face, appearing at once wary and haughty, peered at me from the cover of *Time* magazine's January 18, 1993, international edition.

A year after taking office, Boutros-Ghali will not admit to disappointment, but it is evident that his ambitions to help shape the architecture of a new world order have run into trouble. Under his stewardship, the UN has dramatically expanded its peacekeeping mandate—only to find itself stymied, even rejected, on several of its recent initiatives. Though the Secretary-General acts at the behest of the Security Council, he is being saddled with much of the blame. Rightly or wrongly, the Secretary-General has become the lightning rod for dissatisfaction with the UN, and, more generally, widespread frustration at the way in which nationalist ambitions and ethnic hostilities are threatening to convert the desired new world order into the very opposite. Never mind that the UN, for all its good intentions, lacks the military force, political leverage, perhaps even the moral suasion to fulfill its expanded mandate.

A New American Administration

January 1993 saw the arrival of a new American administration. President Bush sent me a warm farewell letter: "My intent has been to be supportive of the UN and of you personally, based on my philosophy that together there is much we can do. I have appreciated very much your efforts, and I believe much has been accomplished." He added a handwritten note: "Boutros—I will miss working with you."

I heard from the incoming Clinton administration only via messages passed at the staff level: Richard Thornburgh would have to go. So would Bush's friend Joseph Verner Reed, who was in charge of preparations for the United Nations' fiftieth anniversary, a year-long series of events to take place during 1995. To replace Reed, I appointed Gillian Sorensen, New York City's commissioner for the United Nations and the diplomatic corps and wife of Theodore Sorensen, the well-known lawyer and former speechwriter for President Kennedy. Reed had done an outstanding job of representing me at functions around the world that I could not attend myself. So I was pleased when he offered to serve as special adviser to me on public affairs and management-staff relations for $1 a year. Later I was told that because Reed was a Republican, the White House was "very unhappy" that I had retained him.

To assure the Clinton administration of my goodwill, I suggested that it might want to name an American whom I could appoint as under secretary-general for public affairs. In this way, I said, the United Nations and the United States might begin to speak if not with one voice, at least coherently. The Clinton administration rejected my offer, apparently regarding it as an attempt to substitute the public affairs post for the administrative job, which I had given to an American, Thornburgh, for the first time in UN history. As a replacement for Thornburgh, it proposed Melissa Wells, a U.S. Foreign Service officer. Wells had worked with UNDP in Uganda and had been the American ambassador to Zaire, with a fine record. Her appointment would advance my self-set goal of "50-50 by 50," that is, 50 percent women in top UN jobs by the fiftieth UN anniversary. I had a long meeting with Wells, who was bright, pleasant, and enthusiastic. I emerged feeling that her African experience would be put to excellent use at the third-world-focused United Nations. I offered her the job and she accepted.

Thornburgh, who had seemed distant and inactive throughout his year at the United Nations, marked his departure by leaking a highly critical report on reform of the United Nations. I agreed with nearly all of his criticisms and regretted that he had not made any of them to me when he was in office.

On May 14, 1993, representatives of the U.S. Commission on Improving the Effectiveness of the UN came to see me. Among its leading members were Senator Claiborne Pell, Congressman Jim Leach, Senator Larry Pressler, Charles Lichenstein, who had been Jeane Kirkpatrick's deputy when she had been American ambassador to the United Nations (Kirkpatrick was also a member of this commission), and Jerome Shestack, a well-known lawyer. I told them of the Volcker-Ogata commission's recommendations and said I hoped President Clinton would read that report. As for administrative reform, I had appointed Thornburgh at the request of the Bush administration and then appointed Wells at the request of the Clinton administration. I noted that 50 percent of the staff assigned to the United Nations' administration and management were Americans. "I have given Wells a full and complete mandate," I assured the group. "What Wells decides must be done to reform the UN, I will do." But within a year I had to remove Wells, who proved ill suited to the job. Like Thornburgh, she was able to point to problems in the UN bureaucracy but unable to propose solutions. I thought I had delegated these Americans the authority to bring about change, but after several months went by, I realized that the problems had simply been passed back up to me.

There were also changes across First Avenue at the U.S. Mission to the United Nations. I was introduced to the new American ambassador by a note from former President Jimmy Carter on February 1, 1993. He wanted me to know "what a knowledgeable and competent person is Madeleine Albright . . . she's very close to me and I know her to be a heavyweight in every respect." I wanted very much to establish close relations with Ambassador Albright, for I knew that I could not perform effectively without the goodwill and cooperation of America's chief representative. Ambassador Albright seemed shy and very nice. Short and plump, she had sharp blue eyes that were dazzling when set off by a blue dress. She presented her credentials to me with Warren Christopher protectively at her side. The UN ambassadorship was her first diplomatic post, and she recognized that it would involve on-the-job training. We exchanged remarks about the transition from academic to diplomatic life that we both had made. She was excited and eager to get to work. She asked me to help her learn. She was, she said, in her "freshman year at the UN school." This was also my first encounter with Warren Christopher and the impeccable cut of his suits. I was intrigued by his strange voice. He seemed detached yet at the same time uneasy in his new role.

As the Clinton administration got under way, Madeleine Albright and I worked together cooperatively and cordially. She praised my determination to reform the United Nations and declared that I was "a ringmaster determined to prod this elephantine bureaucracy into action." I was puzzled, however, by what seemed her desire to strike attitudes rather than address substantive issues. She seemed to have little interest in the difficult diplomatic work of persuading her foreign counterparts to go along with the positions of her government, preferring to lecture or speak in declarative sentences, or simply to read verbatim from her briefing books. She seemed to assume that her mere assertion of a U.S. policy should be sufficient to achieve the support of other nations.

Bosnia: A New U.S. Approach

By early 1993 it had become clear that the United Nations had been given responsibilities that not only far exceeded traditional peacekeeping but also were virtually open-ended, extending to almost every area of human activity. In Cambodia, Somalia, and the former Yugoslavia, the United Nations' new duties were vast, encompassing food, water, land mines, disease, refugees, democratization, human rights, social and economic development, and governance at every level. But above all, the tragic situation in Bosnia was absorbing our attention and draining our resources. Throughout most of the past year, the Security Council, in sharp contrast to its traditional mode of operation, had been meeting almost every day, issuing resolutions and presidential statements at an unprecedented rate. More than 2 million people in Bosnia were being assisted by the United Nations. UNPROFOR had delivered more than 40,000 tons of humanitarian aid to besieged cities and towns, and it was providing help to countless displaced people. Through an airlift greater than any in Europe since the Berlin blockade, the United Nations had prevented the mass starvation predicted for the winter.

As a presidential candidate, Clinton had called for multilateral military action in Bosnia and entered office declaring Bosnia to be America's most urgent international crisis. But the new U.S. administration quickly threw up barriers against effective action. Cyrus Vance felt certain that the United States would accept the peace plan that he and David Owen had negotiated. The key figures of the new Clinton foreign policy team had been colleagues appointed fifteen years earlier, when Cy had been secretary of state. Cy's former deputy, Warren Christopher, was now secretary of state. Cy's policy planning chief, Anthony Lake, had become Clinton's national security adviser. And Cy's chief of staff, Peter Tarnoff, had become under secretary of state for political affairs. But Cy's peace plan was rejected. The new Clinton team seemed to want to have little to do with him and even less to do with David Owen.

Worse, the chances of peace were being thrown away, as Clinton and Christopher, using strong language, attacked the Vance-Owen plan as appeasement of the Serbs. They were wrong. The plan delineated a ten-province structure that would reflect all groups fairly, reconstituting Bosnia as a multiethnic and progressively demilitarized state. It would have blocked the Serb goal of creating a "Greater Serbia." It would have required the Serbs to give up great areas of conquered territory and to return property seized by force.

All this effort was tossed aside by Clinton and Christopher, who declared that the United States would come up with its own peace plan. They called for lifting the embargo on arms for Bosnia. They said they wanted air strikes against the Serbs, though they knew that France, Britain, and Russia would not agree. An end to the arms embargo would not "level the playing field" to the benefit of the Muslims, as the United States claimed it would; instead, as Owen said, it would create a "killing field." And if the United States did carry out air strikes, they would lead only to retaliation on the ground by Serb forces against the UN Protection Force, which was made up largely of European troops from NATO member countries carrying out a Security Council mandate that dispersed them in small groups all over Bosnia to carry out peacekeeping tasks while the war raged on and there was no peace to keep. Washington turned a blind eye to the danger of retaliation against them but refused to contemplate putting U.S. forces into this risky situation. To the world outside the United States, the Clinton administration's approach made sense only as the product of some obscure Machiavellian calculation.

Vance and Owen came to my office on February 2, 1993. The previous evening Vance had met with Christopher to brief him on the Vance-Owen plan. Though the EC had just announced its full and unequivocal support for the plan, Christopher seemed skeptical and negative. The

Serbs had agreed to it, but the Bosnian Muslims were the holdouts, largely because the negative attitude of the incoming Clinton team had convinced them that the United States would give them a better deal. The previous evening Vance had asked Christopher to telephone President Izetbegović of Bosnia simply to urge him to come to New York for further negotiations on the plan. Christopher had coolly turned the request aside, simply "taking note of it." The meeting concluded with Christopher stating that the United States wanted to study its options and would not lend its support at this point, critical as it was.

While recognizing the limits to my authority, I wanted to do all that I could to seize the moment. I decided to issue a report to the Security Council immediately, urging acceptance of the Vance-Owen plan. On February 8, 1993, Vance, Owen, and I met with Bosnian Croat leader Mile Akmadžić, prime minister of Bosnia. "In my opinion," he said, "and that of most citizens of Bosnia and Herzegovina, the Vance-Owen plan is the best; there is no alternative to it but war. In our view, we cannot finish a war successfully, and victory for any side is not in prospect." But in Washington Bosnian Foreign Minister Haris Silajdžić was not encouraged to accept the plan. U.S. opposition had dealt the Vance-Owen plan a severe setback, if not a death blow.

On February 10, 1993, Christopher announced a U.S. peace plan for Bosnia. By coming up with its own plan, the United States seemed to want to take the lead; instead it thoroughly confused everyone, because its plan seemed virtually indistinguishable from that of Vance and Owen. It appeared that the United States was simply trying to avoid the Vance-Owen plan's requirement of 30,000 troops on the ground to police the agreement, half of whom would have been Americans. Apparently the new U.S. administration did not want to get involved on the ground in a dangerous foreign conflict that Bush had avoided. Clinton had been elected on a domestic-agenda platform, and Bush had been defeated, most commentators said, because he had stressed foreign policy over domestic policy.

Within a few weeks Christopher announced that President Clinton had decided that the United States would "engage actively and directly in the Vance-Owen negotiations, bringing the weight of American policy to bear." Christopher's statement gave the impression that the United States now supported the Vance-Owen plan; read carefully, it meant that the United States intended to take over the negotiations and, as Christopher put it, "build on" the Vance-Owen ideas. Asked to explain what the United States intended, former secretary of state Lawrence Eagleburger said he thought the United States wanted to reduce the 43 percent of the territory that the Vance-Owen plan gave the Serbs. It would take two and a half more years of bloody war and war crimes before the United States, at Dayton, would give the Serbs 49 percent. David Owen later declared that "if George Bush had won the American elections . . . then the war in Bosnia would have been over long ago."

As the United States began the process of supplanting the Vance-Owen effort, NATO planners began to work with the UN Department of Peace-Keeping Operations and UN military advisers to design a force that would be put on the ground to implement a peace agreement. Fifty thousand troops would be needed. I favored something along the lines of the force that was in Somalia at this time, a U.S.-led combat force, joined by forces from a coalition of several other countries and authorized by the Security Council. As I had argued in the case of Somalia, any such force for Bosnia would have to be ready and willing to take military action to enforce peace should it meet with violent resistance. The United States, however, showed no desire to get involved militarily in Bosnia. Indeed, as any truce or peace agreement would leave the United States with no alternative but to contribute troops, the Americans seemed most uncooperative whenever progress toward peace seemed possible. This created real tension between Washington and some European governments, especially those of Britain and France, which had significant numbers of troops on the ground and were becoming less and less tolerant of Washington's tendency to criticize their performance but not contribute any troops of its own.

In the Oval Office

Snow was forecast for February 23, 1993, so I took Amtrak instead of the air shuttle to Washington. I met President Clinton in the Oval Office, and we sat side by side with our respective advisers lined up on each side facing each other from a double line of sofas and chairs. Flashbulbs lit up the scene, and cameras clicked and whirred like cicadas. As the reporters were being shooed from the room, I tried to make conversation by telling Clinton that I had arrived by train. "I thought Egyptian trains were bad,"

I said, "but American trains make them look pretty good." "Americans like cars," Clinton said tersely. Immediately I feared that I had stupidly offended the president by casting aspersions on his country's railway system. But no, everything was all right. The mood in the Oval Office was, as the Egyptian saying goes, *samme ala assal* ("melted butter on honey").

Clinton praised me, saying that he liked having an activist secretary-general at the United Nations. He knew where to find me at any time, he said, just by looking at the newspaper. As we reviewed the range of conflicts in which the United Nations was involved, Clinton said that I would find the United States to be a good troop-contributing country. He was pleased, he said, by the idea of U.S. troops serving in Somalia under the command of a general from another country. I explained the merits of the Vance-Owen plan to Clinton and asked him for America's support, but Vice President Gore intervened to say that the Vance-Owen plan left the Serbs with an advantage and repeated, insistently, the arguments for lifting the arms embargo in favor of Bosnia. The United States would try to support the Vance-Owen plan, the president said, but "did see a need for a modification of the envisaged borders." Before meeting Clinton I had been told by friends who had encountered him that Clinton would never say "no" and that I would have to listen very carefully to hear when "yes" really meant "no." Clinton's remarks about the Vance-Owen plan, I concluded, amounted to such a case.

The stakes were getting higher. Fighting was intensifying in Bosnia as the Serbs moved forward on the ground in the wake of the rejection of the Vance-Owen plan. Cy Vance was downcast when he, Owen, and I met at the United Nations on March 1, 1993. "We are on the brink of a major war," Vance predicted.

That same day, Ambassador Reginald Bartholomew, who had just been appointed by Clinton as envoy to the former Yugoslavia, came to see me, accompanied by Madeleine Albright. I opened our meeting by arguing once again that the United States should support the Vance-Owen plan. Bartholomew said equivocally that his role would be to work with the Vance-Owen "process." I raised the need for U.S.-NATO troops to enforce a peace agreement. "Speaking as a former American ambassador to NATO," Bartholomew said, "I want to assure you that neither NATO nor the U.S. has any desire for arrangements that would not be under UN control. To put it bluntly, the U.S. and NATO don't want to be on the hook. I hope the secretary-general understands this message," he emphasized. When I asked what "don't want to be on the hook" meant, I was told that it was slang, meaning that the United States and NATO would want the cover of international blessing and UN responsibility for any such mission.

On March 4, 1993, Radovan Karadžić, the Bosnian Serb leader, came to see me in New York. A complaint had been lodged in the U.S. District Court for the Southern District of New York against Karadžić for "genocide, war crimes and crimes against humanity." Cyrus Vance and David Owen were with me when Karadžić, a burly, posturing, pompadoured figure, familiar from his many interviews with television news reporters, arrived. An open letter to the American people, signed by Bosnian Serbs, had appeared in *The New York Times.* It said that the bombing of the World Trade Center in New York was an example of what could happen again if the United States decided to intervene in Bosnia. Cyrus Vance was outraged. "How dare you!" he said fiercely. Challenged, Karadžić swiftly retreated, claiming that he had never really mastered English and that the letter had not been intended to be insulting.

The refusal of the Bosnian Muslims, encouraged by the United States, to accept the Vance-Owen plan had relieved the pressure on the Bosnian Serbs to negotiate seriously for peace. Karadžić, a psychiatrist by profession and an accomplished diplomatic actor, began moaning about the injustice that the Vance-Owen plan would inflict upon his people. The Serbs "would be the most deprived community" if the Vance-Owen plan were to go into effect. I urged Karadžić in the strongest terms to accept the plan. "It has not been easy to get you and your delegation permission to come to New York," I said. "This is the moment. You are isolated. The entire world is against you. Accept now, before it is too late. The Bosnian Serbs will face great condemnation by, and terrible pressure from, the international community. You have seen nothing yet. It is crucial that you understand the commitment and the will of the international community," I told him, though in my heart I had little confidence that any such commitment existed.

But the American abandonment of the Vance-Owen plan had given the Serbs a new opportunity. Karadžić was clearly playing for time as his Serb forces intensified their attacks and seized more territory. Serb paramilitary units had attacked several cities, including Srebenica. Loss of life was heavy, and UN humanitarian shipments were interrupted. Thousands of Muslims had sought refuge in Srebenica from the surrounding areas under attack or occupied by Serb forces. Every day thirty to forty people died as a result of military action, starvation, exposure, or lack of medical treatment or will.

Media Distortion

On Sunday, March 7, 1993, I appeared on the television news program *This Week with David Brinkley.* I said that we had to continue to negotiate within the Vance-Owen framework. There was no alternative. Patience was needed. "Let us continue to work in spite of all the difficulties, and let us give a chance to the Vance-Owen plan," I said. George Will declared that "the Serbs are winning," and that NATO and the United Nations appear to be "impotent." Sam Donaldson pressed me sternly: "Mr. Secretary-General, while you continue to negotiate, the Serbs apparently make progress on the ground. More towns have fallen. Aren't you afraid, at the end of the day, that they will have not just seventy percent more territory, but all of it?"

"Yes," I replied, "but we have as an objective the withdrawal of the Serbs, and if they will not withdraw, then we'll have to take the necessary measures."

"Now, just what necessary measures do you have in mind?" Donaldson asked.

"I believe that if we find that we are not able to achieve their withdrawal, then there is only one solution, which is enforcement. And the member states [of the United Nations] must be ready to send troops on the ground."

Donaldson asked how many troops it would take to drive the Serbs back.

"I'm not a technician; I don't know," I replied, "but certainly it will be a major operation . . . and without participation of the United States it will be very difficult to have this enforcement."

Donaldson then stressed that "a great number of Americans believe the Europeans should lead the way, that the United States should not be in the forefront of any ground action in that territory."

"Yes," I said, "but in fact, who is doing the operation? It is the United Nations, and the United States is a major member of the United Nations. But we are still at the stage of negotiation, of humanitarian assistance, of economic sanctions."

"Well, I suppose you're quite correct, sir," said Donaldson, "but I suppose that many Americans would say that the people dying on the ground would not really be United Nations troops if they happened to be Americans."

"I completely agree," I replied. "This is why we have to continue to negotiate for the time being."

As I emerged from the studio, I tried to make sense of this confusing exchange. At first these television correspondents seemed to be complaining that the United Nations was not doing enough to defeat the Serbs in combat. Then, when I responded that to do so would require U.S. participation, they seemed to accuse me of wanting to draw the United States into the fighting against the wishes of the American people. My attempt at the end to stress the need for negotiation seemed to have no impact.

The next morning the *Washington Post* headline read: UN CHIEF SAYS SERB FIGHTERS MAY BE FORCED BACK UNDER PACT. This raised a wave of alarm. It was not exactly what I had said, but facts rarely catch up with a false report. I was accused of trying to draw the United States into a war in the Balkans and to place American troops under my command. President Clinton's aide George Stephanopoulos quickly declared, on March 9, "We've had no discussions at all on anything beyond what we've said in the past, which is that we would contemplate the use of U.S. forces to enforce an agreement that is already made." Before my appearance on the Brinkley program, the former U.S. ambassador to the United Nations, Jeane Kirkpatrick, had denounced me in her syndicated newspaper column for opposing the use of force in Bosnia. Every time the Security Council approached a decision to enforce a solution, she wrote, Boutros-Ghali "has appealed for more time to find a political solution."

In a subsequent column published after my television remarks, Kirkpatrick declared that, "Boutros Boutros-Ghali wants to make himself the world's commander-in-chief: Last week, he suggested that U.S. and NATO forces be put at the service of the UN and under the command of its secretary-general to drive Serbian troops out of designated areas of Bosnia if they refuse to leave." The Clinton administration, she said, "wisely rejected the suggestion that U.S. forces become involved in a land war in Bosnia." Kirkpatrick's characterization lodged in the American consciousness and could not be dislodged. She had accused me of both trying to avoid a war and seeking to send American soldiers into combat under my command. Why was Kirkpatrick saying these things?

Surely she knew that they were not true. We had met. She knew me. I could conclude only that she saw a domestic political advantage for herself in attacking the UN secretary-general.

The conditions for UNPROFOR's actions in Bosnia steadily deteriorated. With the Vance-Owen plan blocked by the United States, which was neither able to produce a better blueprint for peace nor willing to impose a military solution, the only option left was to ask the United Nations to keep doing more of the same: provide humanitarian relief even as the fighting worsened. Relief operations were obstructed, sabotaged, or diverted for the military purposes of the warring parties. UN personnel were deliberately targeted by fighters from all three sides. By this time, the United Nations had taken 548 casualties with 51 fatalities, and the rate of killed and wounded was steadily escalating.

Creating a War Crimes Tribunal

One of the most heinous aspects of the war in the former Yugoslavia was the massive and systematized violation of human rights. This was "the worst human disaster in Europe since the crimes of the Nazis," wrote Anthony Lewis in *The New York Times*. Pope John Paul II called it an "atrocious drama" that "humiliates Europe and seriously compromises the future of peace." The Security Council had reaffirmed the individual responsibility of all those who committed or ordered grave breaches of the Geneva Conventions or violations of international humanitarian law. The Council requested that I appoint a commission of experts to compile a database of war crimes and begin to conduct field investigations. By its Resolution 808 of 1993, the Security Council requested me to report on all aspects of the matter, including specific proposals for the establishment of an international tribunal. The UN legal department, headed by Carl-August Fleischauer, did wonderful work, enabling me to submit a draft statute dealing with the constitutionally controversial question of the legal basis for establishing such a tribunal. This laid the groundwork for the first war crimes tribunal authorized not by a country victorious in war but by the international community as a whole, acting through its organization, the United Nations. The proposal that an international court at The Hague try the war criminals of former Yugoslavia would be a milestone in international law.

By this time, mid-March 1993, a new factor was shaping the scene. The Russians, recovering their diplomatic footing following the collapse of the Soviet Union, were asserting their traditional role as patron and protector of the Serbs, their Orthodox coreligionists. Russian Foreign Minister Andrei Kozyrev had made it clear that the United States should stop talking about unilateral actions, such as air strikes, if it did not want to risk a real war in the Balkans—a war by proxy of major outside powers. No one could suppress the recollection that the First World War had flared up through just such a struggle by proxy in Bosnia in 1914.

In this context, the UN Security Council, at the end of March, decided not to authorize force to enforce the so-called no-fly zone, the Security Council's ban under Resolution 781 of all military flights in the airspace of Bosnia except those for UN operations. Using force, the United States said, might undermine President Boris Yeltsin by giving an issue to Russian nationalists, who were increasingly calling for NATO and the United Nations to adopt a pro-Serb policy. I held long talks with Kozyrev, who defended the Serbs with heartfelt emotion and accused the United Nations of bias. I reminded him that the Security Council, with his country not openly opposed, had approved all the resolutions under which the UN forces were constrained to operate.

As the fighting worsened and the Serbs gained more territory, the Muslims, at the end of March, decided that they would agree to the map presented in the Vance-Owen plan. At the United Nations the British and the French proposed a Security Council resolution putting the Council's full weight behind the Vance-Owen text, but the United States again turned away from it. Why? An explanation was provided by a current Washington joke: "What's worse than the Bosnians saying no? Bosnians saying yes," because that would require the United States to put American soldiers on the ground to implement the agreement. Clinton had constructed a double bind for himself. On the one hand, he would block efforts to reach a peace agreement because such an agreement would mean sending American troops to Bosnia to implement it. On the other hand, he would reject proposals to pull the United Nations out of its impossible Bosnian situation because such an emergency evacuation—a "Dunkirk," as some termed it—would require American troops to make it succeed. Years later Richard Holbrooke would claim in his book about Bosnia that until 1995 Clinton was unaware of the U.S. commitment not only to send American troops in the event of a peace agreement but also to deploy them to evacuate UN peacekeepers in the event of a debacle. But both commitments were widely known and discussed throughout the United Nations' involvement in Bosnia.

On April 1, 1993, Cyrus Vance resigned. I could only sympathize with his decision. He had been let down by his own country and by his own former State Department colleagues. I proposed that Cy be replaced by Thorvald Stoltenberg, the former defense and foreign minister of Norway. He spoke Serbo-Croatian, had served in a diplomatic post in Yugoslavia, and knew the UN system well, having been UN high commissioner for refugees in the late 1980s. A tall man who spoke English with slow precision, Stoltenberg could listen to the longest and most outrageous diplomatic harangues with never-changing composure. He was as cool as his northern homeland.

Phnom Penh and Hun Sen

By early 1993, the United Nations' electoral component in Cambodia had registered almost 5 million people, a number not far from the total of all eligible voters outside the Khmer Rouge–controlled areas. But the February deadline for all Cambodian parties to register for the national election passed, and the Khmer Rouge, rather than join the process, launched dangerous and destabilizing raids into the countryside, terrifying the population into renewed fear that the genocidal killers of the 1970s would return.

With the situation increasingly grave, I returned to Cambodia in April 1993. Prince Sihanouk awaited me at the foot of the aircraft steps. En route to the royal palace, I found him discouraged and depressed. Before my arrival he had publicly criticized the United Nations and renewed his threat to resign as head of the Supreme National Council. I begged him to stand firm for the good of the people of Cambodia. Our dialogue warmed. At a meeting in the throne room of the palace, in the presence of all the members of the Supreme National Council, I deplored the recalcitrance of the Khmer Rouge. I implored all parties to respect the decision of the ballot and promised that ballot secrecy and voter safety would be secure. The role of Prince Sihanouk was crucial. "The responsibility of the prince," I said, "extends not only over Cambodia but also beyond, to the concerns of the entire world," for if the United Nations succeeded in Cambodia, it would serve as a model for similar operations in other parts of the world. Success in Cambodia would reflect positively on the whole international community to which Cambodia belongs.

Hun Sen, the head of the government of Cambodia and its political arm, the Cambodian People's Party (PPC), was present. I had met him before, when he had called on me in New York early in my term. Young, obviously intelligent, and apparently not in the best of health, he carried himself like the real, if not yet recognized, leader. In the palatial setting of Sihanouk's chambers, Hun Sen looked like a militant peasant in a field of golden grain. A former Khmer Rouge leader himself, he had defected to the Heng Samrin regime established by the invading Vietnamese in 1979 and, as Heng Samrin's successor, had now chosen to work for a new Cambodia under the Paris Agreement. He deserved credit for taking this course. He knew no foreign languages and was never without a translator at his side. His lack of sophistication seemed to magnify the sense he conveyed of someone aggrieved and isolated yet indispensable as a leader at this time in his country's history. Hun Sen wanted the maximum foreign assistance for his country and the minimum international presence. The UN mission in Cambodia was supposed to exercise significant control over the main ministries in his administration, but he resisted this strenuously and denied the UN mission any access at all to the party structures where, as in all Communist regimes, the important decisions were taken. Hun Sen turned to me: "Just this morning, a leaflet was distributed in Phnom Penh, which was a veritable declaration of war on the part of the Khmer Rouge." Khieu Samphan, Pol Pot's mouthpiece, was at the palace representing the Khmer Rouge and denounced all charges against it. Vietnam is the enemy, he said, and the Vietnamese-installed regime in Phnom Penh—referring to Hun Sen. He rejected in advance the UN-organized elections and made it menacingly clear that we could expect even more serious trouble. Though always deferential to Prince Sihanouk, Khieu Samphan and Hun Sen clearly hated each other.

Using UN Leverage

I had known Prince Norodom Ranariddh, Prince Sihanouk's son, for some years, ever since he, as a young assistant at the University of Bordeaux, had been my escort when I lectured there. Ranariddh spoke and acted like his father, but he lacked Sihanouk's deep political craft. Despite the son's shortcomings, he and his FUNCINPEC party were central to the UN objective of creating a multiparty system for Cambodia. I took Yasushi Akashi aside and quietly urged him to try to raise money from Japanese nongovernmental organizations to help create and strengthen the ability of a range of political parties to compete in the election. This could be criticized as outside interference, but I felt it was necessary if a truly multiparty competition were to take place.

When Hun Sen's regime tried to prevent Ranariddh from campaigning by refusing to let him fly his plane around the country, UN forces lent him a helicopter. A democratic election would be essential to give Cambodia a new and legitimized start at self-governance. But the Cambodian people were not yet part of a democratic culture, nor would they be for years to come. Akashi did as I asked and distributed sums of money strategically. Despite all this, I was convinced that Hun Sen was the only true political leader on the scene and that, multiparty system or not, he would inevitably make the key decisions. The election would have to be truly free and fair, and I would do all I could to ensure this. At the same time it was obvious to me that whatever the outcome, Hun Sen would gravitate toward the center of Cambodia's political life; no other figure could match his authoritative demeanor, determination, and political skill.

There in the throne room I repeatedly implored the four Cambodian parties to prove their tolerance toward one another and reminded them that they must not take UN help for granted. The United Nations might even be authorized to employ force, I suggested, although in reality I knew the Security Council would never go that far.

The election campaign began as scheduled on April 7, 1993, the day I arrived in Phnom Penh. By mid-May the supplies needed for the election, most importantly ballots and ballot boxes, had arrived in Cambodia. Some nine hundred supervisors from forty-four countries and the Inter-parliamentary Union were deployed and, with them, more than 50,000 Cambodian election officers. Radio United Nations broadcast fifteen hours a day. Relay stations had been installed to increase the range of transmission, and hundreds of radio sets had been distributed throughout the country, thanks to a donation from the Japanese government. The messages broadcast by radio emphasized the secrecy of the vote, to counter the Khmer Rouge's attempts to spread fear among the people by saying that their votes would not be confidential, thereby raising the specter of reprisals against those who did not vote for the Khmer Rouge.

On April 8 I addressed the people of Cambodia on television. Speaking in French, I said that the huge numbers of people who had registered to vote demonstrated that the Cambodian people wanted a free and fair democratic election. "I have asked your leaders to renounce violence, intimidation, and threats. In turn, you must not be intimidated. Remember that your vote is secret. Nobody will ever know how you vote. Vote with a clear conscience for the party of your choice. Do so for the sake of your children and grandchildren. Do so for the future of peace and prosperity in Cambodia."

Despite the UN presence, the weeks preceding the election were marked by violence and intimidation. Cambodians of all four parties were killed or wounded. I was repeatedly advised by officials of various countries and by reporters to postpone the election, but I refused to do so. In the last days of April, the Khmer Rouge withdrew all its personnel from Phnom Penh. This was taken as a sign of its intent to attack the city. My colleagues urged me to pull UN personnel into safe quarters. Staff members' requests to have their families evacuated would be approved, I said, but I would not order an evacuation. I insisted that the Khmer Rouge was too weak to pose a serious nationwide threat. In fact, I was afraid for the security of UN personnel, but a decision had to be made. I felt I had no choice but to rely on my political intuition, which told me I was right: the United Nations had to risk going forward with the voting as scheduled.

On April 28 Akashi telephoned to say that the situation was worse than ever. The Khmer Rouge was increasingly hostile; UNTAC was taking additional security measures. Prince Sihanouk had been in Pyongyang, where he had been visited by Khieu Samphan, seeking Sihanouk's support for the Khmer Rouge. At the moment Sihanouk was in Beijing, claiming that his doctors had ordered him not to travel. I sent a message to Sihanouk saying that the Supreme National Council scheduled for May 6 could be convened not in Phnom Penh but in Beijing and that Akashi would fly there to be present. I intended this as pressure on Sihanouk to return to Cambodia.

On May 21, 1993, the Khmer Rouge attacked a UN unit, killing two and injuring seven members of a Chinese engineer detachment. The Security Council unanimously condemned the attack and appealed to the Cambodian people to exercise their right to vote. On May 22 Sihanouk returned to Phnom Penh as I had hoped, delivering a symbolic setback to the Khmer Rouge's objective of undermining the election and forcing UNTAC to withdraw in failure.

A New King for Cambodia

The day after Sihanouk's return, the balloting began. A thunderstorm broke over the city, and some feared that the booming sounds were the guns of the returning Khmer Rouge. But hundreds of thousands of voters lined up to cast their ballots in the rain. The Cambodian people, despite their history of fear, their recent experience of intimidation, and the looming threat that somehow the Khmer Rouge would seek revenge upon all who voted, came bravely forward to take the opportunity that the United Nations had given them to restore their country's sovereignty and international legitimacy. Ninety percent of all eligible voters turned out. Until the final hour we awaited an attack by the Khmer Rouge, but it did not come. The Khmer Rouge boycott had failed. The United Nations had succeeded.

The results were released on June 10: Prince Ranariddh's FUNCIN-PEC got 45.5 percent of the vote. Hun Sen's Cambodian People's Party came in second with 32.2 percent; eighteen other political parties shared the rest of the vote. Under the Constitution the two top vote getters would have to coalesce in some fashion to meet the requirements for forming a government.

Ranariddh and Hun Sen flew to Pyongyang to present Sihanouk with two constitutional options, one for a republic and the other for a constitutional monarchy. On September 20, 1993, Sihanouk returned to Phnom Penh and proclaimed Cambodia to be a constitutional monarchy, the kingdom of Cambodia. I received the following message from Akashi:

On 24 September 1993, Norodom Sihanouk, after having been elected King of Cambodia (by the Conseil Royal du Trône), signed the Royal Decree by which Prince Ranariddh was appointed as the First Prime Minister and Mr. Hun Sen as the Second Prime Minister respectively. This constitutes the creation of the new Royal Government of Cambodia. It was followed by the taking of a joint oath of office by the King, the Government, and the Legislative Assembly. The mandate of UNTAC has thus terminated.

Addressing the international press, King Sihanouk declared, "From this moment forward, the Cambodian people are the masters of their own destiny." I congratulated the people of Cambodia on this historic achievement, which, I said, "shows what the international community can achieve when it is united and determined in pursuit of a worthy goal, and when the people concerned are willing to make mutual accommodation and concessions." The United Nations remained committed to supporting Cambodia in postconflict nation building, I said. But with the elections over, Hun Sen insisted that the United Nations leave Cambodia. In this he reflected a growing unease amongst the political class in Cambodia, including the king himself, about the extent to which the Security Council's mandate had caused the United Nations to intrude into the country's domestic affairs and about the sometimes devastating economic and social impact of so many well-paid foreigners on a wartorn country whose national income per head was less than $200 per annum. There was no way the United Nations could stay.

Fearing a coup by Hun Sen in the aftermath of the election, Sihanouk had the idea of declaring a "National Government of Cambodia" with himself as head of state and prime minister and Ranariddh and Hun Sen as first and second deputy prime ministers. The United Nations had no say in this plan, which was criticized as a "coup from above." Stung by this reaction, the king returned to Beijing to undergo further chemotherapy, leaving Ranariddh and Hun Sen to make their own political arrangement. The result came out much as Sihanouk intended: in a deal to share power, Ranariddh and Hun Sen were installed as co–prime ministers, and Sihanouk was confirmed as head of state. It was, as "old hands" knowledgeable about the country said, a "Cambodian solution." To the surprise of many outside observers, Hun Sen and Ranariddh proceeded to cooperate in the government for the next four years.

Bosnia: "Safe Areas"

As Cambodia was pulling itself together with the United Nations' help, Bosnia was falling apart. In April 1993 Srebenica was about to be seized by Serb forces. The Security Council adopted a resolution demanding that all parties treat Srebenica as a "safe area" free from any armed attack or hostile act. I was asked to increase the UN presence in Srebenica and arrange for the safety of the sick and wounded and the delivery of humanitarian aid to the civilian population of the city. A few weeks later the Security Council declared that Sarajevo and the threatened cities of Tuzla, Žepa, Goražde, Bihać, and their surroundings, would also be "safe areas." To "strengthen" the UN operation, the Security Council authorized fifty more observers to monitor the humanitarian situation in those areas.

In a closed meeting of the Security Council on May 4, 1993, I presented a "working paper" proposing that a force of 70,000 troops be authorized. NATO would have operational and tactical control. Ultimate strategic and political authority would reside with the Security Council. It would be a Blue Helmet force under the UN flag. My proposal was the only way to meet the concerns of France and Russia, who were not part of NATO's armed forces and would not agree to an all-NATO operation with a UN blessing. Under my plan, I would be able at any time to ask the Security Council for "any measures judged necessary to re-orient, correct or conclude the military operation." Without a force of this magnitude, I said, the United Nations might have no choice but to withdraw should it come under heavy military pressure in Bosnia.

The United States declared my proposal to be "totally unacceptable," which suggested that, for Washington, keeping the UN operation on the scene served two purposes: as a substitute for direct great-power intervention and as a scapegoat for problems created by the great powers' continued unwillingness to act decisively. Madeleine Albright and Peter Tarnoff came to see me on May 18, 1993. In a very relaxed and cheerful way, Albright proposed that "once and for all" we simply drop the approach set by the London Conference of August 1992. "I hate being involved in arguments over the Vance-Owen map," she said. Instead, she proposed we move to "a Balkan conference." Yes, Tarnoff added, we want "a Balkan perspective." I asked what this meant. "All the countries of the Danube," Albright said. I could make little sense of this and gently tried to explain that while changes and new thinking were necessary, they should be simply modifications to the present process. The London Conference was the agreed international framework for dealing with the conflicts in the former Yugoslavia. The United States had fully participated in it; it could not simply drop it. I suggested instead that the London Conference hold a second session.

After Albright and Tarnoff left my office, I sat in amazement, wondering about their insouciant disregard for what was, after all, a formal international diplomatic process accepted by the United States. I could not fathom what they wanted, but I knew that the United States would never go along with the Vance-Owen plan. After Vance's resignation, Owen's diplomatic achievement had been impressive, but his outspoken style undercut the substance of his work. Owen was openly contemptuous of the Clinton administration's policy on Bosnia and felt, as he later wrote, that its effect was to prolong the war, with all its casualties and ethnic cleansing. As a result, Owen became persona non grata in Washington, and the administration's strong feelings about him personally spilled over to taint the United States' attitude toward the United Nations itself. Every time I mentioned Owen's name to Albright, she blew up. "Never mention that man's name to the president," she warned me.

On May 27, 1993, the Secretariat was given less than a day by the Security Council to produce working papers on (1) the humanitarian situation in each of the "safe areas," (2) the military situation, (3) maps of the front lines of the "safe areas," and (4) the concept of a "safe area." Under intense pressure we did, in fact, produce the papers, only to have the United States object to our "oil slick" recommendation to try to use force to gradually enlarge the safe areas, which might require using U.S. forces. Back in February, Christopher's announcement of the Clinton administration's Bosnia policy had been interpreted in Europe as meaning that the United States would put troops on the ground, but it was now clear to everyone that the United States would do no such thing.

In response to U.S. criticism of our twenty-four-hour response to the Security Council, I could only assure everyone that the question of the safe areas was the exclusive responsibility of the Security Council and that I wished only to provide the members with points for consideration. The United States' position was incomprehensible. In the spring of 1993 Under Secretary of State Tarnoff publicly declared that the United States would no longer be the world leader in monitoring international security. Yet the United States continued its tough talk and pushed the United Nations into ever less tenable positions, only to deny the resources that decisive action would require and to shy away at any sign that the United States might itself be expected to become directly involved. As one of my UN colleagues noted, the United Nations was being "taken for a ride" by the United States and some other NATO powers.

The Struggle over Air Strikes

On June 6, 1993, in Resolution 836, the Security Council authorized UNPROFOR—if acting in self-defense—to take necessary measures, including the use of force, in reply to bombardments against the safe areas or armed incursions into them. The Council also decided that member states, acting nationally or through regional arrangements (that is, the United States alone or with NATO), might take, under the authority of the Security Council, "all necessary measures," through the use of airpower, in and around the "safe areas," to support the UN forces.

In this way, the Security Council, in the words of the White Queen in *Through the Looking-Glass,* asked the UN forces to perform "six impossible things before breakfast." The "safe areas" could not, in fact, be safe, because the United Nations lacked the means either to prevent attacks launched from inside these areas or to deter attacks from outside. At the same time, the United Nations was expected to agree to the use of NATO airpower against Serb targets that could result in Serb retaliation against or hostage taking of essentially defenseless UN personnel.

The Security Council invited me to report to it on the requirements for implementing Resolution 836. On June 14 I replied that it would be necessary to deploy additional troops on the ground and to give them air support. I agreed with the UN force commander that some 34,000 more troops would be needed. But I was told in no uncertain terms by Sir David Hannay, the British permanent representative, and other Western ambassadors to the United Nations that no such number would be authorized. Hannay pressed me hard to recommend a "light option" of 7,600 troops. Reluctantly I agreed to do so, but I told the Security Council that this could be only a start and that with so small a reinforcement UNPROFOR would be able to do nothing without the consent and cooperation of the warring parties. In fact, the 7,600 troops were authorized but not provided for many months, and then only in part and inadequately armed.

I asked NATO to coordinate with me on its use of air support for the UN operation. The first decision to initiate the use of airpower would, I said, be made by me in consultation with the Security Council. The difference between "air strikes" and "close air support" was important. Throughout the Bosnia crisis, politicians, officials, the public, and the press constantly confused the two operations. Close air support was limited, by resolution, to protection of UN troops under attack. Air strikes were a strategic matter, the use of which would signal that a peacekeeping mission had given way to a war by NATO and the United Nations against the targeted forces and their political authorities.

The UN forces on the ground had no hesitation about calling for close air support when a specific UN operation was under attack. What the

UN commanders could not readily accept were requests for air strikes against targets that were not threatening the UN operation. The difference, in essence, was between defense and offense. The United Nations had to defend itself, of course, but to go on the offensive through air strikes would be regarded as a belligerent act in an international war against the Serbs. That would violate the central purpose of the entire body of Security Council resolutions concerning the former Yugoslavia, under which the United Nations was to remain impartial.

Throughout these weeks the UN operation in Bosnia, given its mandate and its weakness, had the opposite of the desired effect. By helping to evacuate populations threatened by terror or death by advancing forces, the United Nations could be said to be helping ethnic cleansing. And by trying to negotiate cease-fires, the United Nations could be helping to seal the results of the acquisition of territory by force. The phrases "safe areas" and "air strikes" conveyed to the world that the United Nations could not maintain the former and was blocking the latter.

The U.S. Mission to the United Nations leaked a letter from Madeleine Albright that recommended air strikes, and the press reported that President Clinton was considering air strikes. But this ignored the problem of the UN personnel on the ground, who were hostages-in-waiting should the air strikes be launched. No one addressed the problem of what would happen when air strikes forced a halt to the United Nations' humanitarian assistance. No one asked what would happen when air strikes brought an end to the negotiation process. No one acknowledged that air strikes could affect the situation positively only if the UN operation were either withdrawn entirely or given an enforcement mandate and the resources it required, including an effective combat force on the ground. And neither the United States nor its NATO allies were ready to meet those conditions. To some observers at the United Nations, it seemed that Washington had devised a way to gain domestic political benefit from tough talk about air strikes, knowing that it was shielded from acting because its European allies would never agree to put their personnel serving with the United Nations in Bosnia in danger. Moreover, my insistence that, as secretary-general, I had a say about the use of air strikes—since UN troops were at risk—let the United States blame me for blocking decisive action. The British, French, and other governments that were against air strikes followed the American lead and also blamed the UN secretary-general.

By this time, the spring of 1993, the war in Bosnia was virtually over.

The Serbs had taken territory almost at will. A. M. Rosenthal wrote in his *New York Times* column of May 4, 1993, "The revilers of the Vance-Owen Plan should apologize." The West had done nothing, through a complicated set of self-blocking steps, to stop the advance of the Serbs and their ethnic cleansing. And the Russians by this time were asserting themselves in ways that seemed to make it impossible for the United States to act. The press was reporting that the United States and Russia were in basic agreement to accept Serb gains for the time being. All that remained was for the United States to continue to appear desirous of taking forcible action while counting on America's NATO allies to prevent any such action and using the United Nations as the scapegoat.

Then, on July 30, 1993, President Clinton sent me a letter. "The Bosnian tragedy has reached a critical point," he wrote. "The Serbian stranglehold risks derailing the negotiations and UNPROFOR's heroic humanitarian mission." If the Serbian efforts to strangle Sarajevo continued, Clinton said, "we should put NATO air power at the service of our diplomacy." Warren Christopher would call me with specific ideas, the president said. He wanted me to know how important he believed this initiative was.

Christopher's "Nonpaper"

The next morning Christopher telephoned to repeat this message and to say that he would be providing me with a letter giving full details of the American initiative. Christopher's two-and-a-half-page letter, with a "nonpaper" attached, arrived that afternoon. "Dear Boutros," Christopher wrote, "the commendable efforts of UN forces in Sarajevo and elsewhere in Bosnia are not enough to cope with this Serb offensive." The collapse of Sarajevo "would jeopardize the very existence of the state of Bosnia-Herzegovina and could fatally undermine hopes for restoring a normal life to Bosnia's Muslim population."

The United States regarded the situation as "intolerable," Christopher wrote. The letter reached me on Saturday. On Monday, August 2, the United States would ask its NATO allies to "be prepared in full coordination with the UN to use air power against Bosnian Serb targets at times and places of NATO's own choosing." The air strikes, the secretary of state said, would be conducted by NATO "in full coordination with the United Nations, consistent with the authority already provided by United

Nations Security Council Resolutions 770 and 836. We believe the time for action has come and must not be delayed. . . . President Clinton has instructed me to tell you that the United States is determined to move forward quickly on this initiative. I hope we can count on your full support and cooperation."

A "nonpaper," such as Christopher attached to his letter, is a form of authoritative yet nonofficial and deniable diplomatic communication. In his nonpaper Christopher revealed the hope that the Serbs would take U.S. warnings seriously and stop threatening Sarajevo. If so, it said, "it might not be necessary for NATO to carry out any air strikes." The nonpaper went into considerable detail to argue that this initiative would be fully coordinated with the United Nations and that authorization for it already existed in UN resolutions. But, it made clear, "we would not envisage the need for a specific request from UNPROFOR or specific authorization from UN headquarters."

Meanwhile, the United States had made it known publicly during the weekend that it would use air strikes on its own. This was soon translated into an ultimatum, with the United States citing authority under previous UN Security Council resolutions. Christopher received my reply on August 2. I had expressed misgivings about this U.S. initiative during our Saturday telephone call, and I wanted to make it clear why. As he knew, the Security Council had adopted several resolutions bearing on the question of the use of airpower. Taken together, the resolutions had established the parameters within which the use of airpower might be contemplated; they dealt with humanitarian relief and with protection of the "safe areas" under Resolution 836. These arrangements would soon reach the stage "where there is adequate capability on the ground to enable the UN force commander to request authorization of [close] air support should the need arise." In other words, I was saying to Christopher that the NATO countries with soldiers on the ground as part of the UN force had already been discussing this issue and had concluded that no air strikes should be conducted without the approval of the commander on the ground.

I explained my position carefully in my reply to Christopher. There were two fundamental responsibilities, and I had no choice but to carry them out. I could not agree that the United States or any other power could, entirely at a time and on a scale of its own choosing, run air strikes that would risk the lives of UN personnel on the ground without coordinated agreement. Nor could I agree to military measures taken by the

United States that exceeded what the Security Council, with full U.S. participation in the vote, had authorized in the resolutions.

"I would welcome the use of air power to support the work of UN-PROFOR in the performance of the mandate given to it by the Security Council," I wrote to Christopher. "At the same time, I am sure you will appreciate that the use of air power will have far-reaching consequences for the security not only of UNPROFOR troops, but also of civilian United Nations personnel on the ground, as well as on the progress of the peace negotiations in Geneva and the delivery of humanitarian assistance. It is for these very pragmatic reasons that I have consistently taken the position that the first use of air power in the theatre should be initiated by the Secretary-General, on the basis of advice received from the Force Commander and from the Special Representative of the Secretary-General in the area." As Christopher knew, I had reported to the Security Council on this on June 14, 1993, and the Council had endorsed this approach.

I, too, produced a "nonpaper" and enclosed it with my reply to Christopher on August 2, 1993. It set out a clear and simple process by which air strikes would be run by NATO—which everyone knew meant U.S. Air Force bombers based in Aviano, Italy—against the Bosnian Serbs or any other forces. The only difference from the U.S. initiative was that the air strikes would have to be called in by the UN force commander on the ground and approved by the secretary-general in consultation with the Security Council.

My letter to Christopher was leaked to Jeane Kirkpatrick, who quoted from it in her syndicated column and denounced me: "How can Boutros-Ghali pretend that he alone has the authority to initiate the use of force in Bosnia?"

The Three-Step Tactic

With the possibility of air strikes featured in the media, the Serbs pulled back from Sarajevo. While this was a welcome development, it was the start of what would become a distressing and detrimental pattern on the part of Karadžić, a clever three-step tactic worthy of his training in psychology. First, Serb fighters would seize territory and inflict horrors upon the civilian population. Then, when an outraged United States threatened forceful intervention, Karadžić would halt the Serb advance and the West would sigh with relief and postpone preparations for action. Then Karadžić would publicly demand something for the Serbs' "concession." In the resulting confusion the Serbs would be left alone to consolidate their grip on the territory they had seized and to regroup in preparation for launching the next three-step move. No matter how many times this dance step was repeated, the United States never seemed to catch on.

The United States wanted the UN operation to continue, without the participation of American personnel, and at the same time wanted full U.S. freedom to run air strikes whenever it desired to demonstrate U.S. resolve. This was absurd and impossible; the Clinton administration's NATO partners would not permit it. America's NATO allies were the ones who had personnel on the ground, and it was those allies who insisted that the United States not be granted any such unilateral authority. There was also little or no confidence among the UN commanders on the ground, primarily British and French, that the United States, even if it did run air strikes, could be relied upon to pursue them to the extent necessary, despite losses of aircraft, to bring an end to the war. It was time to call the United States' bluff. The "misgivings" that I expressed to Christopher were reinforced by the British and French, and the Clinton administration backed away from this initiative. On August 6, 1993, the United States agreed that UN commanders would have control over air strikes: whether they would be run, when they would be run, and against which targets. The NATO allies approved this procedure a few days later. Thus the United States backed away, but I would be blamed for preventing the use of NATO airpower to solve the Bosnia crisis and would pay for my "obstinacy" from then on.

Within a few days National Public Radio broadcast a long report about my attempts to reshape the United Nations for a new era and the sharp criticism being mounted by the United States against me. My insistence on a veto over air strikes had angered Congress, the report said, and Madeleine Albright had publicly rebuked me. But one administration official was quoted as saying that the United States "wanted a dynamic, outspoken secretary-general, and we got one."

On September 20, 1993, I recommended that the Security Council renew the mandate of UNPROFOR for six months, the usual extension for UN peacekeeping operations. I said that I had been "sorely tempted" to recommend the withdrawal of the force altogether because of the criticism by both sides and the dangers and abuse to which its personnel were exposed, but I had concluded that such a step could result only in further conflict.

This, of course, presented an almost intolerable situation: continued carnage on the ground, claims of UN helplessness, and media pressures on the United States to "do something." The "something" seemed to be air strikes, which would punish the Serbs and provide the United States and NATO with the appearance of decisiveness without risking unacceptable military losses on the ground. The system I had put in place through an exchange of letters with NATO was this: if the UN commander in the field wanted air support and the top UN civilian in the field agreed, I would approve an air strike. By the end of 1993, I could not recall having received a single request to do so, a fact reflecting the refusal of the Europeans to put their troops at risk.

Somalia: Over to the United Nations Again

The troubles in Bosnia and Somalia proceeded in parallel in 1993. Once into Somalia, the United States was eager to depart. On March 3, 1993, I submitted to the Security Council my recommendations for the transition from the U.S.-led Unified Task Force (UNITAF) back to the UN Somalia Operation, now to be known as UNOSOM II. While the security situation had improved, incidents of violence continued. I concluded, therefore, that this second UN operation should be given enforcement powers to enable it to establish a secure environment throughout Somalia. At the request of U.S. National Security Adviser Anthony Lake, I named Jonathan Howe, a retired U.S. Navy admiral, as my special representative to take charge, as a civilian, of UNOSOM II. Our understanding was that Howe would serve for a short period and then be replaced by a non-American, but this did not turn out to be the case. Howe created an impeccable impression of efficiency and integrity. His attitude was unfailingly calm and openly cooperative toward everyone. I never regretted my decision to make Howe my special representative for Somalia.

The Security Council agreed. On March 26, 1993, in its Resolution 814, the Council decided that the new UN force, instead of resuming the peacekeeping mandate of the earlier UN operation, could conduct enforcement operations, as necessary, under the authority of the Security Council. This too was a new approach.

But as the handover date approached, the United Nations was not being given the required capability. I wrote to Ambassador Albright on May 3, 1993. The Security Council had envisaged, I said, that the transition would be effected progressively, area by area, when adequate troops, command, and control were available to the United Nations in a given area:

> To this end, it was my expectation that there would be a force of 28,000 on the ground under UNOSOM II command prior to the departure of the United States troops. As you know, this is not the case. The present strength of UNOSOM II is barely 18,000. . . .
>
> However, in the light of the position of your government, as you explained to me, I have concluded that I have no alternative but to accept the transfer of command from UNITAF to UNOSOM II on 4 May 1993. You would agree with me that this transfer is taking place under less than ideal circumstances. The bulk of the United States contingents and their equipment have been withdrawn before they could be replaced by contingents from other countries.

When the U.S.-led operation came to an end on May 4, 1993, a strange and fragmented operation replaced it. Marine Lieutenant General Robert Johnson lowered the UNITAF flag. UNOSOM II came into being under Turkish Lieutenant General Cevik Bir, a strong and silent representative of the Turkish military tradition established by Mustafa Kemal Atatürk. Bir's deputy was U.S. Major General Thomas Montgomery. After the UNITAF pullout, nearly 4,000 U.S. troops remained to perform logistics and support duties while wearing blue berets and patches identifying them as under UN command.

In addition, the United States inserted three other American military units independent of the UN chain of command. There was the U.S. Quick Reaction Force (QRF), consisting of a light battalion with helicopter support, under the command of an American colonel. The QRF was stationed at various locations in Somalia, with the purpose of stepping in as needed should UN personnel run into trouble. For a brief period the United States also positioned a marine amphibious group on ships just off the Somali coast, operating entirely under U.S. command.

In addition, Jon Howe in June requested the United States to provide a special commando force. No response came until about three months later, in late August 1993, when the United States sent in the Delta Force, composed of U.S. Army Rangers and special commandos. This force reported directly to the U.S. Joint Special Operations Command in Tampa, Florida. The Delta Force took up positions at Mogadishu Airport and was totally independent of other operations within Somalia.

This complex arrangement would lead to trouble.

Negotiations for Somali national reconciliation had been going on in Addis Ababa, Ethiopia, attended by fifteen of the main Somali factions, clan elders, and other Somali leaders. The conference had been extremely difficult to manage, but the agreement concluded on March 27, 1993, set out a careful two-year program for progress toward peace. Communities would first establish organs of local government. These "district councils" would send representatives to each of eighteen "regional councils." Three representatives of each regional council, one of whom would have to be a woman, would then make up a Transitional National Council that would become the repository of Somali national sovereignty, which had been dissolved in the national collapse of 1992. The Transitional National Council would draft a Constitution, guided by the Universal Declaration of Human Rights and traditional Somali ethics. These measures would lead the country back into membership in the international community. As part of this effort the leaders of the fifteen factions committed themselves to complete and simultaneous disarmament. This commitment, however, would soon be violated.

Aidid's Surprise Attack

As UN forces attempted to carry out an inspection of weapons storage facilities in and around Mogadishu on June 5, 1993, gunmen using women as screens assaulted Pakistani UN troops as they were returning to base. A Pakistani unit guarding a food distribution center in south Mogadishu was also hit. Twenty-six Pakistani peacekeepers were killed and fifty-six wounded. These losses left me horrified and heartsick. An internal UN investigation revealed that General Mohammed Farah Aidid was responsible. At the Security Council's request, I engaged an expert consultant, Professor Tom Farer of American University in Washington,

D.C., to go to Somalia to investigate. His report confirmed that the attacks could have been carried out only under Aidid's orders.

If the United Nations did not respond, a dangerous precedent would be set, and other factions would assume that assaults against the United Nations could be carried out with impunity. The Security Council, with the U.S. vote powerfully influential, unanimously adopted Resolution 837, authorizing me as secretary-general to take "all necessary precautions against all those responsible for the armed attacks," including their arrest and detention for trial and punishment. Thus, on June 12, UN forces began a systematic drive to restore law and order in south Mogadishu, Aidid's stronghold and the most disrupted and dangerous place in the country. The offensive continued for several days, with aerial bombardments and ground assaults on weapons sites, as well as on the broadcast facilities of Radio Mogadishu. On June 17, Howe publicly called for the arrest and detention of General Aidid pursuant to Resolution 837, and plans went forward to carry out the Security Council's decision.

The African countries neighboring Somalia were increasingly burdened by refugees fleeing the conflict. I needed their support but feared that they were beginning to see this as a U.S. and UN operation conducted without reference to their concerns. On June 22, 1993, I wrote to the presidents of Djibouti, Eritrea, Ethiopia, and Kenya reaffirming that the United Nations' "complex military operation" was designed to end the flagrant violations of the cease-fire, to restore law and order, and "to initiate the process of disarmament" to which all Somali factions had committed themselves. These efforts, I hoped, would "contribute to the enhancement of peace and stability in Somalia and thus in the Horn of Africa."

Aidid's faction resorted to urban guerrilla tactics and also mobilized crowds of civilians. Gunmen mingled with women and children, making it impossible for UN and QRF troops to defend themselves without risking civilian lives. I shared the widespread horror at the callous way in which women and children were forced into the line of fire.

On July 12, 1993, the QRF, acting at the request of the UN forces in Somalia, bombed a compound in south Mogadishu believed to be the command headquarters from which Aidid was directing attacks on U.S. personnel. QRF troops swept through the area, confiscating weapons and communications gear and taking prisoners. After they withdrew, journalists from the international press drove to the scene. A large crowd of Somalis, some armed, surrounded and attacked the reporters and murdered four of them.

A debate arose: Should we continue to pursue Aidid, or should we try to make a political deal with him? I had no option, because the Security Council resolution had mandated that Aidid be captured and brought to justice. Moreover, I agreed with the resolution. Aidid had ordered his gunmen to starve the Somali people and to use women and children as shields in combat. He had no compunction about killing people sent on a humanitarian mission. Madeleine Albright also agreed. On August 10, 1993, she wrote on *The New York Times'* op-ed page that "some criticize the UN mission in Somali for supposedly departing from its humanitarian purpose by conducting military operations against the renegade warlord Mohammed Farah Aidid. . . . The decision we must make is whether to pull up stakes and allow Somalia to fall back into the abyss or stay the course and help lift the country and its people from the category of a failed state into that of an emerging democracy. For Somalia's sake, and ours, we must persevere." Albright was correct. This was nation building, a task once regarded as great and noble, but the task of nation building was increasingly being denounced by politicians as an expensive and endless waste of U.S. money and effort on behalf of ungrateful people in far-off lands.

Pressure for a Political Solution

During this time I found myself in trouble with the government of Italy. Because Italy was the former colonial ruler of Somalia, it should not, according to UN practice, contribute troops to serve there. But I had been in desperate need of troops for the UN operation in Mozambique, and in order to get an Italian contingent there, I was compelled to accept Italian forces in Somalia. This was a mistake. The United Nations' established policy was correct. Once on the ground in Somalia, the Italian forces, under instructions from Rome, pursued their own agenda at the expense of the common UN effort.

The Italian troops assigned to the UN forces under General Bruno Loi had been unilaterally conducting talks with Aidid, and it was suspected that the Italians were tipping him off to UN military movements. On July 5, 1993, I received a report that Italian troops assigned to the United Nations "simply stopped their counteraction at a critical moment, with

Quick Reaction Force helicopters poised to destroy thirty [of Aidid's] militia, they have hunkered down ever since, abandoning some strong points and letting roadblocks remain in the area. Intelligence indicates that Aidid forces are boastful" as a result of the Italian collapse. As the former colonial power in Somalia, the Italians had convinced themselves that they "understood" the Somali people, and this became the litany of proponents of a "negotiated solution." They "understood" Somalis, which those who saw Aidid as a dangerous warlord supposedly did not. Aidid had been communicating with Jimmy Carter during this period, and Carter was now an influential voice for opposing the military option and pursuing a political solution. But Aidid would never allow another Somali clan leader to lead the country, while other clan leaders resisted Aidid's own efforts to rule, because he belonged to a small subclan. It was useless to try to solve the Somali crisis by negotiating with Aidid.

This was a crucial moment in UN history. For the first time since the 1950 Korean War, UN forces had been mandated to engage in military operations against an adversary specified by the Security Council. This came as something of a shock to those who identified the United Nations with impartial peacekeeping under a cease-fire agreement. For UN personnel, major adjustments were necessary. As Admiral Howe reported to me, "Security and intelligence are new words to UN operations." For the U.S. units involved, the mission was clear: Stop Aidid's forces from reinstituting a reign of terror in Mogadishu. Meanwhile, domestic political pressure on the Clinton administration to end the fighting and feed the people was approaching an unacceptable level.

Looking for Friends

On August 26, 1993, Madeleine Albright visited me on the thirty-eighth floor. She mentioned congressional complaints that the United States was too extensively involved and said the Clinton administration wanted to show that the Somalia effort was being "internationalized." She wanted me to announce that I would form "a group of friends of the secretary-general," referring to a technique I had used in UN peace operations elsewhere and in which representatives of concerned countries would advise and assist me. I said that such a core group for Somalia had already been formed a year before under the chairmanship of President Mubarak—it was made up of the Arab League, the Organization of

African Unity, and the Organization of the Islamic Conference—and that before adding others I would need to consult with those organizations. That was not sufficient, Albright said. The United States wanted to be able to state right away that it was my intention to form a "group of friends." Arguing was useless, so I agreed. Although I had already done so by involving the governments of Somalia's neighboring states, as well as the African, Islamic, and Arab international organizations, I was happy to do as she wished and let the Clinton administration take credit for it with the Congress.

Albright then stressed the importance of getting Egypt to send troops to join UNOSOM II. I confirmed that Egypt wanted to send six hundred peacekeepers but had not been paid for its earlier contributions to other UN operations. Albright replied with a not-so-veiled threat: the United States gave Egypt billions in aid every year, and "Frankly, this could be a big problem for Egypt."

But Albright's main reason for calling on me was to discuss, tête-à-tête, the question of what to do with Aidid. Aidid's capture, she said, was imminent. We discussed at length the options for transporting Aidid to detention in some other country and of placing him on trial. The United States, I was told, would begin to approach other countries for this purpose. "Our problems might be less," I said to Albright, "if Aidid had been arrested three months earlier," when Admiral Howe had tried to obtain the assistance of U.S. special forces without success. "Now that the effort to arrest him is no longer a secret, capturing him will not be easy." With that, our meeting ended.

Warren Christopher and I met at the United Nations on September 20, 1993. Albright was with him. Visibly pleased, he told me that the United States would be paying the United Nations $420 million in arrears and would be bringing the United States current on its peacekeeping account. The total payment would amount to $680 million. That was good, I said, but "the problem is that the UN is now spending $400 million every month." The mission assigned to UNPROFOR in the former Yugoslavia was devouring the UN budget. "The U.S. payment will not cover even two months of UN expenses," I noted with regret. When the meeting was over I thought that Christopher and I had had a mature and mutually respectful exchange of views on a difficult subject, but word came from Washington that Christopher had been deeply annoyed by my reaction. He had expected to hear expressions of gratitude and appreciation from me for the United States' decision to do partially what it was legally obligated to do entirely—pay its debt.

Albright was also upset with me. I was beginning to realize that she tended to react to discussions of problems between the United Nations and the United States as though they were criticisms specifically directed at her performance as the American representative to the United Nations. Such sensitivity is not uncommon among unseasoned diplomats, who are inclined to feel that they are expected to solve all the problems of the relationships they are assigned to work on. Nonetheless, the reactions of Christopher and Albright to our meeting made me wonder about my own style. The importance of the United Nations' relationship with the United States was such that I should have found a way to keep both of them on my side. I had failed to do so. I realized that I was not the easiest person to deal with—but then, neither were Christopher and Albright.

Somalia was most urgently on Christopher's mind. He said that public support for U.S. involvement had declined dramatically: "The American public sees only a UN military operation and wonders why there is no long-term political effort to find a solution." I replied that initiatives were under way. I had convened a meeting of fourteen states to seek help (I did not, however, call them "friends of the secretary-general"). I would go to Somalia myself in a few weeks. And a new conference on Somalia to be held in Ethiopia would demonstrate momentum toward a political solution. In fact, a great deal of progress had been made diplomatically and on the ground in Somalia, but the outside world was getting only television reports about Aidid's defiance in Mogadishu, which was an exception to the pattern.

Christopher asked whether we had tried to get Aidid to agree to a cease-fire. I pointed out that the second UN operation in Somalia was obliged by the Security Council—which included the United States—to arrest Aidid and bring him to trial. A new resolution would be needed to authorize the United Nations to seek a cease-fire. "Is there any basis to follow up on President Carter's initiative?" Christopher asked, referring to Carter's proposal to give up the military solution and negotiate with Aidid. "Not under the present mandate," I replied. In twenty days, Christopher said, "The U.S. might lose the support of Congress for continuing the operation."

Christopher handed me another "nonpaper," which I read as soon as he departed. He wanted my cooperation on a new approach: We would stop the search for Aidid, start a campaign to draw the media's attention to the UN operation as a humanitarian effort, and explore ways to get Aidid out of Somalia and placed under house arrest in some other country. It was clear that the United States, having failed to disarm the Somali factions at the start, was under strong congressional pressure to get itself out of the resulting mess.

However, I was still mandated by the Security Council—with the Clinton administration's vote making it unanimous—to continue on course. Moreover, on September 22, 1993, the Security Council adopted yet another resolution (Number 865) supporting the strategy of the UN operations in Somalia and affirming that those who committed or ordered attacks against UN personnel, such as Aidid, would be held individually responsible for their deeds.

I replied to Christopher in a nonpaper of September 25, 1993. The reality was that while the bloodshed in Mogadishu was making headlines around the world, throughout much of the rest of Somalia real gains were being made by the UN effort. The Somali people deeply desired the United Nations to continue its work and were working hard to get their lives back in order. There was progress toward interclan reconciliation. Local and regional government was being reconstructed. Starvation had been largely arrested. Harvests had improved and now met about half the country's cereal needs. Hospitals and schools were beginning to operate again, and refugees were being resettled.

I told Christopher I was working hard with the World Bank on the next steps in Somalia's rehabilitation. I planned to go to Mogadishu in mid-October to oversee the nonmilitary aspects of UNOSOM II's mission. I had asked Admiral Howe to explore the feasibility of establishing a Somali "interim government" to cooperate with our efforts.

"I believe," I wrote to Christopher, "that these initiatives will, with your support, help to shift media attention away from the hunt for Aidid. None of them, however, enables me to side-step the problem he creates. It was his refusal to share power after the overthrow of [Mohammed] Siad Barre, the last president of Somalia, that led to civil conflict in Somalia. That conflict, in turn, led to human suffering which the international community could not tolerate." From the beginning, I stressed, my colleagues and I had made every effort to bring Aidid into the political process and the search for national reconciliation, and initially we had received a good deal of cooperation from him.

"However," I said to Christopher, "the killing and mutilation of twenty-four United Nations soldiers on 5 June created a new situation and obliged the Security Council to instruct me to detain and bring to trial those responsible for that crime. Until the Security Council decides to change those instructions, I am obliged to make every effort to bring Aidid to justice." I wrote to Christopher that "I know that you understand and support this operation," but, in fact, I was not at all sure that he did. The Clinton administration was feeling the pinch of adverse public opinion and wanted to extricate itself from this painful situation.

I then told Christopher that my mind was not closed to exploring "other ways of neutralizing Aidid, by which I mean bringing about his removal from Somalia to controlled residence in another country from which he would not be able to direct military operations by his supporters in Somalia or otherwise block our efforts to achieve national reconciliation." But, I said, the feasibility of such a solution should not divert us from the mandate set by the Security Council.

I finally told Christopher that all this strengthened my conviction, expressed to the United States almost a year earlier, when the Unified Task Force had been about to enter Somalia, that our efforts "will not succeed unless we can disarm the clans and factions. I made that position clear in my letter of 29 November 1992 to the president of the Security Council. I repeated it in my letter of 8 December 1992 to President Bush and again in my report of 19 December 1992 to the Security Council."

The fact that the U.S.-led task force had not disarmed the factions was the principal reason I had not wanted to hand over responsibility to the UN operation prematurely and, when the handover had taken place six months before, had wanted a significant U.S. combat force to remain in Somalia. "Any restrictions now on the use of the Quick Reaction Force would greatly undermine the UN force's ability to disarm the parties and would be contrary to the understandings we reached when the transition from the Unified Task Force to the second UN operation took place. Actual withdrawal of the force would in my judgment lead to the rapid decomposition of the whole UN operation."

If adverse public opinion should lead the United States and the Security Council to withdraw the UN operation from Somalia, I told Christopher, "not only would that condemn the people of Somalia to a resumption of civil war and all the horrors that would result; it would also represent a humbling of the United Nations and of the efforts of the United States and other countries to restore peace and human decency to Somalia. This would have a devastating effort on your and my efforts to strengthen the capacity of the United Nations to contribute to a better world."

Meeting Clinton in GA-200

President Clinton came to the United Nations to address the General Assembly on September 27, 1993, and we met in GA-200, a small room just off the Assembly chamber. Christopher, Albright, and Lake accompanied the president. Clinton said that in law school they had debated whether falsely shouting "Fire!" in a crowded theater is protected by free speech. "I hope that no one shouts 'Fire!' in this tiny room," he said. "Don't worry," I said, "it's the UN's job to go around the world putting out fires." Everybody smiled at my lame joke. I felt real warmth and mutual understanding in the tiny room.

The president told me of his strong belief that the United States should pay its bills to the United Nations in full and on time. But Congress had gotten used to not paying, and it would be hard to turn it around. To do so, he said, "I will have to assure them that I have spoken to you about UN reform." I replied by describing my reform program. But without the agreement of member states, I said, my efforts to achieve reform could go nowhere. "Like Dr. Jekyll and Mr. Hyde, states push me in one direction and then oppose measures I have undertaken at their request." Clinton laughed. "You mean they want it all!" He had a similar problem, he said, with the Congress. I was pleased with our brief but pleasant encounter.

No Loaves, No Fishes

Three days later, in the evening, I met with the foreign ministers of the Permanent Five of the Security Council: Qian Qichen of China, Alain Juppé of France, Andrei Kozyrev of Russia, Douglas Hurd of Britain, and Warren Christopher of the United States. This was an annual event, but this year, I said, "because of the UN financial crisis I am unable to offer you lunch."

Christopher spoke very warmly. "On behalf of the United States," he said, "I want to assure the secretary-general of our continued support and admiration for your efforts in your daunting tasks, some of which are undoable. People hold you, Mr. Secretary-General, and the United Nations to a standard of perfection which it is impossible to achieve on so many fronts." Christopher assured me that if the United States asked for changes in the UN organization, "the requests should be seen as coming, to quote Ambassador Albright, 'from a first friend.'" As for Somalia, Christopher expressed appreciation for my decision to go there in mid-October. He hoped that I would look for alternatives that would maintain pressure for a political solution. The session was warm and productive on every issue, and all joined in what Foreign Minister Kozyrev called the "round of congratulations for the Secretary-General" and the "really indispensable" role of the United Nations.

"*Inshallah* [Allah be willing]," I said, "next year I shall be able to offer you lunch."

The Delta Force Moves In

In a report to the Security Council I had raised the issue of command and control in Somalia. There was always a threat of casualties, I stated, when the Council mandated an action under Chapter VII, but the danger could be minimized "if there is effective command and control on the ground by the Force Commander."

I had expressed my views publicly in an op-ed article in *The New York Times* on August 20, 1993. The United Nations, I said, was "attempting to deal with threats from micronationalism and the ethnic or tribal forces that cause states to fracture and fall apart. In Somalia, the state and its sovereign authority and integrity ceased to exist as a result of these pressures. What the UN is trying to accomplish there is the restoration to legitimacy of one of its members. When it is suggested that the UN abandon this effort as violence worsens, or when the multilateral effort is undercut by the uncoordinated decisions of those contributing to it, the failure of a mission and the loss of a nation's hopes are at risk."

Much later I learned that five days after my report to the Security Council the U.S. Delta Force of commandos and Rangers left the Joint Special Operations Command in Fort Bragg, North Carolina, for deployment in Somalia. On the night of October 3, 1993, in an operation planned, decided, and launched entirely without the knowledge of United Nations officials, the U.S. Delta Force staged a raid against a house in South Mogadishu where their intelligence reports led them to believe that the key lieutenants of Mohammed Farah Aidid were meeting. The Delta Force stormed the house and seized twenty-four Somalis as U.S. helicopters fired antitank missiles into the surrounding area. But as the U.S. troops began their withdrawal to base, the Somalis shot down two of their helicopters. As the Delta Force moved to protect the downed airmen, they were surrounded by hundreds of Somali men, women, and children. Trapped, the U.S. force poured devastating firepower into the Somali crowds, killing, by later press investigations, as many as a thousand Africans. The battle went on for hours. UN peacekeeping troops, primarily Malaysian and Pakistani, were called in by the United States to help extract the Ranger force. By the time they did so, eighteen U.S. soldiers and one Malaysian soldier had been killed, ninety U.S., Malaysian, and Pakistani soldiers had been wounded, and one U.S. pilot had been captured. The catastrophic failure of the raid was made vivid in television pictures flashed around the world of the body of a U.S. soldier being dragged through the streets of Mogadishu by jubilant, jeering supporters of Mohammed Farah Aidid.

Forty-eight hours later former President Jimmy Carter sent me by fax a copy of a letter he had just sent to President Clinton. Carter had been active, at Aidid's request, in mediating between Aidid and the Security Council. Aidid, Carter reported, was surrounded by forty thousand fervent supporters, most of them women and children. Aidid is their hero, and they will give their lives in his support, he said. His 2,000 to 3,000 troops are experienced guerrilla forces. Other Somalian tribes are now "strongly supportive of Aidid." All this, Carter told Clinton, was "totally contrary" to the views of Admiral Howe and Boutros-Ghali. I could not guess what Carter meant by this other than that we were reporting that the UN operation was going well in Somalia everywhere but in Aidid's stronghold of south Mogadishu and that we were seeking to arrest him in accordance with the orders of the Security Council.

During his recent travels in East Africa, Carter told Clinton, he had found unanimous agreement "that Admiral Howe has been a disaster, with an almost fanatical belief that he must win some kind of military victory in Somalia." Even Boutros-Ghali, Carter wrote, "would have accepted a more peaceful way." The United Nations, Carter concluded, is now seen by Somalia as a colonial power, and the United States has become the hated enemy. The way out, Carter said, is to "try a political solution that doesn't appear to be a capitulation."

Secretary of State Warren Christopher, Secretary of Defense Les Aspin, and Anthony Lake were called before the Congress on October 5 and criticized harshly for the debacle of the U.S. Rangers in south Mogadishu. At 8:30 that night, Robert Oakley, who was a dinner guest at the Syrian Embassy in Washington, received a call asking him to come to the White House immediately. Oakley, who had overseen the U.S.-led Unified Task Force phase in Somalia from December 1992 to March 1993, had been back in Washington for six months but had been neither debriefed nor consulted by the Clinton administration; now it wanted him to return to Somalia. With the president and all his advisers in the cabinet room, the talk about what to do went on past midnight in, as one participant said, "Renaissance Weekend style." Through all the hours of agonizing discussion, one participant told me, Secretary of State Christopher said nothing. In the end it was decided that the U.S. forces must withdraw from Somalia but that Oakley would be sent back to Mogadishu as a sign that the United States was in charge of events. As a cover for the American withdrawal, another U.S. task force, under another U.S. general, would be sent in as a show—but only a show—of strength.

On October 7, 1993, President Clinton spoke to the American people. He announced that U.S. forces in Somalia would be more than doubled and "will be under American command," as if that were a change in status. Clinton's inclination was to blame the United Nations for what had been entirely an American disaster. Clinton said he would send Oakley back to Somalia to try to gain the release of the captured American pilot and seek a political settlement. U.S. forces would be out of Somalia by March 31, 1994. The United States had run into trouble, and it wanted out.

I admired Oakley; tall, lean, and articulately taciturn, he reminded me of the honest sheriff in a classic American cowboy movie. Oakley and Howe had known each other as friends for many years. But sending Oakley back to the scene could only undercut Howe and strengthen Aidid. As Oakley said to me later, "The Somalis wanted me to be governor-general." I told Madeleine Albright, "You have already confused the military situation; now you want to confuse the diplomatic situation too." Albright reacted by telling Oakley not to meet with me before his departure for Somalia, but he came to see me in New York anyway.

The next day, October 8, Albright sent me "a selection of documents pertaining to U.S. participation in UNOSOM II," revealing that Carter's proposal that Clinton "try a political solution that doesn't appear to be a capitulation" was being adopted by the Clinton administration. In other words, the U.S. would try to accommodate Aidid rather than apprehend him. A week later Carter wrote to tell me that "it is almost inevitable that, on occasion, you and I will have some disagreement." He added that "although I have no specific request of you at this time," he would urge me to focus my attention away from Somalia and on Liberia. In one sense I was pleased by this; no other leader of Carter's stature cared as much about Africa. Nonetheless, I was puzzled. The United Nations was already deeply involved in Liberia, and how could I turn away from Somalia when the Security Council, including the United States, had instructed me otherwise?

Thus it was clear that Clinton and his administration were going to blame the United Nations for the U.S. Rangers' debacle in south Mogadishu. On October 16, 1993, Clinton, in a statement made after the Senate endorsed his decision to withdraw U.S. troops from Somalia, accused the United Nations of assigning American troops the "police function" of finding those responsible for killing twenty-six Pakistani peacekeepers in June.

Under the headline UN's GLOW IS GONE, a *New York Times* page-one article declared, "After embracing the UN as the global peace-maker of the future, President Clinton has broken sharply with it over Somalia, signaling the Administration's intense displeasure with Secretary-General Boutros Boutros-Ghali and complicating U.S. participation in peacekeeping operations elsewhere." But, it went on, "the U.S. could not blame the United Nations for last Sunday's attack since the raid that led to it was carried out on purely American orders" and by a U.S. force with which the United Nations had no contact.

Despite the Rangers' losses, the October 3 raid had in fact dealt an almost devastating blow to Aidid's position. But the psychological cost to the United States was all that seemed to matter. American public and congressional opinion surged strongly against the U.S. presence in Somalia.

Television news programs, which earlier had aroused a groundswell of public sympathy for the victims of famine imposed by Somali gunmen, now broadcast, over and over again, distressing scenes of the captured American helicopter pilot and the footage of the dead U.S. Ranger being dragged through Mogadishu streets. Congressman Charles Rangel, an old friend, told me that the American public was particularly outraged by this event because those who were dragging the body of the American soldier were black.

"Now that the manhunt [for Aidid] has failed," *The Economist* wrote, "and too many Americans have been killed in the course of it, somebody has to be blamed: so finger the UN in general, and Mr. Boutros-Ghali and Admiral Howe in particular. With a chutzpah level high even by American standards, Congressmen and columnists are busy rewriting history with the discovery that America was diverted from its pure humanitarian purpose in Somalia by the UN's obsessive vendetta against General Aidid."

The White House quickly warmed to this theme. On October 16 President Clinton accused the United Nations of assigning U.S. troops the task of finding those responsible for killing the twenty-six Pakistani peacekeepers in June. A *New York Times* headline of October 18, 1993, declared, AFTER SUPPORTING HUNT FOR AIDID, US NOW BLAMES UN FOR BATTLE LOSSES. And far more than this was at stake. Senator Mitch McConnell of Kentucky declared that "Multilateralism is dead, killed . . . in the alleys of Mogadishu" (*The Christian Science Monitor,* October 17, 1993). More specifically, *The Nation* of Thailand reported that "By failing even to thank the Malaysian soldiers who rescued the Ranger survivors, Clinton has effectively made the United Nations the scapegoat."

The Somali Syndrome Reaches Haiti

The catastrophic Ranger raid would send a message around the world: Kill U.S. soldiers, and Washington will order American armed forces home.

In mid-1993 the Security Council had applied sanctions against Haiti. This decision produced unexpected results: General Cedras agreed to meet with President Aristide. The talks took place in July at Governors Island, a U.S. Coast Guard station about a thousand yards off the lower tip of Manhattan in New York Harbor, across from the Statue of Liberty. The talks were difficult because of the refusal of Aristide and Cedras to meet face-to-face. The go-between was Dante Caputo, the joint special envoy of the secretaries-general of the United Nations and the OAS, who shuttled between the two in an extended bout of "proximity talks" through which Aristide and Cedras were finally brought to a fragile agreement.

The Governors Island Accord called for dialogue among the Haitian political factions; for designation of a prime minister by Aristide; for restoration of the integrity of Parliament (Cedras had packed the Parliament with extra deputies; Aristide insisted that they must go); for the suspension of sanctions; for modernization of the armed forces and police force; for an amnesty granted by the president of the republic; for a new chief of police named by Aristide; for the departure and retirement of Cedras as commandant of the armed forces; for Aristide's return to Haiti on October 30, 1993; and for UN-OAS verification of all these points.

At the last minute Aristide refused to sign the agreement, and my colleagues urged me to intervene. I telephoned Aristide, and we talked over every complication and concern in detail. I was able to persuade him that any omission in the agreement could be rectified once he returned to Haiti. The point was to get him back into his rightfully elected office. At the end of our telephone talk he promised that he would sign. During July, August, and September 1993 the Governors Island Accord was put into effect. Aristide designated Robert Malval, a businessman, the new prime minister, and sanctions were suspended on August 27, 1993. They would be reimposed, the Security Council declared, if I informed it that the Governors Island Accord was not being carried out in good faith.

The date set for President Aristide to return to Haiti was October 30, 1993. To assist in reestablishing law and order and justice, the Security Council authorized the immediate deployment of the United Nations Mission in Haiti (UNMIH) with a military component and 567 civilian police.

On the morning of October 11 Dante Caputo, the UN-OAS envoy, was riding in an American Embassy car, along with U.S. envoy Lawrence Pezzullo, Clinton's special envoy, and the American chargé d'affaires. They were on their way to the harbor to meet the USS *Harlan County,* carrying U.S. and Canadian soldiers to join the UN mission in Haiti. As they approached the harbor, their vehicle was rocked by demonstrators, apparently hired by the military regime. Ignoring this political theater, they proceeded to the dock. The *Harlan County* arrived offshore and anchored. On the quay, more thugs shouted and gesticulated, declaring that Haiti would become "another Somalia" for the United States, and protesters held up a sign saying, "Welcome to Mogadishu." Within a few hours the *Harlan County* weighed anchor and steamed away, apparently ordered by the White House to return to Norfolk, Virginia. The dockside demonstration had succeeded. Port-au-Prince did appear to be another Mogadishu for the United States.

The seaward retreat of the *Harlan County* inflicted a humiliation not only on the United States but also on the United Nations and undermined the Governors Island Accord. Madeleine Albright publicly declared that the defeats suffered by the United States in Somalia and Haiti were unconnected, and she played down the significance of the *Harlan County* incident.

General Cedras quickly took advantage of this opportunity. In a letter of October 12, 1993, he accused Caputo of unjustly blaming the Haitian Army for stimulating the anti-American protests on the dock. On October 13 I reported to the Security Council that the *Harlan County* incident had constituted violation of the Governors Island Accord and recommended the reimposition of sanctions. The Security Council adopted a new resolution that not only reimposed the sanctions but also confirmed that it was "prepared to contemplate with urgency the imposition of supplementary measures, if the Secretary General informs the Security Council that the parties to the accord, or any other authority in Haiti, continue to obstruct the activities of the mission."

President Aristide wrote to me on October 15 to request the immediate application of these supplementary sanctions. I have never been in favor of sanctions, but in this case it was absolutely necessary to save the prestige of the United Nations, held up to ridicule by the incoherence of American policy. From the time of the *Harlan County* incident, General Cedras had refused to meet with Dante Caputo, who became isolated, his ability to fulfill his mission impaired.

October 30, 1993, passed without the return of President Aristide, as had been required by the Governors Island Accord. A series of endeavors to reinstate the dialogue failed. A meeting scheduled for November 5 in Port-au-Prince had to be adjourned, despite my efforts, because the chairs reserved for the representatives of the military remained empty. Prime Minister Malval favored convening a national convention. I encouraged this initiative, only to learn later that President Aristide did not favor it. Malval gave up his plan and resigned on December 15, 1993.

The Friends of the Secretary-General for Haiti—Canada, France, the United States, and Venezuela—met in Paris on December 13 and 14. The French position differed from the American one. Whereas Washington blamed the military, Paris claimed that neither party had fully respected the Governors Island Accord but that the military was principally responsible for the delays in its application. By the end of 1993 a major campaign was under way in Washington to discredit Aristide, stimulated largely by a leaked CIA "psychological profile" depicting him as mentally unstable. From the United Nations' vantage point, it appeared that the U.S. government was divided. The civilian side was firmly opposed to the Haitian junta. The military and intelligence side regarded the Haitian Army as a critical factor in national stability and as a bulwark against Aristide's radical followers. The United States never made its aims and intentions clear to the United Nations.

Against U.S. Wishes in Somalia

Shortly after the *Harlan County* episode, I was in Africa on my way to Somalia on a trip planned long before the October 3 disaster in south Mogadishu. Only two weeks earlier, Christopher had welcomed my plan to go to Somalia. Now a brusque message came from him stating that my presence in Somalia would only "aggravate the situation." The United States wanted to extricate itself unilaterally from Somalia and then to see the international community's involvement there closed out. Madeleine Albright urged me to cancel my planned stop in Mogadishu "in order not to jeopardize this fragile process." The only fragile process was the recent U.S. effort to appease Aidid. In Washington, U.S. officials were telling the press that my presence in Somalia would "fuel unrest."

My UN colleagues urged me to do what the United States wanted and stay away. I was about to take their advice when the White House revealed to the press that the United States had told me not to go to Somalia. This put me into an impossible situation. Under the UN Charter the secretary-general is not to accept instructions from a member state. The United States could be oblivious to this principle, but I could not. Now I had to go.

Shortly before leaving for Africa, I spoke to a group of heads of state who were in New York for the opening of the General Assembly. In reference to Aidid, I said that "those who were responsible for Somalia's collapse now seek to prevent Somalia's rescue and to destroy all that has so far been achieved. They must not succeed." I knew that the United States would leave Somalia. Nonetheless, I said, "We must not abandon Somalia." Somalia showed the United Nations at the service of one of its weakest members—indeed, assisting a state whose very statehood was in doubt. "The principle of universality is relatively new in the history of the United Nations," I said. "It is something which we must nurture and cherish, for it means universality not only in the composition of the membership of the organization but also in the scope of the support and assistance it provides for its members."

In Cairo in the presidential palace, I met with the regional "friends group" under the chairmanship of President Mubarak. Present were the secretaries-general of the Arab League, the Organization of African Unity, and the Organization of the Islamic Conference. Mubarak was then chairman of the OAU and spoke in that capacity: "As soon as the United States pulls out of Somalia, all the other countries will follow. The French, the Belgians, and all the Western countries will pull out as soon as the Americans leave. And one hour after the U.S. leaves, I will pull out also."

Heading toward Somalia, I stopped in Djibouti on October 13 to see President Hassan Gouled Aptidon, who was at his mountain retreat out-side the capital. An old Soviet-built helicopter was "put at my disposal." When I saw it, I was truly afraid to get aboard, but to refuse would have been an insult to the government of Djibouti. I clambered into my seat and prayed. The machine rose with a terrible grinding noise. A crew member next to me circled his arms around a part that was shaking vio-lently. Ten minutes later we landed safely for my appointment with the president. "Be serious, you have to go to Somalia. You're the UN boss," he told me. "If you don't make an appearance among your UN troops, no one will take you seriously." Aidid, he said, "is a *baudruche*—a hot-air bal-loon inflated by the UN and the U.S.; he represents absolutely nothing in Somalia." My survival of the first helicopter flight had not strengthened my courage for the return trip, but the stuttering aircraft arrived safely again. The crew beamed at me with pride at their accomplishment.

I stopped next in Nairobi, Kenya, and met with President Daniel Arap Moi. October 24 was United Nations Day, the national holiday, so to speak, of the United Nations. It would be celebrated at Nairobi at the African UN headquarters, where I was to deliver a speech attended by Kenyan officials. But I decided instead to spend that day with the Blue Helmets in Somalia. I asked UN Under Secretary-General James Jonah to represent me at the Nairobi celebration and telephoned Admiral Howe to tell him of my change in plans, and he dispatched a small plane for me. We left the hotel at a very early hour. It was cold. En route to the airport we came across Kenyans walking toward the capital. They were inhabitants of the suburbs, too poor even to afford the cheap public bus. We took off as the marvelous African sun rose gently over the plain. There were four of us on the small plane: Rolf Knutsson, a high-ranking UN official from Sweden; Thérèse Gastaut, the spokeswoman; and Stanlake Samkange, a young Zimbabwean acting as note taker. After less than two hours in the air, the plane landed at Baidoa in the interior of Somalia.

Jonathan Howe greeted me at the airport, as always calm and self-effacing, with perfect manners and steely determination despite the recent turmoil. We drove through the center of the town, which was calm and quiet. The inhabitants recognized Howe and waved and smiled. In a frank discussion at the general headquarters of UN forces, the concern was that the United States' decision to pull out was causing other troop-contributing countries to conclude that Somalia was not worth the effort. Even worse, the Somalis believed that the United States was now pro-Aidid.

When I met with local Somali leaders, I stressed that I had come to show solidarity with the UN Blue Helmets. Chief Mukhtar Malaag Hassan declared that before the fighting and the eruption of famine, this had been "Baidoa the paradise." After having been transformed into a town of death, Baidoa had revived, thanks to aid from the United Nations. The Somali chieftains spoke in turn, at great length. To enable the translator to do his job, I periodically punctuated their talks by declaring, "Long live the new Baidoa!" and each time the audience enthusiastically repeated my slogan.

I visited a school run by the Ananda Margu Universal Relief Team, an Indian nongovernmental organization; then I went to a Catholic orphanage, where two young Irishwomen looked after four hundred children. After touring a police station staffed by UN-trained local police officers, Admiral Howe and I flew on to Mogadishu. Around a table in a room at the airport, generals of diverse troop-contributing countries portrayed a difficult but improving situation in Somalia. One general from Kuwait recalled that he had been my student at the University of Cairo years before. At a hospital run by a Romanian organization, I found an Egyptian soldier and asked the general accompanying me how the man had been injured. The general whispered with a smile, "It's an appendectomy."

As I returned to board the plane that would take me to Nairobi, I was mobbed by a group of Egyptian soldiers who wanted to greet and embrace me. My security contingent, at first alarmed, realized that I was being assailed by admirers and did not intervene. Later, television film of the jostling was used to show that I had met with angry protests in Mogadishu.

At Nairobi I found an agitated and worried James Jonah, who told me that incredible stories had been spread about hostile demonstrations, bloody confrontations with troops, and Boutros-Ghali being hurried away to a secure compound for his own safety. I quickly held a press conference to convey the truth and calm the situation. Above all, I wanted to reassure UN personnel in Baidoa and elsewhere in Somalia that the situation was not as depicted in the media. But in the following days journalists continued to report that my visit to Somalia had provoked massively hostile and dangerous demonstrations. I was deeply concerned about the morale of the UN troops. They knew that the United States was about to pack up and go and were naturally afraid of what would follow. The next morning I flew to Addis Ababa to meet with President Meles Zenawi. There have been two policies toward Somalia, I said, one U.S. and one UN. Now the United States is leaving. The United Nations could continue its work without the United States, I said, but not unless the United States, so used to playing a major role in any UN activity, allowed the United Nations to do so.

CHAPTER 4

Policies Have Consequences

(1994)

All through 1993 I had tried, in speeches and articles, to generate a serious debate about the importance of multilateral approaches to conflicts like that in Somalia. Almost as though in response, the Clinton administration attempted to set out its policy in a series of four major speeches given in September 1993. The UN operations in Somalia and Bosnia provided the leitmotif for these statements. At the UN General Assembly, President Clinton said that the "scourge of bitter conflict has placed high demands on UN peacekeeping forces. Frequently the Blue Helmets have worked wonders. In Namibia, El Salvador, the Golan Heights, and elsewhere, UN peacekeepers have helped to stop the fighting, restore civil authority, and enable free elections. In Bosnia, UN peacekeepers, against the danger and frustration of that continuing tragedy, have maintained a valiant humanitarian effort. . . . In Somalia, the United States and the United Nations have worked together to achieve a stunning humanitarian rescue, saving literally hundreds of thousands of lives and restoring the conditions of security for almost the entire country." The United States had supported UN peacekeeping, Clinton said, "not, as some critics in the United States have charged, to subcontract American foreign policy, but to strengthen our security, protect our interests, and to share among nations the costs of pursuing peace. Peacekeeping cannot be a substitute for our own national defense efforts, but it can strongly supplement them." But, Clinton said, it was time to put on the brakes regarding further peacekeeping missions for the United Nations, a position I fully shared—because we had no more money available for such operations.

"The United Nations simply cannot become engaged in every one of the world's conflicts," Clinton said. "If the American people are to say yes to UN peacekeeping, the United Nations must know when to say no." Clinton may have forgotten that the United States had voted "yes" on UN involvement in all those operations, including Bosnia, where I had recommended "no."

National Security Adviser Anthony Lake, in a speech at Johns Hopkins University, expressed his hope that "the habit of multilateralism" would one day "enable the rule of law to play a far more civilizing role in the conduct of nations, as envisioned by the founders of the United Nations." But, he concluded, only one overriding factor could determine whether the United States should act multilaterally or unilaterally, and that was America's national interest.

At Columbia University, Secretary of State Christopher's speech called multilateralism a means, not an end, and warranted only when it served the central purpose of American foreign policy. If the United States displayed a willingness to act alone, Christopher said, that fact itself would "generate effective multilateral responses."

Ambassador Albright, at the National Defense University, listed questions that the United States would insist be answered before it would agree to a new UN peace operation. There would have to be a real threat to international peace and security, a clearly defined objective, a cease-fire in place, agreement to a UN presence by the parties to the conflict, necessary financial and human resources available, and an identifiable end point to the UN operation.

Albright's speech was the most specific and definitive of the four American statements. She had earlier been criticized for favoring "assertive multilateralism." But if her newly stated conditions were to be carried out to the letter, the United States should at that moment have been calling for the withdrawal of the UN missions from Bosnia as well as Somalia.

Searching for an American Policy

Since the summer of 1993 we at the United Nations had been aware of the drafting of what was called Presidential Review Document 13, an effort to set down with some precision the conditions under which U.S. forces would work in and with UN peacekeeping missions. As a quid pro quo for serving under UN control, the Pentagon insisted that the U.S. chain of command remain intact, that U.S. forces retain the ability to report separately to Washington, and that U.S. commanders be instructed not to comply with orders that were beyond the UN mandate, were illegal, or were militarily imprudent or unsound. This was General Colin Powell's own language, I was told. I had no objection. There was no reason why a system could not be arranged that would satisfy the American requirements for sovereignty and still permit a coordinated, unified peacekeeping mission to be carried out under UN Security Council resolutions.

On October 27, 1993, the director of the State Department's policy planning staff telephoned my office to say that all the hopes that he and many others in Washington had had for close UN-U.S. cooperation over the next years "blew up in our faces" in Mogadishu. "In PRD 13 we were on the brink of a far-reaching policy," he said, under which American forces could have participated in UN peace operations. Now that draft policy had been "put on the shelf forever. Somalia will have a devastating impact on the future of UN peacekeeping operations. No more big ones. Maybe that's best." The director, Ambassador Samuel W. Lewis, soon resigned.

At the very end of October, I went to Washington, D.C., where I was scheduled to address the United Nations Association of the USA, a private, pro–United Nations group with a nationwide membership. I also wanted to speak with Warren Christopher about the positive signs I had seen in Somalia. As I was about to leave for Pennsylvania Station to board the train for Washington, Madeleine Albright telephoned my chief of staff to argue vehemently that I should not accept *The Washington Post*'s invitation to meet with its editorial board. This was becoming a familiar practice on her part. My very presence in Washington, she insisted, would only stir up anti–United Nations feeling in the press and the Congress. In fact, I had always been well received by both, so I began to wonder whether there was some other purpose behind her efforts.

On board the Amtrak train to Washington an aide gave me a selection of current political cartoons from *The Washington Post*. In one I was depicted brandishing a riding crop and shouting "Tally Ho!" as I rode on the helmet of a U.S. soldier. "So many trouble spots, so little time" was the caption. The other cartoons all made fun of Clinton's ineptitude and vacillation in foreign policy.

When I met with the board of *The Washington Post*, I repeated my conviction that no solution for Somalia could ever succeed as long as the factions remained armed to the teeth. Now, however, the United States would never disarm them.

That evening I spoke to the United Nations Association of the USA audience in the magnificent colonnaded hall of a pre–Civil War building. "I have many friends in Washington," I joked. "They always have my best interests at heart. They didn't want me to go to Mogadishu. They said it wasn't safe. But when they learned that I was coming to Washington, they didn't say a thing. So I take that to mean that I am safe here."

Madeleine Albright had also told me not to be critical in my speech of the United States' failure to pay its arrears to the United Nations. I did not follow her instructions. I said, "Let me say this frankly: I need the United States. The United Nations needs the United States. Finding the right relationship between the United Nations and the United States may be one of the most important tasks of our time. In peacekeeping, the United Nations budget arrears approach a thousand million dollars. That is not an oversight. It is a decision. And it will have consequences.

"If the United States, despite its legal obligations under the Charter, decides not to fulfill its financial undertaking, it can do so. If the United States wants to condition its contribution or withhold part of it or re-schedule it—the United Nations can do nothing. But I ask that such steps not be taken lightly. I ask that those who decide consider carefully what such steps may mean—for American influence at the United Nations and for the precedent it would set for others."

Before giving these remarks, I had been sitting at a table with Vice President Al Gore. Early in my term as secretary-general, when he was still a senator, he had come to see me at the United Nations and had autographed a copy of his book on the environment for me. This evening we had a long and lively talk about the world's water shortage. But during my speech, when I criticized the United States' failure to pay its UN dues, Gore was the only person in the hall whose face displayed no emotion whatsoever.

A week later I went back to Washington to attend a seminar on ethnic conflict at the invitation of the National Defense University. This time I got into and out of town before Albright or Christopher knew of my presence. My name, however, was much in the news. The conservative press was referring to me as the "Secretary-Generalissimo." An article in the November 1993 *American Spectator* declared, "Since Bill Clinton doesn't seem to want to do it, Boutros-Ghali is finding it easy to run U.S. foreign policy." And *The New York Times* had shifted its generally positive view of me to heavily emphasize negative aspects of my personality and policies.

A Misleading Meeting

On the afternoon of November 8 I went to the State Department for a meeting with Christopher and Albright, which the young UN official who accompanied me to take notes called "worse than a disaster." At first, it appeared that all three of us—Christopher, Albright, and I—had been misinformed by our aides on key issues. I later realized that I had not been misinformed, but the truth, it turned out, was not enough. Misunderstandings resulted in harsh, bitter exchanges on one issue after another.

My UN colleague James Jonah had told me repeatedly that U.S. forces in Mogadishu were holding prisoners taken in the raids against Somali factions the preceding summer and that the United Nations was being denied access to these detainees. I protested to Christopher in the strongest terms.

"But the prisoners are being held by UNOSOM II!" Christopher's aide, Peter Tarnoff, exclaimed. I was embarrassed to have spoken on the basis of mistaken information provided by my own people and to have appeared misinformed in the presence of Christopher and Albright. Later I learned that Jonah had been correct—the prisoners *were* being held by the United States—but the damage had been done as far as the meeting was concerned.

Madeleine Albright then raised the issue of a Commission of Inquiry to be set up by a UN Security Council resolution to find whether Aidid had in fact ordered the June 5 Mogadishu ambush of the Pakistani Blue Helmets. "What Commission of Inquiry?" I asked. "What resolution?"

Albright turned red with embarrassment. "I *told* you about that," she said. "Well, tell me more," I replied, "because I have heard nothing about it from you." Now Christopher appeared to be irritated with Albright. "We just now thought of this idea," he said.

Eagerly changing the subject, we turned to Haiti. I mentioned that the principal UN official dealing with Haiti, Alvaro de Soto, had told me that "different parts of the U.S. government are giving different messages to the Haitians." This was, in fact, a long-standing problem. The State Department was pursuing one policy in Haiti, while other American officials, apparently from the CIA, were taking quite a different line. We had raised this with the Clinton administration before.

Christopher lost his self-control, something I had never seen him do before. "Are you telling me," he asked angrily, "that there are people in this administration who are not carrying out the president's unified policy on Haiti:?" Christopher's tone implied that I was the one at fault. "No, no," one of my aides said, "but the Haitians *are* getting back-channel messages." Now it was Christopher who was embarrassed by appearing to be out of touch with his own government. Unfortunately, what Soto told me was true; different parts of the U.S. government held differing views about Haitian President Jean-Bertrand Aristide. The State Department, the Defense Department, and the CIA each seemed to have its own position and to be conducting its own policy in Haiti.

We then returned to the issue of Somalia. Because of the United States' declaration that it would withdraw by March 31, 1994, several European and other governments had decided to pull out their contingents as well. The Security Council, of which the United States was the major member, had called upon me to offer a plan on what should be done next. "How can I plan if you just walk out of Somalia?" I asked. "You do not understand the political issues involved," Christopher said. "You are going to have trouble with the United States government. You and the UN are not being helpful." I replied that Jonathan Howe was out there on the ground in Somalia. He and Oakley agreed on what the situation required. "Howe must know better than we do what is needed," I said.

"We're having our problems with Howe," Christopher muttered. "We are upset at the lack of progress toward a political solution. Howe is a barrier to progress." I objected strongly: "You Americans insist that I hire Admiral Howe. So I hire him. Then you want him to report directly to Tony Lake at the National Security Council, who then gives him his instructions from Washington. Then things go wrong. Then you blame him. Then you blame me for relying on him. I can't function this way."

On and on we went, with Christopher repeating again and again that the United States was upset with the slow progress toward a political solution, by which he meant appeasing Aidid, and my repeatedly asking him to explain the United States' long-term intentions toward Somalia.

"All right," Christopher said finally, "the U.S. will keep you advised more about our intentions, but the U.S. expects to be respected more by you." "I respect you one hundred percent," I said, "but I need to be told more about what you want, what you are doing, and where you want to go."

In the end Christopher and Albright expressed their unhappiness that I had accepted an invitation to go up to Capitol Hill to meet with members of Congress the next day. "It won't help if you criticize us," Christopher said. "This is not a good time to come here," Albright added. "They'll try to divide you and us." Don't worry, I assured them, "I won't betray you. My only message to the Congress will be 'Please don't harm the United Nations too much.'"

The staff aides, both U.S. and UN, emerged from the meeting shaken. "It was bad between Christopher and BB-G," a young American said, "but not as bad as between Albright and BB-G." The State Department spokesman described the meeting as "frank and candid," the diplomatic vocabulary for "brutal." News of the meeting got into the press when an anonymous U.S. official told a *New York Times* reporter that "they got in each other's faces."

I was beginning to realize that I had no margin for error with either Christopher or Albright. In my diplomatic experience, personal relationships were key. But I had not been able to consolidate a friendship with Christopher because of his immensely heavy schedule and his occluded personality, and because Albright insisted on mediating between us. As for Albright, we had an apparently warm friendship, but warmth turned to fury the instant problems surfaced. Christopher seemed to regard such problems as how to deal with Aidid as an affront to his dignity; Albright regarded them as a veiled attack on her competence. They both seemed unsure of their roles. I could only contrast this meeting at the State Department with my earlier meeting with Pentagon leaders on the same topic, Somalia; the atmosphere had been totally different, cordial and mature. Secretary of Defense Les Aspin, Assistant Secretary Frank Wisner, and I had been able to disagree without the perception of a personal challenge. I took heart from our talk, regarding it as proof that it was possible for me to work cooperatively with this U.S. administration.

With the House and Senate

At breakfast the next day with the House International Affairs Committee, I was given a warm welcome by Congressman Tom Lantos of California, who congratulated me for my "frankness." But "why couldn't the date for all U.S. troops to leave Somalia be December 31, 1993 rather than March 31, 1994?" Congressman Benjamin Gilman wanted to know. I gave strong arguments to justify the later date, but it was clear that Congress wanted the United States out of Somalia as soon as possible. After two hours of vigorous debate, Lantos declared that our talk had been a success and asked me to come back again, several times a year.

At lunch with the Congressional Round Table on Post Cold War Issues I got a taste of the deliberate misinformation that was now being generated against the United Nations from somewhere within Washington. A congressman asked me whether I held any personal animosity against Aidid. "Never," I said, somewhat ironically. "When we met, we embraced." But wasn't it true, my questioner said, "that you owned a farm in Somalia that was confiscated—and that is why you are out to get Aidid?" I laughed and replied that if ever I bought a farm, it wouldn't be in Somalia; it would be in America. But this was one of the poisonous allegations that were circulating about me in Washington.

As the luncheon was ending, Congressman Neil Smith simply said, again and again, "The U.S. will not pay for peacekeeping operations; peacekeeping is not popular." I defended peacekeeping with every argument I could muster. The United States had spent $1 billion a day on weaponry during the cold war; by comparison, peacekeeping was cheap. "No," Smith said, "we won't pay." "What about morality?" I asked. "About saving lives, about giving people a chance?" "No," Smith repeated, "we won't pay." We could not have been farther apart on the issue, but our debate was marked by mutual respect, as was my session with the Senate that afternoon.

That evening, Christopher's personal assistant telephoned my aide to ask for a "readout" of what I had said in the restricted sessions; Christopher was going to be on the Hill the next day, and his staff wanted to get him ready to repair whatever damage I might have done. There was no cause for concern, I said; I had praised President Clinton's decision to keep American troops in Somalia until March 31, 1994. I wanted them there longer, of course, but Congress wanted them out at once, so I found myself speaking as the strongest supporter of Clinton's decision.

To their credit, both my aides and those serving Christopher tried to rescue the relationship between the secretary of state and the secretary-general. Christopher reached out first in a telephone call to me on November 11, 1993, two days after our turbulent meeting in Washington. He apologized for his "anonymous spokesman" who had told *The New York Times* that we "got in each other's faces." I joked that whereas the United States and the USSR had used to have a "hot line" to prevent war from breaking out, perhaps we should have a hot line between the United States and the United Nations. We rang off in good spirits and promised to stay in closer touch. But all through the winter months, whenever my staff tried to arrange with Christopher's staff a way for us to meet in person, they were rebuffed.

The United States had ended the United Nations' effort to restore Somalia to nationhood. There was nothing to do but try to help the United States depart with as little lasting harm as possible. This was not easy. Madeleine Albright informed me that the United States wanted the Commission of Inquiry to be headed by Jimmy Carter and the presidents of Ethiopia and Eritrea. This would be an incredible blunder, I said, "To ask Christians, including those from two Christian countries next door to Somalia, to pass judgment on the killing of Muslims by Muslims in a country beset by Islamic fundamentalism." I said to Albright, "Don't you have an intelligence service to advise you?" Albright threw her head back, rolled her eyes, made a face, and slapped her thigh with a loud *whack,* all in one smoothly flowing display of exasperation with me.

My protest made an impact. I soon received a workable list of names from the State Department and began to consult with the Security Council to ensure that the Commission of Inquiry would not simply be dictated to by the United States. On November 16 the Security Council adopted Resolution 885, authorizing me to appoint the commission.

Two days later the Council adopted Resolution 886, renewing UNOSOM II's mandate until the end of May 1994, two months after the U.S. withdrawal would be completed. Pending the outcome of the Commission of Inquiry, the warrants for the arrest of Aidid and others were suspended, and the UN forces began releasing the forty-two detainees suspected of involvement in attacks on their personnel. The eight close aides to Aidid were released later. I would have held them longer to demonstrate at least a modicum of consistency in our policy, but Christopher insisted on their release. The Commission of Inquiry was restricted by the United States to investigating the June 5 killing of the Pakistani UN soldiers, an indication that the United States hoped it would exonerate Aidid because he had publicly and proudly claimed responsibility for the October 3 killing of the U.S. Rangers. And by this time we had received an intelligence document revealing that Aidid, on October 19, 1993, had ordered the execution of fifty-four members of his own clan and subclan apparatus. To me this rendered the "inquiry" meaningless, but the United States continued to search for some way to exonerate Aidid so that he could play the leading role in a political reconciliation process for Somalia that would justify the United States' withdrawal under conditions that might appear honorable.

The United States proceeded to put Aidid at the center of its "political solution." Aidid was its man. He was flown to Addis Ababa by a U.S. aircraft for talks from which the United Nations was excluded. "Bizarre and unseemly," *The Wall Street Journal* called it. But the other faction leaders would not sit down with Aidid unless he reaffirmed the United Nations' role in Somalia. "If he won't deal with the United Nations, we won't deal with him" was their attitude. A year or so later Aidid was ousted by his party, and not long afterward he was attacked in a factional fight and died of his wounds. With the United States gone from the scene, the news was hardly noticed. Aidid was replaced by his son, but the Somalian factions did not cease warring on each other.

The United States' departure from Somalia precipitated a stampede of other nations pulling out as well, demonstrating that the international community did not have the will to act in support of a failed state. A state that loses its government—a failed state—loses its place as a member of the international community. Even so, I was determined that the United Nations continue to offer assistance, within the means at its disposal, to the suffering people of Somalia.

Presidential Decision Directive 13

The debate over multilateralism and U.S. policy toward UN peacekeeping operations had moved from speeches to policy documents. Paul Lewis of *The New York Times* revealed on November 19, 1993, that

Madeleine Albright had allowed him to see a classified draft of PRD 13. The original draft had been shelved after the U.S. debacle in Mogadishu; the new draft, upgraded in title to Presidential Decision Directive 13 (PDD 13), would prevent rather than facilitate U.S. participation in UN peacekeeping operations. The document, not yet signed by President Clinton, elaborated on the conditions set out by Albright in her September 23 speech at Johns Hopkins University. The message was clear: the United States was preparing to set almost insurmountable conditions for any future UN peacekeeping operations other than those of the "classic" kind, where a cease-fire had been agreed on, all parties wanted the United Nations to come in, and no trouble was anticipated. It was a declaration by the Clinton administration of opposition to any but benign, small-scale, and U.S.-directed peace operations.

Henry Kissinger had entered the debate with a newspaper column calling PDD 13 a "recipe for chaos," in that it would nominally put U.S. troops under UN command but expect U.S. commanders to ignore UN orders if the U.S. officers thought they were "imprudent or outside the UN mandate." I agreed. Multilateralism, Kissinger wrote, was "not policy but a flight from it," a form of American isolationism, a way for the United States to avoid taking action on its own. I disagreed; American unilateralism, it seemed clear to me, was even more isolationist, because it could become a means of avoiding decisions on any but the most direct and dire threats to the national interest.

Paradoxically, on the same day that the article on PDD 13 appeared in the *Times,* I was on the parade ground at windy, chilly West Point at the invitation of the superintendent of the U.S. Military Academy. The first UN secretary-general to visit West Point, I met with officers and faculty, attended a seminar, addressed the Corps of Cadets, and, prodded by my gleeful staff, exhorted the cheering gray-clad throng in the gigantic mess hall to "Beat Navy!" At West Point I was given one message clearly and repeatedly: "U.S. military cooperation with the United Nations in peacekeeping and peace enforcement is a good thing."

But West Point and Washington were not of the same opinion. PDD 13 would drive a wedge between the United Nations and the United States, making relations ever more problematic. My responsibility was to promote multilateralism; the emerging U.S. policy was unilateralism, with multilateralism providing a fig leaf as needed. "Relations between Boutros Boutros-Ghali and the United States government have taken a sharp turn for the worse," declared *The Economist.* "Not since U Thant—

the only other UN chief executive from the third world—incurred the wrath of Lyndon Johnson for his opposition to the Vietnam War has there been so much rancor between the two ends of the New York–Washington political corridor." I asked my staff to propose to National Security Adviser Anthony Lake that I come to Washington to meet briefly with President Clinton to "clear the air."

An aide to Christopher at the State Department telephoned my aide at the United Nations on December 20, 1993. Secretary of State Christopher and National Security Adviser Anthony Lake, I was told, had had a "very long talk on the weekend about how to respond to the secretary-general's request for a meeting with President Clinton. The message to you is that we would like very much to discourage such a meeting." The president is tired, the U.S. official said. "Maybe Boutros could come to Washington later." Off the record, the U.S. official said, Christopher had inadvertently revealed to Madeleine Albright that I had approached the State Department directly and that Albright was "very unhappy" that I had not made my request to see Clinton through her.

Encounter with the "Great Leader"

Once again I was going against Washington's wishes regarding my travel. This time the issue was whether I should go to North Korea. When tests had showed that plutonium had been produced there, and Pyongyang refused International Atomic Energy Agency requests to visit the suspected site, the General Assembly had passed a resolution urging the Democratic People's Republic of Korea (DPRK) to open for inspection two undeclared nuclear complexes north of the capital, Pyongyang. My friend Dr. Hans Blix, the director general of the International Atomic Energy Agency, a specialized agency of the United Nations, declared that by blocking inspection the North Korean regime had "damaged the continuity of monitoring," to which it had committed itself in an agreement signed in 1992. Blix carefully avoided saying that the DPRK had broken the Nuclear Nonproliferation Treaty. This meant that the issue would not go to the Security Council yet. Nonetheless, there was widespread fear that the North Koreans were building a nuclear weapon. The General Assembly's message was that of international consensus against the DPRK's actions. Because of this, I asked to meet with President Kim Il Sung in Pyongyang. The State Department's chief of staff telephoned my chief of staff. "We don't think he should go" was the message. Madeleine Albright nonetheless came to brief me on the status of U.S.-DPRK contacts. The United States was considering "a comprehensive package" of assistance for Pyongyang if it would agree to inspection. Over and over again Albright said to me, "This meeting is not taking place. We will say nothing to the media."

I urged her not to worry and to try to calm Washington's concerns. I was simply going to Pyongyang to ask the government to be wise and to avoid turning the international community further against it. I was not doing so only as UN secretary-general, I explained; Kim Il Sung had a long and close relationship with Egypt.

During the 1973 October War between Egypt and Israel, Kim Il Sung had sent to Egypt a squadron of MiG fighter aircraft with North Korean pilots. They had patrolled Egyptian airspace throughout the war. The general in command of the Egyptian Air Force at that time was Hosni Mubarak. As a result of this support for Egypt by the DPRK, President Mubarak would never agree to establishing full diplomatic relations with the Republic of Korea (ROK). As for myself, over many years I had constructed a network of personal ties to North Korean officials through contacts at various conferences of the third-world and nonaligned countries. At the same time, the Korean government in Seoul was well aware that I was persistently arguing in Cairo for the establishment of Egypt-ROK relations in view of the fact that nearly half the world's nations had diplomatic ties to both Koreas. My efforts were repeatedly doomed as soon as Mubarak realized that I was making progress. He would never disappoint the DPRK. So there were several good reasons for my decision to go to Pyongyang: I had access on both sides of the Korean peninsula; I was the UN secretary-general; and a General Assembly resolution legitimized a UN role in the current crisis. Nonetheless, the United States maintained its pressure to prevent me from going.

As I left the South, I was saluted by an honor guard of Korean and UN soldiers; no American troops were to be seen. As I entered the North, I was saluted again, by a contingent of the Korean People's Army. It was the first time that the DPRK had allowed a foreigner to use this road to Pyongyang. A vice minister of foreign affairs met me and accompanied me during the long limousine ride north. Leia followed in a second car; Under Secretary-General Marrack Goulding rode in a third. It was Christmas Eve in the Western calendar. The road was excellent but empty; we saw scarcely another car throughout the nearly four-hour ride.

Large factory buildings could be seen from the road, all apparently vacant. I asked why. "It is Friday afternoon," the vice minister said, "and the workers all have departed for the weekend." In reality, they were "Potemkin" factories.

Arriving in Pyongyang, I was greeted by the minister of foreign affairs, whom I had often met at international gatherings. Now that I was representing the United Nations, he wished to explain to me that because the United Nations had been the belligerent party in the Korean War in 1950, he should not even talk to me. But as I was an old friend, an exception was being made. There were no problems to discuss; North Korea was developing a very good relationship with the United States and needed no help from the United Nations. My visit, therefore, was based on "constructive confusion"; I would be received as UN secretary-general even though, as such, I was the head of an organization with which the DPRK was still "at war." To get around this, everywhere I went I was called "the *Egyptian* secretary-general."

The atmosphere in Pyongyang was strange indeed. Huge Soviet-style buildings stood dark and apparently empty in the bitter cold. There was obviously a shortage of electric power. As soon as we left a room, people would rush in to turn off the lights. Only official automobiles were on the streets. Yet in the concert hall where we were treated to a cultural presentation, all was a glorious blaze of light, and fountains danced with colored water dazzlingly illuminated. Food appeared in exaggerated abundance. Everyone talked incessantly about the "Great Leader," Kim Il Sung, but there was no sign of his son and successor, Kim Jong Il, the "Dear Leader," and no one said a word about him.

The next morning I sat in a gigantic room empty except for the Great Leader, the translator, and me. I found Kim Il Sung quick-witted and well informed. His aides appeared to be in terror of him. He was somewhat deaf, and I was asked to speak loudly even though he could not understand me. Nonetheless, I did raise my voice to a near shout. The interpreter would relay my words with a shout, and then Kim would shout back.

My message was simple: The United Nations had two Koreas as member states. The UN Development Program had offices in both Pyongyang and Seoul. "You therefore have a structure for communication at your disposal," I said to Kim, "and the UN is ready to help you arrange a meeting with the president of the Republic of Korea, Kim Young Sam," the first civilian president in the history of South Korea. The Great Leader spoke in surprisingly warm tones about his hopes for relations with the South. "The obstacles," he said, "all come from their side." As evidence, he cited small details of protocol or affronts to the ego, such as anniversaries not marked or letters not answered. I told Kim Il Sung that I believed in all sincerity that Pyongyang's policy was distorted by exaggerated fears of dangers that did not exist. As a result, the DPRK was missing new opportunities to promote the welfare of its people, to enhance its international standing, and to further the objective of early reunification.

"But now," Kim Il Sung declared, "I have a surprise for you!" Because it was Christmas Day, he invited my staff and me to a grand luncheon banquet and seated Leia on his right. The table was heaped with food and the atmosphere was cordial, but conversation seemed impossible. There was a long, terribly awkward silence, which the Great Leader overcame by asking me to expound on the history of Arab literature, which I gladly did at some length, to everyone's apparent relief. In the afternoon I was taken to the home of Kim Il Sung's late father; the significance of the visit was not entirely clear. In the course of this excursion, I emphasized to the North Koreans the strength of international support for nonproliferation. Although the current crisis with North Korea centered on its refusal to allow International Atomic Energy Agency inspections, I deliberately focused on reunification of the two Koreas and the importance of North Korea's endeavoring to gain acceptance as a responsible world citizen.

Near the end of my visit the North Koreans showed me the latest issue of an Arab-language magazine. On the cover was a cartoon depicting me as America's most hated enemy. I was surprised that they were aware of, and could so rapidly acquire, such publications. The fact that I was said to be hated by the United States seemed to create a bond of esteem for me in North Korea. My visit to Pyongyang, they declared, had been so successful that they would put an aircraft at my disposal to take me to the next stop on my itinerary, the People's Republic of China—"The United Nations will only have to pay the tax for landing at Beijing Airport."

When I arrived in Beijing, I briefed Chinese officials on my visit to Pyongyang. I then traveled to Tokyo and did the same with the Japanese Foreign Office. I sent my representative to Seoul to brief the South Korean government. Back in New York on December 28, I told Madeleine Albright the details of my trip. "It is imperative," I said, "that the U.S. send a high-level emissary to Pyongyang; this alone would ease fifty percent of the psychological problems that affect North Korea." I had found a consensus in Beijing, Seoul, and Tokyo that the mere dispatch by the United States of an important envoy to Pyongyang could defuse tensions there and open a possibility for constructive change. I gave Jimmy Carter the same message.

Before leaving for Asia, I heard an American expert on North Korea interviewed on National Public Radio saying that "Boutros-Ghali's trip to Pyongyang can't hurt, and it might help." But to the Clinton administration it was just one more item on its growing list of grievances against me and the United Nations.

As Pyongyang continued to reject international inspections and talk was heard of the need for a U.S. air strike on the Yongbyon complex, Jimmy Carter stepped in. Although at first disavowed by the Clinton administration, Carter returned from Pyongyang with a deal that deferred a confrontation.

Rwanda: Tropical Nazism

A direct connection can be drawn from the U.S. debacle in South Mogadishu to the new U.S. policy toward UN peacekeeping under PDD 13, and to the United States' refusal to act to stop genocide in Rwanda.

Fighting between the armed forces of the government of Rwanda, consisting largely of members of the Hutu tribe, and the Rwandese Patriotic Front (RPF), a primarily Tutsi group, first broke out in October 1990 along the border between Rwanda and Uganda. After a number of cease-fire agreements failed, fighting resumed in February 1993. To support peace negotiations, the Security Council asked me to send a mission to try to further peace talks and to examine the possibility of deploying UN military observers along the Rwandan-Ugandan border. As a result, on June 22, 1993, the Security Council authorized a UN military observer mission on the Ugandan side of the border.

A peace agreement was successfully concluded in Arusha, Tanzania, on August 4, 1993. At the request of the parties to the agreement, the Security Council established the United Nations Assistance Mission in Rwanda (UNAMIR) to monitor the peace agreement and assist in maintaining the security of Kigali, the capital city of Rwanda, as well as to provide humanitarian assistance and help with refugee repatriation. I appointed General Romeo Dallaire of Canada as the force commander and Jacques-Roger Booh-Booh, the former foreign minister of Cameroon, as my special representative for Rwanda. As a West African, Booh-

Booh would be objective about the situation in Rwanda. In addition, I wanted to reinforce the African presence in the United Nations. With this appointment there would be two special representatives helping a secretary-general from Africa deal with issues of war and peace in Africa, the other being Alioune Blondin Beye of Mali, whom I had appointed as special representative for Angola.

At the end of 1993 I reported to the Security Council that the parties in Rwanda had failed to fulfil the Arusha Agreement and that the situation remained fragile. Therefore, although the Council had earlier requested me to consider ways to reduce UN troop strength in Rwanda, I urged it to authorize the deployment of a second infantry battalion. The Council accepted my recommendation in a resolution passed on January 6, 1994.

President Juvénal Habyarimana was sworn in as president of Rwanda on January 5, 1994, in accordance with the Arusha Agreement, but the parties failed to install a transitional government as agreed upon at Arusha, and increasingly violent demonstrations erupted as political leaders were assassinated and civilians murdered.

Throughout most of January 1994 I was away from UN headquarters in New York and not in close touch with the Rwanda situation. Not until three years later did I learn that a cable had been sent by General Dallaire to the UN Department of Peace-Keeping Operations (DPKO) reporting an informant's claim that weapons were being stockpiled by Hutu forces in preparation for mass killings of Tutsis. Dallaire requested authorization to try to seize the weapons, but his request was denied by DPKO on the ground that the United Nations' mandate for Rwanda did not cover such operations. The next day, January 12, 1994 Dallaire, acting under UN instructions, told the ambassadors of Belgium, France, and the United States about the informant's report. In other words, the powers that could have acted to prevent the ensuing massacre—the United States, France, and Belgium—had indisputably and immediately been informed by the United Nations of the severity of the threat.

On February 10 my senior political adviser, Chinmaya Gharekhan, informed the Security Council about the increasingly tense situation in Rwanda, and in a report to the Security Council on March 30 I expressed my concern over the resurgence of violence in Kigali and the increase in ethnically motivated crimes and murders.

On April 6, acting on my recommendation, the Security Council, by

Resolution 909, extended the mandate of the UN force through July. That same day, UN military observers at Kigali Airport and at Camp Kanombe, a post for Rwandese government troops, reported a loud explosion from the camp. Although forcibly prevented from investigating the explosion, they soon monitored a report from the airport tower that the presidential aircraft had crashed. It was confirmed that the president of Rwanda, Juvénal Habyarimana, and the president of Burundi, Cyprien Ntaryamira, both Hutus, had been killed. A plausible interpretation was that the two presidents had been killed by Hutu extremists who were opposed to the concessions that the Hutu presidents had been making to the Tutsis in Rwanda and Burundi. But Hutu leaders declared that the assassins were Tutsis and launched a campaign aimed at slaughtering the entire Tutsi population. Elements of the presidential guard then took violent action against political opponents of the president and launched a campaign of terror and violence against suspected supporters of the Tutsi-led Rwandese Patriotic Front. Hundreds were killed. Youths of the Hutu militia poured into the streets. Armed with machetes, clubs, and sharp homemade weapons, they roamed through Kigali, killing, looting, and setting buildings ablaze. A mass of people seeking safety surged into UN facilities. As Tutsi fighters of the Rwandese Patriotic Front rushed out to protect their supporters, urban warfare broke out.

Killing became widespread across Rwanda, apparently driven by both ethnic and political factors. The country collapsed into bloody chaos. On April 7 Rwanda's interim president, Agathe Uwilingiyimana, sought refuge in the UN Development Program compound. When General Dallaire sent armored personnel carriers to protect her, they were held up by roadblocks. The United Nations, under its mandated rules of engagement, was not authorized to use force to break through. The force commander had been instructed that UN personnel should fire only in self-defense. Thus the interim president's guards were overpowered, and she was taken away and killed. Ten Belgian Blue Helmets were butchered in the rampage that followed. The next day I informed the Security Council that the United Nations was attempting to secure agreement on a cease-fire in Kigali and promote the establishment of some sort of interim political authority. I alerted the Council that the evacuation of UN civilian personnel might become unavoidable. General Dallaire, I said, estimated that an evacuation would require two to three additional battalions. Over the next few days, disorder continued to spread. Manhunts and ethnic killings, mainly of Tutsis, were under way. We were facing a kind of "tropical Nazi genocide." The International Committee of the Red Cross was reporting thousands killed.

The arrival of French and Belgian troops in Kigali to evacuate expatriates enabled the United Nations to maintain several safe havens for displaced Rwandese civilians. By April 11 French and Belgian troops had evacuated almost all their nationals. I recommended to the Security Council that all UN troops be drawn into Kigali for security reasons and in order to maintain a very visible UN presence in Rwanda. "A sudden disappearance of the UN forces," I said, "could lead to degeneration of the whole situation and result in violence of incalculable proportions."

A Night Visit in Bonn

The Belgian foreign minister, Mark Eyskens, flew to Bonn to meet with me. Belgian troops made up the greatest part of the UN operation in Rwanda, and the Brussels government was in shock over the killing of the ten Belgian Blue Helmets. Very excited, the foreign minister asked me to withdraw all UN forces from Rwanda, because Belgium had decided to withdraw the entire Belgian contingent. Belgium was afflicted with "the American syndrome": pull out at the first encounter with serious trouble. I argued against a Belgian pullout, but if the Belgians were determined to leave, I asked that they at least leave their heavy weapons behind so that they could be used by the remaining UN troops, which otherwise would be in a very weakened position. The foreign minister promised to pass my request on to Brussels. But the Belgian troops took all their arms with them as they went, later explaining that their weapons were incompatible for use by other forces. I sent a letter to the Security Council on April 13, stating my view that Belgium's withdrawal made it extremely difficult for the UN operation in Rwanda to carry out its responsibilities unless the Belgians were replaced by another well-equipped contingent. In an attempt to put pressure on the Security Council to authorize such a new force, I said that I had requested the force commander and my special representative to prepare plans for the withdrawal of the United Nations from Rwanda unless we received additional forces.

The next day I was informed that in the Security Council the United States, France, and Britain had received my letter "with varying degrees of indignation" because of my supposed insinuation that the withdrawal of the Belgian contingent would be a cause of further instability and a reason for UNAMIR to shut down. Ambassador Albright suggested that a "small, skeletal" operation be left in Kigali "to show the will of the international community" and that "Later, the Council might see what could be done about giving an effective mandate." I hastened to send word back, assuring the Council that I was not recommending the immediate withdrawal of the UN force, which was neither advisable nor feasible. The options that the Council should consider, I said, were either phased withdrawal or a strengthened UN mission authorized to conduct enforcement operations. It was clear that I favored the latter, but again my views were not well received.

On April 17 General Dallaire reported that the United Nations would have to employ one battalion to defend Kigali Airport, the country's lifeline to the outside world. This left only half a battalion to escort humanitarian relief efforts, which in any event was no longer possible without a change in the mandated rules of engagement. Dallaire reported that a "third force," apparently the young Hutu militia, had in recent days emerged, bold, aggressive, and brazen. "They work to their own unruly/ drugged tune," he said. "They are a very large, dangerous and totally irrational group of people. Force Commander considers them to be the most dangerous threat." Dallaire called for a new mandate. The United Nations, he said, "cannot continue to sit on the fence in the face of all these morally legitimate demands for assistance/protection. Nor can [the UN peacekeepers in Rwanda] simply launch into [enforcement] operations without the proper authority, personnel and equipment. . . . Maintaining the status quo on manpower under these severe and adverse conditions is wasteful, dangerously casualty-causing and demoralizing to the troops."

On April 20 I reported to the Security Council that UN personnel could not be left at risk indefinitely when there was no possibility of their performing the tasks for which they had been dispatched. I offered three options: (1) immediate and massive reinforcement by several thousand additional troops mandated to coerce a cease-fire, which was my preference; (2) leaving a small group behind under Dallaire to attempt to mediate a cease-fire; or (3) complete withdrawal, which I said I did not favor.

The next day the Council, by Resolution 912, reduced the UN force to a token level of 270 personnel and restricted its mandate to mediation and humanitarian aid. Reports from Kigali depicted a horrendous scene: "There is no electricity or running water, and dead bodies are on the roads for two weeks now. Dogs eat them at night." It was becoming clear that the world was watching nothing less than genocide taking place in Rwanda. On April 29 I addressed a letter to the Security Council urging it to consider again what action, including use of force, it could take, or could authorize member states to take, to end the massacres in Rwanda. The scale of human suffering and the implications for the stability of neighboring countries left the Council with no alternative but to examine this possibility, I said. I asked the Security Council to reconsider its decision to withdraw most of the 1,700 UN troops. The few remaining, I said, did not have the power to take effective action to stop the genocide. The Security Council debated through most of that Friday night but took no action. Nor did it act during the following week.

PDD 25 Requires . . .

Then, on May 3, 1993, while the massacres were raging, President Clinton signed PDD 13. Rechristened Presidential Decision Document 25, the document dealt a deadly blow to cooperative multilateral action to maintain peace and security. Entitled "The Clinton Administration's Policy on Reforming Multilateral Peace Operations," the new rules were so tightly drawn as to scope, mission, duration, resources, and risk that only the easiest, cheapest, and safest peacekeeping operations could be approved under them and many current UN operations could not. It was the end of what Madeleine Albright two years earlier had declared to be a policy of "assertive multilateralism." A headline declared, THE US WASHES ITS HANDS OF THE WORLD.

I understood full well that the American public did not want the United States to become the world's policeman. But there was certainly a broader interest in having a properly mandated United Nations ready to fill the gap in places where the United States did not want to employ its military. Clinton's PDD 25 was issued at a moment when UN peacekeeping was at an all-time high. Some 70,000 peacekeepers from seventy countries were serving in seventeen UN peace operations around the world. More operations had been launched in the past four years than in the previous forty. All had been approved by the Security Council, with the United States voting in favor, but the United Nations' member states were not willing to pay for what they ordered. The bill was some $3 billion a year, of which one third was unpaid.

It was one thing for the United States to place conditions for its own participation in UN peacekeeping, even to set conditions that must be met before the United States would vote for a UN peacekeeping operation manned by the armed forces of other countries. It was something else entirely for the United States to attempt to impose its conditions on other countries. Yet that is what Madeleine Albright did. With the publication of PDD 25 she argued with members of the Security Council for the new Clinton conditions to apply before Resolution 918 of May 17, 1994, which increased the strength and expanded the mandate of UN-AMIR, was carried out. For example, a cease-fire should be in place; the parties should agree to a UN presence; UNAMIR should not engage in peace enforcement unless what was happening in Rwanda was a significant threat to international peace and security. Were the troops, funds, and equipment all available? What was the "exit strategy"?

On May 9 I distributed as a Secretariat nonpaper a text that outlined "a possible mandate and force structure for an expanded UN force, capable of providing support for displaced persons and assisting in the delivery of humanitarian assistance to those in need." The nonpaper contemplated a UN force of some 4,000 soldiers, 721 support troops, and appropriate headquarters and other personnel. I sent the paper to General Dallaire, who found it "truly excellent" and stressed, perhaps with the Somali example in mind, that he could achieve the goals with this mandate and force structure "if, and only if, the force made at his disposal will demonstrate the desire, the determination and the courage to implement the clear rules of engagement that have been proposed for these tasks."

Two days later the U.S. position was presented by Ambassador Albright: "We have serious reservations about proposals to establish a large peace enforcement mission which would operate throughout Rwanda with a mandate to end the fighting, restore law and order and pacify the population." Recalling what had happened in Somalia, Albright warned that "the parties to the conflict would use force to oppose such a mission." Indeed, Albright said, "It is unclear precisely what the peace enforcement mission would be or when it would end." Of course, Albright and everyone else knew perfectly well that the mission was to stop the genocide then in progress. The behavior of the Security Council was shocking; it meekly followed the United States' lead in denying the reality of the genocide. Although it was a clear case of genocide, U.S. spokesmen were obviously under instructions to avoid the term in order to avoid having to fulfill their treaty obligations under the 1949 Genocide Convention. U.S. representatives simply said that "acts of genocide may have occurred and need to be investigated."

Two more weeks of unrelieved horror passed before the Security Council made a decision. In Resolution 918 of May 17, 1994, the Council increased the strength of the UN mission—which then stood at about 500 of all ranks—to 5,500 troops and expanded its mandate. I was asked to redeploy immediately to Rwanda the UN military observers who had been evacuated to Nairobi, to bring the infantry battalion already in Rwanda up to strength, to report on human rights violations, and to accelerate efforts with the OAU to obtain personnel for rapid deployment. I sent a mission to Rwanda to discuss details of a new cease-fire and the new UN mandate. I was soon able to inform the Council that the parties had agreed to begin cease-fire talks under UN auspices and had agreed to cooperate with the expanded UN force. I emphatically urged that the additional troops be deployed at once, and I called again on member states to provide the necessary personnel and equipment to bring an end to the slaughter. There was, I stated, no doubt that the killings in Rwanda constituted genocide. At this moment, there was a chance to bring the killings to a halt. The Kigali radio station Mille Collines (A Thousand Hills) was a powerful voice inciting genocide every day. I asked the United States to jam these inflammatory broadcasts, but I was told that it would be too expensive.

Albright employed the requirements of PDD 25 to pressure the other Security Council members to delay the deployment of the full 5,500-man contingent to Rwanda until I could satisfy her that all of the many U.S. conditions had been met. "Sending a UN force into the maelstrom of Rwanda without a sound plan of operations would be folly," she told the House Foreign Affairs Committee. Albright would not have taken this position, I felt sure, without clear authorization from the White House. She was always, in my experience, very cautious and "awaiting instructions." As the Rwandan genocide continued, she was apparently just following orders.

Sausage in the White House

Some months earlier, Madeleine Albright had asked me to deliver the commencement address on Saturday, May 28, 1994, at the School of

Foreign Service at Georgetown University, where she had been a professor. I had readily agreed and conveyed a request, through Albright, that
when in Washington I be permitted to call on President Clinton. I had to
go to Washington on Thursday, May 26, to give another long-scheduled
talk at the Johns Hopkins University School of Advanced International
Studies. This meant that I would be available to go to the White House at
any time on Friday, May 27, I said when reminding Albright of my request. "Oh, but the president is very busy," she said. "He is preparing for
his European trip." I nonetheless asked her to help arrange a meeting,
even though it once again appeared that she did not want me talking
directly to Clinton. I also asked to meet with Warren Christopher while I
was in Washington.

I heard nothing from the White House. An appointment with Christopher was scheduled and then canceled. So on Friday I had nothing on my
schedule for the entire day. One of my aides quietly pointed out to a
member of Christopher's staff that the press might take note of me sitting all day long in a Washington hotel room, shunned by the Clinton administration. Suddenly a call came from the White House: Come see
President Clinton at once. I went to the Oval Office to meet with the
president, who was surrounded by a huge entourage.

When I began to talk about Rwanda, Clinton said that if other countries were willing to provide troops for Rwanda, the United States would
be willing to fly them there, but he quickly changed the subject to two
"special issues" that he said he was most interested in. One was the
creation of an inspector general for the United Nations, which he said
Congress was making a condition for U.S. payments. I said that Joseph
Connor, the U.S. administration's nominee, whom I had appointed as
under secretary-general for administration and management, the position held earlier by Thornburgh and Wells, was doing a superb job, but
that I was nonetheless entirely in favor of an inspector general. In fact, I
said, I was about to appoint a diplomat from Germany to the job. "I guess
that'll start a bunch of sausage jokes," Clinton said, and all his advisers
chuckled. Later I asked my staff what this meant and was told that there
was an old American expression, "sausage inspectors," and that Americans associated Germans with sausages.

The second item on Clinton's agenda—apparently of far more importance to him, although I never learned why—was his desire that I appoint Dr. William Foege, an epidemiologist attached to the Carter Center
in Atlanta, as executive director of the United Nations Children's Fund

(UNICEF). I told President Clinton I was sure that Dr. Foege was an excellent man, but that, as Ambassador Albright knew, I had publicly committed myself to try to fill 50 percent of the United Nations' top jobs with women and that UNICEF was an agency of particular concern to women. Clinton's many aides stiffened and looked displeased.

To ease the tension, I told the president the old Arab story of the vizier who promised the sultan that he could teach a donkey to talk in five years. In return, the sultan, who had been about to have his courtier beheaded, stayed the execution for five years. "You idiot!" the vizier's wife said later. "You can't teach a donkey to talk!" "Maybe you're right," the vizier said, "but in five years the donkey might be dead, the sultan might be dead, I might be dead—or I might even teach the donkey to talk!" So, I said, "four options are better than one. It's better to buy some time." Clinton and all his viziers laughed at my story. "But," I said, "I really cannot follow the example of the story and promise you that I will appoint Dr. Foege. To do that may be harder for me than teaching a donkey to talk." That ended the laughter and closed our meeting, but the Foege matter would later return to haunt me.

While the president and I joked in the Oval Office, the genocide in Rwanda went on. On that same day, May 27, 1994, I told the press that Rwanda was a scandal: "It is genocide . . . and more than 200,000 people have been killed, but the international community is still debating what to do."

Operation Turquoise

The U.S. effort to prevent the effective deployment of a UN force for Rwanda succeeded, with the strong support of Britain. The international community did little or nothing as the killing in Rwanda continued. On June 19, in a letter to the Security Council, I reiterated the need for an urgent and coordinated response to the genocide that was engulfing Rwanda. I enumerated the offers the United Nations had received after I had approached many potential contributers to the UN force in anticipation of the expansion of its mandate as authorized in Resolution 918 of May 17, 1994. I asked the Security Council to consider France's offer to undertake an operation under Chapter VII to ensure the security and protection of civilians in Rwanda. The French would remain until the

UN force was strong enough to take over. The Security Council agreed. The French were acting out of bitter frustration with the United States' obstruction. If the Security Council, guided by the United States, would not agree to strengthen the UN force, the French would act on their own. The French intervention in effect highlighted the Security Council's refusal to strengthen the UN presence in Rwanda. France had long been deeply involved with the Hutus and therefore was far from ideal for this role. But multilateralism had been rejected, so no other course of action was available.

Outraged, General Dallaire sent an angry message:

Since the passing of Resolution 918 of 17 May 1994, UNAMIR has patiently waited for its expansion in order to fan out and help stop these massacres. . . . The ineffective reaction to meeting the critical needs of the Mission . . . has been nothing less than scandalous from the word go, and even bordering on the irresponsible to dangerous towards the personnel of the Mission here in theatre. This has directly led to the loss of many more Rwandese lives, to the casualties among our troops and of course to the French initiative.

Dallaire denounced the failure of the Security Council to act and pointed out that "an early and determined effort to get troops and resources on the ground under the UN's mandate could have avoided all this and already saved so many lives." He was entirely correct.

Dallaire concluded his message with an uncharacteristic departure from form: "At this point, Force Commander finds 'regards' very difficult to express."

The French initiative, named Operation Turquoise, was launched on June 23, 1994, and authorized by Security Council Resolution 929 to continue until August 21, 1994. The French sent 2,500 troops to establish a "humanitarian protected zone" in southwest Rwanda that covered about one fifth of the country's territory. Some observers claimed that the French were using their area of operation to provide a refuge for France's Hutu friends who had launched the genocide. Others pointed out that the French zone served to protect large numbers of civilians threatened by the slaughter.

On August 1 I told the Security Council that the United Nations was as far from attaining the 5,500 troops authorized as it had been on May

17, the day Resolution 918 had been adopted. Nineteen governments that had originally pledged a total of more than 30,000 troops had been approached. Of the very few that did not decline outright, the offers were conditional, entailing impossibly complicated efforts to match troops from one country with equipment from another. Fewer than 500 troops were now on the ground, and the French forces had already begun to withdraw.

The swift UN intervention in April that I had recommended to the Security Council would have been far preferable. If the UN forces had been augmented at that time, rather than depleted, tens of thousands of lives might have been saved. Moreover, if the United Nations' standby force for rapid deployment that I had proposed two years earlier had been agreed upon, the Rwandan genocide might never have taken place. Perhaps I had not been insistent enough with the Security Council. In private talks with ambassadors I was repeatedly told that my effort was hopeless; no government had any intention of stepping in to stop the Rwandan holocaust. Many of them cited PDD 25, but this seemed to me merely a convenient cover for their own reluctance to get involved.

By August 1994 a rebellion launched against the Hutu-led regime by the Tutsi-dominated Rwandese Patriotic Front from its exile base in Uganda had established military control over most of Rwanda and was moving toward setting up a government in Kigali. The RPF's swift advance and inflammatory broadcasts by its radio stations caused masses of Hutus to flee into neighboring Zaire. So the genocide precipitated by the Hutus was followed by a gigantic refugee crisis, and the United Nations was left to try to cope with the human disaster as well as it could. "Unless this exodus ceases," I warned, "the stability of the whole region will be endangered." Again, I failed to gain Security Council approval for the forces needed to control the refugee camps.

Not so long ago the world thought it could recognize and then stop genocide. "Never again" was the watchword. But here was genocide once more; in Cambodia, where more than a million victims fell to the Khmer Rouge; in the former Yugoslavia, where genocide was called "ethnic cleansing"; in Somalia, where genocide by starvation resulted when warlords deliberately withheld food aid from the starving and sick and where 350,000 died before the Security Council decided to step in. In Rwanda close to a million people were killed in what was genocide without doubt, yet the Security Council did nothing.

Frustration

Time magazine, in its August 1, 1994, issue, carried an interview with me in which, as the magazine said, I vented my frustration at the inaction of the world community. I said that when I had been elected in 1991, the world had thought that the United Nations could handle conflicts with a few thousand troops. Suddenly we discovered that the United Nations was running seventeen different operations, and, rather than a few thousand troops, more than 70,000 were in the field. Rather than $600 million for peacekeeping, we now needed more than $3 billion as states collapsed, war crimes proliferated, and genocide raged.

Those countries with the means to save the situation were fatigued, distracted, unwilling, bereft of vision. The United States, which had spent some $1 billion a day overall during the cold war, had now prevailed upon other governments to withhold the relatively trivial sums to stop genocide. In a letter to the Security Council on August 3 I declared that it was "all the more tragic that the international community hesitated for so long to intervene, despite the fact that most of its member States have signed the Convention on the Prevention and Punishment of the Crime of Genocide." And speaking specifically of the United States, I said to the press, "Why don't they make as much fuss about Rwanda, where between a quarter- and a half-million people have been murdered, as they do about one dissident in China?" I pointed out that the numbers killed in Rwanda were on the same scale for that country as 9 million to 18 million deaths would be for the United States.

Bosnia: The Struggle over Air Strikes

As Rwanda was building toward horrible bloodshed in the first six months of 1994, I was still struggling with the question of airpower in Bosnia.

Yasushi Akashi had done a good job in Cambodia. When the Europeans had proved unwilling to make the difficult decisions required in the former Yugoslavia, I appointed him as my special representative to head UNPROFOR. Akashi was in every way qualified for the task, but I had also chosen the distinguished Japanese diplomat as a rebuke to the Europeans for their failure to deal with this conflict on their own continent. More seriously, Akashi would be 100 percent immune to Yugoslav political pressures. A Catholic would be accused of being pro-Croat, a Muslim would be accused of being pro-Bosnian, an Orthodox Christian would be accused of being pro-Serb. As a Japanese, Akashi would be spared such accusations, but nothing could protect Akashi or me from Washington's angry vacillation.

On January 18, 1994, I instructed Akashi to draw up "detailed plans for military operations, with the use of air power as required" and to co-ordinate closely with NATO's Southern Command in Naples. The NATO summit at Brussels that month had affirmed NATO's readiness to use airpower to defend Srebenica, but the United States still appeared indecisive and unwilling when the question arose. "This summit is not about airpower," Christopher said in Brussels. And President Clinton noted that the use of U.S. aircraft would depend upon congressional approval. Nevertheless, the summit declaration stated, "We affirm our readiness under the authority of the United Nations Security Council . . . to carry out air strikes to prevent the strangulation of Sarajevo, the safe areas, and other threatened areas in Bosnia-Herzegovina."

The key point, still not directly acknowledged by either U.S. or NATO leaders, was that if air strikes were not coordinated with an army capable of taking and holding territory, the bombings would endanger UN peace-keeping personnel on the ground more than they would damage the Bosnian Serb military. Three elements needed to be coordinated: combat infantry on the ground; potential UN hostages being pulled back to safety; and a protracted air campaign. Two of the three requirements were missing, and no one was willing to address them seriously. Only the third point, air strikes, was being advocated. As the American military expert Elliott Cohen put it, "Air power is an unusually seductive form of military strength because, like modern courtship, it appears to offer gratification without commitment." Soon after the NATO summit, a senior NATO military adviser, British Field Marshal Sir Richard Vincent, said it directly: "Bombing is not of much use unless conducted in coordination with infantry." There was no NATO, U.S., or UN infantry on the ground in Bosnia, nor would there be for as long as the conflict continued. Apparently forgotten were the forty days of intensive bombing in 1991 that had failed to get Iraq to withdraw from Kuwait; it had taken a ground invasion to do that. Not until the summer of 1995 would such a ground offensive take place in Bosnia.

Field Marshal Vincent's position was supported by British Defense

Minister Malcolm Rifkind, who affirmed that air strikes should be conducted only "in very special circumstances." I expressed full agreement with this position in the letter I sent to the Security Council stating that I was opposed to the use of air strikes to open Tuzla Airport, because the United Nations on the ground lacked the other necessary means to make such strikes successful. UNPROFOR would need additional military assets in excess of those currently available to use in conjunction with airpower.

There was an added factor: it was an open secret by now that Bosnian forces had been receiving substantial financial assistance from Muslim countries to acquire arms. The Serbs believed that Tuzla Airport was the entrepôt for weapons shipments. There was considerable danger that if NATO air strikes were used to open Tuzla while UN forces on the ground were vulnerable, the Serbs would overrun the Blue Helmets.

Despite these concerns, I declared at a press conference in The Hague on January 21, 1994, that I favored the use of airpower and was ready to give the green light if asked, but so far I had not been. In an interview in *The New York Times* I said, "Everyone in Europe thinks I'm blocking the use of air power in Bosnia. But I'm not, if my advisers want to use it." I also revealed that I had received a letter from the Russian government conveying its expectation that I would seek its consent before I authorized air strikes in Bosnia. At this point the only country pressing for air strikes was the United States, which had no forces at risk on the ground.

The United Nations was an easy target. Critics of the United Nations from within the Clinton administration, Congress, and the media asserted that war making was possible but was being prevented by pusillanimous peacekeepers. The fact was the opposite: peacekeepers had been deployed precisely because the United States and NATO were not willing to go to war.

Jeane Kirkpatrick continued her assault against me in a column headed BOUTROS-GHALI BLOCKS USE OF AIR POWER IN BOSNIA (*The New York Times*, January 17, 1994). I was, she said, "guilty of the most sweeping power grab in the history of international organizations." I must be firmly rebuffed, she declared. "No country and no president can assign his forces to the 'operational control' of such a command structure." Thus was born the outlandish assertion, later to be trumpeted incessantly by Senator Bob Dole, as Republican candidate for the presidency, that I, not President Clinton, was the commander in chief of the American armed forces.

The Sarajevo Market Massacre

On Saturday, February 5, 1994, a mortar attack on the Sarajevo market killed sixty-eight civilians and wounded hundreds. Outrage swept through Europe and North America. While American opinion overwhelmingly opposed U.S. involvement on the ground, pressure mounted for Clinton to strike back from the air. On that first weekend in February I was at home with a mild case of the flu. It gave me time to think. Madeleine Albright telephoned me to say, "Something has to be done." The French ambassador called to say the same thing, as did Akashi, calling from Bosnia. Something had to be done. On February 6 I wrote to NATO Secretary-General Manfred Woerner: "The mortar attacks last week against civilian targets in Sarajevo . . . make it necessary to prepare urgently for the use of air strikes to deter further such attacks." I asked Woerner to seek a decision "to authorize the Commander-in-Chief of NATO's Southern Command to launch air strikes, at the request of the United Nations, against artillery or mortar positions in or around Sarajevo which are determined by UNPROFOR to be responsible for attacks against civilian targets in that city."

Woerner replied on February 9, "I am able to inform you that the North Atlantic Council has today agreed to your request to authorize air strikes to prevent further attacks on Sarajevo." If the Serbs did not pull their heavy artillery away from Sarajevo, they would be hit by NATO from the air.

To specify the procedures involved, I wrote back to Woerner on February 10:

> I have today instructed my Special Representative for the former Yugoslavia, Mr. Yasushi Akashi, and through him, the Force Commanders of UNPROFOR, to finalize with the Commander in Chief Allied Forces Southern Europe, detailed procedures for the initiation and conduct of air strikes. I have asked my Special Representative to ensure that these procedures, like those already in place for close air support, take adequately into account my responsibilities vis-à-vis the Security Council, as well as my responsibilities for the humanitarian operations and for the security of United Nations military and civilian personnel on the ground in Bosnia and Herzegovina. On this basis I have delegated the necessary authority to my Special Representative, including, as sug-

gested by you, authority to approve a request from the Force Commander of UNPROFOR for close air support for the defense of United
Nations personnel anywhere in Bosnia and Herzegovina.

My letters made headlines and were interpreted as meaning that I
favored air strikes; if the force commander on the ground wanted them,
NATO could conduct them. I remained fearful, however, that air strikes
would lead to hostage taking. Late in the afternoon of February 10,
Christopher telephoned me. "I did not want to end the day without
thanking you for your splendid cooperation," he said. I replied that I had
been on the phone almost incessantly with Ambassador Albright about
this matter. I told Christopher I had done what I had done "to save the
image of the United Nations." I had delegated authority to Akashi. "We
both know quite well," I said to Christopher, "that the decision will be
taken by the military. But at least we will have the presence of a civilian
who understands the risks involved in an air strike and who will give a
civilian dimension to the decision." I told Christopher that Akashi reported that the mortar round that had exploded in the Sarajevo market
on Saturday might have been fired by Bosnian Muslims in order to in-
duce a NATO intervention. Christopher replied that he had seen many
intelligence reports and that they went "both ways." President Clinton,
Christopher said, was well aware of my cooperation and was "looking forward to working closely with you during this difficult period ahead."

I told Akashi that I favored air strikes should Serb forces interfere with
UN efforts to rotate the garrison at Srebenica to relieve Canadian UN
troops there or to open the airport at Tuzla. Christopher "endorsed" my
position.

In reality I was caught between the opposing positions in the Security
Council. Britain and France, which had forces on the ground, did not
want the United States to conduct air strikes. The Russians, historically
the patrons of the Serbs, did not want air strikes either and were furious
that an ultimatum had been issued without a Security Council vote,
thereby depriving Russia of the use of its veto. The Duma, the Russian
parliament, had passed a resolution opposing air strikes by 280 to 2.

At that point the Russians intervened to defuse the situation. In a dramatic and unilateral move, Russian troops were deployed around Sarajevo, inducing the Serbs to start pulling their big guns away from the city
on February 21. These steps, Russia said, negated the NATO ultimatum
and threat to use air strikes. Russia had reasserted its "big-power" cre-

dentials and carried out a diplomatic coup. The war for Sarajevo seemed to be over.

But the apparently successful threat to use force to relieve the Serb pressure on Sarajevo only deepened the opprobrium directed toward me. The earlier criticism that I had blocked air strikes was soon followed by attacks for having "overstepped" my role. BEND THE UN TO OUR WILL was the headline of a *New York Times* op-ed piece by a former high official at the Pentagon. The United Nations, he charged, had become a "a sort of super-state, with the secretary-general, Boutros Boutros-Ghali, ensconced as the chief executive officer of the world." Throughout the cold war, the article said, the United States had circumvented the Soviet veto–bound Security Council by promoting the secretary-general from chief clerk to chief conscience of the world, and I should be instructed to revert to my proper status as "functionary." Somehow, within the space of a few weeks, I had been transformed from the secretary-general who supposedly rejected any use of decisive military force to the secretary-general who sought to be commander in chief of the world. And the Americans seemed close to adopting the old Soviet position that the secretary-general was nothing more than the chief administrative officer of the organization.

The Dual-Key Duel

On March 2, 1994, I made the keynote speech in a seminar in Vienna sponsored by the government of Austria called "Peacemaking and Peace-keeping for the Next Century." In the course of a general review of the dramatically increased number and complexity of UN peace operations responsibilities, I focused on the "double-key" approach. UN troops, I said, must first make the request and then obtain the agreement of NATO; thus the term "double key." Because NATO and the United Nations might differ in their assessment of certain situations, with NATO believing that it is important to use airpower while the UN forces on the ground say, "For the safety of the forces, we do not want to use that power," it would be crucial to maintain the principle of the "double key."

My use of the term "double key," on which NATO and I had agreed, was transposed by the media into "dual key," the term applied to the system by which the U.S. keeps control over the use of nuclear weapons in the hands of its allies. Hereafter I would be portrayed in the media as possessing "dual-key" authority over the use of American armed forces.

In April 1994, as Serb forces massed to take Goražde, U.S. Secretary of Defense William Perry, a quiet, serious man with great technological and diplomatic experience, declared that the United States would "not enter the war" to stop Goražde from falling. Chairman of the Joint Chiefs of Staff General John Shalikashvili added that airpower would be ineffective around Goražde. Nonetheless, on April 9 I instructed the UN forces to use "all available means" to get the Serbs to pull back to positions held before this latest offensive. Though I had delegated my authority to Akashi and no longer needed to be involved on a daily basis, I issued the instruction simply because I was engaged in a regularly scheduled discussion with Akashi when the moment for decision arrived.

The next day, with the city under heavy artillery fire and the Serbs advancing, UN observers requested NATO intervention, and two U.S. F-16s based in Aviano, Italy, bombed tank targets around Goražde. A second raid followed less than twenty-four hours later. The raids were guided by UN forward air controllers. The *Daily Telegraph* of April 11, 1994, noted that "The air strikes were triggered by Mr. Boutros Boutros-Ghali" and added that the Russians were angry that they had not been consulted. Radovan Karadžić declared that from then on, the Serbs would treat UNPROFOR as a potentially hostile force. Commentators who had been pressing for just this kind of decisive action now began to worry about the dangers involved. One prominent Washington news analyst, Daniel Schorr, asked, "Is this stumbling across the Rubicon?" A BBC commentator given to anatomical clichés called it a "knee-jerk reaction. Washington was sitting on its hands; now it could get its fingers burnt." Perhaps most disconcerting was that after all these months of chest thumping, the attacks were brief, only a few bombs were dropped, and NATO did not react forcefully when British and French units were targeted and fired upon in retaliation by the Serbs.

On April 18 I wrote to Woerner that the Serb attacks on Goražde demonstrated the need to authorize the use of airpower to defend the five other "safe areas" declared by the Security Council: Sarajevo, Tuzla, Žepa, Bihać, and Srebenica and their surrounding areas. I asked for such a decision at the earliest possible date.

Throughout this period I was acting under diametrically opposed pressures. Russia was opposed to air strikes; I wrote to assure the Russian foreign minister that procedures agreed with NATO ensured that none would be launched without UN consent. But Islamic governments wanted air strikes; I wrote to assure the prime minister of Pakistan that I would "not hesitate to authorize the use of air strikes" should Bosnian Serb forces endanger the safe areas.

The Goražde Test

The Bosnian Serbs shelled Goražde throughout the morning and early afternoon of Saturday, April 23, 1994. NATO's Southern Command requested UN agreement to initiate air strikes. Akashi telephoned Woerner to ask that NATO hold off, as he had just negotiated a cease-fire with Karadžić that involved deployment of an UNPROFOR contingent to Goražde. Woerner argued strongly against delay; the Serbs were testing the Security Council's ultimatum and the credibility of both UNPROFOR and NATO. I had just then arrived in Barbados for the UN global conference on small island states. I hoped my presence there would symbolize the United Nations' determination to fulfill its long-term responsibilities for development despite the debilitating way it was being used in Bosnia. The very existence of small island states is threatened by rising ocean levels caused by development-driven climate changes, yet the powerful countries were paying no attention. As soon as I reached my hotel in Barbados, I telephoned Woerner, and the two of us agreed to authorize air strikes immediately if the Serbs did not comply with the withdrawal deadline of 1600 GMT, just two hours away. I then telephoned Akashi and asked him to authorize air strikes.

Christopher and Alain Juppé also telephoned me in Barbados. Both were unhappy with Akashi's reluctance to approve air strikes. But, as expected, the British and French generals on the ground did not want air strikes for fear of the risks to their troops and the integrity of their mission. Akashi really had no choice but to respect the advice of these military men. Yet back in the capitals of the same countries that had assigned those commanders to UNPROFOR, politicians and Foreign Ministry officials were demanding air strikes. The controversy was really a confrontation between NATO military commanders on the ground and NATO political leaders in national capitals—a confrontation conducted through, and, as usual blamed on, the United Nations.

By April 27 Akashi reported that the Serbs had complied with NATO's ultimatum by removing their heavy weapons from around Goražde, the latest in the seemingly endless series of dramas staged by Karadžić, who always emerged with more territory than he had had before.

At a press conference at the end of April, Akashi said that if the United States wanted to be taken seriously about Bosnia, it would contribute troops for deployment on the ground. Albright, infuriated, declared that Akashi was out of line. "International civil servants should remember where their salaries come from," she said, a strange comment in that the United States refused to pay its UN dues. "Thanks to you," I said to Akashi, "I am no longer scapegoat number one."

Aristide's Obsession with Death

The first half of 1994 was scarred not only by the genocide in Rwanda and the continuing horrors in Bosnia but also by mounting tensions and talk of the need for an American invasion of Haiti. I met tête-à-tête with President Aristide on March 5, 1994, in New York and found him in a sour and complaining mood. I was firm with him. His volatility, I said, was being used by his enemies as leverage to build support against him. At a UN lunch a few months previously, President Clinton had raised Aristide's mental attitude with me. "We have to work together to cope with him," Clinton said.

My private talk with Aristide only seemed to irritate him more. After we had rejoined our aides, he repeated the fears he had expressed to me when he had signed the Governors Island Accord. He had signed, he said, only under pressure from me. "This adventure ended in death," he said. The ideas he was hearing now "are only repeating a strategy leading to death." Death was his obsession. "Death, death, death": He repeated the word countless times.

Aristide seemed in no hurry to name a new prime minister and rejected the Haitian Parliament's initiative designed to lead to a new government and to Aristide's return to take up his presidential duties in Haiti. As long as the junta led by Cedras remained in power, Aristide was justified in his fear. Goulding explained that the parliamentary initiative conformed to the Governors Island Accord and that it would get the support of the international community. Yet Aristide's gloom persisted. "The military is hiding itself behind the parliamentarians, using the latter like mari-onettes," he said bitterly—and accurately.

As I was leaving, Aristide asked me not to give the media the impression that he had rejected a plan submitted by the secretary-general. I acquiesced, and we drafted a press release saying that the president did not think that the parliamentary initiative conformed to the Governors Island Accord. Aristide insisted on adding a sentence to emphasize that the new initiative would "end in death."

Claudette Werleigh, Aristide's minister of foreign affairs, intervened delicately to say that what the president meant was that this parliamentary initiative would bring about more repression and so, possibly, more death. I proposed that in place of "death" we say "destined for failure," which seemed to satisfy everyone.

After Aristide's rejection of the parliamentarians' plan, the question was: What to do? More sanctions? Or more negotiation?

By this time Haiti had become a major American political problem as thousands of "boat people" set sail for Florida. Many were turned back by the U.S. Coast Guard, and others were interned at the U.S. naval base at Guantánamo, Cuba. During the American presidential election campaign, Clinton had criticized President Bush for repatriating Haitian refugees. But so great had the number of fleeing Haitians become that Clinton tightened the Bush administration's restrictions on Haitians' entry and imposed a naval blockade to fend off the boat people.

In the spring of 1994 critics of the U.S. administration's Haiti policy, particularly the Congressional Black Caucus, pressed hard for action, and talk grew of U.S. intervention or even invasion to restore Aristide as president. Tension over the crisis was rising in Washington.

The Return of Father Aristide

To my great surprise, Clinton turned to the United Nations, and on May 6, 1994, the Security Council adopted supplementary sanctions: a total commercial embargo, a ban on noncommercial flights, and denial of visas and freezing of the assets of the military junta. The sanctions were not to be lifted until the Haitian military and police high commands, led by General Cedras and Colonel Michel François, retired or departed from Haiti. The resolution also required a "proper environment" for deployment of the UN mission and the return of "the democratically elected president."

On the evening of May 18, 1994, Ambassador Albright and Under Secretary of State Peter Tarnoff met with me in my UN office. I told my guests of Dante Caputo's complaint that his job was still complicated by the fact that we were hearing one policy from one branch of the government and a second from another. Tarnoff said that the United States was aware that different lines of communication existed. Christopher wanted to assure me that Ambassador Lawrence Pezzullo, the U.S. special envoy on Haiti, was Christopher's representative. They would report to me and to the secretary of state. "If others present themselves as channels of communication," Tarnoff said, "they have no standing. Pezzullo is our man." But Pezzullo soon resigned, apparently in opposition to the United States' decision to intervene militarily.

My own concern, I said, was that the United Nations not be accused of fronting for U.S. intervention. UN member states of the third world warned me not to allow the United Nations to legitimize an intervention intended to serve only Washington's interests.

Tarnoff said that he had spoken twice that very day to Secretary of State Christopher, who had asked him to respond to my concerns. "We view Haiti as an opportunity for the international system, namely the UN, and including the United States, to come to closure in a situation where an example of a successful operation will have implications not only in Haiti but elsewhere," he said. Christopher did not view an operation in Haiti as purely a U.S. operation, but he did attach urgency to it, Tarnoff said. I would prefer that the operation be conducted without the United Nations, I replied, but if the UN were involved, other, non-U.S. militaries should be included. Tarnoff said that could be done.

"Would it be possible to have a commander from a country other than the United States?" I asked. Albright said that Congress would resist this. I agreed and said that the UN task force on Haiti had no objection to the appointment of a U.S. commander.

Not long after, we presented a package of proposals to the Haitian leadership, offering UN monitors and trainers to help the Haitian police and army take constructive roles in the economy and society. The Cedras regime flatly rejected our proposals and stepped up propaganda attacks on both the United States and the United Nations.

With negotiations broken down, sanctions ineffective, and the status quo intolerable on humanitarian grounds, force became almost inevitable. The problem, as I said to Albright on June 22, was obtaining Aristide's agreement. Then tensions in Haiti increased drastically with the military junta's illegal installation of Émile Jonaissant, a judge, as "provisional president," an act carried out at two in the morning of June 28, 1994. Aristide, who was still based in New York, wrote to me requesting that the UN presence in Haiti be intensified, the total number then being less than 1,200. On July 11 the Haitian regime ordered the joint UN-OAS human rights monitoring team to leave the country at once. On July 15 I reported to the Security Council that a stable and secure climate had to be established in Haiti. I proposed three options for armed intervention: a UN force; a multinational force mandated by the Security Council; or a multinational force for an initial phase, to be replaced, once a peaceful climate was reestablished, by a UN operation.

As July wore on, a U.S. invasion seemed near. Assault ships carrying marines moved into Haitian waters. The exodus of Haitians increased. Some 8,000 "boat people" took to the sea in a three-day period. Under domestic political pressures, Clinton ordered offshore asylum hearings. It was reported that of some 15,000 picked up at sea by the U.S. Coast Guard, 30 percent screened on board a hospital ship in Kingston, Jamaica, were granted asylum. This, of course, only stimulated a greater rush to depart. Reversing itself, the United States stopped granting asylum and offered instead to send the fleeing populations to "safe havens" in Panama and elsewhere in the Caribbean, where they would be looked after, U.S. spokesmen said—to my surprise—by the United Nations. I telephoned President Guillermo Endara Galimany of Panama and listened to his lengthy complaint that the United States had imposed this decision upon him. I made no comment; this was a bilateral matter between two member states of the United Nations, and the arrangement soon fell apart.

As speculation on an invasion mounted, Albright proposed that the Security Council adopt a new resolution, one that drew heavily on the third of the options I had offered the Council in my report of July 15. The language was similar, with mention of the need for "a stable and secure environment throughout Haiti in order to facilitate the early restoration of the legitimate authorities" as the first order of business. A subsequent UN operation, for which I had envisaged 15,000 troops and 550 police, would "assist the legitimate authorities," maintain order, and "professionalize" Haiti's armed forces.

On July 29 I obtained—not without difficulty—a letter from President Aristide. He did not want to sign it, fearing that he would be denounced as a traitor who had brought the U.S. Marines back to occupy his country. The best I could get from him was a rather vague statement that "the moment has arrived for the international community—a party to the Governors Island Accord—to take prompt and decisive action." To avoid any misunderstanding, the next morning I obtained a complementary and unmistakably clear letter from Haiti's permanent representative to the United Nations, Fritz Longchamp, who conveyed the consent of the legitimate Haitian government to the Security Council's decision. As for Aristide, he never openly accepted either U.S. or UN intervention. He wanted to be able to disclaim any responsibility for it and to oppose those who had asked for the international operation.

Military Intervention Authorized

On July 31 the Security Council adopted Resolution 940, authorizing member states to form a multinational force and use "all necessary means" to facilitate "the departure from Haiti of the military leadership . . . the prompt return of the legitimately elected president . . . and to establish a secure and stable environment that will permit implementation of the Governors Island Agreement." The reaction of the military in Port-au-Prince was to proclaim a state of siege, to form "voluntary" militias to counter an invasion and to proclaim "Mr. Jean-Bertrand Aristide and Mr. Fritz Longchamp guilty of the crime of high treason for having addressed to the UN letters which have served as the bases for Resolution 940."

I was in Asia, receiving hourly reports on Haiti to keep the United Nations closely coordinated with the U.S. operation. On September 12, 1994, from Tokyo, I advised Haiti's military leaders to leave the country. The United Nations, like the United States, I said, had lost patience with the failure to restore democracy; UN diplomacy on the issue had been exhausted. Three days later President Clinton issued a public ultimatum to the Haitian junta: "Leave now, or we will force you to give up power."

Back in New York I made a final bid for an alternative to military intervention by sending my aide, the Swedish diplomat Rolf Knutsson, to Haiti to seek a last-minute compromise, but the junta refused to meet with him.

Suddenly Jimmy Carter was on the scene again, seeking a way for the U.S. military to enter Haiti unopposed. Madeleine Albright indicated to me her deep displeasure with Carter, who once again was both solving and creating problems for the U.S. administration. Carter drafted an agreement en route to Port-au-Prince. He arrived early Saturday afternoon on September 17 and negotiated deep into the night.

We had passed some advice to Carter: The key to a solution might be in the hands of Cedras's wife, Yannick, a beautiful and highly manipulative woman able to influence both the leader of the army and the leader of the police. Carter gave the Haitian dictators a face-saving "honorable" way to avoid conflict with the U.S. armed forces by signing an agreement with Haiti's provisional president, Émile Jonaissant, providing for the retirement of the key junta leaders. Carter apologized to Cedras, stating that he was ashamed of his country's policy. With this successful move Carter seemed to have become the de facto minister of foreign affairs for the United States.

The American intervention force would have met little or no resistance whether Carter had gone to Haiti or not. But Carter succeeded where we had failed. It was a swift diplomatic triumph. But some important principles had been ignored. Carter's agreement, if actually carried out, would have allowed the junta to stay in Haiti, thereby undermining democracy; it would have produced a general amnesty that would let all wrongdoers escape justice; it was signed by the false president of an illegal regime; and it abandoned the standards of the Governors Island Accord. Carter's agreement was later cast aside when violence obliged the U.S. military to use force. Only then was Aristide able to return.

On September 19, 1994, 2,000 military personnel under U.S. command disembarked at Port-au-Prince. On the same day, Dante Caputo submitted his resignation. He did not want to represent the United Nations and the OAS during a foreign military occupation, which reminded him of the "big stick" policy America had followed in the early twentieth century. Caputo had been marginalized and unhappy ever since the *Harlan County* incident.

The American deployment proceeded rapidly, and one week later 15,000 men were in place. Speaking before the UN General Assembly on September 26, President Clinton praised UN-U.S. cooperation in Haiti as demonstrating that "multilateral cooperation" is necessary and can succeed. "The efforts [the United Nations and the United States] have taken together in Haiti are a prime example. Under the sponsorship of the United Nations, American troops, now being joined by the personnel of an ever-growing international coalition of over two dozen nations, are giving the people of Haiti their chance at freedom." I was delighted that the United States and the United Nations had worked well together. Proof had come that each, in some circumstances, needed the other, and that a poor country could benefit from that cooperation.

General Raoul Cedras resigned as head of the Haitian junta and arrived in Panama on October 13. The provisional Haitian president and his government gave up power, and on October 15 President Aristide returned to his country after more than three years in exile.

On October 25 President Aristide named Smarck Michel, a businessman, prime minister. The Parliament ratified his choice, and the new government, which included several members of the opposition, began its session on November 8, 1994.

I flew to Port-au-Prince from New York on November 15. Prime Minister Michel greeted me at the airport, and the two of us departed for the presidential palace. An American armored personnel carrier led the way and soon got lost. We informed the American officer that he was going the wrong way, but he insisted that he had his orders and had no authority to change them. Eventually, after a slow drive along steep, narrow, potholed roads, the APC retraced its way and led us to the presidential palace. During the long ride I found Michel to be an optimist, who seemed to have the trust of both President Aristide and the propertied class, which was hostile to Aristide's populist politics. When I finally arrived at the presidential palace, Aristide met with me in an office that had just been refurnished and repainted. He showed me a small room, where he pointed to a stark camp bed on which he said he slept after working late at night.

Aristide complained that the Americans were not doing enough to disarm the remnants of the armed gangs, successors to the Tontons Macoutes, whom the regime used to do their dirty work. I told him that I had pleaded with the United States to disarm the factions in Somalia and that my failure to persuade them had resulted in disaster. But in Haiti, U.S. forces were willing to take the risks of disarmament, I said. Haiti was in the United States' backyard, and the Clinton administration could not afford to fail in this case. First, they took control of heavy weapons stored in camps; then they launched an arms-purchasing program. More than 30,000 weapons were recovered, of which the United States bought 13,000. The U.S. roadblocks and arms searches were effective in ways I had wished for in Somalia. I was gratified to see that what I had advocated in vain for one part of the world was finally shown to be indispensable for the success of a major operation in another part.

Haiti remained marked by profound economic and cultural disparities. Aristide's natural constituents were the peasants and homeless persons who represent more than 80 percent of the population with an annual per capita income of less than $100. The other 20 percent form a hierarchical bourgeois society ranging from the Creole-speaking lower middle class to the solely French-speaking "aristocracy."

With Aristide I emphasized the importance of national reconciliation and of obtaining the support of the bourgeoisie. In doing so I tried hard to avoid the paternalistic tone that I realize results from my many years of teaching, but I doubt that I was successful. Aristide's reaction was unknown to me; he had an uncanny ability to conceal his true feelings whenever he wished to do so.

Before lunch at the newly restored presidential palace, Aristide showed me his library and the books that the military junta had damaged. We learned that we admired the same French writers and had discovered them at the same age. President Aristide provided excellent champagne, classical music, and fine food.

I found President Aristide in Haiti to be more moderate and conciliatory than Aristide in exile. I worried about what would happen when the American troops departed and the United Nations remained. But I felt certain that the United States would not leave Haiti in the state of anarchy and despair in which it had left Somalia.

Despite my assurances to Aristide about the United States' willingness to disarm the Haitians, I worried about rancor on the part of demobilized Haitian military personnel who were allowed to keep their arms; about frustration on the part of the Haitian people, faced with gangsterism and economic stagnation; and about tensions mounting as the date for elections approached. Most of all I worried that Aristide's ideology, forged under the terrible pressures of the Duvalier regime, might be too narrow to permit economic success. As I left Haiti, Port-au-Prince seemed to me like any provincial African city: the same climate, same vegetation, same color of earth, same disarray, same poverty, same sense of hopelessness.

CHAPTER 5

Africa in the World

(1992–1995)

I had been elected as Africa's candidate to take "Africa's turn" in the job of UN secretary-general. Because of this, and because of my decades of involvement with the economic, political, and diplomatic problems of Africa, I committed myself to try to advance the cause of the continent throughout my term in office. As time went by, I became increasingly frustrated yet reinforced in my determination as I saw my worst fears coming true. The UN member states were so preoccupied with post–cold war conflicts—particularly in the former Yugoslavia—that the United Nations' responsibility to the poorest countries was increasingly neglected, while peacekeeping duties, without the mandates required for success, were heaped on the organization.

During the cold war, the United States and the USSR had competed to address the political and economic needs of African countries. The shift of an African country from one side to the other was taken as a serious loss—or victory, depending on where you stood. The African powers soon learned to play the superpowers against each other for their own advantage.

With the end of the cold war, the interest of the outside world in Africa declined sharply. A truly global economy came into being and made dramatic advances. Africa, lacking the necessary levels of training, technology, and infrastructure, was largely unable to grasp the opportunities of the post–cold war world. The continent was burdened with unfavorable terms of trade and a huge foreign debt. The gap between rich and poor was becoming morally insupportable and economically irrational, even for the wealthiest nations of the world. Without development, conflict in Africa would become endemic. Democratization would be impossible, and a downward cycle of famine, disease, mass illegal immigration, ecological devastation, and crime would not only burden the poorest countries but reach the shores of the developed world as well.

Starting in the spring of 1992, I ventured into controversial territory on behalf of African development. I addressed a letter to the presidents and prime ministers of the Group of Seven (G-7)—Britain, Canada, France, Germany, Italy, Japan, and the United States—the wealthy industrialized nations of the world, which hold an economic summit each June. In my letter I asked them to take up the plight of Africa. There was urgent need for debt relief and fundamental assistance so that Africans might take advantage of the new dynamism of a global market economy. It was, my advisers told me, presumptuous for a UN secretary-general to address such an appeal to the G-7.

Each year thereafter—1993, 1994, 1995, 1996—I would send a letter in advance of the G-7 summit repeating my request for collective measures to help Africa. Each year I would receive perfunctory acknowledgments. Each G-7 summit would mention Africa's needs in passing, but no action followed.

Setback after setback projected a hopeless image for Africa and a hapless image for the United Nations.

Another Agenda

Following my 1992 report, *An Agenda for Peace,* I suggested that an "agenda for development" should come next. At the end of 1992 the General Assembly, in Resolution 47/181, asked me to prepare such a report. I took on this assignment with enthusiasm but also with trepidation. I hoped to shift the focus from short-term emergencies to the longer-term work of real development.

In its formative stage, the idea of "development" was often confrontational. Generations of colonial exploitation made development seem to be a debt owed by the postimperial powers to those they had once sought to rule. Development was taken not only as a cause but also as a right of newly liberated peoples. Failure to develop was attributed to the legacy of colonialism and to its successor, neocolonialism. The only solution, it was thought, was "to expropriate the expropriators"—to take over foreign economic interests in developing countries. When Gamal Abdel Nasser's decision to nationalize the Suez Canal in 1956 was followed by a military attack on Egypt by France and England, a link between development and confrontation was forged for the entire developing world.

The reaction of the nonaligned movement in the 1960s institutionalized a "third-world" or "South" approach to global politics, which during the cold war enabled the developing countries to play East and West off against each other. The South set forth its own model for development. Neither communist, capitalist, nor socialist, the countries of the South inclined toward planned economies with authoritarian features, and often a one-party system considered uniquely appropriate to the post-colonial condition.

The second stage brought a sharp decrease in confrontation. The end of the cold war removed the third world's main source of leverage with the industrialized powers. The failure of centrally planned economies compelled recognition of the importance of the marketplace and democratization to development. Leading developing countries sought to find a vehicle to bring the case of the South into the councils of the major industrial nations of the North. In 1989, as minister of state for foreign affairs for Egypt, I participated in shaping a common African position during an extraordinary summit meeting of the OAU in Addis Ababa on the question of foreign debt. In July 1989 in Paris, we attempted to establish a Group of Four—Egypt, India, Senegal, and Venezuela—capable of dialogue with the G-7 major economic powers. But opposition by some members of the G-7 and a lack of political will among the G-4 destroyed this fledgling effort.

Now, however, the age-old problems of poverty, unemployment, and social dislocation, once considered virtually the exclusive province of national policy, have become global problems and require global attention. Environmental change is transnational in scope; it is not susceptible to sustained improvement by states acting on their own. Some 94 million people are added to the world's population every year. Driven by conflict and ecological and economic pressures, large numbers of people are moving across national borders in ways that defy conventional measures of response. Terrorism and crime, particularly trafficking in narcotics, have become a worldwide concern. Such global problems grow from the poor soil of underdevelopment. If positive change is to come, a new rationale for development will have to be conceived, articulated, and made convincing to the widest audience.

The Dimensions of Development

This was the intellectual framework in which I took on the task of trying to produce an agenda for development. The global context was not favorable. The rich countries feared the rise of another movement from the poor regions of the world demanding redistribution. They were inclined to dismiss the entire subject with the assertion that development was a concept whose time had gone; any country nowadays, they said, could emulate the "Asian Tigers" if it could just summon the will to adopt the market economy. Yet this was patently impossible for the poorest of the poor, particularly in Africa. They lacked the human resources, the capital, and the infrastructure to take advantage of the new global economy. And soon the Asian model itself would falter.

A second set of obstacles came from the multitude of bureaucracies, national and international, that had emerged and entrenched themselves over the many years and phases of the development effort around the world, each with its own career interests and established ideologies. They were not opposed to new approaches but tended to substitute new slogans for new ideas. "Development" became "human development" and then "sustainable human development," as labels attached themselves like a row of elephants, trunk to tail.

Then there were the developing countries themselves, many of them governed by military or political elites who fed on the flow of overseas development assistance. They feared, often rightly, the conditions on aid and loans imposed on them by international financial institutions. They saw the United Nations in its institutional role as their voice and advocate. They would be happy if I simply called on the rich to aid the poor. They grew suspicious and resistant at any sign that the old development prescriptions on which they depended might be declared a failure or be replaced by a fresh approach.

I nonetheless began eagerly to work on an agenda for development. Soon it became apparent that this effort would be far more difficult, both intellectually and politically, than *An Agenda for Peace*. First, the drafters of the UN Charter had, in 1945, confidently filled that document with specific provisions on maintaining international peace and security but had had much less to say about development. From the "legislative history" of the UN Charter it appeared that the ideas and agencies of economic and social progress had been deliberately dispersed and left ambiguous. Second, development economics was conceptually a shambles. The theories and practices of decades had provided neither consensus on the concept nor satisfaction in the results. The field was, I found, intellectually all but bankrupt. Third, at the United Nations the issue was politically explosive. Every statement, every meeting, was subjected to the closest and most critical scrutiny, primarily out of fear of the poor countries that the United Nations, under pressure from the rich, would cease to play its role as the major voice of the developing world.

As I thought about my agenda for development, I saw that traditional approaches presuppose that development takes place under conditions of peace. Yet that is rarely the case. Most peoples strive for development in a context of past, present, or threatened conflict. Peace is not the norm. It has to be achieved for development to go forward. Next I stressed that economic growth is the engine of development. And growth depends on national policies favorable to creating a healthy private-sector economy; without this, no amount of international support will help. Yet at the same time, without international support, debt and protectionism will doom any development effort. The political dimensions of the environment, with bitter conflict over the use of natural resources, must be taken into account. Since social conditions govern the priorities and direction of development, the most obvious and difficult task is to attack both the causes and symptoms of poverty, hunger, disease, and illiteracy. Productive employment, I stressed, is fundamental to reducing poverty and enhancing social stability. Most controversially, I insisted that development and democracy are fundamentally linked. Responsive and representative government may be the single most important factor of all.

Each of these five dimensions seemed obvious. But new forms of conflict were proving unmanageable by the international community, and economic growth was impossible under conditions of chaos and strife. A protected environment would make development sustainable, but governments that had committed themselves to curtailing harmful practices were not following through. The social fabric was being weakened by the weight of transnational crime, migration, disease, drugs, and other social ills. Even democracy, which, at the end of World War II, had commonly been held to be "the wave of the future," was being challenged by regimes claiming that too much freedom undermines discipline, efficiency, and central authority. The reality, I pointed out, is that democracy fosters the good governance and stability that are necessary for development over time, as well as the creativity essential for success in the new age of information; the two agendas—peace and development—are inextricably intertwined.

Over the next months the president of the General Assembly held hearings on my report, and development became a focus of debate. Six months after setting out my five theoretical considerations, I sent to the General Assembly a barrage of specific recommendations, including equitable access to global trade, technology, investment, and information; agreed new levels of assistance; debt reduction; and outright cancellation of the debts of the poorest countries.

Development is as important as peace for the United Nations. But, unfortunately, development was becoming an ugly word. A difficult, long-term process, it is dealt with by too many overlapping parts of the UN system. And many states prefer to provide aid bilaterally, rather than multilaterally; they are willing to be generous in emergency cases but not in meeting long-term development needs. They seem oblivious to the fact that prevention costs a lot less than reconstruction.

A Concatenation of Conferences

My ideas in *An Agenda for Development* were put forward within a larger political effort for development. Africa needed to be part of a worldwide focus on all the dimensions of development. During my years in office, the United Nations conducted a series of world conferences to this end. All these conferences had been decided on by the General Assembly before my term as secretary-general began. But I quickly adopted these conferences as my own and made them a continuum, so that each would draw upon those that had come before and contribute in a cumulative way to those coming after. We agreed to take issues common to all the conferences, such as the advancement of women, and track them across the entire conference spectrum, thus creating the first fully integrated effort to follow through on the various conference decisions.

International conferences are all too often a chance to pad expense accounts and engage in pleasant but pointless palaver at expensive hotels in beautiful cities. But the UN series of world conferences between 1992 and 1996 was not that at all. A great deal has been written about these conferences, both pro and con, but it remains to be recognized how they added up to an entirely new method for reaching international agreement on critical transnational problems.

Each of the six major conferences took up a problem that affects every society, nation, and state: the environment at Rio, human rights at Vienna, population at Cairo, social development at Copenhagen, women at Beijing, cities at Istanbul. Each was based on a principle or concept that is controversial, disputed, or neglected. Each achieved or reaffirmed —not without considerable difficulty—a consensus. Each set standards to which governments committed themselves. Each strengthened the new understanding that problems that cross national boundaries are the legitimate concern of the international community and that offending governments cannot avoid their responsibilities by asserting their sovereignty as a way of fending off critical scrutiny. And each conference established a follow-on process by which progress or its lack could be assessed.

Rio and Sustainable Development

At the 1992 Rio Conference on Environment and Development, despite protests from some business and commercial interests, the international community agreed that environmental deterioration affects economic development globally. For the first time ever, governments—at the level of head of state or government—committed themselves to take international environmental consequences into account in their domestic economic policy making. From that point forward it became legitimate to hold a government to account for its performance as measured against the standards set at Rio.

The environment had not been at the top of my list of concerns when I entered office. But once on the job my attention was focused by three figures deeply concerned with the environment. Senator Al Gore was deeply knowledgeable and committed, and whenever we met we talked about the world's water needs. Tommy Koh, Singapore's quintessential diplomat, with whom I had worked in the nonaligned movement, pushed me toward a more active environmental role. Koh's work would be critical in making Rio a success. And Maurice Strong, a Canadian businessman who had been asked by Secretary-General U Thant to coordinate the first international conference on the environment, at Stockholm in 1972, and had then become the first director of the United Nations Environmental Program, came to get my support for his coordination of the Rio summit, which he had been working on since being appointed to do so by Pérez de Cuéllar in 1990.

I regarded my role as that of a public relations officer and my goal as persuading the maximum number of heads of state and government to attend, particularly President Bush, who seemed reluctant to go to Rio, fearing it would stir up domestic "antigreen" opposition to him in a presidential election year. Bush announced his decision to attend after I went to the White House to stress how important his presence at Rio would be. I gave myself some credit for the 116 leaders from 172 countries who attended Rio, plus the more than 9,000 journalists and some 3,000 representatives of nongovernmental organizations.

But when I arrived in Rio on June 2, 1992, I was outraged by the number of UN officials on the scene. Scores of them were using the conference simply as an opportunity for a holiday. As a newcomer to the United Nations, I had not realized that every department and agency made its own decision to send one or more representatives. From that moment on, *I* would decide how many UN officials would be allowed to attend conferences.

In a gigantic conference hall an hour's distance from Rio, I declared the conference open on June 3, 1992. On the platform with me was President Fernando Collor de Mello of Brazil, handsome as a movie star and very aware of his looks, which were complemented by those of his young wife. Collor was in political trouble. Brazilian critics were calling him—at one and the same time—an elitist playboy and a radical with dangerous economic policies. Also with us were the king and queen of Sweden and Portugal's prime minister, Mário Soares, and his wife.

Before beginning my speech I asked the hall for two minutes of silence on behalf of the earth, a tribute that was at that moment being observed all over the planet. The paradox of our time, I said, is that the earth has been made sick by overdevelopment at the same time that it is being sickened by underdevelopment. The words "ecology" and "economy" have their origin in the same Greek word, *oikoulogos,* "the science of the house," and the link between the two is not only etymological but actual. We have to pursue the science of managing our own house, the earth, I said; we do not own the world's wealth; we hold it on loan, from our ancestors and in trust for our children.

In Rio, I discussed with Jacques Cousteau, the explorer of the undersea depths, how to ensure that the conference would have continuing influence. We debated whether it would be best to create a new UN organization, shift the conference's mandate to the UN General Assembly, or create a commission. As I was trying to streamline the United Nations, I deeply opposed establishing any new department within the Secretariat to deal with the environment. It would be far better to reconvene at a high level and review what had been done to meet the commitments made at Rio. And this was in fact done five years later at a major review meeting held at UN headquarters in New York, at which Britain and several other nations reported that the commitment that they had made at Rio to reduce environmental damage was being met, a demonstration that the Rio process remained alive.

On June 10 I received a telephone call from Marcos de Sa Coimbra, the director of the Brazilian president's cabinet, who was also the president's brother-in-law and a former ambassador from Brazil to Cairo, where I had met him. He insisted that I participate in the inauguration by President Collor of a school in a Rio suburb to be named the United Nations School. I was not keen to go, but under pressure I agreed. Together with foreign and Brazilian dignitaries I flew by helicopter for about forty-five minutes to the site of the ceremony. The woman president of Iceland, Vigdís Finnbogadóttir, led the protocol list. The archbishop of Rio and an array of generals were present. Of course, in the starring role was the debonair president of Brazil. We toured the school premises and saw its facilities for vocational training. As television cameras followed our inspection tour, I was astonished to note that the students were all wearing brand-new clothes. Then I realized that they were really too old to be students and that the school was not a real school but a "Potemkin" school. I went over to the president's brother-in-law and asked him what was going on. "This is a gimmick," I said. "None of this is real!" He pulled me aside with a smile and whispered, "Yes, of course, but one day it *could* be a real school." He asked me to please keep my discovery quiet, which I did.

At the Rio closing session, we had lunch for the heads of state at one gigantic table. On my right was George Bush, president of the United States. On my left was Maumoon Abdul Gayoom, the president of the

Maldives, a republic of more than a thousand tiny islands some three hundred miles south of the Indian subcontinent. Each of my luncheon partners had a major worry. The president of the world's great superpower feared that his very presence in Rio, which was politically controversial in Washington, might harm his reelection chances; in fact, he chose to sign the Rio agreement not at Rio but later, at a less conspicuous moment, elsewhere. The president of the small and scattered Maldive Islands had an even more distressing worry: that his country might disappear, swallowed by the rising waters caused by global warming. Despite their worries, each head of state listened politely to me as I defended the concept of sustainable development, the watchword of the conference.

In my closing speech I said that we had come to a new point in human consciousness. Thousands of years ago, a moral contract between God and humankind had been consummated. Hundreds of years ago had come the social contract between citizens and the state. Here today we were called to a living contract between human beings and the earth. For the ancients, the forests, rivers, mountains, deserts, and seas had been alive; each had had a spiritual essence. We needed to reawaken that sense, to recognize that the earth has a soul and to find it and protect it. That would be the spirit of Rio.

Vienna and the Right to Development

The Vienna World Conference on Human Rights took place at a time when the Universal Declaration of Human Rights of 1948 and the concept of fundamental rights belonging to all peoples regardless of race, religion, gender, class, culture, or ethnicity had come under criticism. The conference affirmed the legitimate and long-standing cultural and historical practices of a multitude of disparate societies. But it also pointed out that many claims of difference and exception were designed to cloak the repressive actions of brutal regimes. The "U-word," the universality of human rights, was reaffirmed. Vienna gave new life to the proposition that how governments treat their citizens is not a matter exclusively within a state's domestic jurisdiction; at least I hoped so.

As an academic, a journalist, a politician, and a diplomat, I have always been concerned about human rights. I have been a member of nongovernmental human rights organizations. I also served on the Interna-

tional Labor Organization's commission of experts. I have participated in
UNESCO's efforts on behalf of cultural rights. And I was one of the leading advocates for the proposal of President Léopold Senghor of Senegal
in 1978 for an African Charter of Human Rights, a proposal that eventually was adopted along with the specific inclusion of the rights "of peoples" as well as of individuals.

Because of this experience, I felt that I had developed a special sense
of how to deal with—and how not to deal with—these issues as they affect third-world peoples. The most challenging problems of human
rights do not arise in the countries of Europe or North America but in the
Muslim world, in China and Southeast Asia, in the Indian subcontinent,
in Africa, and in parts of Latin America. In these areas, which make up
most of the world's geographic and demographic entirety, are located the
religious, cultural, ethnic, and economic concerns that can complicate
the application of universal human rights norms, especially when asserted from outside the third world.

On May 14, 1993, a few weeks before the Vienna World Conference
on Human Rights opened, a delegate from the Human Rights Division of
the Carter Center in Atlanta came to meet with me at the United
Nations. Former President Jimmy Carter had chaired a convention of experts in anticipation of the Vienna Conference. The experts had produced, I was told, an "Atlanta Statement," and President Carter had sent
them to inform me of its significant ideas. Foremost was the need to create a "UN high commissioner for human rights," a high authority to coordinate all activities on behalf of human rights worldwide.

I declared immediately that I was not in favor of it. The Carter delegation stiffened in their chairs and looked stricken. This might simply create one more big bureaucracy, I said. I was having a hard enough time
dealing with the United Nations' new human rights center in Geneva.
Moreover, the effort to "coordinate" would be regarded as an attempt to
consolidate pressure against countries of the third world, and that would
only strengthen their resistance to progress in human rights. The very
title "high commissioner" was a vestige of British colonialism and should
be abandoned.

"There is no urgent need for such a position," I told my guests. It will
waste money and arouse nationalist opposition. It will also undermine
the idea of "universal" human rights. Human rights are best advanced
case by case, I said, and without a big fanfare. "This proposal can have
been made only to please the nongovernmental organizations and the

public opinion of the West." I urged them to reconsider, offering the example of democracy. The United Nations was being requested, by countries from every corner of the globe, to help in their efforts to make the transition to democracy. "But," I went on, "if I named a 'Special Representative of the Secretary-General for Democratization,' it would kill all hope of progress. An institutionalized approach like this will only generate suspicion." My guests were shocked. After a long and disputatious debate, they departed. I knew that in the end, they would win and I would lose.

A Chinese Dissident

Simultaneously a case had arisen to demonstrate the complex ramifications of human rights in the UN context. The United Nations Correspondents Association (UNCA) had invited a Chinese dissident, Shen Tong, to hold a press conference on May 25, 1993, at UNCA's club room on the third floor of the UN Secretariat building. The ambassador from the People's Republic of China rushed in to protest to me. To try to resolve the situation, I telephoned the president of the correspondents' association to ask that the event be moved to another location. He agreed, and I informed the Chinese ambassador of this compromise. But when the UNCA president announced this, he was met with a storm of protest from his members. I was charged with censoring free speech, suppressing human rights, and abandoning the assurance given by Secretary-General Dag Hammarskjold more than thirty years before that UNCA would have full freedom in the use of its clubroom.

Nevertheless, I decided that the dissident's press conference should not be staged inside the UN Secretariat building, since the event was designed as an act of political opposition to the People's Republic of China, a UN member state. And I had given my word to the Chinese ambassador. I made space available for Shen Tong's press conference in the UN Institute for Training and Research, located across First Avenue from the Secretariat.

On May 19 I issued a statement that I had decided that "it would not be appropriate for this event to take place on the premises of the Secretariat in view of its apparent opposition to a member state of the United Nations." I said that I was "unalterably committed to free speech and to the cause of human rights worldwide" and at the same time, as secretary-general, I would "maintain the integrity of the United Nations Head-quarters complex as a location dedicated primarily to diplomacy among the Member States." I kept open my offer of the use of alternative UN space, but in any event the "press conference" took place on the sidewalk of First Avenue facing UN headquarters. Reporters were less interested in Shen Tong than in the theater of confrontation provoked by his appearance at the United Nations.

My decision also stirred criticism within the Congress. Representative Christopher H. Smith of New Jersey wrote to me, with a copy to Secretary of State Christopher, urging me "in the strongest terms to reverse your unfortunate decision." What I had done, the congressman declared, would certainly weigh on the mind of Congress as it considered "funding levels and conditions relating to [U.S.] participation in United Nations programs." A *New York Times* editorial accused me of "careless indifference" to the UN Charter, asserting that I had taken orders from China. Madeleine Albright joined the attack on my decision in a letter to the United Nations Correspondents Association expressing sentiments that a UN reporter said "would have shaken a less-insensitive Secretary-General to his senses." This was, to my knowledge, Albright's first public attack on me.

I could understand how the congressman, and perhaps even the newspaper's editors, might not understand how the United Nations works, but the American ambassador surely was aware that rationally no other decision could be made. The United Nations is not a government. A government can have a foreign policy; it can favor someone who opposes another government. But the United Nations is the world organization of its member states; it cannot give over its premises for the purpose of attacks on a member state. Dag Hammarskjold's assurances notwithstanding, the press club had never been used for that purpose before. Many speakers, both official and nonofficial, have denounced the governments of UN member states from podiums within the United Nations' walls, but only when they have been sponsored by another member state. No member state had sponsored a Chinese dissident. I asked Egypt's UN ambassador, Nabil Elaraby, "What if UNCA invited Sheikh Abdul Rahman [the fundamentalist leader convicted of directing the bombing of the World Trade Center and of an attempt to assassinate President Mubarak] to speak at their room in UN headquarters?" Elaraby jumped to his feet. "Impossible!" he exclaimed. "Well," I said, "for China, Shen Tong is like Abdul Rahman, but on the other side of the political spectrum." Nevertheless, the UN press corps never ceased to express its unhappiness with me over this episode.

I arrived in Vienna for the conference on human rights on June 10, 1993. I had specifically reserved a room in a hotel with a swimming pool, but after one swim, I had no time for another. A major problem had emerged. Without informing the United Nations, the Austrians had invited the Dalai Lama to attend the conference. The Dalai Lama was not only a world-revered religious figure but also regarded by many human rights activists as the symbol of political efforts to assert Tibetan rights against the People's Republic of China, of which Tibet is a part. China declared that it would withdraw from the Vienna Conference if the Dalai Lama was permitted to attend, meaning that one quarter of humanity would not be represented at the conference.

My first event in Vienna was to deliver the Bruno Kreisky Lecture, an invitation I had accepted in tribute to the long and friendly association I had had with the late Chancellor Kreisky. I told my audience that years before, when negotiations to get Israeli withdrawal from the West Bank and Gaza had not been going well, Kreisky saw that I was depressed. "How long have you been working on this?" he asked me. "Three long years," I replied. "Three years!" Kreisky exclaimed. "It took three times that long just to get the Soviets and the Americans out of *Austria!*" So Bruno Kreisky made me remember that diplomacy requires patience and perseverance. The trouble was, I did not have years, only days at best, to solve the problem of the presence of the Dalai Lama.

I dined at the home of Karl Kahane, an Austrian Jewish multimillionaire who had been a friend of Bruno Kreisky and who did useful work for the Egyptian-Israeli relationship. He wanted to help me solve the Dalai Lama problem and so had also invited the chancellor of Austria, Franz Vranitzky, and the Austrian minister of foreign affairs, Alois Mock. But try as I might, I was unable to learn who in Austria had invited the Dalai Lama and on what terms.

As it happened, the problem was easily solved. The Dalai Lama graciously accepted an invitation to participate in the nongovernmental session at Vienna. The world summit had been convened by and for states. NGOs were warmly welcomed but participated as observers and within their own forum. The Dalai Lama understood this and acted accordingly. It was not he but others with political agendas who sought without success to create a confrontation that would have threatened the conference and the cause of human rights. When I opened the Vienna world summit on June 14, 1993, the Dalai Lama was not in the room and the full Chinese delegation was present.

Four months after the Vienna Conference, the post of high commissioner for human rights was established, and I nominated for the General Assembly's approval the Ecuadoran foreign minister, José Ayala Lasso. He had lobbied successfully for the resolution adopted by the General Assembly creating the post, and his name had been proposed by the U.S. delegation. He had no human rights background but was of the third world and skillful politically. I remained convinced, however, that no one would be able to make such a position into anything more than one more bureaucratic layer.

It is patently obvious that a human rights culture is not shared by all peoples in the same way. The answer lies in its application. Principles may be universal, but the manner of carrying them out must include considerable flexibility. Human rights will continue to be a major problem as long as the third world perceives them as an instrument of intervention to serve the political objectives of the developed world—and as long as those wealthy countries remain convinced that their way to impose human rights is the only way.

Copenhagen and Social Development

The World Summit for Social Development at Copenhagen in March 1995 stressed the interconnectedness of the entire continuum of conferences. It is obvious that economic problems have social consequences and that social deterioration in turn undermines economies. The ills that societies feel most acutely all have social origins and social consequences, and the Copenhagen summit focused on these: the urgent and universal need to eradicate poverty, expand productive employment, reduce unemployment, and enhance social integration.

The decision to focus a summit entirely on the most deprived segment of global society was a dazzling statement. One hundred and eighty-seven countries were represented at Copenhagen, no fewer than 117 of them by their heads of state or government. The most innovative idea of the summit was endorsement of the principle of spending 20 percent of overseas development assistance on basic social services, in return for which poor countries would agree to devote 20 percent of their budgets to such programs.

At Copenhagen, in a pleasant office made available at the center of the conference site, I had a warm and informative meeting with Hillary Rodham Clinton. She spoke of the difficulty of maintaining the media's interest even in medium-term issues, let alone the long-term problems being addressed by the Copenhagen summit. I explained to her my view that this cycle of summit meetings was a way of ending the economic and social cold war between North and South, to parallel the end of the political and strategic cold war between East and West. The conferences were helping us move beyond the old confrontational ways. Mrs. Clinton said that it was important to project the United Nations' multilateral point of view and to tell the United Nations' success stories "over and over again" to build up support. "This would strengthen your hand in other efforts," she said, such as in Bosnia. "In the U.S. Congress and elsewhere, it seems, only negatives are discussed." She suggested a stepped-up public relations campaign to focus on UN successes. I showed her the "Blue Book" series on UN operations that I had initiated. She said she would give them out herself and urged that they be made available at public locations, such as international airports. Mrs. Clinton praised the entire series of world conferences, saying that they "are the true purpose of multilateral diplomacy."

When our meeting was over, I escorted her from my UN office to her office in the conference complex area marked for the U.S. delegation. Just as we were about to enter the U.S. pavilion, I stopped and said, "Here end my territorial waters" and kissed her hand as she laughed. The next day, after she delivered her speech, I again accompanied her to her office. As we approached the U.S. site, she leaned over to me to say with a smile, "Beware, you are entering *my* territorial waters!"

The Perils of Protocol

At the Copenhagen summit I attended the strangest dinner in my experience. The practice of protocol is much maligned. To a populist age it seems foolish, old-fashioned, and undemocratic. But it is absolutely essential if international relations are to flow smoothly. To abide by a set of unchallengeable criteria for rank ordering prevents an unseemly and sometimes dangerous struggle for precedence by other means. When an ambassador is seated below the salt, his nerves are calmed by the knowledge that those above him are there only because they arrived at post at an earlier date than he did. Nonetheless, protocol rankings are of an infinite variety and present protocol officers with endless series of headaches. Debates have been held over whether coffee outranks tea. And sometimes the correct order of precedence seems to go against instinct. I have heard that American diplomats, for example, perennially find it "counterintuitive" to place state governors above U.S. senators, as proper protocol demands.

The official who sketched out the seating chart for the table at which Queen Margrethe II of Denmark was to be the hostess undoubtedly believed that it was based upon a surefire protocol principle: those at the table would be the most senior—in terms of years in office—of all the heads of state and government attending the World Summit for Social Development. Leia and I would be there as well, because the United Nations was cohost of the summit with Denmark.

Seated to the queen's right in the place of most senior guest was Fidel Castro, Cuba's maximum leader. Counterclockwise from Castro were President Hassan Gouled Aptidon of Djibouti, who had led his country since it had gained its independence from France in 1977; Mrs. Suharto, wife of the Indonesian president; General Suharto, who had first been elected in 1968; German Chancellor Helmut Kohl, who was in his thirteenth year in power and at that moment also serving as president of the European Union; then Leia; and to her right Mobutu Sese Seko, the head of state of Zaire since 1965; then Mrs. Mobutu and me. Behind each head of state except for President Gouled stood a translator.

At every international gathering Castro is always the most applauded whenever he appears in public. This had been true at Rio, where astounding crowds, predominantly young girls, had jumped up and down shouting, "We love you, Fidel!" It was true even when Castro appeared at the inauguration of Nelson Mandela as president of South Africa, upstaging Mandela in his moment of glory. Over the years Castro had become a universal symbol of opposition to American power. Adulation and admiration have given him an attitude of superiority over his surroundings and associates wherever he goes.

Once we had taken our seats, Castro clearly seemed annoyed by Kohl's presence. "On what basis are you sitting at this table?" he demanded of the chancellor of Germany. "This table is for only the most senior heads of state or government," Castro added, as if no one knew this. Kohl reddened. "I am an old politician," he replied in a self-deprecating attempt to deflect Castro's assault. "You have been chancellor for only a few years!" Castro declared. I leaned over to Queen Margrethe and whispered, "Music, your majesty"—"*La musique adoucit les moeurs!*" (Music sweetens behavior). By a happy accident the orchestra's sound at that moment grew loud, suppressing all conversation.

When the fanfare subsided, Castro started again. "You eat too much," he said to Kohl. "You should watch your diet." Kohl was ready for him: "I hadn't realized, Mr. Castro, that you had become so Americanized that you worry so much about weight." All this was translated from Spanish to German and from German to Spanish, which only heightened and prolonged the tension.

"Could you explain the so-called German miracle to me?" Castro asked with a smirk. Kohl took the thrust and struck back: "Work, Mr. Castro, work—not words." "Please, your Majesty," I said, "more music." The queen was prepared this time, and music flowed over the table. Kohl turned to Leia and said, "I can't believe the composition of this table!" Later Chancellor Kohl told me that when he returned to his suite that night, he drew up a seating diagram of the table so that he could remember this event. "I did the same," I replied.

The next day Vice President Al Gore arrived and came to see me, along with Madeleine Albright and Richard Holbrooke, the assistant secretary of state for foreign affairs. Gore congratulated me on the success of the Copenhagen summit, saying he was impressed by the huge turnout of world leaders. President Clinton, he said, had rebuffed the attacks on the United Nations in the Congress and was turning American public opinion around toward greater understanding of and support for the United Nations. I told Gore of my conversation earlier that day with Prime Minister Narasimha Rao of India. Referring to the U.S. administration and Congress, I had said, "Isn't there an Indian saying that 'When the elephants fight, the grass gets trampled'?" Rao had replied indignantly, "The UN isn't grass; it is the Parliament of the world!"

The UN world summits of the 1990s emerged as a wholly new factor for achieving change on the world stage. A bitter critic of these conferences described them accurately: "UN meetings are not just talkathons. They are opportunities to seed international law with new norms and rights, many of them hidden in apparently routine language. Though not immediately binding on any nation, after some time they may be cited as 'customary' interpretations of international law and acquire some legal force. . . . UN conferences now have a precise use in hardball international politics." Although some criticized the conferences as a way of circumventing national parliamentary or congressional politics, they were in fact democratic in a larger sense and the beginning of a new form of peoples' control of their own destinies on issues too large or too suppressed by special interests to be handled by domestic national politics.

I had not been back from Copenhagen very long before Madeleine Albright came to see me with a complaint about the next UN world conference, which would be held in China and focus on women's issues. "Your preparations for Beijing are going too slowly," Albright declared. It was obvious, she said, that Gertrude Mongella, from Tanzania, the United Nations' director for the Beijing summit, "doesn't know how to organize a conference. She's the main problem." I tried to reassure Albright that we were on schedule and effectively addressing all problems as they arose. I had established a special team of experts to deal with all the difficult conference issues. "But they *don't* deal with the problems," Albright insisted. "They will deal with them, I promise you," I replied. "All will come out right in the end." So far the United Nations had run the entire cycle of large conferences almost flawlessly. We knew what we were doing. But Albright was not to be reassured. She warned me, "The U.S. will remember this conversation," and she would throw it back in my face when the Beijing Conference failed, she said. In any event, the Beijing World Conference on Women, the first global summit conference ever held in China, was a success, a fact that nonetheless seemed to give Albright no satisfaction.

A Prisoner of Expectations

One year after the genocide in Rwanda, I traveled to Africa once more. The conflict in Bosnia was coming to a climax; Srebenica and Žepa had fallen, and the Serbs were on the verge of defeating the international effort in the former Yugoslavia. How could I justify my absence from Bosnia or from United Nations headquarters in New York at this critical time? Reporters pressed me for an answer again and again. "Because," I said, "if I cancel this trip, which I scheduled long ago, the Africans will say that while there is genocide in Africa—a million have died in Rwanda —the secretary-general pays attention only to Srebenica, a village in Europe."

Michael Ignatieff, a writer for *The New Yorker* magazine, traveled with me and described the scene. Years later Ignatieff was still being denounced by fellow journalists for having reported favorably on my activities (see, e.g., David Rieff, *The New Republic,* April 27, 1998). His description of my Africa trip nonetheless captured my mood and the nature of the crisis of the time:

> Thursday, July 13, 1995: Boutros Boutros-Ghali's plane is heading south from Cairo, a small, cramped executive jet, a crush of luggage and people—his team of seven, plus three journalists. I have been called forward for a briefing. He is an intense, wiry, sallow-skinned man in his seventies, sitting alone in a window seat, looking out at the Sudanese desert. He wants to talk about Africa. I want to talk about Bosnia.

For a very long while on this trip it appeared that the reporters could not, and would never, take their minds off Bosnia. But slowly the reality and the magnitude of Africa began to impose itself upon them. Ignatieff wrote:

> Monday, July 17th: Bujumbura, Burundi. The tour is in its fifth day, and the only one who doesn't look exhausted is the briskly energetic seventy-two-year-old at the center of it. I never see him relaxing—I've never seen his tie loosened—and this morning he appears, bursting from an elevator, with his stooped and slightly hunched gait. The members of his entourage behind him are exhausted: you can see them in the corridors of the Hôtel Source du Nil, long after midnight, in their dressing gowns, taking cables into his rooms, fielding calls from New York, their beds strewn with paper. He drives them hard. His American security guard, an ex-policeman from Darien, Connecticut, recalls the days with Pérez de Cuéllar or Waldheim, when there was time for sightseeing on the tours. "Not with this one," he sighs. "When he looks down the schedule and spots a visit to the zoo, out it goes. In goes another meeting. . . ."

At last the writer touched the core of the problem:

> I am invited to sit in on the process of preventive diplomacy at work. Boutros-Ghali is at the head of a baize table in his hotel and listens to the Hutu and Tutsi leadership, ranged on opposite sides, facing each other. The Hutus insist that the Tutsi-dominated Army is waging a campaign of extermination; the Tutsis say that night attacks by Hutu ex-

tremists have rendered all constitutional dialogue impossible. The atmosphere in the room thickens with accusation, counter-accusation, stares, and contempt.

Boutros-Ghali says nothing until everyone has finished speaking. He then tells them they make him ashamed to call himself an African. You seem to assume, he says, staring along the two rows of eyes that will not meet each other, that the international community will save you. You are deceived. Remember Beirut. Many good friends of mine died there, deceived by the same assumption. The international community is quite content to let you massacre each other to the last man. The donor community is fatigued. It is tired of having to save societies that seem incapable of saving themselves. He brings the flat of his palm down upon the baize table. "You are mature adults—*majeurs et vaccinés*," he says. "God helps those who help themselves. Your enemy is not each other but fear and cowardice. You must have the courage to accept compromises. That is what a political class is for. You must assume your responsibilities. If you don't, nobody will save you." He then sweeps up his papers and strides out.

Later that night, in the Hôtel Source du Nil, I ask him if he always chooses such caustic language in private.

"When I have to, yes." There is nothing personal about it. The anger is a professionally modulated set piece, designed to bring a craven, local élite to its senses.

Will it work?

We are only the doctors, he says. If the patient won't take the medicine, what can we do?

The metaphor is not quite accurate. These patients aren't refusing the medicine. They are setting fire to the clinic. Is there a point at which they should be left to it—a point at which even a Secretary-General succumbs to the seductiveness of moral disgust?

Everywhere he goes, he appears to be the prisoner of the expectations that those beggarly places have of the United Nations and of that exalted fiction the international community. These expectations validate his organization: they are its real mandate, its raison d'être. And yet, in one way or another, he deliberately tries to reduce these expectations, to contain the inevitable disappointment and force people to rediscover their own capabilities.

I ask him if he is tired.

"Not at all. You see me as I am."

Will he run again?

"I have fifteen months to decide."

He recently said that the achievement of the United Nations' fifty years was to create a workable international system. I tell him that after five days on the road I don't see a workable international system; I see a jungle, kept at bay by desperate improvisation.

He shakes his head. It is not that bad. There is more reason to be hopeful. He is not discouraged. "We bring hope to the international community." And then he is gone, upstairs, meeting another militia leader with blood on his hands, taking another phone call from Akashi in Zagreb or the Secretariat in New York.

Night settles on the Hôtel Source du Nil. The swimming pool is still. In the corridors, where his staff has been scurrying to and fro, there is silence, but it is soon broken by a round of gunfire and the sharp, concussive report of a grenade. Ethnic cleansing is under way half a mile from where the Secretary-General is sleeping.

On April 17, 1996, I sent the last of my series of letters to the leaders of the G-7 in advance of their summit, that year to be held in Lyons, France. I referred to my previous letters and wrote, "The economic, social and environmental challenges facing Africa are of unparalleled severity. At the same time, Africa's development prospects are in many ways better now than they have been for many years. Realizing these prospects will require renewed determination within Africa. It will also require renewed commitment by the international community."

In this spirit I urged the G-7 leaders to give their strong support to the United Nations Special Initiative on Africa, which I had launched just a few weeks before. The initiative, I explained, "is an effort to strengthen the collective impact of the actions of the United Nations, the World Bank, the International Monetary Fund, the World Trade Organization and other agencies in support of Africa. With the G-7's support," I said, "The outcome can be a freer, more peaceful and prosperous Africa and thus a freer and more peaceful and prosperous world."

At Lyons the G-7 adopted a resolution on Africa, and I soon received a letter from the president of the G-7, Jacques Chirac, asking what the United Nations had done to follow up on their resolution. Together with the heads of the World Bank, the World Trade Organization, and the International Monetary Fund, I signed a letter to President Chirac describing in detail what the United Nations and the Bretton Woods institutions had been doing for Africa. Somehow the leaders of the great wealthy powers had evaded the subject once more. I had, after years of trying, finally gotten them to address the question of Africa's plight, only to have them demand to know what *I* had done to implement their declaration. A year later, after my departure from the United Nations, President Clinton introduced what he called his "Africa Initiative" before the G-7 summit held in Denver, Colorado. And a year after that, in 1998, he made an extended trip to Africa, where he was warmly welcomed but understood to be only conveying a message that security and development needs would have to be met locally or privately, that in a global market economy the role of the world's governments would be marginal at best.

When I was a boy in Egypt, I was awed by the Nile, as children on the banks of that river have been for eons. When grown, I traveled southward again and again, deep into the center of the African continent to the sources of the Nile. I learned that not only the river's sources but those of humanity itself lie deep in Africa. We all come "out of Africa." Africa is the mother of us all, and Egypt is the oldest daughter of Africa. This is why I have loved Africa and tried so hard throughout my life to help her. This is why the horrors inflicted in and on Africa cause such pain. But anyone who knows Africa knows that its people will endure and ultimately succeed.

CHAPTER 6

The Arab World and Israel

(1992–1993)

Just as my commitment to Africa was a theme running all through my UN years, so my identification with the Arab world provided an ever-present backdrop to my work. The relations between the United Nations and the Arab world are complex and difficult. The United Nations had contributed to the decolonization of the majority of Arab countries and the creation of the state of Israel, but it still had not resolved the decolonization of Palestine, nor had it succeeded in managing the Arab-Israeli conflict. UN resolutions numbering in the hundreds, adopted by both the Security Council and the General Assembly, served only to sharpen a double crisis of confidence regarding the United Nations. To Israel, the United Nations was a veritable war machine made for condemning, isolating, and undermining the Jewish state. To the Arab world, the United Nations was an organization feudally dependent on the United States in which pro-Arab resolutions in support of the Palestinian cause were never implemented.

This double crisis of confidence tremendously complicated my role as secretary-general. I tried to surmount it by attempting an authentic reconciliation between the United Nations and Israel. My message to the prime minister of Israel before and after my election was "At Camp David I contributed to the achievement of the peace treaty between Egypt and Israel. I would now like to conclude a peace treaty between the United Nations and Israel."

To the Arab world my message was "I am an Arab. Your problems are my problems. This is an opportunity that will not recur for decades. Help me in order that I can help you."

To the problems of Palestine was added a list of other, often related, troubles besetting the Arab world: the Israeli occupation of southern Lebanon, the conflict in Western Sahara, the civil war in Yemen, the sanctions against Iraq and Libya, the turmoil in Sudan. And the problems of the Arab world were interwoven with the goal of pan-Islamic solidarity. Not only for fundamentalists but for many Arabs, the sole entity is the Muslim nation, the Umma, which must take precedence over the Arab nation. One must without reservation support Muslims in Bosnia, in Kashmir, in Chechnya, in Cyprus, in Nagorno-Karabakh. Not to do so would be anti-Muslim and thus anti-Arab. At the third Popular and Arab Conference in Khartoum in March 1995, the Sudanese fundamentalist leader Hassan al-Turabi declared that "the international mechanism that is called the UN now functions incorrectly and has become a weapon against Muslim countries." Al-Turabi and I knew and distrusted each other heartily.

Books and pamphlets sold in the streets of Cairo and the Arab capitals accused me of treason against the Muslim world, of being an agent of American imperialism. One cartoon depicted me as Dracula, about to sink my fangs into the countries of Islam. But in American political circles I was assumed to be biased against Israel and against the United States in general. So in Arab capitals I was regarded at best as nonsupportive; in Washington I was regarded at best as nonneutral.

Faced with this double bind, I took refuge in strictly interpreting the resolutions of the United Nations to legitimate my decisions and support my actions. When dealing with any problem in any part of the world, I would always consult as widely as possible with others, both inside the United Nations and out. And I would always try to form a team or a task force so that any UN position could be viewed as taken by consensus and not by the secretary-general alone. When dealing with problems of the Middle East, I tried to do all this and more, to go the extra mile to be as objective as possible. I tried my best to calm suspicions on all sides. To avoid stirring up passions, I never visited either Libya or Lebanon, or the Israeli-occupied territories, and never went to Israel except for the funeral of Yitzhak Rabin.

Against this background, three Arab issues stand out: those involving Palestine, Libya, and Iraq. This is not to say that other problems to which

I devoted extensive attention and effort—such as the civil war in Sudan or Yemen or the future of Western Sahara—were less important but that they were given far less time on the agenda of the Security Council. I did not so much choose problems as be chosen by them.

Resolution 242

I had hardly settled in behind my desk on the thirty-eighth floor when I found myself in trouble over a Middle East issue. At a press conference on March 19, 1992, I stated that UN Security Council Resolution 242 of 1967 was not binding because it was not based on the chapter of the Charter that deals with enforcement of the Council's resolutions. This brought down upon my head the weight and clamor of a falling piano. Resolution 242 deals with the Arab-Israeli conflict and declares that territory is to be given up in return for peace. If I said that Resolution 242 was nonbinding, my Arab friends howled, then I must be saying that Israel need not withdraw from the West Bank and Gaza.

An hour later my spokesman issued a clarification: "The Secretary-General's observation regarding Security Council Resolution 242, made in reply to a question at his press conference this morning, should be understood to mean that that resolution is not enforceable since it was not adopted under Chapter VII of the Charter of the United Nations." I had simply meant that no means of enforcement had been provided for the achievement of the resolution.

This statement satisfied my critics not in the least, and I was soon presented with a lengthy legal analysis by an Arab-American group declaring that my statements were "contrary to the principles of the United Nations Charter, UN resolutions and the principles of International Law." To be fair, I sent the Arab memo to the UN legal adviser, who replied in a memo of similar length, the bottom line of which read, all in capital letters: NO SECURITY COUNCIL RESOLUTION CAN BE DESCRIBED AS UNENFORCEABLE. I got the message. I decided that I would let some time pass before pronouncing myself on an Arab-Israeli issue again.

As the months went by, I found that my hope of making "peace" between the United Nations and Israel, as I had helped to do between Egypt and Israel, was making headway. Over the years the United Nations had served as an internationally sanctioned mechanism for isolating Israel. But with the new atmosphere that attended the end of the cold war, the General Assembly had repealed its "Zionism is racism" resolution. And as the Israeli government itself happily pointed out, with the achievement in 1993 of the Israel-PLO Declaration of Principles negotiated at Oslo and the Israel-Jordan Common Agenda, the United Nations began to welcome achievements in the Arab-Israeli peace process. This was in stark contrast to the United Nations' refusal to provide a peacekeeping force for the Sinai after the achievement of the peace treaty between Egypt and Israel, a refusal that remains the most disgraceful moment in UN history.

But in the 1990s several positive steps were taken toward a new UN-Israeli relationship. Arab representatives at the United Nations abandoned their annual ritual of challenging Israel's credentials in the General Assembly, thus implicitly recognizing Israel's legitimacy in the family of nations. With the consent of most Arab countries, Israel was admitted to the UN Committee on Information. An Israeli was elected to the administrative tribunal dealing with UN employee issues, whereas for decades Israel and Israelis had been totally excluded from elected positions in UN bodies. The annual resolution submitted by the Arab group calling for cooperation between the United Nations and the Arab League was cleared of all provisions hostile to Israel and the peace process, enabling both Israel and the United States to support the passage of the resolution. Taken together, these developments helped Israel and the United Nations begin a new chapter in their shared history.

Libya: Charged with Airline Terrorism

My relations with the Libyan government had been extremely difficult ever since President Sadat's visit to Jerusalem in November 1977. Libya accused Egypt of betraying the Palestinian cause and the Arab world, and Egypt accused Libya of involvement in acts of terrorism. There were regular verbal confrontations between Libyan Minister of Foreign Affairs Ali Turayki and me at the time of the African summits and conferences of the nonaligned movement, as well as in the UN General Assembly. Toward the end of the 1980s relations improved between President Mubarak and Colonel Muammar Qaddafi, an important matter for Cairo because of the hundreds of thousands of Egyptian workers employed in Libya and because, with better relations, Egypt had a better chance to moderate Qaddafi's policy. Having been one of Egypt's principal spokesmen against Qaddafi during the years when Egypt had been isolated from the Arab world because of its peace treaty with Israel, I was naturally kept in the background during this diplomatic reconciliation.

But early in 1990 President Mubarak, returning to Cairo from a tour in which I was involved, decided to land in Libya for a brief meeting with Qaddafi. I was not relaxed about the prospect of encountering Qaddafi face to face. The presidential airplane landed at a military airfield somewhere between Bengazi and Tripoli. We were met by Colonel Qaddafi, who awaited President Mubarak at the foot of the airplane steps. He embraced the president, as he did the other members of the president's entourage. When my turn came, he greeted me but without the kiss and embrace that he granted to the others. I understood that even if reconciliation had taken place at the level of heads of state and high-ranking officials, it had not taken place at my level. I still bore the weight of the past. This discrimination did not go unnoticed by President Mubarak, who, during the lunch offered by Colonel Qaddafi in a modest desert house—Libya is all desert—teased me, "Have some macaroni. I won't tell your wife." Then, speaking to Colonel Qaddafi: "His wife has him follow a very strict regimen when it comes to food. She forbids him bread, pasta, and, above all, macaroni."

Qaddafi, very interested, addressed his words to me: "You like macaroni?"

"Yes, Mr. President, I have a great weakness for macaroni," I replied. Qaddafi arose and served me macaroni himself, specifying, "This is made in Libya." As a former colony of Italy, Libya did indeed produce superb macaroni.

After returning to his seat, Qaddafi leaned across the table and asked me, "If your wife forbids you macaroni, why don't you divorce her?"

"Because I'm scared of her," I said, trying to make a joke.

Qaddafi declared that my marriage would have to be very strong indeed, because he was going to instruct the Libyan ambassador in Cairo to deliver crates of macaroni to my residence. There was a burst of laughter, and the atmosphere relaxed.

As we were leaving to fly back to Cairo, the colonel embraced President Mubarak and then embraced me. As he did so, I whispered, "Don't forget the macaroni."

Later, a huge crate of macaroni—twice the size of an office desk—was delivered to me in Cairo from Qaddafi. Egyptian security guards were alarmed and refused to let me accept the shipment. I telephoned President Mubarak at once: "Qaddafi has sent me a ton of macaroni. Should I keep it? What can I do, open a macaroni shop?"

"Put down the telephone and go get a pencil," Mubarak said. I did so and picked up the receiver again. "Number one," Mubarak said, "No shop. Number two: you may not give any macaroni to your friends. Number three: You must eat all the macaroni yourself, alone."

This soon became a standing joke with Mubarak, not only about me but as a comment used to describe anyone who said or did something out of line. At a press conference he gave in London, before an audience made up largely of Egyptians living in Britain, a fundamentalist sheikh stood up and asked Mubarak, "Why don't you appoint as Egyptian vice president a man of religion?" Mubarak turned to me, seated next to him on the podium, and said loudly, "This man has eaten too much macaroni." Hearing this, people rushed up to me afterward demanding that I explain the secret meaning of "macaroni."

Later, just after my election as secretary-general, President Mubarak, in a telephone conversation with me, said, "Boutros, try to find a solution to Qaddafi's Pan Am problem." I replied that I would try to do so if he would send me more macaroni. "Boutros," Mubarak replied, "he is ready to send you a macaroni factory!" It seemed that Colonel Qaddafi felt that my election as secretary-general could resolve all his problems with France, Britain, and the United States.

The Montreal Convention

In November 1991 the United States and Britain issued warrants for the arrest and surrender of two Libyan citizens accused of violating the laws of Scotland and the United States by planting a bomb that destroyed Pan Am Flight 103 over Lockerbie, Scotland in December 1988. At the same time, France requested Libya's cooperation in investigating an apparent terrorist bombing of Union de Transports Aériens (UTA) Flight 772 in September 1989 over the African country of Niger.

In response, the government of Libya asked the United States, Britain, and France to cooperate in Libya's own investigation of the bombings. Libya expressly denied any involvement in the downing of Pan Am Flight 103 and offered to submit the case to the International Court of Justice at The Hague. The United States and Britain rejected Libya's proposal.

The Lockerbie outrage was precisely governed by an international treaty: the 1971 Montreal Convention for the Suppression of Unlawful Acts Against the Safety of Civil Aviation. Libya, the United States, Britain, and France had all signed the treaty, which falls under the International Civil Aviation Organization (ICAO), a specialized agency of the United Nations. The Montreal Convention requires a government to prosecute or extradite any person accused of placing on an aircraft "a device . . . which is likely to . . . cause damage to it which is likely to endanger its safety in flight."

There were, however, no extradition treaties between Libya and the United States or Britain. The Montreal Convention speaks to this situation by declaring that each party to the treaty agrees that "if it does not extradite" those who are accused, it is "obliged without exception whatsoever and whether or not the offense was committed on its territory, to submit the case to its competent authorities for the purpose of prosecution."

By doing so, Libya thus fully complied with the Montreal Convention. It arrested the suspects, notified the accusing states, asked for evidence, began an inquiry, and invited the United States and Britain to participate. Libya also responded positively to France by offering a high degree of cooperation between the investigations conducted by the two countries.

In addition, the Montreal Convention provides recourse to the International Court of Justice for solving problems related to the interpretation or application of the convention. The World Court would provide a very visible forum at which U.S., British, and French evidence could be presented and assessed. If Libya refused to carry out the decision of the International Court of Justice, it would be in violation of the UN Charter, and action by the Security Council could follow. But in this case the United States and Britain rejected Libya's offer to go to the World Court and instead went directly to the Security Council, requesting the Council to endorse the request for the surrender of the two accused Libyans.

First Condemnation

On January 3, 1992—one of my very first days in office—the ambassadors of France, Great Britain, and the United States came to my temporary residence at the Waldorf-Astoria to discuss Libyan responsibility for the destruction of Pan Am Flight 103 and UTA Flight 772. There was extensive evidence against the two suspects, they said. They were about to propose a Security Council resolution that would pave the way for imposing sanctions on Libya. In the days following, representatives of Libya came to consult with me. On Sunday, January 19, I met with Ali Turayki, formerly the Libyan minister of foreign affairs and a former adversary of mine. The Libyans had been told the resolution would not pass. I knew that they were mistaken and tried to convince them that the resolution would pass by a unanimous vote, which is just what happened. Resolution 731 was adopted on Monday, January 20, 1992. The resolution required that the Libyan authorities provide a complete response to the demands of the United States, Britain, and France and that the secretary-general seek the cooperation of the Libyan government in obtaining this response. The demands, as we discovered later, concerned four points: the destruction of Pan Am Flight 103, the destruction of UTA Flight 772, the training of terrorists in Libyan camps, and military aid given by Libya to terrorist groups, notably to the Irish Republican Army (IRA).

The problem was complicated by uncertainties and misunderstandings.

First, the Libyans were surrounded by intermediaries. Some were small-time con men, some were big-time international deal makers, and some were British and American lawyers. All were telling the Libyans that they could go around the Security Council and solve the dispute directly with high political figures in the United States, Britain, and France. With the Security Council resolution passed unanimously, the Libyans, like a patient with an incurable disease, were ready to turn to quacks for help.

Second, although allied and united against Libya, the three powers had different bilateral relations and divergent interests in this affair. The United States was concerned above all with the destruction of Pan Am Flight 103, on which the majority of victims had been students from Syracuse University in New York State. Great Britain was most interested in Libya's supplying of arms to the IRA. France was focused on UTA Flight 772.

Third, legal scholars as well as Libya's lawyers were deeply divided on the legality of the demands made by the three powers because of the lack of an extradition treaty. There were multiple legal interpretations of what Libya was being asked to do.

Fourth, the Libyans did not understand how the UN resolution would work. Would Resolution 731 be the whole story, or would it be the start of some vast effort to change the government of Libya, to unseat Colonel

Qaddafi? From my own conversations with the ambassadors of the three powers, I did not think that they themselves could answer that question.

Moreover, the Libyans did not know what consequences awaited them should they fail to obey Resolution 731. Here again the advice they received was contradictory. The three powers will do nothing. . . . Stall. . . . Appeal to the International Court of Justice. . . . Let us take care of it . . . said the intermediaries and courtiers swarming about Tripoli.

In Mexico, at the ceremony to sign the peace agreement for El Salvador in January 1992, I had met Secretary of State James Baker before the UN sanctions resolution was passed. He told me he had heard that North African countries were inclined toward conciliation with Libya, with me as secretary-general as the mediator. He asked me to avoid the issue. The United States wanted a UN resolution passed calling on Libya to turn over the suspects.

I met with the Libyan delegation at its request on January 22, 1992, at the Waldorf-Astoria and with Ali Turayki, who was operating alone, on Saturday, January 25. I tried to convince them that another resolution would be adopted if they did not respond immediately to the demands of the three powers. Through the Libyan delegation I obtained Qaddafi's agreement to receive an envoy from me, an under secretary-general of Russian nationality, Vassily Safronchuk. I chose a Russian in hopes that now, with the cold war over, Russia would play a constructive role in world affairs. I also thought that using a Russian national would help win the Libyans' trust. Later I learned that my choice had only raised suspicions.

On Sunday, January 26, I met with Ambassador Thomas Pickering, my neighbor at the Waldorf. He assured me that the United States intended to apply sanctions if Libya did not respond. Tall, bald, and almost unbearably intense, Pickering spoke in a soft, rapid-fire cadence, yet every word was precisely enunciated. He was a superb ambassador, unendingly patient and never showing emotion. If Libya did not comply with Resolution 731, the United States wanted a follow-on resolution imposing sanctions. The United States wanted me to make sure Qaddafi knew that.

Colonel Qaddafi met with my emissary on January 25 and promised to take the necessary measures to respond to the demands of the three powers but asked for more time. A month later I sent Safronchuk to see him again, but Qaddafi stuck to the same line.

On February 26 I met in Geneva with a Libyan delegation that simply repeated that it could do nothing more for the moment. The delegates gave no explanation, but I knew that they were stalling in hopes that their hired lawyers and other intermediaries would fix the problem. They also seemed convinced that I could somehow magically resolve the affair. I explained, in vain, that my power was extremely limited and that it was the Security Council that, in the final analysis, decided these matters.

In the Arab world rumors spread that Security Council Resolution 731 was actually a U.S. payoff to Syria and Iran for having supported—or at least acquiesced—in the war against Iraq. Both Syria and Iran had been suspected of being behind the bombing of Pan Am Flight 103. *The New York Times* of April 1, 1992, reported that investigators "cannot rule out the participation of their original suspects—Iran and Syria."

Speculation thus arose that the United States had promised not to charge Iran or Syria with this crime in return for Syria's willingness to provide a small unit to the Persian Gulf War coalition and for Iran's willingness to stay out of the conflict. Instead, the United States would focus on Libya alone as the culprit in the Lockerbie disaster.

In New York on Sunday, March 1, 1992 I met again with Ambassador Pickering, this time at Sutton Place. Our meeting was easy and pleasant. We agreed that Qaddafi was trying to delay and confuse the situation by involving a multiplicity of intermediaries. At the same time, I said, the Libyans were confused by the United States' position. If Libya agreed to extradite the two men accused of bombing Pan Am Flight 103, would that be the end of it? Or would it be only the start of a new series of demands? Pickering could not supply a definitive answer. He could only confirm yet again that the United States intended to apply sanctions against the Libyans, who did not believe that it would. On Monday, March 23, I met with Libyan Ambassador El Houderi. A timid man, very polite and discreet, he was full of goodwill but seemed overwhelmed by the contradictory instructions he was receiving from Tripoli. We discussed the possibility of giving up the two suspects to the Arab League in order to avoid the sanctions and to offer an initial response to the demands of the three powers.

New Sanctions Against Libya

On March 3 Libya filed suit against the United States and Britain in the International Court of Justice, requesting the court to declare that Libya had fully complied with the Montreal Convention, that the United States and Britain were in violation of the convention, and that they should cease threats of force against Libya. On March 31 the United States, Britain, and France put through another Security Council resolution, 748, declaring that Libya's failure to respond to Resolution 731 amounted to "a threat to international peace and security," language that brought Chapter VII of the Charter into play and made it possible to impose new sanctions upon Libya. In effect, the resolution declared Libya to be guilty of terrorism.

Resolution 748 came as a great shock to the Libyans, who were certain that it could not pass. Five members of the Security Council abstained—Cape Verde, China, India, Morocco, and Zimbabwe—quietly expressing their disapproval of the resolution. The resolution accused Libya of promoting international terrorism and of assisting terrorist groups; insisted upon an immediate response to the demands of the three powers concerning the destruction of Pan Am Flight 103 and UTA Flight 772; and scheduled a series of sanctions, to begin on April 15. These included a boycott of air traffic to or from Libya; a boycott of all military assistance to Libya; reduction in the level of Libyan diplomatic missions; and adherence of all states to any one state's ban on the entry of suspected terrorists. The resolution also requested the secretary-general to seek the cooperation of the Libyan government in implementing it.

Tremendous demonstrations condemning Resolution 748 and the United Nations broke out in the streets of Tripoli. The Venezuelan Embassy was destroyed because the Security Council had been under the presidency of Venezuela when the resolution was passed. On April 12 the Security Council condemned these acts of violence and insisted that Libya compensate Venezuela for the damages.

On April 7 I sent Vladimir Petrovsky, a former Soviet vice-minister of foreign affairs and now the highest-ranking Russian at the UN, to Libya to see Colonel Qaddafi. Qaddafi proposed that a commission of inquiry, composed of Chinese and Indian representatives, be sent to Libya to certify that there were no more terrorist training camps there. This was something to work with. In Geneva on April 11 and 12 I met with a large Libyan delegation and proposed that we undertake a step-by-step process. I had in mind the Arab-Israeli peace process, in which the hardest issues, such as Jerusalem, had been left until the very end of the process: "Start with what is most tolerable for your government. . . . Above all, avoid delay, which only runs the risks of new sanctions.

"First, provide hard evidence that there are no more terrorist training camps in your country. This means you will have to accept the presence of a commission of experts to visit and inspect the territory of the Libyan Jamarihya. Second," I said, "give precise information to the British authorities concerning Libya's shipment of arms to the IRA in Ireland." I placed this issue ahead of Pan Am Flight 103 and UTA Flight 772 because it could be satisfied by information rather than action.

"Third, settle your dispute with the French government concerning the destruction of UTA 772." I knew that Libya would have an easier time dealing with the French than with the Americans. I recalled that one result of the American-Libyan confrontation had been the U.S. bombing of Tripoli in retaliation for the terrorist bombing of a Berlin nightclub in which Americans had been killed and injured. France had opposed the bombing and denied overflight rights to U.S. Air Force F-111 bombers en route from England to their targets in and around Tripoli. The Pan Am Flight 103 case was entangled in a bitter cycle of violence and because it was such a difficult case, I said, should be placed last on the agenda.

"Fourth," I said, "deliver the two suspects to a country allied with the three powers or to a neutral state or to the Arab League—a transitional step, it being understood that Libya will accept the competence of the Scottish court."

I emphasized to the Libyans that this was my personal initiative. I had not obtained the agreement of the three powers concerned and could give no guarantee that taking these steps would lead to a lifting of the sanctions. The Libyan delegation raised the same questions over and over: If Libya met these demands, what guarantee would it have that the three powers would not then make new demands? If Libya extradited the two suspects to Great Britain, how could it be sure that Britain would not reextradite them to the United States?

I sent Petrovsky to Libya again but without results. I arranged meetings of the British and the Libyans so they could discuss the problem of arms shipments to Ireland. The British complained that the information they had received was incomplete. The Libyans assured me of the contrary. What was important was that the process was under way.

I obtained the permission of the three powers to send a commission of inquiry to Libya to determine whether there were terrorist training camps there. But before this could take place, they changed their view. An American military officer came to show me photographs taken by satellite that showed that where once there had been terrorist training camps, there were now peaceful rural landscapes. So, the United States declared, there was no need for a commission to go to Libya, because it would not find any such camps there.

After many contacts, the three powers provided me with a "tripartite nonpaper," the contents of which I transmitted to Colonel Qaddafi in mid-August 1992. The three allies had no secret agenda; they would not make new demands after Libya fulfilled the Security Council resolutions; and the British would not extradite the two suspects if they were tried in a Scottish court, the Pan Am aircraft having been destroyed over Lockerbie, Scotland.

On April 14 the International Court of Justice decided to defer to the fact that the Security Council had taken action. But several judges wrote opinions expressing their unease that the Security Council had stepped in while the case was sub judice. This concern was not unlike that in *Marbury v. Madison,* in which Chief Justice John Marshall had established the principle of judicial review, giving the Supreme Court the power to declare null and void a legislative act repugnant to the Constitution. In this case the International Court of Justice could have challenged the Security Council on the interpretation of the Charter, but it chose not to do so at this phase of the process.

As secretary-general I was duty-bound to carry out the resolutions of the Security Council to the letter. But as a lifelong student of international law, I lamented this situation, which both disparaged international law and displayed the United Nations not as an organization of sovereign states equal under the Charter but as a political tool of the major powers.

On October 6 in New York I asked the new Libyan minister of foreign affairs, Ibrahim Bishari, why I had received no reply to the tripartite nonpaper. I warned the minister about the many lawyers and other self-appointed intermediaries who claimed to have contacts in high places; they were spreading confusion and rendering the process much more difficult.

On November 19 Libya accepted in principle that the two suspects should stand trial, but it would extradite them only in exchange for certain guarantees, a response that displeased the three powers because it simply multiplied the conditions precedent to a solution. I met with Senator Edward Kennedy of Massachusetts, who was concerned with the issue because of the Massachusetts residents killed aboard Pan Am Flight 103. I called in the Libyan ambassador to inform him that Kennedy favored an embargo on Libyan oil and to inform him that the three powers considered the Libyan response to their nonpaper unsatisfactory.

As 1992 gave way to 1993, I returned to Cairo to join my family for Christmas according to the Coptic calendar. While there I met with Omar Mustafa al-Muntasser, the new Libyan minister of foreign affairs, on January 7, 1993. He came from one of the old Libyan families and had studied at Victoria College in Alexandria. A charming and debonair spirit, he seemed able to navigate serenely in the Qaddafian labyrinth. He told me of his coming visit to New York, where he expected to take the entire affair in hand and find a rapid solution to the problem of Libya's compliance with Resolution 731.

Palestinians Deported

My first battle with the Clinton administration and, as it would later turn out, my last battle as well, was over an Arab-Israeli issue. The 1992 American presidential election voted into office a candidate who had campaigned on a domestic agenda. But at the very moment President Clinton entered office, he found himself facing a tense foreign policy challenge. One month earlier, on December 17, 1992, Israel had deported to south Lebanon more than four hundred Palestinian residents of the West Bank and Gaza. According to the Israelis, about one hundred were Islamic religious leaders. I immediately put out a statement noting that the Security Council over the years had repeatedly reaffirmed the applicability of the Fourth Geneva Convention of 1949 to the territories occupied by Israel. Such deportations were expressly prohibited. Israel had expelled the Palestinians into Lebanon in reaction to an escalation of violence in the West Bank and Gaza. I condemned the violence and urged all sides to avoid worsening the situation. Under the Geneva Convention the Israelis were obliged to rescind their decision and permit the safe and immediate return of all those deported.

The next day, December 18, the Security Council, with the Bush administration voting in favor, unanimously adopted Resolution 799, strongly condemning the Israeli action and declaring that Israel's actions contravened the Geneva Convention. The Security Council demanded that Israel return the deportees and that I send a representative to Israel and report back to the Council. To Washington, the word "demands" was understood as a first step toward recommending sanctions on Israel under Chapter VII of the Charter, a resolution that the United States would, of course, be forced to veto. The controversy was urgent, involving not only the United Nations and Israel but also the United Nations and the United States. The Israelis looked to the new Clinton administration to relieve the Security Council's pressure on them.

"It could hardly be a more desolate scene," the press reported from Marj al-Zuhour in Lebanon; "an anonymous stretch of barren hillside in the remotest corner of southeastern Lebanon. It is in the middle of nowhere. But not, it seems, a Godforsaken spot. There, on the twisting mountain road, more than 400 men are lined up in ranks, a block of humanity kneeling, prostrating themselves and rising in unison, sending the cry of 'Allahu Akbar'—God is greatest—echoing through the hills."

These, Israeli authorities claimed, were activists of Hamas and Islamic Jihad, fundamentalist organizations committed to the violent destruction of Israel. Many of them had been kept in Israeli jails under "administrative detention" for months before their deportation. But many claimed that although they supported the anti-Israel cause, they were not active in the movement and had not been in trouble with the Israeli authorities before.

At the end of December 1992 I dispatched James O. C. Jonah to the Middle East. I was then in Addis Ababa, Ethiopia, attempting to promote talks between the faction leaders of Somalia. Jonah telephoned me in Addis to say that he had run into a stone wall in Israel. The Israelis had undercut Jonah as being "nonobjective" when it came to Arab-Israeli issues. I rejected this utterly, but there was no sense in struggling with the problem. I telephoned Prime Minister Yitzhak Rabin to say that I would like to send one of my senior political advisers, Chinmaya Gharekhan of India, to the Middle East to seek a solution.

On January 4, 1993, I dispatched Gharekhan, saying that if Resolution 799 were not respected by Israel, I might have to recommend that the Council take further steps to gain compliance. A State Department official telephoned my office that same day to say that Rabin was "furious" with my statement and that Israeli Foreign Minister Shimon Peres had asked the United States to veto any further action in the Security Council. The Israelis were convinced, the State Department officials said, that they had "the U.S. veto in their pocket."

I had offered Gharekhan a compromise solution to put to Rabin: release the deportees in phases, stretched out over time, even a year or more. If we announced quickly that some would be returned—say about a hundred—the crisis would be defused. If Rabin agreed, I felt that I could sell it to the Security Council. But when Gharekhan put this to Rabin, the Israeli prime minister declared that to return a hundred would be a humiliating capitulation by Israel. Besides, Rabin said, his hands were tied. The case had been put to the Israeli Supreme Court, he said, and nothing could be done until it handed down its decision

After further discussions got nowhere, I began to suspect that the Israelis did not want to solve this problem precisely because they wanted to confront Clinton, from his first day in office as president, with a crisis. If Israel demanded that the United States veto any further UN action and Clinton, under pressure, agreed, it would set the tone for the Israeli-U.S. relationship throughout the Clinton presidency.

On January 13 in Paris, after talks with outgoing U.S. Secretary of State Lawrence Eagleburger, I met with Shimon Peres but to no avail. I called Prime Minister Rabin and asked him to accept a second visit by Gharekhan. World political pressure was mounting rapidly. I wanted to demonstrate that the United Nations was active, fair, and flexible. Above all, I wanted to resolve this crisis before Clinton became president, so that he would not enter the Oval Office facing pressure to cast the first post–cold war veto. This could turn the newly positive atmosphere in the Security Council sour. The United States would be blamed and, in turn, would blame the United Nations.

I sent a message to President Bush on January 17, asking his permission to communicate directly with President-elect Clinton. I was under enormous pressure to report to the Security Council and to recommend that steps be taken against Israel. I received no reply from Bush. I realized that at that moment he must be busy moving out of the White House.

So without Bush's permission, I passed an informal message to Clinton via the State Department and Clinton's transition team. I asked to speak to Clinton right away on an important matter and added that I very much looked forward to close and warm relations with both President Clinton and Secretary of State Christopher. The answer came back informally from an aide: "The transition is in chaos. No contact with the Clinton team is possible for the time being." I sent another message saying that I would like permission to come to Washington to meet with President Clinton and Secretary Christopher. I had cleared my calendar and would be able to meet at any time on any day between January 20 and February 12, 1993.

No answer came back in any form to my message. Gharekhan arrived in Israel on January 17 and began his second round of intensive talks. After meeting twice with Prime Minister Rabin, Gharekhan reported again that he could detect no sign of flexibility in Israel.

Many commentators had said that Secretary Christopher had been chosen in order to keep foreign policy problems out of the headlines so that President Clinton could focus on the American domestic agenda that he had been elected to address. But as I had not been able to communicate or consult with the Clinton administration beforehand, on January 20, Warren Christopher walked into his State Department office to confront the Palestinian deportation crisis, whose focal point was now the United Nations and which was getting major media attention.

On January 21 Assistant Secretary of State Edward Djerejian telephoned me "on instructions" from Secretary Christopher: "Keep Gharekhan in the Middle East. Christopher will make the pitch to Rabin on this. If it comes to another UN Security Council resolution, the U.S. will veto." In effect, the message said that the United Nations should continue to fail to find a solution, thereby giving the United States time to find that solution itself.

After Djerejian had spoken with me, his deputy in the State Department's Middle East Bureau followed up with a telephone call to my aide: "Boutros-Ghali is perceived as the driving force behind pressing for a confrontation. Christopher is *really upset* that this is developing this way." The next day, January 23, yet another call came from the State Department to my office. "Don't put the U.S. in a veto dilemma spot," was the message. "Christopher is loath to get off to a bad start." For some reason my staff did not convey this to me at the time.

I had very little room to maneuver. I could not simply let Gharekhan stay in Israel with the sole prospect of being rejected. My old friend Ezer Weizman, the president of Israel, telephoned from Jerusalem to ask me to delay my report to the Security Council, which I did, wanting to give Israel all the time it needed, within reason, to make its decision. But by January 25 I had no choice but to issue my report. In it, I said, "The refusal by Israel to ensure the safe and immediate return of deportees as demanded in Resolution 799, in my view, challenges the authority of the Security Council." In these circumstances, I added, "I would be failing in my duty if I did not recommend to the Security Council that it should take whatever measures are required to ensure that its unanimous decision, as set out in Resolution 799, is respected." The State Department conveyed a private message to my office: "Boutros-Ghali is seen down here as confrontational."

Work then began in the Security Council to draft another resolution, one that might move closer toward Chapter VII sanctions on Israel. On January 29 the Israeli Supreme Court ruled that the deportations were legal under Israeli law, as long as individual appeals were allowed. This seemed only to solidify Israel's defiance of international law and accepted practice, for it meant that collective deportations without a prior right of appeal were legal.

Lunch with Christopher and Albright

I sent a message to Secretary Christopher, inviting him to lunch on February 1, and he accepted. Shortly before Christopher was to arrive at Sutton Place, the State Department telephoned to say that it had achieved a breakthrough: Rabin had agreed to release a sizable number of the deportees, a number, the U.S. official said, "in the range of the original number proposed by Gharekhan." That number had been 100; the Israelis had just announced that they would return 101, and the rest would come out later in phases. Just before our luncheon meeting Christopher announced, "President Clinton and I are pleased to announce that, based upon intensive efforts and consultations over the last several days, there has been a breakthrough in our efforts with respect to the deportation issue."

The Israelis had scored a victory over the brand-new Clinton administration. They had obtained U.S. agreement to veto any resolution aimed at Israel. Then they had rejected the UN compromise in order to save it as a gift for the new American president. The United Nations and I had been depicted as difficult to deal with and confrontational toward the United States.

The day before my lunch with Christopher, the U.S. Mission telephoned to say that I must also invite Ambassador Albright. I did so at once. After the first course, I asked Christopher and Albright if I might speak honestly, but off the record, to them. "Mr. Secretary, Madame Ambassador," I said, "I am deeply aware that the U.S. is the major actor on the world scene. I know that I must have U.S. support if I am to succeed. I will always seek and try to deserve that support. But," I said, "please allow me from time to time to differ publicly from U.S. policy. This would help the UN reinforce its own personality and maintain its integrity. It would help dispel the image among many member states that the UN is just the tool of the U.S." To do so, I said, "would also be in the interest of the U.S. It would give the U.S. more options in its foreign policy if on some occasions it were able to use the UN credibly."

I was sure that Christopher and Albright would understand my point of view. I was completely wrong. My words appeared to shock them. Christopher and Albright looked at each other as though the fish I had served was rotten. They didn't speak. I was horrified and quickly changed the subject. A bit later I tried again. "Perhaps I was unclear," I said. "I was merely trying to propose an approach that would offer greater flexibility in both U.S. and UN diplomacy." Again there was a silence. I recalled the words of the late Israeli prime minister Golda Meir: "If you are with me ninety-nine percent, you are not with me."

It would be some time before I fully realized that the United States sees little need for diplomacy; power is enough. Only the weak rely on diplomacy. This is why the weak are so deeply concerned with the democratic principle of the sovereign equality of states, as a means of providing some small measure of equality for that which is not equal in fact. Coming from a developing country, I was trained extensively in international law and diplomacy and mistakenly assumed that the great powers, especially the United States, also trained their representatives in diplomacy and accepted the value of it. But the Roman Empire had no need for diplomacy. Nor does the United States. Diplomacy is perceived by an imperial power as a waste of time and prestige and a sign of weakness.

Once the awkward moment I created passed, lunch resumed in a pleasant way. After Christopher and Albright had departed, I sat in my study looking out over the barges and tugs in the East River and thought about what had happened. I concluded that Christopher and Albright had not really been shocked by what I said. I had been the one who was shocked. They had simply thought that I must be a fool even to raise such an idea.

The New York Times in its editorial of February 3, 1993, accused me of "taking sides" by issuing a report on Israel's deportation of Palestinians while the issue was before the Security Council. I felt that this stance, like so many such characterizations by the American media and officials in Washington, could stem only from ignorance of how the United Nations works. Security Council Resolution 799, for which the United States had voted, required me to dispatch a representative to Israel and to report back to the Council. After three such missions over the course of a month, I had had no choice but to report to the Council on January 25 that these efforts had failed to produce compliance with the resolution.

Libyan Labyrinth

On May 27, 1993, as I was about to go to North Africa to deal with the Western Sahara problem, the Libyan ambassador came to see me with an "urgent and important" message from Colonel Qaddafi. He invited me to come to Tripoli to find a definitive solution to the problem of Pan Am Flight 103. I explained that I could not change my itinerary at the last moment and proposed a meeting in Geneva or Cairo in June at the time of the OAU summit. Instead, I met in New York with Omar Mustafa al-Muntasser, who had completely changed his attitude. He was no longer flexible. He declared, legalistically, that Resolution 731 did not require Libya to extradite the two suspects. I disputed his opinion but promised that I would immediately request a legal opinion from the office of the United Nations' legal adviser, which I received at the beginning of April 1993. I explained to al-Muntasser that the resolution referred to and was based on four other official UN documents, which explicitly required the extradition of the two suspects in order that they might be judged in an American or British court. Because these documents constituted an integral part of the resolution, it was incontestable that surrender was required.

Ambassador El Houderi, who accompanied al-Muntasser, seemed unable to comprehend this juridical subtlety. "Why isn't the surrender of the two suspects mentioned in the resolution?" he asked. I repeated that there was no need for it to do so because it was explicitly based on the other official documents, which did require surrender. Al-Muntasser then said, "The secretary-general is an eminent jurist. We must respect his interpretation, even if we do not accept it."

On August 13, 1993, the United States, Britain, and France declared to the Security Council that if Libya did not hand over the two suspects by October 1, 1993, the three powers would table a new and stronger resolution against Libya. As a result, in August, Abdel Ati al-Obeidi, the

Libyan ambassador in Tunis, was put in charge of the case. He was, above all, a man whom Colonel Qaddafi trusted. Al-Obeidi had worked as a young assistant with Professor Khairy Issa, with whom I had coauthored a textbook, often reprinted, on international relations.

"In other words, I am your student," al-Obeidi said to me by way of introduction. Intelligent, extremely frank, and direct, he cleverly defended Libya's case, but it was clear that Libya wanted at all costs to avoid a new resolution by the Security Council.

The draft of just such a new resolution was presented to me on September 9 by the representatives of the three powers. Further sanctions would be imposed on Libya if it did not respond to the demands of Resolution 731 before the end of the month.

"If the Libyans deliver the two suspects, do you plan to lift the sanctions?" I asked. The three responded that they would suspend the sanctions pending the compliance of Libya with their other demands.

I insisted that if the suspects were handed over, the sanctions should be lifted; this prospect would encourage the Libyans to comply. Suspending the sanctions would only increase their suspicions that the extradition of the two suspects would simply stimulate other demands. I proposed that the new resolution be put off for two or three weeks.

On September 14, al-Obeidi presented me with a thirty-three-page Libyan memorandum filled with detailed questions about the trial of the two suspects, the definition of terrorism, the French judicial system, the procedures for lifting sanctions, and long digressions of a political and ideological order. Al-Obeidi requested that the Security Council refrain from passing a new resolution before responding to this questionnaire, which would permit Libya to comply with Resolutions 731 and 748. When I handed this memorandum over to the ambassadors of the three powers, the French ambassador asked me, "In all honesty, do you think they intend to hand over the two suspects?"

I chose my words carefully: "A response to their questionnaire might encourage them to accede to the demands of the Security Council." British Ambassador Sir David Hannay probed further for my views. Madeleine Albright, as a newcomer to this diplomatic problem, watched silently.

In the end the three ambassadors agreed to answer the Libyan questionnaire in a single document, on the understanding that certain responses might differ because the French, Scottish, and American legal systems differ. Personally I thought that Qaddafi was stalling for time again. He did not want to surrender the two suspects, one of whom was his relative. Sending them to trial might stir up opposition in Libya that could destabilize his regime. Moreover, Qaddafi was still being told by British, French, and American attorneys and agents that they could solve his problems. By delaying the UN process, Qaddafi thought he was buying time for those lawyers to find a way out for him. But with each new Security Council resolution his attorneys would tell him that they would have to start all over again.

Omar Mustafa al-Muntasser wrote to me that Libya was encouraging the two suspects to go to Scotland to stand trial. He asked for Scottish lawyers to come to Tripoli "to see the efforts we are making, to meet the two suspects, their families and lawyers and to contribute to the efforts designed to convince them to appear before the Scottish courts." As a result, on October 1, 1993, the Americans, British, and French extended their deadline by two weeks. Relatives of those killed on Pan Am Flight 103 reacted angrily. There was great political pressure in America for stronger U.S. measures against Libya.

On November 11 Security Council Resolution 883 ordered new sanctions against Libya, to take effect on December 1, 1993. These new sanctions were to be suspended if I, as secretary-general, informed the Security Council that Libya was ready to extradite the two suspects in the bombing of Pan Am Flight 103 to be tried before a British or American court.

A Gentleman's Agreement

Faced with an escalation of the confrontation by the three powers in the form of a new resolution, on the one hand, and Libya's claim to be ready to discuss a major concession, on the other, I decided to drop back to an "easier" agenda item: the issue of arms transfers to the IRA. I met often with the Libyans in Paris or Geneva to manage this case. Despite my efforts, the negotiations between Britain and Libya did not go forward. The British maintained that the information given them was not complete, and the Libyans accused the British of bad faith. In a long and candid conversation with al-Obeidi, I discovered that the Libyans were concealing certain information out of mistrust. Al-Obeidi asked, "What guarantee do we have that if we give all the information, the British will say they are not satisfied with it, just to please the Americans? We would have given up something for nothing in return."

"In other words," I said, "you want something in exchange immediately?"

Al-Obeidi smiled and responded in the affirmative: "If we give the information, what will the British give us in return?"

I restrained myself from saying, "The British declare that you are guilty; you can ask for nothing in return." I could not promise anything on behalf of Britain, so I said to the Libyan, "The only thing you can do is ask for a receipt, a document declaring that this case is closed."

Meanwhile, reports were being carried in the American press that some terrorist experts were tracing the Lockerbie bombing to Iran and charging that the United States had "jumped the gun" by blaming Libya from the outset. Tiny Rowland, the head of the private firm Lonrho (London-Rhodesia) and an influential figure in African affairs, who was working on Libya's behalf, came to see me. He had earlier helped me make contact in Addis Ababa with John Garang, the rebel leader in southern Sudan, and had played a positive role in Mozambique. Rowland had produced a television film attempting to demonstrate that the accused Libyans had had nothing to do with Pan Am Flight 103. I invited the Moroccan ambassador to watch the video with me. I found the film too long and complicated to be convincing. Nonetheless, the media reports had created some uncertainty about Libyan guilt.

In any event, al-Obeidi accepted my proposal. Now it was my job to get Libya to provide Britain with information about arms for the IRA and get the British to state their satisfaction with it. This would take me almost two years.

Israel: Prayer and Massacre

On November 12, 1993, Prime Minister Yitzhak Rabin was the guest of honor at a dinner at the residence of Israel's ambassador to the United Nations. I was asked to speak. As I began, I could see that Rabin was apprehensive about what I would say. But as I continued, Rabin slid back in his chair and relaxed. I said, "I recall the first words of the book *Joseph and His Brethren* by Thomas Mann: 'Very deep is the well of time.' Deep indeed is the well of history—and the time before history—in the Middle

East. The source of the divine spirit, the spark of human greatness, and the scar of violence all go back so far in time in that land of ours. As for my own history, I cannot remember a time when I was not emotionally, intellectually, or professionally deeply involved in the conflict of the modern Middle East. And so was my family before me. Theodor Herzl came to Cairo at the start of the twentieth century to negotiate with my grandfather for a Jewish colony in Sinai. Thirty years later, when Egypt entered the League of Nations, my uncle's speech proposed a dialogue among Jews, Muslims, and Christians and called for peace in the mandated territory of Palestine. Forty years later I officially accompanied President Anwar Sadat to Jerusalem. . . . I hope that additional generations will not be added to the well of time before comprehensive peace is achieved." The dinner took on a warm family atmosphere. The Israeli ambassador, Gad Yaacobi, said a prayer, and for a moment one could feel that peace had come to the Middle East too.

Three months later an American-born Israeli, Dr. Baruch Goldstein, from the Jewish settlement of Kiryat Arba, entered the tomb of Abraham in Hebron, sacred to both Muslims and Jews, opened fire with an automatic weapon, and shot Palestinians at dawn prayers on Friday, February 25, 1994. Between forty and fifty Palestinians were killed and more than seventy wounded. Goldstein himself was killed, beaten to death by outraged witnesses to the massacre. Stone throwing and rioting erupted throughout the West Bank and Gaza. Israeli soldiers firing on protesters killed nineteen Palestinians. Many more were wounded. More blood was shed on that Friday than on any single day since the Israeli Army had taken the territories during the 1967 war.

I had long believed that the United Nations had a legitimate and positive role to play in the Middle East. So I wrote to Prime Minister Yitzhak Rabin that same day to say that the United Nations was ready to help ease the tensions caused by these events, including—should all parties wish it and agree to it—a UN presence in Hebron. I sent a similar letter to Chairman Yasser Arafat of the Palestine Liberation Organization (PLO). James Rubin, the U.S. Mission to the United Nations' spokesman, kept up a steady barrage of attacks on my motives and declared that "we do not think the secretary-general's suggestion is particularly helpful or useful." When asked about this by an Arab reporter, I said that it was strange that I had sent a letter to *Rabin* in Jerusalem but gotten a reply from *Rubin* in New York. This brought mail accusing me of making an anti-Semitic remark. *The New York Times* reported that the Clinton administration was irritated with me because news of my letter to Rabin had come just as the United States was attempting to prevent efforts in the Security Council to pass a resolution deploring the Hebron mosque massacre. This was another version of the trouble I had encountered two years earlier involving the Security Council resolution on the deportation of the Palestinians.

A week had passed since the Hebron massacre. The United States was stalling on the resolution before the Security Council, hoping that the Israelis and the PLO would get together to issue a joint announcement that would make a resolution unnecessary. This delay was dangerous, for the time of Friday prayers was approaching, and Muslims in mosques all across the Islamic world were likely to be exhorted by fiery preachers to take violent action. I contacted the State Department to urge the United States to let some form of draft resolution go forward for Security Council consideration. This would give the United Nations a responsible role and Arab governments a way to calm the situation. To my satisfaction, the United States responded positively and let the word be passed that an American draft had been submitted *ad referendum* to the PLO. Nonetheless, it was my letter to Prime Minister Rabin and the criticism of me by the U.S. Mission to the United Nations that stuck in people's minds.

This "is the most recent of a number of quarrels between the Clinton Administration and Mr. Boutros-Ghali involving Somalia, Bosnia, and the United States failure to pay its United Nations bills on time," commented *The New York Times.* Indeed, my persistent effort to solve the UN financial crisis by urging the United States to pay up was a leitmotif running through all the disputes over regional conflicts. "There is nothing people like less than to be badgered," Madeleine Albright said, "and Mr. Boutros-Ghali has a tendency to badger."

Recalling Sadat

Sitting on the White House grounds at the September 1994 ceremony to mark the signing of the Oslo Accords, a major step forward in the Arab-Israeli peace process, I seemed to be seeing a rerun of my past. I remembered Sadat and Begin together at the same White House podium fifteen years before to mark the Camp David Agreement. I found myself among others who had been present at that earlier time. Presidents Carter and

Bush and former Secretary of State Henry Kissinger were there. I took personal satisfaction in seeing Arafat, Rabin, and Clinton do what Sadat, Begin, and Carter had done before. But as I listened and watched this new ceremony of peace, I was astonished—and appalled—that no one— not Arafat, nor Rabin, nor Peres, nor Clinton—in all their speeches ever mentioned the name of Anwar Sadat, the Egyptian leader who had started it all by going to Jerusalem.

I had tried, back in 1979 and again in 1994, to have the United Nations make a contribution to Arab-Israeli peace. There was much in the UN record in the Middle East to deplore: the pullout of UN peace-keepers from Sinai before the 1967 war; the United Nations' refusal to accept the Egypt-Israel Treaty of Peace; the Zionism-equals-racism reso-lution. Nonetheless, I had increased the United Nations' role as much as I could. I had moved the United Nations Relief and Works Agency for Palestinian Refugees in the Near East (UNRWA) office from Vienna to Gaza, despite a great bureaucratic outcry. I had appointed a special coor-dinator for UN assistance to the occupied territories, and I had worked to enhance bilateral aid to the region. Despite all this, the United Nations' role remained marginal.

I had worked with Yitzhak Rabin for many years, reaching back to my earliest service as Egypt's minister of state for foreign affairs. I was im-pressed by his intelligence and his frank convictions. On November 4, 1995, Prime Minister Rabin, who had led a rally in downtown Tel Aviv where he had joined in singing a song of peace, was assassinated by a fanatically fundamentalist Jewish terrorist. It was a terrible shock and called for the solidarity of all who sought peace in the Middle East and who would not be cowed by terrorism. As soon as I learned of the assassi-nation, I telephoned the Israeli ambassador to the United Nations, Gad Yaacobi, to say that I intended to go to Jerusalem for the funeral, and I booked myself on El Al the next evening.

Leaders from many countries paid moving tribute to Rabin at the Knesset. Rabin's death was a terrible loss, for he truly had the strength of will to be a peacemaker. At the Knesset service I felt strange about being placed in a protocol ranking above that warranted by the position of UN secretary-general; that is, I was placed above heads of state or govern-ment. I did not want to make a scene by moving elsewhere, so I reassured myself with the thought that my place in the order of protocol might be an unusual Israeli tribute to the United Nations. When my time to speak came, I took care to mention the name of Anwar Sadat, who, like Rabin, had been assassinated because he had believed in peace, but I was alone in mentioning Sadat. When the body of Yitzhak Rabin was laid in the earth, I thought, "Will this death mark the end of the time of hope that Sadat started? Are we fated to return to the hatreds of the pre-Sadat days?"

Last Round with Libya

A month after Yitzhak Rabin's death, I met with British Foreign Minister Douglas Hurd to take up Britain's demand for Libya's information about arms for the IRA. I knew that if the British were satisfied with the information provided by Libya, it would not be easy for her Majesty's government to confirm that in writing. So I said to Hurd, "You need only give me your response orally; I would provide Libya with a written document."

"Fair enough," Hurd said.

I then told al-Obeidi that if all information pertaining to Libya's support for the IRA were handed over to the British, I would provide him with a document, signed by myself, declaring that the arms-transfer case was closed. My declaration would be transmitted to the Security Council as an official document. Soon thereafter, Hurd resigned and was replaced by Malcolm Rifkind. Al-Obeidi sent me an urgent message, worried that the deal was off, but Rifkind confirmed that he was bound by Hurd's commitment.

At the beginning of 1996 the new British ambassador to the United Nations, John Weston, informed me that Britain had received all the information it had requested from the Libyans but insisted that my letter not imply that Britain had dissociated itself from the U.S. case. Weston's manner indicated mistrust in the entire process.

"It is my letter, not yours," I said. "Therefore, I am responsible for its contents, not you." Negotiation was difficult with Weston, who was less independent than his brilliant predecessor, Sir David Hannay, and more eager to follow the American lead. I was sometimes unsure whether Weston was acting on instructions from his foreign office or on his own.

The Security Council was informed that Britain was satisfied with the information it had received from Libya about the IRA.

With the momentum of this first success, I wanted to speed up Libya's compliance with Resolutions 731 and 748. But the opposite happened.

In the fall of 1996, in response to a Libyan campaign, the Arab League, the OAU, the nonaligned states, the Group of 77, and the General Assembly of the United Nations denounced the sanctions and demanded that they be lifted. I received a sharp letter from Qaddafi, expressing his bitterness over the injustice to which the Libyan people were being subjected. In a play on the name of Lockerbie, Qaddafi recalled the U.S. air attack against his country in 1986, calling it the "Locker-A Massacre" and saying it was the cause of the current crisis.

Originally Qaddafi had operated on two levels, negotiating with the three powers through me and working behind the scenes through his many go-betweens. Now he was appealing to third-world public opinion as a victim of the major Western powers. Qaddafi could point to the sanctions as an attempt by the West to humiliate the Libyan people. In April 1995, wearing his flowing robes and speaking from the Aziziyah barracks in Tripoli, Qaddafi compared his determination to get Libyan pilgrims to Mecca to the medieval Crusaders who fought to gain access for Christians to Jerusalem. "We do not want to violate the resolutions of the Security Council," Qaddafi said, "nor do we demand that any state violate them," but "Mecca is a separate affair that has nothing to do with the embargo or the Security Council resolutions."

Libya's defiance of the ban on international air travel by sending aircraft filled with Muslim pilgrims aroused sympathy, support, and pride in the Islamic world and among third-world nations for Qaddafi and his case against the West. They increasingly condemned the sanctions imposed on him by the Security Council. The forces of Islamic fundamentalism point out that in virtually every case the international community's sanctions regimes or arms embargoes are directed against, or act to the detriment of, Muslims: from Pakistan and Afghanistan, to Iraq, to Sudan, to Libya, to Bosnia.

The first item on my list—Libya's aid to the IRA—had been dealt with. Next would be to settle the French-Libyan dispute over UTA Flight 772. The standoff could not simply be ignored, for its effect on international relations went beyond Libya's position as a "pariah" state.

Near the end of my term of office, Qaddafi was furious with me. He criticized me publicly, which I took as proof that I had performed my role effectively. An active, independent secretary-general will come under fire from both sides—as I did.

Iraq: Oil for Food?

While attempting to resolve the terrorist case against Libya, I was also trying to ease the burden of sanctions on the people of Iraq. While fighting raged in the Iraq-Kuwait war, the United Nations in February 1991 sent a team to evaluate the humanitarian needs of the Iraqi people. This mission, led by Sadruddin Aga Khan, proposed the sale of Iraqi oil to finance the purchase of "foodstuffs, medicine, and materials for essential civilian needs."

On the basis of Sadruddin Aga Kahn's report, the Security Council adopted Resolution 706 on August 15, 1991, authorizing states to import Iraqi oil at the rate of $1.6 billion each six months, and provided for that sum to be deposited in an account managed by the secretary-general. Resolution 712 of September 18, 1991, described in detail the system of supervision for Operation "Oil for Food."

From this point on, "Oil for Food" became the story of my own quixotic attempt to obtain Iraq's approval of this program. The Iraqi people, not Saddam Hussein's regime, were the ones who were suffering under the sanctions. Their jobs had been lost, their children's health affected, and their general well-being reduced by the severe restrictions imposed on the flow of goods and services into and out of the country. The scheme would also generate funds to compensate thousands of expatriate workers, whose livelihoods had been at risk and their property seized or destroyed when Iraq's army had swarmed over Kuwait in 1990. The program provided for the secretary-general to transfer 30 percent of the proceeds from the sale of oil into a compensation fund that had been created by the Security Council but was still without resources.

There was virtually no international interest in the concept of oil for food. The impetus for it, such as there was, came mainly from the UN. Saddam Hussein seemed to care nothing at all for the welfare of the poorest Iraqi people; his attitude toward the negotiations would shift back and forth according to his own shadowy instincts for self-preservation or self-aggrandizement.

I first met Saddam Hussein in Baghdad during the Iran-Iraq war. I was on a mission for President Mubarak to try to get Iraq to reestablish diplomatic relations with Egypt, which Iraq had broken in reaction to Sadat's decision to make peace with Israel. The Iraqis refused my request on the grounds that, as they had led the Arab world effort to isolate Egypt, they could not be the first to reverse that policy. I argued that true leadership would never be hindered by such a precedent. Whenever I saw Saddam Hussein, he was in uniform. All his ministers wore uniforms too and saluted him in a military way. When I asked why, I was told that Iraq was in a state of war. Saddam thrived on the tension created by his claims that Iraq was perpetually threatened by an array of enemies, a claim that he used to justify the exceptional powers he assumed under a state of continuing military emergency.

The first negotiations took place in January 1992. But Iraq reversed its decision to participate in a second round. The Security Council deplored this action and declared that the government in Baghdad must assume entire responsibility for the humanitarian problems of its civilian population. In another U-turn, Iraq came back to the table in the spring of 1992, but the talks went nowhere. Again we confronted the fundamentally contradictory character of sanctions: the innocent population suffers greatly but the oppressive regime feels little or nothing, while the process only deepens its control over the people.

The following year, on June 29, 1993, I met in Geneva with Deputy Prime Minister Tariq Aziz. I pressed him to give "Oil for Food" a chance. It is not only a humanitarian program, I said, but also "contains the seeds of reconciliation between Iraq and the international community."

New talks began in July 1993 and by all appearances were successful. The UN legal adviser, Carl-August Fleischauer, came to my office looking immensely pleased. "The Iraqis have agreed," he said. "Of course, their agreement is *ad referendum*. They have gone back to Baghdad to get final approval. They'll come back to New York next week, when we may sign the agreement." I predicted to Fleischauer that this would not happen. I was right. Saddam ordered his negotiators not to return to the talks. His team did not apologize or even bother to say why.

Some speculated that Saddam was playing this game as a way to manipulate the world oil market. This was not implausible. Whenever the oil-for-food talks were reported to go well, the world market price of oil fell in anticipation of Iraqi oil coming onto the market; when Saddam Hussein broke off talks, the price of oil rose as the market expected oil supplies to tighten. I did not, however, accept this theory. Saddam Hussein thinks of himself as a romantic hero confronting the forces of evil. He is totally isolated and shielded from hard information about world affairs. He has no sense of the way international affairs are conducted, let alone the intricacies of the oil futures market. He has another logic, a logic all his own. His logic was, I believe, that the suffering of the Iraqi people was in his interest because it undermined international support for the sanctions against his regime. This was why he was always so reluctant to come to closure on "Oil for Food."

Among the five permanent member states on the Security Council, China, France, and Russia were disposed to compromise, each for its own reasons: the desire to sell goods to Iraq, the desire to buy oil, the desire that Iraq be enabled to pay what it owed them. In contrast, the United States and Britain were suspicious of Saddam but willing to see if "Oil for Food" could work. The Arab states, notably Kuwait and Saudi Arabia, were deeply hostile to any relaxation of sanctions but would never say so openly.

Parallel to the oil-for-food effort was the work of the UN Special Commission (UNSCOM), led by Ambassador Rolf Ekeus of Sweden, to ensure that Iraq gave up its weapons of mass destruction. In the hope of obtaining Iraq's cooperation on arms inspections, Ekeus left open the prospect that sanctions would be lifted in their entirety. This encouraged the Iraqis to reject every partial lifting of the embargo scheduled by Operation "Oil for Food," in the expectation that they might get rid of the embargo all at once. Thus, one UN effort tended to work against the other.

In October 1994 Iraqi troops began to deploy toward the Kuwait border, raising fears that another invasion might be at hand. As a deterrent, the United States began the movement of some 30,000 troops to the Persian Gulf region. I immediately expressed deep concern and instructed the UN Iraq-Kuwait Observation Mission (UNIKOM) to report any potentially hostile action or violation of the demilitarized zone established in 1991 at the end of the Gulf War. I called upon Iraq to immediately recognize, without qualification, the border between the two countries as defined in Security Council Resolution 833. A month later, as the result of strenuous Russian diplomacy, Saddam Hussein announced Iraq's recognition of Kuwait's sovereignty. In return, Russia pledged to work to persuade the Security Council to lift the oil embargo, but the United States continued to insist that Iraq would have to display a long-term pattern of compliance with all UN resolutions regarding weapons of mass destruction before it would agree to lift the sanctions.

CHAPTER 7

Outcomes Without Endings

(1994–1996)

In diplomacy nothing is ever settled. Anyone who expects to solve a problem and then move on will be thwarted. A problem may shift in size or shape or urgency but rarely disappears; continual effort is a necessity. This was reaffirmed by what was going on in the autumn of 1994 in the widely differing cases of Cambodia, Bosnia, Haiti, and Iraq.

Cambodia: Sihanouk's Dismay

In September 1994, while in Beijing, I requested an audience at Sihanouk's residence. Instead the king came to my quarters in the government guest house, the Diao yu Tai. He was as full of pep and sly intelligence as ever and seemed in no way weakened by his illness. "This is my first time out since I became ill," he said with a big smile. He criticized Hun Sen's government for restricting press freedom and the army for refusing to root out corruption. Complaining about the deterioration of the situation in his country, he asked, "Has all the money you spent been useless?"

"The UN was a doctor," I said. "We restored Cambodia to a state of basic health. But in the long run, the patient is responsible for his own health. A doctor can't compel a patient to live a healthy life or swallow unpleasant medicine."

Sihanouk stared out over the lake. *Diao yu tai* means "fishing pavilion," and we viewed a scene landscaped to resemble an ancient Chinese painting. "The UN should not have withdrawn," he said.

"Perhaps," I said, "but the UN lacks the money, and the Security Council lacks the will to keep the UN on the scene."

I told Sihanouk that the intense diplomatic effort and the millions of dollars spent to repatriate refugees, monitor the cease-fire, conduct elections, produce a constitution, and start to reconstruct the country had not only been worth it; it had been indispensable to the future of Cambodia. UNTAC had enabled the people to express their will freely. A legitimate if imperfect government had emerged. Cambodia, an ancient nation, had risen to its feet and regained international recognition. Beyond this, the United Nations could not, and should not, go. The United Nations' achievement was essential not only because it was comprehensive but also because it was limited in time. Building a new Cambodia, I told Sihanouk, was up to the Cambodian people themselves, and it would take decades. There would be repeated setbacks, but the UN operation had been a success.

Perhaps the United Nations' most serious mistake had come in 1993, when we had urged that the election produce a government in which all three main parties would participate. That precedent reinforced the unwillingness of the second and third parties in the 1998 election to accept the results of the ballot. A healthy democratic system for Cambodia will require a true "opposition," one that accepts an election as legitimate, serves as a check on the winning party, and works to win more votes for itself in future elections.

The Cambodian situation today has been described in the media (*The New York Times, The New Yorker, The New York Review of Books, The Economist,* August 1998) as a virtual disaster, and the government has been denounced as an oppressive dictatorship.

Some basic facts, however, are clear. The national election results of 1998, certified by dozens of international observers, some with more than a thousand people stationed around the country, as reasonably free and fair, substantially resembled the outcome of the UN-conducted elections of 1993, a further sign of their validity. No party got a majority of the votes cast by a huge turnout, and the proportion of votes going to the top three parties was about the same in 1998 as in 1993. In 1998 Hun

Sen's party came in first, but with only 41 percent. Under the election law this would require him to enter into a coalition with his opponents to form a government, hardly the kind of result associated with dictatorship. Ironically, one correspondent, Henry Kamm, in an article entitled "The Cambodian Calamity" (*The New York Review of Books,* August 13, 1998), concluded that he saw "no other way but to place Cambodia's people into caring and disinterested hands for one generation, administer it for its own sake, and gradually hand it back to a new generation of Cambodians, who will have matured with respect for their own people and will be ready to take responsibility for them." This is exactly what the United Nations had been sent to Cambodia to do, but instead of being allowed a generation to complete the work, it had been hurried out of the country in less than two years.

Bosnia: Entangled Again

A few weeks after my talk with Sihanouk in Beijing, as the situation in Bosnia continued to deteriorate in the autumn of 1994, I received a letter from NATO acting Secretary-General Sergio Balanzino saying that "in the spirit of your previous requests of 6th February and 18th April to Secretary General Woerner for increased protection of Safe Areas, the North Atlantic Council agreed that the following standards should apply to the conduct of NATO air strikes." The letter reiterated the double-key system: once both keys were turned, strikes would be conducted "without tactical warning to the offending party," and each action would be on a larger scale: "For each use of air power, a minimum of four targets will be authorized by the commander in chief of NATO's Southern Command and Force Commander UNPROFOR." But which targets were actually attacked would be determined by NATO according to tactical considerations. The new standards were in accordance with existing Security Council resolutions; my agreement was requested.

I replied that I could not agree. If the UN forces were not to be consulted about the relation between a violation and the proposed target of an air strike, reprisals would result, as at Goražde. And if the UN force had no say as to how many targets were to be attacked, the principle of proportionality would be abandoned. I cited as an example the case in September 1993 when Serbs had attacked an armored personnel carrier but inflicted no casualties. Several reprisal targets had been suggested. If all had been hit, the reaction would have been disproportionate; even the limited use of NATO airpower at that time had led the Serbs again to close Sarajevo Airport.

So I was again entangled in a dispute about air strikes, and the fundamental problem—the mandated impartiality of UNPROFOR and the denial of the means to do the jobs given it by the Security Council—had still not been addressed. I pointedly told the NATO secretary-general, "I believe you will agree with me that we should not willfully put ourselves into a position where we have to implement the contingency plans for a withdrawal of UNPROFOR in a hostile environment, which, as you are very well aware, would require the deployment of a substantial number of combat troops to extricate the peace-keeping force."

On November 30, 1994, with the situation further deteriorating and at the insistence of Madeleine Albright, who telephoned me in Morocco, where I was struggling with the Western Sahara problem, I went to Sarajevo to tell the parties that the UN force would withdraw unless a countrywide cease-fire were established. My warning, *The New York Times* reported, "which is a virtual ultimatum, amounts to an act of desperation after the worst spell in Bosnia that the UN has endured." I asked to meet Karadžić at Sarajevo Airport, but he insisted that I travel to Pale, the Bosnian Serb headquarters, to be received by him. I refused because this would signal acceptance of his "Republika Srpska" by the United Nations, and no meeting between us took place. The state of Bosnia and Herzegovina was a legitimate member state of the United Nations. Karadžić's "Republic" sought to break Bosnia apart.

Capitol Confusion

In Washington, Secretary of Defense Perry made a public comment suggesting a confederation between the Bosnian Serbs and Serbia proper with its government in Belgrade, capital of the former Yugoslavia. This, the press reported, "sent the State Department into a tailspin." I learned from *The New York Times* of December 4, 1994, that the United States had made a major policy change. When on vacation at his New England farm, the report went, Anthony Lake had written a memorandum concluding that there were inherent contradictions in trying to use NATO airpower coercively against the Bosnian Serbs when NATO-country troops were on the ground with the United Nations attempting to maintain impartiality in performing a humanitarian mission. U.S. demands for action were hurting the NATO alliance for no tangible gains, not to mention hurting the United Nations. Thus Lake recommended that the United States stop pushing for air strikes and seek a cease-fire and a diplomatic solution. The United States conveyed nothing to me directly. All I knew was what I read in the newspapers.

On December 8, 1994, the U.S. Mission to the United Nations formally conveyed to me "The following decisions, made by President Clinton." Clinton had decided "that the U.S. would participate with ground troops in a NATO-led withdrawal of allied forces in Bosnia." But "the U.S. is not in favor of a withdrawal of UNPROFOR at this point in time since it has an important humanitarian role to play. With winter approaching in Bosnia, a withdrawal would have disastrous humanitarian consequences." Nevertheless, the démarche went on, "NATO and UNPROFOR contingency plans for a withdrawal operation should be completed as soon as possible since the situation in Bosnia may deteriorate. . . . Moreover, the U.S. would only be prepared to agree to a withdrawal of UNPROFOR in the context of discussions on what steps the international community should pursue in the aftermath."

What on earth did this incoherent message mean? Was the United States saying that it intended to assist the British and French UNPROFOR units to withdraw, leaving the non–NATO nation units participating in UNPROFOR behind? I asked my UN colleagues to try to get clarification from Washington. What I wanted to know was whether the United States wanted the United Nations to pull out of Bosnia and, if so, precisely what the United States was prepared to do about it. In a few hours the answer came back, apparently from Secretary of State Christopher, that "The U.S. wants UNPROFOR to continue as is, for the time being." The U.S. message to the United Nations was "Just keep doing what you are doing." But if diplomacy fails, we were told, *then* the UN force should be withdrawn. But the United States would not agree to UN withdrawal unless the arms embargo on Bosnia were lifted, and then the United States would not assist non-NATO personnel serving with UNPROFOR to leave.

This was a recipe for a debacle. The United States was ready to provide troops to liquidate its own policy toward Bosnia but not to help it succeed. The United States would evacuate NATO troops assigned to the

United Nations but refuse to help other UN personnel. In an op-ed piece in the *Christian Science Monitor,* a former high State Department official declared, "When the UN's most powerful member fails to understand its mandate or to support its mission, it is little wonder that the UN role is marked by frustration and failure." Here at the midpoint of President Clinton's four-year term, U.S. foreign policy seemed utterly confused. Oddly enough, as if in reaction to the signs of disarray, my staff at this time received several telephone calls from embassy officials overseas. Rumors had begun to sweep through the diplomatic community that Christopher was about to be replaced as secretary of state by Madeleine Albright. Did we at the United Nations happen to notice whether Madeleine was packing her bags?

Into this morass stepped former President Jimmy Carter. When reporters asked me about Carter's decision to go to Bosnia, I recalled his mastery as a negotiator in 1978 at Camp David, where his efforts had led to the Egypt-Israel treaty of peace. "Diplomacy is a multifaceted art," I told the press, "and President Carter understands every aspect it requires: psychological, historical, religious, cultural, and personal. He achieved success then, in the mountains of Maryland, because above all he conveyed to those he encountered a sense of absolute integrity and conviction."

Once again, as in other instances when Carter intervened to rescue a muddled American foreign policy, Madeleine Albright suggested that I try to persuade Carter to stay out of it. The cases of North Korea, Haiti, and Bosnia all deeply involved the United Nations, so presumably my views would carry some weight. Albright was surprisingly open with me concerning the Clinton administration's view of Carter's intervention. "Can't you do something to stop him?" she challenged me. "I can do nothing," I said. "The UN does not possess a monopoly on diplomacy." The United States was not used to this, I said, but the United Nations was. We knew from experience that whenever the United Nations was expected to conduct a diplomatic endeavor, the United States and other permanent members of the Security Council would be diplomatically active as well and would not bother to coordinate, inform, or act in any way compatible with what they, through the Security Council, had asked the United Nations to do. So, I said to Albright, "Jimmy Carter is simply doing to the U.S. administration what the U.S. administration constantly does to the UN." Perhaps Jimmy Carter could help get us out of this confused situation. On December 16, 1994, I sent Carter a five-page letter briefing him on the state of negotiations and wishing him every success.

So at the very end of 1994 Jimmy Carter, at Karadžić's invitation, moved intensively back and forth between the Bosnian Serb and Muslim leaders and then produced a signed cease-fire—just what the Clinton administration wanted. There were negative aspects: the 70 percent of the country then held by the Serbs would remain in their hands, and Karadžić's "Republika Srpska" had been given new legitimacy. In my December 16, 1994, letter to Carter, I had informed him that the Bosnian government was "apprehensive that an open-ended cease-fire might freeze the existing military status quo to their disadvantage." That, in fact, is what Carter's intervention achieved, but with the signed agreement of Bosnian President Alija Izetbegović. Both sides agreed to an immediate cease-fire, the release of prisoners and detainees, interpositioning by UNPROFOR, and a four-month cessation of hostilities from January 1, 1995. The United States declared that the understandings arrived at by Carter were a historic opportunity that the United Nations should now develop in the form of more precise implementation agreements. Skeptics said that Karadžić had achieved acquiescence in the acquisition of 70 percent of Bosnian territory by force and a respite during the winter months just to prepare for the Serbs' spring campaign.

On March 31, 1995, the Security Council welcomed the Carter-negotiated cease-fire and adopted three resolutions that restructured the UN presence in the former Yugoslavia. The newly independent republics had become increasingly unhappy that a single force should be operating in all of them; each wanted its own tailor-made and separately titled UN force. So UNPROFOR, whose original mandate had related to Croatia but had then been extended to Bosnia and Macedonia, was split into three—UNPROFOR in Bosnia, UNCRO in Croatia, and UNPREDEP in Macedonia—with an overall commander and his staff located with my special representative, Akashi, in Zagreb, the capital of Croatia. But then Croatia terminated the UN mission there, an ominous sign of hostilities to come.

During the first quarter of 1995, when the cease-fire negotiated by Jimmy Carter was in place and winter had set in, action in Bosnia eased. Tensions between the United States and the United Nations eased, and once again I could turn my attention to Haiti.

Haiti: The Changing of the Guard

The American and multinational forces would depart, it was decided, on March 31, 1995. In spite of—or perhaps because of—our fears, the relief of the American and multinational force by the United Nations took place without difficulty. The transition had been prepared meticulously by my special representative, Lakhdar Brahimi, first in New York and then in Port-au-Prince, where he set up his office in February 1995. The handover took place so smoothly that the Haitian population scarcely noticed the difference between the UN and U.S. phases of the operation. In fact, about two thirds of the military component and one third of the police force component came from the multinational force, with the United States furnishing the largest military contingent. The commander of the military component was American, and the commander of the police was Canadian; they were overseen by an Algerian. The international dimension of the UN presence was respected, as the military force comprised troops from twenty-one countries.

The ceremony for the changing of the guard was set for March 31, and President Clinton was to participate. My UN colleagues asked me to come one day earlier to show the blue flag. "With President Clinton present, the media won't even look at you," a young colleague said.

Prime Minister Smarck Michel and Foreign Minister Claudette Werleigh met me at Port-au-Prince Airport. They wanted to discuss the elections. They needed offices so they could open voting stations. "You couldn't rent some houses?" I asked. No, explained the prime minister. Years of intimidation had left few people prepared to visibly associate themselves or their houses with an election. "Then set up the voting stations in the schools," I said. "It's not necessary to close the entire school, just one or two rooms." Again the prime minister was negative: "During the 1987 elections families would not send their children to schools sheltering voting stations."

Our arrival at the hotel put an end to this discussion, which revealed the formidable attitudinal obstacles to democratization in Haiti. The hotel had a great deal of charm, with an unimpeded view over the city. In the bathroom I found ants. This gave me great joy. In Egypt, in the third world, ants are part of our everyday life and share our daily bread with us. I love to contemplate them as they transport bread crumbs or twigs.

Lakhdar Brahimi knocked on my door, interrupting my daydreaming. I was to go meet the prime minister. With its armored car in the lead, the American unit responsible for my security took me to the prime minister's residence while he was waiting for me at his office. When we finally met, our talk was brief, fruitless, and somewhat strained. I was then taken to President Aristide, where our talk turned again to the question of how to get places to serve as voting stations. That evening Aristide held a sumptuous dinner for me, which concluded with lengthy speeches in French. Mine was a standard and boring text written by a tired bureaucrat; his was improvised, brilliant, and vibrant.

When I returned to the hotel, the Haitian night was oppressively hot. I looked for the ants in the bathroom again, but they had departed, so I found myself alone, weighed down by the food from the presidential dinner and the problems facing Haiti.

The next day, we gathered in the ballroom of the presidential palace for more speeches. In a preliminary tête-à-tête with Aristide I found him in a somber mood, even less conciliatory than he had been a year earlier, when we had met alone in New York. Soon Aristide, Clinton, and I were led to a newly built podium in front of the presidential palace. Photographers and cameramen were to the left of the stand, the best place to get pictures, but the American president had to be on the right for reasons of precedence. I was oblivious to this teleprotocol until made aware of the frantic but vain efforts the Americans had made to avoid this situation. The White House wanted to make this ceremony an American victory celebration; my entourage wanted to feature the United Nations. The Americans, of course, won the contest. Even so, Madeleine Albright was overheard complaining about the number of "UN people" on the platform. Trying to be a good diplomat, I was ready to disappear, leaving the place of honor to the politicians who need it.

After President Clinton's address, I spoke in French, delivering my final words in Creole, which won me frenzied applause. President Aristide then took the floor and improvised a speech in French, interspersed with Creole. His sentences sent a series of shocklike impulses resonating through thousands of Haitians galvanized by this exceptional orator. Having experienced several of Aristide's performances, I was more interested in observing President Clinton, who seemed to be regarding this spectacle as an opportunity to learn Aristide's secret of electrifying the crowd. The ceremony ended, we congratulated one another, and then we left Haiti with a shared recognition that the story of Haiti's recovery was far from over.

Iraq: Ceaseless Circularity

Considering the worsening food and health situation of the Iraqi people, in April 1995 the Security Council prepared to adopt Resolution 986, which would allow Iraq to sell $2 billion in oil over six months in exchange for $1.3 billion worth of food, medicine, and humanitarian supplies. The rest would go to compensate victims of Iraq's aggression and meet the expenses of the United Nations' inspection and compensation programs. The vote on Resolution 986 was postponed for twenty-four hours so that I might obtain Baghdad's agreement. On the afternoon of April 14 I met with Tariq Aziz at Sutton Place. Knowing he was a Catholic, I stressed the symbolic value of the resolution's being adopted on Good Friday, but he did not appreciate my remark. He objected to the resolution because it focused on Iraq's northern provinces, which constitute Kurdistan, and because it would require that most of the oil be exported via the Kirkuk pipeline to Turkey. I ardently defended the resolution, emphasizing that it mentioned Iraq's territorial integrity and sovereignty. Moreover, the text authorized the secretary-general, not the Security Council, to approve Iraq's food distribution plan and posed no obstacle to lifting the sanctions totally if Iraq met its conditions. "This resolution," I said, "could reestablish confidence between Iraq and the international community."

"Look," I said to Tariq Aziz, "in eight months the American election year begins. If you don't accept this resolution, we will not return to this issue until the end of 1996 if President Clinton is elected or even a year beyond that if he is not elected."

Tariq Aziz listened, smoking his Havana cigar, his face displaying the slight tic that appeared at moments of tension or fatigue. I knew the decision would be made by Saddam Hussein. I knew that Iraq had a greater goal: to prevent any international supervision of the production of Iraqi oil and to obtain, sooner or later, the end of the embargo.

Resolution 986 was passed unanimously on April 14, 1995. The next day, Baghdad announced its refusal to accept it. "Oil for Food" collapsed again. Despite the recommendations of my colleagues, who argued that I would be accused of bias toward Iraq, I met later in the year with Saddam Hussein's brother, Iraq's representative to the UN office in Geneva. Again I argued in favor of Resolution 986. "Agree to negotiate," I said. "You can withdraw at any time from the negotiations if you are not satisfied, and you can always stop producing oil. The key is in your hands. Why delay? Once the American election year starts, Washington will not want to show flexibility toward Iraq by signing such an agreement." But again my arguments got nowhere.

UN50 Celebrations in Excess

Lasting throughout the 1995 calendar year, the United Nations' fiftieth anniversary celebrations were conducted under an American cloud. In Bosnia, Somalia, and Rwanda, the United States had respectively abused, scapegoated, and obstructed UN peacekeeping operations, placing the future of UN peacekeeping in doubt. More immediate was the UN financial crisis, exacerbated by Washington's refusal to pay.

The world outside the United States saw a solid record of UN accomplishment and a significant effort under near-impossible conditions to adapt to the new responsibilities of the post–cold war period, but in the United States, the United Nations was called an inefficient and bloated bureaucracy and—laughable though this was—a danger to American sovereignty.

I had hoped to arrange a Security Council summit for January 1995 to mark three years after the first historic UN summit that had called forth *An Agenda for Peace.* I raised the idea with Argentinean President Carlos Saúl Menem, because Argentina would hold the Security Council presidency during January 1995. Menem liked my idea, but resistance arose in the Security Council. Peacekeeping had become too controversial a topic to risk discussion by the world's most powerful countries in such a prominent forum. So no second UN summit took place. Instead, I set out to use UN50 to demonstrate that my efforts at reform were real and to try to persuade critics that the United Nations was an indispensable mechanism for achieving the goals sought by the world's nations, including the United States.

Dr. Waldheim's Request

On June 16, 1993, I had addressed the Austrian Parliament, the first secretary-general to be invited to do so, I was told, since Trygve Lie had spoken there some four decades earlier. I decided to speak on human rights in the context of views I had heard at the Vienna World Conference on Human Rights. As I was delivering my speech, I looked up at the visitors' gallery, which had been closed to the public. Only one man sat there: Kurt Waldheim. About a year later I received a letter from the mayor and governor of Vienna, Dr. Helmut Zilk, telling me of the preparations under way to mark UN50 in Austria. October 24, 1995, would also be, he wrote, "no doubt a reunion of all those eminent personalities who over the years have held the office of Secretary-General of the United Nations. I hope," the letter went on, "it is not inappropriate to ask you to assist Dr. Waldheim in being able to travel to the United States to attend the celebrations, and I most sincerely appreciate your understanding."

In 1987 the attorney general of the United States had placed the name of Kurt Waldheim on the U.S. Immigration and Naturalization Service's "Watch List" of undesirable aliens prohibited from entering the United States. Under U.S. law, the borders of the United States were to be closed to any and all alleged war criminals and Nazi collaborators—that is, any alien who, in the view of the attorney general, had "ordered, incited, assisted, or otherwise participated in the persecution of any person because of race, religion, national origin or political opinion" during the 1933–1945 Nazi era. A year earlier, in March 1986, after Waldheim had concluded his second five-year term as secretary-general of the United Nations and while he was campaigning for the presidency of Austria, reports emerged that Waldheim, while serving as an officer in the German Army in World War II in the Balkans, had participated in what in 1994 would become known as "ethnic cleansing."

Nothing like the U.S. decision to bar Waldheim had ever happened before. Waldheim was the head of state of Austria, a friendly neutral country with which Washington had full diplomatic relations. And now I was being asked to get the United States to acquiesce in Waldheim's coming to New York for a UN celebration.

On the one hand, how could I not invite a former secretary-general of the United Nations? The United States had supported him twice with its vote for his election as secretary-general and even backed him for an unprecedented third term until Waldheim had dropped his candidacy in the face of opposition from China, which wanted the next secretary-general to come from the developing world. Waldheim had not been convicted of any crime. And he was the freely elected leader of a democratic country. Moreover, there was what was called the Headquarters Agreement, under which the United States obligated itself to allow representatives of other nations to come to the United Nations regardless of Washington's political or policy position toward them. The United Nations could not function if the United States insisted on being the "bouncer" at the door.

On the other hand, I realized full well that the U.S. government would never allow Waldheim to enter the country; or if it did, it might be only to arrest him if it had the evidence to do so. In 1988 the United States had barred Yasser Arafat from coming to speak at the United Nations because he was on the Watch List, charged by the United States with involvement in terrorism. The United States would certainly do it again in the case of Waldheim. I could invite him and let the United States take the praise or blame for the consequences. But such a controversy would not be good for the United Nations. It would strain the U.S.-UN relationship ever further, and it would be another example of the United States' capacity to exercise political domination over the United Nations whenever it suited it to do so.

At this very time the U.S. Department of Justice, which to my knowledge was unaware of the issue of Waldheim's attendance at UN50, released its 1987 report, which was the basis upon which Attorney General Edwin Meese III decided to put Waldheim's name on the Watch List. The report stated that Waldheim's German Army unit had been responsible for the deaths of 1,200 Greek Jews who had been placed on board barges that were then scuttled in the Mediterranean. "The portrait of Waldheim that emerges from the report is that of a canny and amoral functionary who went out of his way to sacrifice innocent victims on the altar of his ambition" was one analysis in the press.

I consulted the United Nations' legal counsel, who informed me that "While the case of Mr. Waldheim can be seen as a legal matter, it is essentially a political issue and should be dealt with as such. . . . Informal soundings could be conducted with the United States authorities and in the light of their reaction we could decide how to proceed." On the basis of this, I asked my chief of staff to reply to Mayor Zilk in a general, noncommittal way. With regard to this matter Jean-Claude Aimé wrote on April 7, 1994, without mentioning Waldheim's name, "Your observations have been noted and will be borne in mind as arrangements are finalized." I did not feel a need to address this issue directly at that time; I felt it was better to wait and see what developed. I asked one of my aides to make the State Department aware of the issue so there would be no surprises. I did not ask for Washington to give me its position or its advice, but word came back that the State Department would be grateful if I would handle this matter in a way that would not put the administration in a difficult or embarrassing position.

Alois Mock, the foreign minister of Austria, discussed the matter with me several times and then presented me with a memorandum rejecting the "renewed slander" of Waldheim. Mock gave me a private message as well: Invite Waldheim, and he won't come; either he'll decide not to, or the United States will bar him. That is our proposed compromise to you. I discussed this with my staff, some of whom had worked with Waldheim when he was secretary-general. "We know him," they said. "If you invite him, he *will* come, and *you* will be embarrassed." Again, I decided to wait and do nothing for the time being.

As the Forty-ninth General Assembly was opening and autumn was arriving in New York, I received a remarkable letter from Waldheim. Above all, it was physically impressive, written on rich, stiff paper, each page longer by a third than regular stationery. Waldheim's signature was also larger-than-life-size. Such a letter made me feel as if I were the recipient of a papal bull in medieval times.

"I have long hesitated to bother you with my personal problems arising from my military service during the Second World War and the regrettable fact that in April 1987 the US-Ministry of Justice has put [*sic*] my name on the so-called watch-list which forbids my entry into the United States. With the recent publication of my file by the Attorney-General in Washington 7 years (!) later a new but brief revival of the media campaign had taken place without no new elements or any evidence for personal guilt." The Austrian Embassy in Washington, Waldheim said, had officially rejected the accusations and asked the United States for "a revision of the case." Two British inquiries, Waldheim said, had come to the conclusion that the accusations and allegations against him were unfounded.

"Recently some newspapers raised the question of my possible attendance of the 50th anniversary of the UN next year," Waldheim wrote. "The Mayor of New York, Mr. Giuliani—when asked about it—was very careful in his answer referring the matter to the United Nations.

"It is in this context that I thought it important for you to have my personal explanation and the attached memorandum of the Austrian Government which puts the record straight. Needless to say that the big powers before electing me twice to the high office of UN-Secretary General have—I am sure—carefully examined my political and military record."

Again I consulted the UN legal counsel, who suspected that Wald-heim's letter was an attempt to involve me in an effort to seek a review of the case by competent authorities. Under Secretary-General for Legal Affairs Hans Corell again reviewed for me the United States' commit-ment not to impede invitees of the United Nations "in their transit to and from" UN headquarters in New York and to issue the necessary visas promptly. Corell also went over the "national security reservation" under which the United States reserved to itself the right "to bar the entry of those who represent a threat to [its] security." The United Nations had never accepted or recognized this reservation, Corell said. Indeed, the United Nations took the legal position that the Headquarters Agreement required unrestricted access to UN invitees. Again I was advised by coun-sel that this matter was "quintessentially political" and that I should "take it up informally with the U.S. and decide how to proceed depend-ing upon their reaction."

Some on my staff urged me to remain noncommittal and to wait. Others urged action, fearing that the longer I delayed, the more Wald-heim's attendance would become a focus of the New York media, direct-ing unwanted and politically damaging attention to the UN and me. Equally important, these advisers said, would be for me *not* to follow legal counsel's advice to take this up with the U.S. government and pro-ceed in light of its reaction; I must make the decision on my own.

Gillian Sorensen, whom I had put in charge of UN50, was worried: "Local groups have advised me that if he comes there will be major demonstrations. Dr. Waldheim and his past could become *the* story, quite apart from the historic UN commemoration." The matter will not go away, Sorensen added, "and has potential to embarrass us all and create vast negative press coverage."

In November 1994 the Simon Wiesenthal Center of Los Angeles urged me not to invite Waldheim. Rabbi Martin Hier of the center declared that Waldheim's record had "forever disgraced him and diminished the office of the chief executive of the world's most important human rights address." Privately, some American Jewish leaders indirectly hinted that my decision on this matter would have a bearing on my own reelection as secretary-general. "Thank you," I said. "I will continue to study the matter."

Whatever the truth about Waldheim's service in Hitler's Wehrmacht, it was indisputable that he had concealed that period of his life and that those UN member states who had supported his election and reelection as secretary-general had done so in ignorance of this (unless one or another of the "big powers" had, as Waldheim suggested, "carefully examined" his record and themselves covered it up).

I telephoned my predecessor, Pérez de Cuéllar; he and Waldheim were the only other living secretaries-general. "I need your help," I said. "If I were to invite you to the Fiftieth Anniversary and not Waldheim, it would be a mess. But if you will agree to go along with it, I would let it be known that I do not intend to issue any invitations to UN50 for former secretaries-general or former presidents of the General Assembly."

"Can't you find some other solution?" Cuéllar asked. "Can you provide me with another solution?" I asked in reply. "No," Cuéllar said, "so I'm ready to help you."

I telephoned Kurt Waldheim and told him that I would not be inviting former secretaries-general or presidents of the General Assembly because I could not justify spending the money to do so in the present UN financial crisis. Waldheim immediately telephoned Cuéllar, who confirmed that he, too, would not be invited. On February 1, 1995, *The New York Times* reported my decision, stating that "the move avoids a confrontation with Washington."

No one remarked upon my decision, positively or negatively. But I immediately came under pressure from the living former presidents of the General Assembly. "Why don't you invite us?" they demanded. They were frustrated and unhappy with me. The General Assembly, I was told, was ready to pass a resolution calling for all the ex-presidents to be invited. In UN protocol terms, the president of the General Assembly outranks the secretary-general. Again I said that the United Nations could not afford it. "Invite them, but say that you can't pay; then only the one or two of them who actually are willing to pay for their own airfare will come." No, I said, I have promised to invite no one.

Later in the year I went to Vienna, where one of the major UN offices is located, to celebrate UN50 with its staff. When Kurt Waldheim invited me to lunch at his residence, the topic never came up. Photographs of our luncheon meeting were taken and published in the Austrian press, which noted that although most visiting officials refused to be photographed with Waldheim, Boutros-Ghali was not one of them.

A few months later, on January 25, 1996, I heard from Waldheim again. He sent me an excerpt from a book published "by a former agent of Mossad, the clandestine Israeli service." The book alleged that in 1987 agents had secretly entered the United Nations' archival storage building on Park Avenue South and placed several incriminating documents into Waldheim's file "for future use" and that the documents had been "discovered" by Benjamin Netanyahu, then Israel's ambassador to the United Nations, as part of a smear campaign against Waldheim, who was critical of Israeli activities in South Lebanon.

I ordered an investigation of the UN archives. On May 22, 1996, I wrote to Waldheim to say that based on a careful review of the archives, "it has been concluded that there is no foundation for the allegation made in the book that United Nations archives were tampered with." The "discovery" of the Waldheim file was not made in the UN archives. There were no "documents" in Waldheim's file other than a single standardized form that contained little but identifying information.

In view of all this, I was interested in the *New York Times* column of June 24, 1996, written by my friend Abe Rosenthal, the former managing editor of the *Times*. My interest was heightened by the fact that the United States had just declared publicly that it would cast a veto to bar me from a second term as UN secretary-general.

Rosenthal wrote, "Did the U.S. know when it backed [Waldheim] for Secretary-General that he had been put on the A list of war-crime suspects, adopted in London in 1948. . . . If not, isn't that real strange, since a U.S. representative on the War Crimes Commission voted to list him? A report was sent to the State Department. . . . And when he was running for Secretary-General why did State Department biographies omit any reference to his military service—just as he forgot to mention it in his autobiographies. How did Mr. Waldheim repay the U.S. for its enduring fondness to him? Twice it pushed him successfully for the job. The third time it was among few countries that backed him again but lost. Nobody can say the U.S. wasn't loyal to the end."

I wondered myself. Why, in 1988, had Washington seemed to welcome confrontation by turning Yasser Arafat away from the United Nations as a demonstration of U.S. policy but now, in 1995, wanted the Waldheim case resolved quietly and without controversy?

Cherchez la Femme

If the Clinton administration gave me any credit for solving its Waldheim problem, it soon evaporated in the heat of a dispute that seemed to irritate Albright more than any previous issue between us. The case of the selection of a director for the United Nations Children's Fund (UNICEF) reveals in microcosm how differences could arise between me and the American administration.

In January 1995, with the end of the term of James P. Grant, a popular and tremendously effective director of UNICEF, Madeleine Albright informed other countries of President Clinton's desire that the job go to Dr. William Foege, an epidemiologist and former head of the U.S. Centers for Disease Control and an associate of the Carter Center in Atlanta.

When Albright came to inform me that Dr. Foege had been selected by the United States, I recalled that President Clinton had pressed me to appoint him when we had met in the Oval Office in May 1994. I replied to her as I had then to President Clinton: that while Dr. Foege was without doubt a distinguished person, unfortunately I could not comply. As I had told President Clinton, I was personally and publicly committed to increasing the number of women in the top ranks of the United Nations and UNICEF would particularly benefit from a woman's leadership. Belgium and Finland had already put forward the names of outstanding women candidates. The United States had been the biggest contributor to UNICEF, and since its founding in 1946, its director had always been an American. Today, because the Scandinavian countries were the largest contributors, because the United States refused to pay its UN dues, and because Washington increasingly disparaged the United Nations, there was no longer automatic acceptance by other nations that the director of UNICEF must inevitably be an American man or woman. Under established procedures the decision was for the secretary-general to take, in consultation with the thirty-six UN member states who sat on the UNICEF board. In practical terms this meant that I would have to conduct a lengthy and careful political and diplomatic effort with the board in order to achieve a consensus behind the person I would eventually name. "The U.S. should select a woman candidate," I told Albright, "and then I will see what I can do." Albright rolled her eyes and made a face, repeating what had become her standard expression of frustration with me.

On March 7 Albright's deputy Edward Gnehm came to see a member of my staff. "The U.S. is very unhappy with Boutros-Ghali for his refusal to accept Foege and for his insistence that the U.S. put up a woman nominee," he said. "Twenty months of U.S. effort has gone into putting Foege across. The secretary-general does not seem to understand that President Clinton cannot be seen to be backing away from another of his nominees."

The question is, Gnehm said, "Can Madeleine take the secretary-general's statement as a commitment? If the U.S. picks a woman, can it be assured that Boutros-Ghali will support her?" My answer was "Yes, if the woman is qualified." The Clinton administration then gave me the names of four women, each of whom I met for a long and searching discussion. At the same time, all through March, I met with other countries' representatives and nominees for the UNICEF job. There was a substantial body of opposition to any U.S. candidate because of resentment over Washington's refusal to pay its UN dues, a mood exacerbated by the fact that at this moment, an assault on the United Nations was taking place in the U.S. Congress. Senator Dole's "Peace Powers Act" would require peacekeeping assessments to be reduced by the amount of direct and indirect Defense Department support. The act would unilaterally reduce the U.S. peacekeeping assessment and provide criminal penalties for U.S. officials who failed to notify Congress concerning U.S. military or financial support of proposed UN peacekeeping activities. This might mean, for example, that the United States could charge the United Nations for U.S. military activities in Somalia that were entirely independent of the UN mission there.

In the House of Representatives, the "National Security Revitalization Act would," Congressman Lee Hamilton said, "probably end U.S. participation in UN peacekeeping operations [and] and leave the UN owing the U.S. money." One columnist wrote, "Is the Contract with America a contract on the United Nations?" *The Wall Street Journal* of April 19, 1995, called UN bashing "fun, but risky spring sport" and noted that the anti-UN sentiment flowed out of the U.S. experience in Somalia and that the rhetoric in Congress was that "the U.S. is being led around by the UN, that American soldiers are being forced to serve UN commanders, that UN bureaucrats are making American foreign-policy decisions"— conclusions that were absolutely incorrect.

Most remarkably, the Washington politicians were out of touch with the American people. A *Los Angeles Times-Mirror* poll of February 1995 found that 62 percent of the American people had a favorable view of the United Nations. And Daniel Yankelovich poll data indicated that the American public did not want the United States to be the go-it-alone policeman of the world and that Americans liked the idea of working with other countries and with the United Nations. In this context the task of convincing the world that a U.S. citizen should again get the job of UNICEF director grew harder, even as Albright was increasingly pressur-

230 · *Boutros Boutros-Ghali*

ing me, with swiftly rising annoyance, to put an American woman candidate across to the world. I was doing my best, but it wasn't easy. On April 5, 1995, I told Albright that it would take me a little longer to line up key countries behind an American candidate. Instead of giving me some leeway, the United States began running its own political campaign for an American woman as UNICEF director without informing or coordinating with me. The United States was making my task more difficult at the same time that it was complaining to me that my effort had not succeeded. Many countries on the UNICEF board were angry and telling me to tell the United States to go to hell.

Gnehm again came to my staff under Albright's instructions. "She is looking bad in D.C.," Gnehm said. "She says Boutros created this by insisting on a woman. She says Boutros said he would take care of it, but Boutros hasn't delivered."

The United States had assumed that the top UNICEF job would remain in American hands, and it wanted to pick the specific American: Dr. Foege. By insisting on a woman, I had opened the search to non-American candidates as well as the women on Clinton's list. This alarmed Albright, who told me bluntly, "If an American is not elected, it will be a defeat for me personally." The decision really was not mine; it was the prerogative of the UNICEF board, composed of UN member states. I worked privately and unofficially, but vigorously, to build support for the American woman I had picked from the Clinton list after serious deliberation: Carol Bellamy. Bellamy was the director of the Peace Corps, a superbly qualified and tough person whom I could unreservedly support. I asked the president of the UNICEF board to take a straw poll of the members. There were fifteen votes for Elizabeth Rehn of Finland and twelve votes for "the American candidate." The remaining votes were scattered. I asked the president of the UNICEF board to try to convince the member states that the United States should retain its monopoly over UNICEF leadership despite its massive arrears in UN dues and Washington's slanderous distortions of the United Nations' record.

After many long and difficult talks in which the board president argued, pleaded, and cajoled, I finally achieved a consensus of the board to accept Carol Bellamy. But I had lost credit with Washington for defying its original decision. And I gained the further enmity of Madeleine Albright because the time it took me to build a consensus for an American woman as UNICEF director "made [her] look bad" in the eyes of the

White House. Despite my efforts to keep the post in American hands, I had displeased the Clinton administration.

Celebration in San Francisco

The first major events to mark the United Nations' fiftieth anniversary centered around June 25, 1995, when San Francisco was to commemorate the signing of the UN Charter in that city at the end of the Second World War. I decided to use this occasion to make my case, in every detail, for why the United Nations was a positive factor for U.S. interests and why the United States should therefore pay its dues and treat the United Nations with respect.

In San Francisco on Sunday, June 25, at an interfaith service in Grace Cathedral atop Russian Hill, I said that fifty years ago, the delegates at San Francisco in 1945 had been asked to "compete with one another not for primacy of power but for primacy of unselfishness." Today, I said, we had to ask ourselves how far we had carried the torch that was lit in San Francisco.

Those at the cathedral service were moved by an impressive prayer and song delivered by Baha'i women. Few of those present realized that the women were singing in Farsi, a matter of significance, since the Baha'i faith has been branded heretical by the Islamic government of Iran and Baha'i followers have been brutally persecuted. On Monday, June 26, I joined President Clinton in commemorating the signing of the UN Charter. I was then invited to meet with the president in an office set aside for him in the San Francisco Veterans Building. Christopher, Albright, and Lake were present. I was invited to report on the full range of UN issues of the moment. I covered Haiti, East Timor, Liberia, Tajikistan, Burundi, Western Sahara, Guatemala, Macedonia, Iraq, and more. It seemed as if the president was in no hurry and was enjoying my lengthy *tour d'horizon,* which he called "heartening."

I caused a stir at San Francisco with my statement to the United Nations Association of the USA, a private organization of pro–United Nations American citizens. Against near-hysterical opposition from my UN colleagues, I directly addressed perhaps the major complaint from Washington: that the United States was asked to pay too much in UN dues. I announced that I favored a significant restructuring of the scale

232 · *Boutros Boutros-Ghali*

of assessments to reflect the current ability of member states to bear their fair share.

Departing from my prepared text, I even suggested a cap on assessments of 15 or 20 percent of the total budget—far below the established U.S. assessment of 25 percent. Later, some of the harshest American critics of the United Nations pressed for a U.S. level of 20 percent by the year 2000, but when I called for a 15 percent cap on assessments, no one paid attention. Being anti–United Nations was smart politics in America.

Not a single Republican member of Congress came to San Francisco for UN50. The feeling behind the bipartisan founding of the United Nations was long gone. President Clinton's remarks at San Francisco, on the other hand, echoed my own speeches as he spoke of cooperation between the United Nations and United States. In the Washington media it was being said, somewhat cynically but not without some truth, that the Republicans wanted the United States *out* of the United Nations because, as neo-isolationists, they did not want to project American power abroad. The Democrats, on the other hand, wanted the United States *in* the United Nations because they were focused on their domestic social agenda and did not want to project American power abroad. For the conservative right, the United Nations was a malevolent magnet, drawing the United States into foreign problems. For the liberal left, the United Nations provided a useful way to appear to be doing something about a foreign crisis while avoiding direct U.S. involvement.

Late in the day in San Francisco a telephone call came from Egypt telling me there had been an assassination attempt against President Mubarak, who was visiting Addis Ababa, Ethiopia. The assassination of President Sadat appeared in my mind's eye. Feelings of love for Egypt welled up in my heart. I wondered what I was doing so far from my country. Being in California seemed like pointless escapism. I had been invited to a reception for President Clinton at the home of a major Democratic supporter. Instead, I caught the next plane to New York, where at least I would feel closer to Egypt and Africa.

Bosnia: Season of Decision

Carter's cessation-of-hostilities agreement in Bosnia expired on May 1, 1995, despite Akashi's persistent effort to renew it. By the end of the first week in May, fighting in Sarajevo was the heaviest in more than a year. On May 7 a mortar attack near Sarajevo killed ten Bosnians. Shelling by both Bosnians and Serbs increased to the highest level in more than a year. My special representative Thorvald Stoltenberg and the overall UN force commander, General Bernard Janvier, opposed air strikes. General Rupert Smith, the UN commander in Bosnia, favored them. I felt that I had to accept the advice of Janvier, the overall commander, and of Stoltenberg. I worried, as always, that air strikes would be followed by Serb retaliation—probably hostage taking—against UN personnel. But if the UN commanders on the ground asked for air support, I was ready to back them up.

On May 12, I convened a meeting with Stoltenberg, Akashi, Janvier, and Smith in a first-floor salon in the Hôtel Crillon in Paris. As we were discussing the United Nations' options in Bosnia, a letter arrived from British Foreign Minister Douglas Hurd protesting my decision to accept General Janvier's recommendation over that of General Smith, a protest that would never take place in a national army. The civilian government would decide the policy, and the general in charge would carry it out. If the second in command did not follow orders, he would be fired. But Janvier was French and Smith was British, so they could argue without fear of dismissal by their respective national governments, and the British government could argue with me. These serious matters were interrupted when the United Nations was presented with a bill for the use of the salon. I lost my temper over this petty indignity and threatened that I would never return to the Crillon. The charge was canceled even as we continued meeting.

Both Janvier and Smith were convinced that the fighting would escalate and that UN personnel would be taken hostage. In fact, they already were hostages in that they were trapped and virtually defenseless inside the "safe areas." Janvier and Smith saw no future for the UN force under these conditions. The choice for the United Nations, they felt, was either, under a new mandate, to wage war or to draw in the UN presence through redeployment out of the safe areas. Such a move would eliminate the greatest barrier to the use of NATO power: the vulnerability of UN personnel to being taken hostage by the Bosnian Serbs in retaliation for air strikes. I strongly favored drawing in and drawing down the UN operation. I asked Janvier and Smith to take this option to the NATO chiefs and then come to New York to present it to the Security Council.

On May 16 there was heavy fighting around Sarajevo and along the Serb-controlled road to Pale with sustained use of heavy weapons. UN civilian and military casualties were increasing. "It appears," I said in the Security Council that day, "that the current mandate of the UN forces, with its complexities and contradictions, is neither desirable nor sustainable and will lead to further frustration for the Force and the troop-contributing countries, continued disillusionment by the parties, and increased risks to the security of UN personnel on the ground." On May 22 I got out a yellow pad and summarized the situation for myself: "Neither General Janvier nor General Smith believes that air strikes will work on an individual or selective basis—only sustained air strikes might make an impact, but they would produce many casualties if UNPROFOR remains deployed as it is." My conclusion was "Redeploy and reduce the number of UN troops." But when Janvier briefed the Council on May 24, his remarks aroused great opposition from the United States. Madeleine Albright furiously attacked Janvier's presentation as "flatly and completely wrong." Janvier was trying to "dump the safe areas," she said, and she announced that the United States would not accept the proposal to draw in UN personnel to make them less vulnerable.

It was a bizarre paradox. The United States was singularly outspoken in its demands for air strikes, but, by opposing UN redeployment, the United States was making a major NATO air assault impossible, because unless the UN could draw in its personnel, those UN troops would remain exposed to the risk of being taken hostage. The United States wanted to continue its rhetorical calls for air strikes but refused to take the steps required to carry them out.

Hostages Taken, as Predicted

On May 22, 1995, heavily armed Bosnian Serb soldiers forced their way past a small, lightly armed French Blue Helmet unit on the outskirts of Sarajevo and pulled artillery pieces out of a UN weapons collection point where they had been placed after the Carter agreement. Soon other Serb tanks and rocket launchers were moved into firing position and began shelling the city. The Serbs even fired weapons still located within the UN storage areas in a deliberate humiliation of the international forces sent to control those points. Meanwhile, Bosnian government forces fired back from within the city. Late on May 24, my special representative and the commander of the UN troops in Bosnia warned the Bosnian government and Bosnian Serbs that their forces would be attacked from the air if all heavy weapons did not cease firing by noon the next day. A second deadline was proclaimed for the removal of all heavy weapons that had been introduced into the area.

When the Serbs failed to respect the deadline, the first air strike was conducted at 1620 hours on May 25, 1995. The target was an ammunition dump near Pale, the self-declared "capital" of the Bosnian Serbs. In retaliation the Serbs began to shell "safe areas" all across Bosnia. In Tuzla some seventy people, many teenagers, were killed and hundreds wounded. Soon a "most immediate" cable came from Akashi: "After consultation with military and civilians I decided this morning to authorize additional air strikes against the Bosnian Serbs." Akashi's rationale for the second round of air strikes, he said, "should be understood to be the direct result of the Bosnian Serbs' failure to return the four weapons taken from the weapons collection points, and because of their continued firing of heavy weapons in and around Sarajevo in violation of [the 1994 agreement on heavy weapons] and related Security Council Resolutions." The second strike was run at 1030 hours on May 26.

In retaliation for the NATO strikes, the Bosnian Serbs, as we had repeatedly predicted, took UN hostages, some 370 in all, and used 17 of them as human shields by chaining them to potential targets of further air attacks. The Serbs then called in the media to make the most of this propaganda-rich blow to the credibility of the international community.

At my monthly Friday lunch with the Security Council, on May 26, 1995, I was bluntly confrontational. "Unfortunately, I was correct in my forecasts," I said. "We now have three unmistakable precedents. Each air strike brings a new wave of hostage taking and takes us a month of negotiations with the Serbs to get the UN personnel released. I gave the instructions for these air strikes. I had no choice. I took the decision that led to the Blue Helmets being seized as hostages, and I knew full well it would happen. So did you."

Next morning in the Security Council chamber, I said, "I am asking for your advice. Should we have a third air strike or not?" This was a decision for me to make, said all the ambassadors, except Albright, who remained silent. "As always," I said, "I will in the end take the decision and take the responsibility. But I am just asking for your advice. You used to give me your advice all the time." No one on the Security Council would give me any advice or guidelines. It was a unique moment. Security Council members who enjoyed micromanaging every detail of a UN operation, offering endless advice at every stage, suddenly had no counsel to offer me.

The air strikes made no lasting impact on the situation. And the United Nations was left with the task of trying to gain the release of Blue Helmets being held hostage. I was shocked at this collective abdication of responsibility. The members could at least have offered to consult their governments, but no one made the slightest effort to be constructive or helpful to the United Nations at this moment of crisis. The absence of U.S. leadership was appalling. The Clinton administration, *The New York Times* commented, was acting like a Halloween prankster who rings a doorbell and runs away. They enjoyed making noise and were thrilled by their own rhetoric but were nowhere to be found when the time came to take responsibility.

The Missing Option

On May 30, 1995, I presented a major report to the Security Council giving four options: The first would be to withdraw UNPROFOR. I said, however, that I could not advocate abandoning the people of Bosnia and admitting the United Nations' failure to help resolve a war of ethnic cleansing.

The second would be to maintain the status quo. Neither could I advocate this, for it was impossible.

The third would be to change the mandate so the force could initiate military action. This would require, I said, that the UN forces be replaced with a multinational force under the command of the major country or countries contributing to it. This would be along the lines of the Desert Storm operation against Iraq.

The fourth option would scale down the United Nations' mandate to include only mediating and humanitarian functions; the size of the force would be reduced.

What was most significant in my report was "the missing option," that is, keeping the UN force as it is but providing more firepower to step in to "protect" it. The United States and NATO argued for this missing option as if the air strikes and hostage taking of recent days had never happened. I had omitted this option because it seemed to promise only an aggravation of the existing situation, portending more forceful action against the Bosnian Serbs and more retaliations. Moreover, was the concept compatible with the impartial peacekeeping and humanitarian role that UNPROFOR was supposed to be playing? I suppressed these worries, however, and recommended that the Security Council approve a British, French, and Dutch proposal for a Rapid Reaction Force (RRF) to help protect UN personnel. I did so because I sensed that we were moving inexorably from peacekeeping to peace enforcement; the extra firepower would help to save UN lives if the fighting worsened. On June 16 the Council approved the proposal and authorized the addition of 12,500 heavily armed troops to UNPROFOR but "noted" in the preamble to the resolution that UNPROFOR remained an impartial peacekeeping operation. I felt that Alice in Wonderland would have enjoyed the resolution.

Two days later, as UN personnel withdrew from the weapons collection points around Sarajevo, the Serbs released the last of the hostages. The Karadžić formula had worked once again: the Bosnian leader would commit a deplorable act, gain from it, then make a "gesture of goodwill" that would make him the center of media attention.

The Serb release of hostages stimulated rumors that I had "made a deal with terrorists" in order to gain the release of the captive Blue Helmets. On June 23 I assured NATO that "neither I, nor my Special Representative, nor the Theatre Force Commander, have given any assurances to the Bosnian Serbs that the use of air power is no longer being considered." I confirmed to NATO that I had delegated to Akashi the authority for requesting the use of airpower to protect UN personnel. However, I said, because it was now indisputable that conducting air strikes for other purposes would bring hostage taking in its wake, I was at this point retaining for myself any UN decision to authorize such action. "You may rest assured," I wrote to the new NATO secretary-general, Willy Claes, "that I will not hesitate to authorize air strikes if I consider that they are warranted by serious transgressions" and that they would further the Security Council's objectives.

Claes had succeeded Manfred Woerner as NATO secretary-general. Woerner's death shortly afterward was a shock, even though I had known for some time of his struggle against cancer. Woerner had always been constructive and optimistic when working with me. Indeed, he had come to believe that a strong NATO partnership with the United Nations might provide the best way for NATO to find a new role in the post–cold war world.

Horror in Srebenica

Then came the worst war crime in Europe since the Second World War. The Netherlands had been the only Western UN member state to respond positively to my June 1993 request for troops to implement the Security Council's "safe-area" mandate, and the "safe area" at Srebenica was assigned to a Dutch battalion of some 450 lightly armed troops. Serb forces under Ratko Mladić began their attack on July 6, 1995, firing rockets that pinned the Dutch in their bunkers.

Akashi agonized over whether close air support would fend off the Serbs or drive them to seize the area with greater ferocity. It was not clear whether the Serbs intended to take over Srebenica. No "safe area" had yet been seized or occupied. Had the Serbs become so bold as to run this risk? On July 11, 1995, at 1225 hours Akashi received a request from General Janvier for close air support for the Dutch. Akashi approved the request immediately, and air attacks were carried out two hours later. But when the Netherlands minister of defense, Joris Voorhoeve, heard that an air operation was under way, he immediately telephoned to say that Dutch troops were so close to the Serb gunners that the air attacks were endangering their lives. Voorhoeve asked Akashi to suspend the close air support, which he had no choice but to do.

The "safe area" of Srebenica was now in Serb hands. Tens of thousands of Bosnian Muslims were seized. Some twenty thousand Muslim women and children were forced to leave in an act of "ethnic cleansing." The Serbs then undertook a concerted massacre of unarmed Muslim men of fighting age. It was not until the last of the Dutch battalion had left Srebenica on July 21 that UN civilian officials were told about the horrors perpetrated by Mladić's men.

That these atrocities had not been prevented suggested that once again the lessons of the past had been forgotten. Nothing can excuse the atavistic cruelty of the Serbs; the incompetence of the international community in no way diminishes their guilt. During the previous three years, their modus operandi had been amply displayed: if they wanted territory, they would use any means to get it. The Western powers and the nonaligned supporters of the Bosnian Muslims had invented the "safe area" concept as a means to "deter" the Serbs from attacking the isolated Muslim communities (and garrisons) in certain cities surrounded by the Serbs.

With the full support of my political and military colleagues, I had repeatedly pointed out that the concept of "safe areas" needed to be better defined, especially the boundaries of the "safe areas" and whether they could legitimately be used by Bosnian government forces as bases from which to launch their own operations into Serb-held territory. I again urged that more resources be provided to enable UNPROFOR to carry out the task it had been given. And I repeatedly told the Security Council that the UN forces in the "safe" areas were losing what little operational capacity they had because the Serbs were systematically obstructing their supplies of food, ammunition, and other necessities. The UN forces in the "safe areas" were there as peacekeepers, and they had neither the authority nor the means to do battle with the parties to the conflict. If the Security Council had responded to my recommendations on these points, the international community would have had a better chance of "deterring" the Serb atrocities in Srebenica.

Srebenica was gone. Then Žepa fell. The fear was that Goražde would fall next. If that were to happen, it seemed likely that the United Nations would be driven out of Bosnia entirely. NATO and UN experts had been at work for some time, planning a NATO-supported withdrawal of UN-PROFOR. The British talked of it as a "Dunkirk"; the French compared it to Dien Bien Phu. It would be a disaster. A second London Conference was quickly arranged with the aim of finding some way to protect Goražde so that the UN mission could hang on in Bosnia. As I arrived in London on July 20, 1995, I saw demonstrators in the street with a huge sign depicting Boutros-Ghali side by side with Radovan Karadžić, the Bosnian Serb leader indicted for war crimes. The sign, a reference to membership in churches of the Orthodox faith, read:

BROTHERS IN FAITH
BROTHERS IN CRIME

At the London Conference I found no two views alike. There seemed to be agreement that the United Nations should remain on the ground but also agreement that the "safe areas" were impossible to secure under the current rules of engagement. I met with Prime Minister Major. "Credible conclusions are needed," he said, "or we can kiss UNPROFOR good-bye." Finally, the two-faced U.S. policy had become untenable. Having avoided the serious military combat operation needed to end the Bosnian horror because it would have required putting U.S. troops at risk, Clinton was now forced to confront the consequences of his long-standing promise to put U.S. forces on the ground to extract UNPRO-FOR if the UN operation collapsed.

The extremity of the situation finally led those present to approve the proposal to draw in UN personnel so that airpower could be used without having the Blue Helmets taken hostage yet again. Agreement was reached that a Serb attack on Goražde or any other of the remaining "safe areas" would result in a major air reaction by NATO. To streamline the decision making, I decided to delegate my part of the double-key authority to the UN commander in the field, who would then agree with the NATO southern commander, Admiral Leighton Smith of the United States.

As this decision was being made, another key development was under way: advancing Croatian forces, built up secretly by the United States, now began to conduct their own military-led campaign of "ethnic cleansing," rolling back Serb forces in Bosnia until the 70 percent of the territory held by the Serbs was reduced to something more like 50 percent. The United States' willingness to arm and accept this Croatian offensive was the price Washington had had to pay to persuade the Bosnian Croats to enter a federation with Bosnian Muslims, thereby balancing the Republika Srpska with a Croat-Muslim Federation inside the borders of Bosnia and Herzegovina. The changing balance of power on the ground would for the first time make airpower a sensible option.

Delegating the Double Key

Back in New York on the night of Sunday, July 23, 1995, the British, French, and American ambassadors came to the Sutton Place residence to ask me to delegate my double-key authority. I had already decided to do so but insisted that a letter be written to me from NATO reaffirming the principle of a NATO-UN double key. When I have a letter confirming that I continue to have such authority, I said, I will be prepared officially to delegate it to the UN force commander. Under this procedure, I would be able to take back the authority delegated whenever I considered it necessary to do so. NATO provided me with such a letter on July 25. NATO Secretary-General Claes's letter asked me to support arrangements that would make air-strike decisions a matter of "the common judgment of NATO and UN commanders" on the ground. The main pressure to maintain UN participation in the airpower decision making came from Britain and France. As *The New York Times* said, "With nearly 15,000 soldiers on the ground in Bosnia who could suffer the consequences if bombing and Serb reactions to it spiral out of control, the countries pressed, in effect, for a series of political fire walls against precipitate American actions from the air."

The next day, July 26, I issued a press statement declaring my full support for the decision of the North Atlantic Council, as conveyed to me in Claes's letter. I stated that I agreed "that an attack by the Bosnian Serbs in Goražde should be met by a firm and decisive response, including through air strikes." To facilitate this, I announced that I had decided to delegate authority regarding air strikes to General Janvier, the overall commander of UN peace forces in the former Yugoslavia, "with immediate effect." Authority to call for close air support, which I had long before delegated to Akashi, I now also delegated to General Janvier. I instructed Janvier and Under Secretary-General Kofi Annan to go to Brussels to work out the operational modalities for implementing this decision. This resulted in a secret UN-NATO memorandum of understanding on how we would respond to the next Serb attack on any of the four remaining "safe areas"—Goražde, Sarajevo, Bihać, or Tuzla—by "the timely and effective use of air power." Despite this, and contrary to the record, President Clinton at a press conference the next day, July 27, blamed the Bosnian situation on the United Nations' failure to use force. Akashi made up a list for reporters titled "SRSG (Special Representative of the Secretary-General) Approval of Employment of Air Power," which showed that he had approved eleven air operations since being assigned to Bosnia, agreeing with virtually every request made to him by the commander in the field.

From that point forward, I expected the course of events to be decided entirely in the field. We had warned the Serbs publicly that an attack on Goražde or any other "safe area" would meet with decisive action. We knew full well that such an attack would come. Despite Albright's rejection in May of my proposal to draw in UN personnel, they had, in fact, under the supervision of the UN commander for Bosnia, Lieutenant General Rupert Smith, pulled back from exposed areas. Thus, for the first time, air strikes were becoming a realistic option. If the Serbs attacked, General Janvier would make the decision in the field for the United Nations, and Admiral Leighton Smith would do the same for NATO. But the air-strike debate was still not settled. On August 11 we received a communication from NATO stating that "General Janvier has been unable to provide his concurrence" to NATO's proposal to conduct preemptive strikes against Bosnian Serb air defense installations. It was true that there was no authority under Security Council Resolution 816 (on the "no-fly zone") for preemptive action against missile and radar sites. But in my reply to NATO on August 15 I affirmed the right of NATO aircraft to take countermeasures against an air defense system showing hostile intent. And, I said, in the context of Security Council Resolution 836 (on the "safe areas") "it is accepted that measures to neutralize integrated air defense systems are a necessary element of graduated air operations against Bosnian Serb targets threatening the safe areas." This provided a more expansive interpretation for Janvier to work with. My letter was drafted both to adhere to Security Council resolutions, as I was required to do, and to make possible the full use of airpower should the Serbs attack again, as they would certainly do.

Then, in a typical example of how the United Nations was expected to fulfill responsibilities even as its member states denied it the resources to do so, the rug was nearly pulled out from under it in Goražde. On August 17 I received a letter from the British foreign secretary confirming Britain's intent to withdraw its troops from Goražde at the scheduled end of their rotation, August 22, and not replace them. We attempted to find another country to replace Britain but without success. Hurriedly we tried to put together a multinational battalion to consist of 100 soldiers each from Russia, Ukraine, an Islamic country, and NATO. But no NATO country was willing to send 100 soldiers; neither was any Islamic country; and Russian and Ukrainian contingents were unacceptable to the Bosnian government unless other countries agreed to join them.

I had no choice but to deploy some twenty military observers to replace the British and to point to the new air actions agreed on by NATO and the United Nations as giving credibility to a purely observer presence. Predictably, this led to reports that the United Nations was preparing to "abandon" Goražde. I issued a public statement on August 18 explaining the situation and assuring that there would be a continuing UN presence at Goražde, albeit in the form of military observers. I stated that I remained "firmly committed to deterring attacks on the safe areas and particularly on the 60,000 civilians who live there." This statement brought down more opprobrium on my head. Jeane Kirkpatrick, in an August 18 *Washington Post* column, declared that I had "shackled NATO."

"A Common Judgment"

On the last weekend in August I was scheduled to fly to Beijing for the World Conference on Women. As I was about to board the aircraft, however, I was suddenly stricken with the flu and was forced to cancel my flight and return to Sutton Place. Therefore, I was in New York when the attack came that set our previously agreed-on arrangement into action. On August 28, Sarajevo was shelled by mortar fire, which killed 37 civilians and wounded nearly 100 others. I immediately issued a statement condemning this despicable act and informing the press that I had instructed the UN military command to "take appropriate action without delay." The situation called for "drastic measures," I said.

It quickly appeared that this was yet another iteration of Karadžić's now-familiar scheme. Richard Holbrooke, the newly appointed American envoy, had warned that force would be used if the Bosnian Serbs did not accept a 51 percent–49 percent division of territory between them and the Croatian-Bosnian Federation. This was followed by the atrocious attack on Sarajevo, after which Karadžić made his usual "concession," declaring that the Holbrooke plan could be a basis for further negotiation. On previous occasions this would have led the NATO powers to hesitate, leaving Karadžić in a stronger position than before. But this time the stakes were enormous and preparations had been laid.

Lieutenant General Rupert Smith and Admiral Leighton Smith held several conversations on August 28 and reached "a common judgment" that the conditions for air strikes as agreed on in the memorandum of understanding between the United Nations and NATO earlier in the month had been met. At 7:25 P.M. Bosnia time, Admiral Smith faxed a letter to General Smith stating that "accordingly I have instructed CO-MAIRSOUTH to commence striking" targets "as depicted in the agreed target list signed by General Janvier and me on 14 August 1995." This decision was conveyed to General Janvier at UN Zagreb and to UN headquarters in New York by telephone at 7:30 P.M. Eastern Daylight Time that same day. The actual launch time for the air strikes was to be determined by optimal weather and other tactical factors.

At about 8:00 P.M. on August 29 (about 2:00 A.M. on the thirtieth in Bosnia), José, the steward at the residence on Sutton Place, handed me a note as I was welcoming dinner guests. After everyone had arrived and conversations had begun over drinks, I read the note. Waves of NATO aircraft had begun striking targets across Bosnia and Herzegovina. I asked my spokesman to inform the media that the NATO raids had my full support.

The situation was summed up well by *The New York Times* of August 31, 1995):

> Such a sweeping attack had often been threatened by NATO and the United Nations. But the political will to go through with it had never previously coalesced among the Western allies, who feared being sucked into a Balkan war. There had also been concern about the reaction of Russia, a traditional ally of the Serbs. Moscow condemned the bombing today, although in terms that were scarcely malignant or threatening.
>
> Differences between the United Nations and NATO have often paralyzed the West's response to the war, but with almost all United Nations peacekeepers out of Bosnian Serb territory and so no longer vulnerable to hostage-taking, greater unity of purpose was achieved.
>
> Boutros Boutros-Ghali, Secretary General of the United Nations, said today that the NATO raids had his "full support." He added, however, that "the United Nations is not at war with the Serbs."

As September began, Janvier reported that the situation was now following a "different logic" than it had in the past, requiring a different approach. The air strikes would continue until the announced objectives—removal of the Serb threat to the "safe areas," withdrawal of heavy weapons from around Sarajevo, and a general cessation of hostilities—were attained in the common judgment of UN and NATO military commanders. The mainly Anglo-French RRF, whose establishment as a part of UNPROFOR had been approved by the Security Council on June 16, had taken up positions in the vicinity of Sarajevo and was able to support the air campaign by engaging Serb artillery and mortars around the city. There was concern, however, that the NATO air strikes, the United Nations' enforcement action against the Bosnian Serbs (through the RRF), and the Croatian campaigns against Serbs in both Croatia and Bosnia not turn into an international war against the Serbs or so unbalance the situation that a fair diplomatic solution would become impossible.

On August 30, hardly a day after the bombing began, Ambassador Albright telephoned Under Secretary-General Annan to ask when the air strikes would end. In a note to me reporting on Albright's call, Annan expressed astonishment that she should ask him such a question. Albright apparently did not understand that the decision-making process for the air operations had been delegated to the commanders in the field weeks ago. She was anxious that the bombing not go to the point where it would derail the peace process. Annan told her that we were in touch with our UN commanders in the field and suggested that she contact her own military authorities on the matter. The bombing was necessary, but Albright was right: too much bombing would be self-defeating.

In an unworthy and gratuitous insult to the United Nations, the United States insisted on excluding the United Nations' chief diplomatic envoy for the former Yugoslavia, Thorvald Stoltenberg, from a meeting to be chaired by Holbrooke in Geneva in early September to discuss a negotiated end to the conflict. I wrote to Christopher to ask that Stoltenberg be included as an observer on the grounds that he, as the United Nations' envoy, and Carl Bildt, who had replaced David Owen as the European Union's envoy, should both be present as representatives of the London Conference, which in 1992 had launched the international community's effort to bring peace to Bosnia. At the last moment, Stoltenberg was permitted to attend but only in closed session. Nothing was said in tribute to the UN operation. The United States was finally ready to get involved and wanted no UN role whatsoever.

As the bombing continued, I called Janvier, Akashi, and Stoltenberg to New York for consultations on September 16. The situation was on the verge of getting out of control; some sense of balance between the warring parties of the former Yugoslavia had to be maintained if a peace agreement were to have a chance. The Russians were alarmed; their ambassador, Sergei Lavrov, urged me to retrieve my "double-key" authority.

On September 18 I told the Security Council that I warmly welcomed the U.S. diplomatic initiative led by Ambassador Holbrooke. I referred to my communications in both 1993 and 1994 to the Council to the effect that member states and regional organizations, such as NATO, were far better suited to the task of dealing with the Bosnian crisis than was the United Nations. I listed the reasons why: the scale of the operation required; the United Nations' difficulties in obtaining civilian and military personnel needed from member states; the United Nations' inability to conduct enforcement actions without the mandates required to do so; and the failure of member states to pay their assessed contributions for peacekeeping on time. I reminded the Security Council that I had said back in May that if it became necessary to use military force in Bosnia, UNPROFOR should be replaced by NATO. In view of the current situation, I urged that an expeditious handover by the United Nations to NATO be authorized. Ambassador Albright reacted sharply to my letter, saying to reporters, "I think the Secretary-General tends to blame the nation-states when things don't work out and take credit when things do."

The next day, September 19, I urged the Croatian-Bosnian forces to show restraint on the battlefield, to pause so as to permit the diplomatic process to work. On September 20 the Serbs withdrew their artillery from around Sarajevo, and NATO air strikes ceased. NATO Secretary-General Claes and I argued over the telephone about whether the bombing halt was temporary or should be declared permanent. On September 22, I wrote to NATO to confirm my position that the military operations initiated with the agreement of the United Nations on August 30 had terminated. I said that the UN field commanders were in agreement that the objectives of the air strikes had been met. Should another situation occur that warranted a similar response, I said, a new decision would have to be made in accordance with the UN-NATO memorandum of understanding.

By this time almost the entire $3 billion peacekeeping budget was being consumed in Bosnia. The United Nations had been used to "internationalize" the United States' and NATO's desire to avoid the war in Bosnia. Hundreds of thousands of refugees and distressed civilians had been helped by the United Nations. Countless lives had been lost, but because of the UN, thousands had been saved. Through preventive deployment in Macedonia the scope of the fighting had been contained. UN mediators and negotiators had upheld fundamental principles and shaped the outlines of ultimate agreement. The United Nations had done an honorable and valuable job in Bosnia, but the damage to its image and the opprobrium heaped upon it would have a lasting effect.

Ironically, the United States, which had sent UN peacekeepers into a combat situation in Bosnia and then, when the war ended, would put its own combat forces on the ground to serve as peacekeepers, adhered to impartial behavior and even refused to arrest indicted war criminals at large in their theater of operations. And whereas UN strength under war conditions had been 22,000 peacekeepers, the United States and NATO took up their peacekeeping duties in Bosnia with no fewer than 60,000 combat troops.

Why was Bosnia a failure? Because the United States was so deeply involved politically and so deeply determined not to be involved militarily. President Bush, having just fought and won a major war in the Persian Gulf in 1991, could not be expected in the immediate aftermath of that conflict to take the United States decisively into yet another war, this time in the Balkans. Bush did not want Bosnia to become a divisive issue between the United States and its NATO partners, nor did he want Bosnia to become a contested issue between the United States and Russia. For this reason, both Bush and Clinton agreed to put the United Nations on the scene under mandates that defined the crisis as "humanitarian" and therefore not within NATO's mission. This was a fundamentally incorrect approach to a major international crisis. By pushing the United Nations to the fore yet depriving it of the tools it needed and using it as a scapegoat, the United States and the West bought time, but at an unwarranted cost. The harm done to the mangled and nearly bankrupt United Nations would not be easily reversed, nor would the damage done to key principles of international behavior: no acquisition of territory by force; no genocide; and guarantees of the integrity and existence of UN member states.

In the late summer of 1995, with the Croatian assault providing the necessary "infantry" on the ground, NATO air strikes shifted the balance of power against the Serbs, and the ratio of territory held provided for the first time an inducement for the Serbs to negotiate. With strength at last joined to diplomacy, serious negotiations could take place. Holbrooke stepped into this wholly transformed situation and within eight to ten weeks produced a cease-fire and settlement eventually known as the Dayton Accords.

In its first weeks in office, the Clinton administration had administered a death blow to a Vance-Owen plan that would have given the Serbs 43 percent of the territory of a unified state. In 1995 at Dayton, the administration took pride in an agreement that, after nearly three more years of horror and slaughter, gave the Serbs 49 percent in a state partitioned into two entities.

The agreement reached through U.S.-led negotiations created two de facto but not de jure states, the Croatian-Bosnian Federation and Republika Srpska, and one de jure but not de facto state, Bosnia and Herzegovina. Under the agreement the two de facto states are free to associate with the state of Croatia or the Federal Republic of Yugoslavia (Serbia and Montenegro). I wrote to Christopher on November 20, 1995, congratulating the United States and welcoming the Dayton agreement, for no alternative was possible, but the agreement is a strange artifact of the diplomatic craft and deeply flawed. Only as long as the governments of Croatia, in Zagreb, and Yugoslavia, in Belgrade, continue to see the fiction of a unitary Bosnian de jure state as a useful buffer between them will the Dayton agreement last. Should that perception change, Serbia and Republika Srpska will become one, as will the "Federation and Croatia, and Bosnia will vanish. President Franjo Tudjman of Croatia never disguised his hope that this will be the outcome, and President Slobodan Milošević's desire for a "Greater Serbia" is well known.

The terrible saga of the former Yugoslavia claimed two principal victims: the people of this unfortunate land, and the United Nations, charged with failing to find a solution to the catastrophe. The blame lies with the war criminals of the former Yugoslavia and with the major powers who, unable to agree on a common policy, evaded their responsibility to support the United Nations' effort to maintain peace and security.

Haiti: In a Grotto with Gore

As the UN chapter of the Bosnia crisis was ending, I returned to Haiti in October 1995 to mark the first anniversary of Aristide's return and to help maintain the momentum of democratization. When the White House learned that I was going to visit Haiti, it was decided that Vice President Al Gore would visit Haiti as well.

Prime Minister Smarck Michel, who met me at the airport, confirmed at once that his relations with Aristide had deteriorated. They were in disagreement about the privatization program, and Michel had submitted his resignation. In a long tête-à-tête meeting with President Aristide, I told him what President Ezer Weizman of Israel—a former RAF pilot and Israeli Air Force general—had said to me: "The hardest part of the flight is landing the airplane." "If you help us," I said to Aristide, "to ensure that these elections are free and fair, to continue economic reform, and to maintain a UN presence after February 6, when our mandate ends, you will land the airplane successfully." I was most worried about economic reform. Aristide, educated in the leftist tradition, was against privatization; Smarck Michel, on the contrary, favored the creation of a vibrant private sector.

The next morning I participated in the anniversary celebration and returned to the airport to make my departure. Everything seemed hypnotically synchronized by American officials so that Vice President Gore would arrive as I was leaving, allowing us only the briefest encounter. In a room called the VIP Lounge, which looked like the grotto of a sleazy nightclub in broad daylight, we began our meeting. I was charmed by the way the American vice president liked to be called "Al Gore." To me it was an Arab name, like al-Hassan or al-Wazzan. Protocol required me to say, "Mr. Vice President" even as I thought "al-Ghor."

I told Al Gore that I had forcefully stressed three issues in my meeting with President Aristide. First, there was little time left before the elections; Aristide needed to get started quickly. Second, Michel had resigned as prime minister because Aristide's Lavalas Party had resisted Haiti's commitments to the International Monetary Fund and the World Bank on privatization; this was sending a negative signal to international investors. Third, the UN presence should extend beyond the current deadline of February 1996. Such a presence need not include Blue Helmets but must involve police and other specialized experts. But we had to get Aristide to request a UN extension. I said that Aristide would have to make a public statement on the next steps to be taken. Only he had the responsibility and the charisma to convince the Haitian people. The vice president said that he would make the same points to Aristide. Having dealt with Aristide in the past, the vice president knew that it could take time to convince him.

Then I mentioned the UN financial crisis, which was linked to the funds required to provide assistance for the coming presidential elections in Haiti. The UN deficit totaled U.S. $3.24 billion. The vice president replied that President Clinton was keenly aware of the fact that the United States was very much in arrears. But Congress needed to be convinced that real UN reform was being undertaken. Reform within the United Nations was probably being resisted by its bureaucracy, Gore said.

"The problem," I said, "stems not from the bureaucracy but from the member states because only they can approve the proposed reforms. Meanwhile, since the U.S. is not paying its dues, other countries are reluctant to do so." I realized that I was, in Madeleine Albright's phrase, "badgering" the vice president. But I had so few contacts with U.S. political leaders that I could not afford to miss this opportunity. I apologized to Gore for raising the financial crisis at a meeting meant to deal with Haiti. But the United Nations, I told him, would not be able to play a useful role in Haiti without the necessary resources. Gore expressed his gratitude for the United Nations' close cooperation with the United States on Haiti, citing examples that showed he had followed the situation closely. Then the vice president and his team left the airport for Port-au-Prince, and I flew on my way to an Ibero-American summit in Argentina.

Disorder and Democracy

Despite our efforts, the local and parliamentary Haitian elections were carried out amid tremendous disorder. Voters searched in vain for voting stations, which had been relocated without announcement. Often a candidate's name did not appear on the ballot, causing demonstrations and, later, annulment of the vote.

However, as a result of what was learned from the defects of the local and parliamentary elections, the presidential election held at the end of 1995 was far better organized. Twenty-four candidates were in the running. The voting was carried out calmly in the presence of more than four hundred international observers, but participation was very low, about 28 percent, which was attributed to a widespread preference that Aristide, who was not eligible for reelection, stay in power three more years. A campaign launched to extend the mandate of President Aristide by three years—the length of his stay in exile—had endangered the election until Aristide had declared unequivocally that he would give up power on February 7, 1996, as scheduled in the Constitution. The poor turnout also seemed to reflect a general disenchantment with the lack of tangible economic progress.

René Préval, who had been President Aristide's prime minister in 1991, was elected in the first round with more than 87 percent of the vote. He took office on February 7, 1996 as the first democratically elected president ever to succeed another democratically elected president in Haiti.

President Préval requested an extension of the mandate of the UN force in Haiti in order to help the government in the process of disarmament and to support the Haitian police. What President Aristide did not want to do, despite our insistence, President Préval did not hesitate to do less than three days after his ascension to power.

The case of Haiti illustrates a constructive division of labor and near-excellent diplomatic and military cooperation between the United States and the United Nations. Although Haiti is far from a democracy, the groundwork may have been laid for democratization. Economic and social development are more remote objectives. Yet the operation may be judged a success. The United Nations proved indispensable to the United States in the effort to help Haiti without resort to neocolonialism. In cases where the United States supports a UN operation but does not directly intervene, as in Cambodia, El Salvador, and Mozambique, the chances of UN success are improved. But where the United States steps in to compete with the United Nations on the ground or criticizes the United Nations from the outside, as in Somalia, Rwanda, and Bosnia, the chances for failure multiply. The challenge is to find a balance between too much and too little U.S. involvement.

The Pope and the Global Polis

October 1995 in New York marked the main observation of the United Nations' fiftieth anniversary. It was dramatically launched by His Holiness Pope John Paul II, who, descending from his aircraft at Newark International Airport, said that he was coming to the United Nations to express his deep conviction that the ideals and intentions that had given birth to that worldwide organization half a century before were more important than ever in a world searching for purpose.

The sheer magnitude of a papal visit is awe-inspiring: the blocked-off streets of Manhattan, the "Popemobile" making its stately progress down the wrong side of Park Avenue, the array of ambulances awaiting excited onlookers who faint, the police protection, the sense spreading over a vast metropolis that something transcendent is under way. All this contrasted strikingly with the man himself, who came to see me on the thirty-eighth floor on October 5, 1995. The north end of the floor is reserved for the business of diplomacy; the south end is where staff and administrative offices are located. Visiting dignitaries never turn south but stay on the north side, as befits their rank. But the pope, emerging from the elevator, saw arrayed along the sides of the south corridor the faces of UN staff from every land. He went among them, and there were tears of joy.

I had met with the pope many times, and we talked again of world affairs as they affect the weakest and poorest peoples. As the Holy Father was leaving, he looked around and asked, "Why do you have only modern sculpture?" "It's what states give us," I replied. The pope's question carried an implication that he expanded upon in his speech a few minutes later to the General Assembly.

The pope's address to the General Assembly was not carried in full by *The New York Times* or *The Washington Post,* which omitted some of the most intriguing references. Although it was a major statement at a symbolically important international occasion, the speech was not closely analyzed. His address was about what he felt was symbolized by the modern art in my office. He said, "It is one of the great paradoxes of our time that man, who began the period we call 'modernity' with a self-confident assertion of his 'coming of age' and 'autonomy,' approaches the end of the twentieth century fearful of himself, fearful of what he might be capable of, fearful for the future."

If the modern age has brought a philosophically stranded humanity, then the question arises, What about the institutions of modernity? The central institution of the past two centuries, of both domestic governance and international action, has certainly been the state. Only a quarter century ago, political thinkers could declare that "today we take the state for granted." That remained true well into the 1980s, but catastrophes such as that in Somalia cause us to wonder.

At the United Nations, the world organization of states, the concept of the state, which is under fire, has had to be pointedly reaffirmed. "The foundation-stone [of human security] is and must remain the State. Respect for its fundamental sovereignty and integrity is crucial to any common international progress" is how I put it in my first major document after taking office as secretary-general.

The pope spoke of matters far beyond the state. Stressing his awareness that he was addressing "the whole family of peoples living on the face of the earth," he provided a chain of logic that stood on its own, regardless of one's culture or religion.

The indisputable quest for freedom around the world, generated by the end of the cold war, the pope said, is based on "universal rights" that reflect a "universal moral law," which is "written on the human heart." This universal moral law is the basis of universal human rights, "which human beings enjoy by the very fact of their humanity." At this point John Paul II paid tribute to the United Nations for formulating, "barely three years after its establishment, that Universal Declaration of Human Rights which remains one of the highest expressions of the human conscience of our time." The universal moral law, the pope said, is a kind of "grammar" for the world's people.

But, continued the pope, unlike the Universal Declaration of Human Rights of 1948, "no similar international agreement has yet adequately addressed the rights of nations." This, he said, raises urgent questions about justice and freedom in the world today.

The pope's declaration on the rights of nations, which, like human rights, are derived from a universal moral law, raises the most serious questions. Nationalism has been considered the cause of the most horrible of modern wars. Indeed, John Paul said that nationalism can take the unhealthy form of teaching contempt for other nations. And religion itself, in the form of fundamentalism, can be no less dangerous. Despite these qualifications, however, the pope seemed at ease with the idea of a renaissance of the nation and nationalism at a time when the concept of the state is under fire.

Thus at the United Nations, on October 5, 1995, John Paul II laid down a major challenge to thought. Must the state remain the fundamental building block of international order simply because no other concept or system is in sight? Or was the pope providing us with the seeds of some future system?

Later, at a mass in a stadium, a driving rain washed the faces of thousands of pilgrims but could not wash away the excited smiles or the spirit of prayer. Many at the United Nations said the pope's visit was "the best UN anniversary gift of all." For me it was the greatest moment of the United Nations' fiftieth anniversary.

Praised by Clinton

One hundred twenty-seven heads of state or government attended the UN50 celebration in New York on October 22, 1995, making it the largest gathering of national and world leaders in history. On this occasion President Clinton was effusive in his praise for me. "Mr. Secretary-General," he said in his toast, "I thank you for your leadership, your energy, your resolve, and the vision of the United Nations and the world for the next fifty years you have painted for us. To be sure, the United Nations will face greater demands, but the potential for doing greater good is there as well. And we believe that your leadership has played a very important role in bringing us to this point."

I have never been known for downplaying my abilities and achievements, but earlier on even I had had to blush, albeit briefly, as I listened to the president of the United States describe my "very strong leadership of the United Nations" to the heads of state on September 26, 1995:

Mr. Secretary-General, you have taken the ideas of peace, help, and security that are at the heart of the UN's mission and worked hard to make them a reality. As the cold war has ended, the world has looked to the UN for even more assistance and leadership. You have met this challenge by effectively placing the UN at the forefront of international affairs. Your leadership has been particularly apparent in the improvement of the UN's peacekeeping operations. There are now approximately 70,000 peacekeepers deployed around the world, some five times the number when you took office. Cooperation among nations is improving, and the operations are growing more efficient.

Your initiatives at the Cairo Conference, your efforts to improve coordination of development assistance, the establishment of an independent Inspector General and meaningful cost controls, and your work to improve the UN's field operations—all these are testaments to your outstanding leadership.

I couldn't believe my ears. People all over the room were craning their necks to look at me, to try to catch my eye and signal their congratulations to me. Clinton, they gestured, was on my side! Clinton continued to heap more praise on me:

Above all, you have focused on the use of diplomacy to prevent bloodshed and conflict, and on building the kinds of permanent institutions that lead to long-term stability within, and, as you have so eloquently stated, among nations. For these things, and more all of us applaud you. . . . Mr. Secretary-General, you have kept our focus on building the kind of organization that can effectively turn our ideals into reality. We thank you for your vision.

I quote these words of praise at length because a few months later, when the Clinton administration excoriated me and declared that it would veto my reelection, the UN spokesman recalled President Clinton's tributes to me and read them out to the press, infuriating Ambassador Albright. In 1995, as President Clinton was extolling my "energy . . . resolve . . . and vision," *The Economist* noted that "Boutros-Ghali is the most effective head of the United Nations in history, and the Americans hate him for it."

Far more important than praise for me was the declaration adopted by the 127 heads of state and government on October 22. Representing the peoples of the world, they solemnly reaffirmed the UN Charter, expressed gratitude to the men and women of the United Nations, especially those who have lost their lives in its service, and agreed to give the twenty-first century a United Nations "equipped, financed and structured to serve effectively the people in whose name it was established."

The "class photograph" of all the leaders in attendance was a sight to see. Who would stand where had to be determined with protocolary precision. At the same time we had to make sure that certain leaders were not placed too near each other. As one staff aide said, "We don't want Castro standing behind Clinton giving him bunny ears." It took more than half an hour for the photographer to line up all the heads of state and government so that everyone's face could be seen. King Hassan II of Morocco was suffering from a fever and understandably impatient, but he put up with it all. When the photograph was distributed, someone noticed that there was one more person in the picture than the total number of leaders supposed to be photographed. The UN staff joked that it was the ubiquitous Joseph Verner Reed, but I never learned for sure who the mystery guest was.

Weeks later, in an article in *The New York Times* dealing not with the United Nations, but with the plight of New York's poorest people, a picture of an overcrowded room, which housed one family, showed, pinned to its wall, a copy of the photograph of the world's leaders at UN50. What could have led these poor people to value such an image? I felt it could only be faith and hope in the United Nations. I wrote to the *Times* to point out my discovery of this hidden dimension of its story and to note that the problem of housing was not peculiar to New York; it was global and needed to be addressed comprehensively, as the forthcoming UN world conference in Istanbul would be doing.

"Massively Unpopular"

Clinton's praise for me notwithstanding, as the end of 1995 approached, my image in the American media was lower than ever. One article, I told Leia, "made me sound like an arrogant, ignorant sheikh speaking broken English." Madeleine Albright's determination to manage my contacts with Washington grew more aggressive. The day before I was scheduled to go to Washington to meet with the Senate Foreign Relations Committee at its request, Albright telephoned my chief of staff to insist that I call it off—something, of course, I could not do. "He is massively unpopular on the Hill," Albright said of me. "He is the butt of jokes. He doesn't present his case well to Americans. He is too elliptical." If I must go to Washington, she said, I should meet with the committee and then quickly get out of town. "He should not try to meet any other people," she insisted.

At the end of 1995 the saga of the United Nations and Bosnia was capped by an appropriately bizarre incident. The United States, having declared that the United Nations would have no part whatsoever in the post-Dayton peacekeeping operation in Bosnia, suddenly announced that it wanted the United Nations to provide a peacekeeping force for eastern Slavonia, the one part of the former Yugoslavia where, despite the cease-fire, conflict might soon resume. Again it appeared that the United States wanted to avoid putting its own soldiers in harm's way by pushing inadequately armed or mandated UN troops out in front. I stated that any force for eastern Slavonia would have to be strong enough to protect itself from attack and that, as would now be the case in Bosnia, it would perhaps be best for a non-UN force such as the NATO/U.S. Implementation Force to be authorized by the Security Council for this mission.

My position immediately aroused the wrath of the United States. "It is a grave mistake," declared spokesman James Rubin, "for the secretary-general to shy away from legitimate operations, supported by key members of the Security Council, that advance the prospects for peace in the Balkans." In particular, the U.S. spokesman announced, "it is misguided and counterproductive to argue that the UN should avoid this operation because of the risk of exacerbating a negative image of UN activities in the former Yugoslavia."

To suggest that the United Nations was "shying away" from a duty after more than two hundred peacekeepers had been killed in Bosnia during a time when the United States would not risk American lives on the ground was despicable. As I had pointed out on innumerable occasions, the United Nations had not been given the capacity to mount, support, and manage large and complex operations in the field that might require the use of force. Nothing could be more dangerous or irresponsible than to ask a peacekeeping mission to use force when its composition, armament, logistical support, and rules of engagement denied it the capacity to do so. Yet that is exactly what the United States and the Security Council had done to UNPROFOR and what they were now prepared to do to the United Nations once again.

Vulgarité

At an informal session of the Security Council, speaking in French and with Albright present, I said that "I was shocked by the statement of the U.S. spokesman . . . and shocked by its vulgarity." Albright declared that my remark was unacceptable. She could not understand how I could say such a thing. The press made much of it. The French tried to defuse the confrontation by saying that *vulgarité* did not mean in French what it meant in English, but around the United Nations my remark was regarded as a slap at Albright that she would never forgive. To me, it was an example of Albright's very effective two-track behavior: in person, she acted as my friend; through her spokesman, she slandered me. She was admired for her tough talk but was offended and outraged when tough talk was directed at her.

A few days later she accepted my invitation to lunch at Sutton Place. Her assistant, fearing an embarrassing incident, telephoned to ask where she would be seated. "Ambassador Albright, as the senior guest present, will be seated directly to the right of the secretary-general" was the reply. She came and we chatted pleasantly, as if nothing had happened.

CHAPTER 8

Defiance, Defeat, and Democratization

(1996)

Iraq: Creative Obstructions

On a cold day in December 1995, Iraqi Foreign Minister Tariq Aziz and I met in a small resort hotel near Geneva. He again denounced Resolution 986 as violating the territorial integrity of Iraq and said that I, as secretary-general, must offer a new and more fair "Oil-for-Food" formula.

I explained to Tariq Aziz that I had no right to do so, because the Security Council had already adopted the highly detailed plan set out in the nineteen paragraphs of Resolution 986 and I was obliged by that text "to do what is necessary to assure the effective application" of that resolution. Then, after a moment of silence, I said, "But 986 authorizes the secretary-general to conclude a memorandum of understanding with Iraq on the application of the resolution. . . . I could invite you to come to negotiate this if you guarantee that you would accept my invitation." Tariq Aziz said he would respond to me soon and asked about my travel plans.

"I have to make an official visit to Kuwait," I said, "and will be in Cairo at the beginning of January. Send an emissary to me there with your response."

In Kuwait, I inspected the UN troops on the Iraqi-Kuwaiti border, where the Kuwaitis had dug a huge trench on their side of the line as a defense against another Iraqi invasion. I urged the Kuwaiti leaders to take a more flexible attitude toward Iraq—"I mean the Iraqi people, who are suffering from the boycott and who will remain your neighbors until the end of the centuries."

No, the Kuwaiti prime minister said, the sanctions must remain in place until the end of Saddam Hussein's regime. And the emir of Kuwait was surprised by my advocacy of "Oil for Food." He reminded me that Iraq still held Kuwaiti prisoners and that Iraq's intention had been to totally eliminate a member state of the United Nations. "One cannot forget such aggression easily," he said gravely.

While in Cairo with my family to celebrate Coptic Christmas, which by the Orthodox calendar took place on January 7, I was given a message from Tariq Aziz: If I invited Iraq to negotiate the "Oil for Food" formula, Iraq would respond positively.

Nothing is simple when it comes to Iraq. First, I had to negotiate the language of my letter of invitation in order to overcome Baghdad's hostility to the mere mention of Resolution 986.

When I finally received Baghdad's agreement on the exchange of letters, I was seized with anxiety. I knew I had started something that ultimately would displease both Washington and Baghdad.

Rumors began to spread about who would negotiate what and where. To quiet the grumbling from the Americans and the British, I announced that negotiations would take place in New York and be led by Hans Corell, the UN's legal adviser.

The negotiations commenced on February 6, 1996, and dealt with how food would be distributed and oil would be sold. Ambassador Abd al-Amir al-Anbari, a shrewd diplomat and a specialist on oil issues, led the Iraqi delegation. Again the Iraqis did not want Resolution 986 to be mentioned. They insisted that I move the negotiations to Baghdad. I refused categorically. Off and on the talks went through March and early April until the Iraqi delegation accepted the mention of Resolution 986 in a memorandum of understanding with the United Nations that would incorporate a new oil-for-food plan.

Then came difficulties from the Americans and the British. They wanted to read the agreed-upon plan before I presented it to the Security Council. But Resolution 986 authorized the secretary-general to conclude the memorandum of understanding and then to inform the Security Council, which was not to participate in the negotiations. I found myself in a dilemma. If I provided the memorandum to all members of the Security Council, I would find myself dealing with fifteen negotiators, plus Iraq. It would take forever to reach agreement. If I gave the text to only the United States and the British, I would displease the other thirteen members of the Security Council, especially the other three permanent members, China, France, and Russia, who had very important financial interests in Iraq, which owed billions of dollars to them. Not surprisingly, these three countries were keen to find a solution, while the United States and Britain were not.

In a difficult—indeed, disagreeable—meeting the U.S. and British representatives explained to me why it was completely understandable that they should receive special treatment. Then the representatives of China, France, and Russia, knowing full well the real causes of the delay, reminded me that the memorandum of understanding was exclusively in my competence and that delay was unwarranted. They wanted me to take responsibility—and blame—for the delay, but they themselves were unwilling to put pressure on the United States.

I told Ambassador al-Anbari that it would be in Iraq's best interest for me to pass the proposed plan to the United States and Britain, because these two "difficult delegations" were sure to block "Oil for Food" if dissatisfied with the text.

Al-Anbari protested energetically, fearing that the United States wanted to restart the negotiations from scratch: "I had a hard time getting Baghdad to agree to this project at all. How do I explain that we are going to begin negotiating a new text?"

"Time is not on your side," I said. "You put off accepting Resolution 986, and the American presidential election will make any negotiations, for all practical purposes, no longer possible."

In the meantime, the increasingly desperate condition of the Iraqi people was beginning to draw the protests of groups in the West. When Madeleine Albright delivered a lecture on U.S. foreign policy at Yale University in April 1996, her talk was repeatedly disrupted by carefully staged demonstrations against the Clinton administration's "murder of Iraqi children." I had two more disagreeable meetings with the Americans and the British in April. They proposed textual changes, some of which were justified, some not.

On Thursday, May 2, as I was passing through Paris en route to New York, Aziz telephoned to tell me that al-Anbari had been recalled to Baghdad for consultations. I replied that we were in a race against time and that al-Anbari's recall would put the entire process at risk. Tariq Aziz was evasive and hung up. Four months of painful negotiations have been wasted, I thought. The United States is now preoccupied with its elections, and other countries will not act because the United States will not take the lead. The Iraqi people will continue to suffer.

As I was about to leave the Hôtel Crillon, there was another telephone call. Al-Anbari was on the line, saying serenely, "I will be in New York on Sunday; my consultation in Baghdad has been postponed."

I arrived in New York at nine on Thursday morning, May 2. Thanks to technology and time zones, one can possess the gift of near ubiquity. I had lunch in my office with Yasser Arafat to discuss UN assistance for reconstruction in Gaza. Arafat told me that he feared Shimon Peres would not win in the coming Israeli election.

"And so what will you do?" I asked. "Await the results of the American election," he said. The shadow of the American election seemed to loom over everything.

I was scheduled to leave for Moscow on the afternoon of May 13. I wanted the "Oil for Food" memorandum of understanding signed before my departure, but the negotiations became entangled in last-minute technical complications. Instead of celebrating an achievement that day, I was visited by Warren Christopher, who came to tell me that the president of the United States had decided to oppose my reelection.

Israel: The Shelling of Qana

While I tried without success to complete the tedious negotiations with Iraq, a horrible crisis in the Middle East deepened Washington's animosity toward me. This would be my final substantive battle with the Clinton administration. Like my first, back in January 1993, it was over an Arab-Israeli crisis. In early April 1996 the Israeli Defense Force assaulted south Lebanon in an effort to root out Islamic guerrilla forces who had been targeting Israel. Scores of civilians fleeing the Israeli onslaught had taken refuge in a UN observation post at Qana (the United Nations had had a peacekeeping force—UNIFIL—in southern Lebanon since the Israeli invasion in 1978, and UN observers had been in Lebanon even longer). The UN compound was considered the safest place in the combat zone. On April 18 Israeli artillery shells fell on the compound. These shells were designed to explode in the air and rain down shrapnel to maximize casualties, which is what happened. Bodies, including those of children, were cut to pieces. At least one hundred refugees were slaughtered in the attack. UN personnel a mile away reported hearing "a sort of chorus of screaming." As secretary-general, I investigated the attack and submitted a report to the Security Council. The situation was unprecedented. The armed forces of a UN member state had launched an attack on a UN peacekeeping post.

The Israelis immediately declared that it had been a mistake, an accident. Clinton declared it "a tragic misfiring in Israel's legitimate exercise of its right to self-defense." The American press reported that the intended target had been a Hezbollah guerrilla position hundreds of yards away from the Qana compound. A *Washington Post* headline read, HIGH-TECH WEAPONRY NOT INFALLIBLE. On the other hand, UN soldiers from Norway said they had seen an Israeli drone, an unmanned aircraft designed to send back images of the territory, flying above Qana before and during the attack. They charged that the Israeli military must have known that the compound was a UN post and that unarmed civilians were inside.

An Israeli spokesman denied that a drone had been in the area. But soon after the attack I was provided with a video taken by Norwegian UN troops that showed the Israeli drone flying overhead, along with the sound of exploding shells. The video then showed the UN compound on fire, with the sound of the drone still audible in the background. The Israeli command stated that the drone had been on "a different mission." It had made a cartographic error, they said, and had believed that the UN compound was some 150 yards from its actual location.

I took every precaution to ensure that my report on the Qana incident was objective and fair. In response to a telephoned request from Foreign Minister Ehud Barak, formerly Israeli chief of staff, I delayed the report so that Israel could revise the position it wished to have reflected in the document. I had dispatched a Dutch general assigned to the UN Department of Peace-Keeping Operations to assess the evidence on the spot. The case received intensive international attention. Leaving aside the Israeli and American media, the consensus seemed to be that there could be only two explanations for the slaughter of civilians at the UN compound at Qana. One was military incompetence on a scale difficult to attribute to the highly professional Israel Defense Force; the other was that Hezbollah fighters had moved their positions close to the UN post in the hope of protecting themselves from Israeli shells, and the Israelis had wanted to demonstrate that this would not be tolerated. But nothing could justify a deliberate attack on the UN peacekeeping post and the refugees who had sought shelter there.

When their investigation was completed, the Dutch officer in charge and his British assistant came to the thirty-eighth floor to brief me on their findings. The Dutch officer stated that, on the basis of his investigation, the video taken at the time of the event, and the testimony of eyewitnesses, including Israelis, he was compelled to conclude that the shelling could not have occurred by mistake and that therefore Israel should bear the full responsibility. I said that the decision to release the report as it was submitted to me was mine alone and that I would bear full responsibility for it. It would be my report. Later my aide Fayza Abulnaga told me that some UN staff members were betting that only some six months before the Security Council was to vote for or against my reelection, I would never publish a report so critical of Israel and unwelcome to the U.S. administration.

My report concluded that it was "unlikely that the shelling of the UN compound was the result of gross technical and/or procedural errors." Israel was enraged. The U.S. administration's spokesman declared that I was "more interested in pointing a finger instead of creating a climate of peace." The spokesman for the U.S. Mission to the United Nations said that Ambassador Albright was "so devastated that the Secretary-General chose to draw unjustified conclusions about this incident that can only divide and polarize the environment rather than the practical lessons that could prevent such a tragedy from happening again."

The Clinton administration had wanted no report at all, fearing that any criticism of Israel at that moment would damage Shimon Peres's chances for reelection as Israel's prime minister. Whether or not my report affected the Israeli election is impossible to say, but it had a major impact on the Clinton administration's view of me. Clinton and Christopher were shocked by Benjamin Netanyahu's victory over Peres, which threw the administration's Middle East policy off the rails. They felt that I had defied their clear wishes and damaged Peres's standing.

In my opinion, this was an incorrect analysis. Netanyahu defeated Peres not because of what happened at Qana but because, for the first time in the history of the Arab-Israeli negotiations, there was no brake on the pressure exerted by the United States for progress toward peace. Previous American administrations had urged the Israeli government to make concessions, which the Israelis would resist. With Peres in office, however, there was no resistance, and the peace process began to pick up speed. The situation was highly desirable from Washington's point of view because it enabled President Clinton to preside over politically valuable ceremonies to mark progress at almost regular intervals. It was also desirable in itself, because both sides had agreed to a process that promised to end hostilities entirely. But the pace of progress alarmed a large segment of the Israeli people, who felt that their government was making concessions while Palestinian terrorism increased. Peres's defeat was a real setback to the Clinton administration—and to the peace process—and it was convenient to blame the United Nations—and specifically me as secretary-general—for my Qana report.

My report on the massacre at Qana provoked an attack in *U.S. News & World Report* by the publisher, Mortimer Zuckerman, who implied that even making such a report was tantamount to anti-Semitism on my part. But among the Arab people the massacre at Qana took on almost epic stature. My role in reporting the incident drew attention to me not only in the Arab and third worlds, but in Europe as well, where I was stopped in the street to be told that I would be remembered as the "last victim of Qana."

Two years later I visited Qana at the invitation of its people, who treated me as a hero who had given recognition to their suffering. I could not hold back my tears when they took me to the grave of the children killed in the shelling of the UN observation post. While I have never tried to hide my support for the Arab and Palestinian cause, I always sought, as secretary-general, to be scrupulously objective, and my report on the incident at Qana met this standard.

Yeltsin's Toast

Later on May 13, the day Warren Christopher came to Sutton Place to tell me that the United States had decided to oust me from the United Nations, I departed for Moscow and the summit meeting of the Commonwealth of Independent States (CIS). Before doing so, as so often was the case, I received a short lecture from the United States, passed by a State Department aide to a member of my staff. The Russians, I was to understand, were pushing hard to have the CIS recognized by the United Nations as a legitimate regional organization. But, the United States message went on, some other member states of the CIS did not want this, fearing that Russia would simply turn the CIS into its own bloc or sphere of influence. The United States shared this concern, I was told, and opposed the Russian plan. "So, have you considered the politics of this?" I was asked.

The between-the-lines message was "Boutros-Ghali should not go to the CIS Moscow meeting, because to do so would confer UN approval on the CIS, something Russia wants but the Clinton administration does not." Madeleine Albright, the State Department aide said, had been instructed to take this up with me earlier, but State had not received her report. I knew why. Albright had in fact raised the issue with me a year earlier at the first world gathering of regional organizations, to which I had invited the CIS. But even as she had recounted her government's concerns to me, she had revealed that she did not agree with Washington's position. "They are being silly," she had said. I too regarded this U.S. position as absurd. CIS members were voluntarily meeting in Moscow, and I as secretary-general was invited to attend. I would do so. My attendance had nothing to do with "legal recognition." I had addressed all manner of regional groups from the Commonwealth to NATO to the Arab League, to the Organization of African Unity, the Organization of American States, and Francophone and Ibero-American groups. There was absolutely no reason for me not to accept the invitation to the CIS session in Moscow.

My first Moscow meeting was with Foreign Minister Yevgeny Primakov, a good friend whom I had known since he was the Soviet Union's Arabist stationed in Cairo years before. I volunteered nothing about my plans, but Primakov declared at the start that he would give me his total support for reelection. I replied that early Russian backing could be counterproductive with regard to the United States; I asked Primakov not to make his position public. The next day, May 16, during a lunch at the Kremlin, President Boris Yeltsin said that he wanted to confirm Russia's support for me. Yeltsin lifted a glass and with a beaming smile proposed a toast to my second term as secretary-general. I looked pleadingly at Primakov. As we left the luncheon, Primakov looked sheepish as he explained that he had no way of controlling Yeltsin.

At the CIS summit on Friday, May 17, in the Kremlin with seventeen heads of state or government in attendance, I spoke about the importance of cooperation between the United Nations and regional groups such as the CIS. As I concluded my address, I had a sense that Yeltsin was about to propose a resolution in favor of my reelection. This would be taken by the United States as a double provocation: it would think I had broken my promise to Christopher not to make public my decision to seek reelection, and it would think that I had come to Moscow to solicit support from Russia and the former Soviet republics. But before Yeltsin could speak, President Nursultan Nazarbayev of Kazakhstan asked me about UN reform, and the moment passed.

Early Saturday morning, I strolled in the garden of what had been Stalin's dacha and peered into a small house built on the grounds for Stalin's daughter. For an hour I walked and thought. I came away with my belief reinforced that, no matter what the difficulties, a secretary-general must always try to maintain good relations with the United States—and that meant it was important not to embarrass the Americans by an early Russian initiative in support of me.

"Strange and Difficult"

Back in New York, I met Hans Corell on May 18. He was jubilant: "The oil-for-food memorandum is settled. Here is the complete text," he said, waving it over his head. "Restrain your enthusiasm," I replied. "With Saddam Hussein, one is sure of nothing." I was not mistaken. The next day, al-Anbari and Corell came to see me at Sutton Place. Baghdad demanded a new guarantee: "You must assure us that once the accord is signed, the Americans will not impose new conditions."

I came close to losing my self-control. "I am sorry. I cannot give you that assurance. I do not have the right, nor do I have the authority, to speak in the name of a member state, still less when that state is the superpower that dominates the United Nations. Let us turn the page on this sad story and go on to something else."

Corell was distraught. Al-Anbari was confused. I pulled myself together and addressed al-Anbari in Arabic: "Try to convince Baghdad that it risks yet again losing a chance to see the end of this story."

After al-Anbari departed, Corell was downcast. "I have negotiated many times in my life," he told me, "but I have never been involved in anything so strange and difficult."

Early on Thursday, May 30, 1996, Baghdad declared that Iraq accepted the memorandum of understanding. Before Saddam Hussein could change his mind again, I decided to sign the agreement at once. Press and television crews were hurriedly assembled for a midmorning ceremony. Beforehand, I telephoned the members of the Security Council to inform them that the agreement had been concluded and to ask them to arrange an informal meeting at which I could brief them on the principal elements of the text. After the signing ceremony, I returned to the thirty-eighth floor to meet and thank Corell and his team for their remarkable work during four months and more than fifty working sessions.

But the United States did not want "Oil for Food" to take place near the time of the presidential elections. The administration feared that the Republicans might cite certain language in the memorandum of understanding as evidence that Clinton had made concessions to Saddam Hussein. This is why the American delegation attached so much importance to form, to sentences, and to any terms that could be interpreted as restoring sovereignty to Iraq. It also feared that Saddam Hussein would trumpet victory following conclusion of the agreement. I was indirectly and discreetly charged by Washington to make sure that Iraq did not portray the signing as a victory for Saddam Hussein and a defeat for the United States. Faced with these contradictions, I asked our spokeswoman to speak of a humanitarian victory that transcended the politics and perceptions of either side.

In early June al-Anbari submitted a plan for the distribution of the humanitarian supplies. According to Resolution 986, legally speaking, it was the secretary-general's responsibility to approve or disapprove such a plan. But Madeleine Albright immediately denounced it, accusing Baghdad of trying to "drive trucks through loopholes." Iraq, she said, was twisting a program to provide food and medicine into one that would include telephone switching equipment and computers. Why this attack? We had only just concluded the agreement. Nothing had yet been implemented. Why would the United States denounce a resolution it had voted for and a memorandum of understanding it had practically drafted itself?

The Mood Turns Nasty

In June, as I flew to Istanbul for what was being called "the city summit," the last in the series of world conferences held during my term of office, I looked over a collection of recent American journals, op-ed pieces, and newsmagazines; most carried nasty articles about me. I had, I read, entangled the United States in Somalia and taken command of its forces there; I had prevented President Clinton from bombing to stop the perpe- trators of war crimes in Bosnia; I had tried to impose global taxes in order to aggrandize my power at the United Nations; and I had blocked the admirable efforts of the United States to reform the United Nations. De- spite polls showing that the vast majority of American citizens favored the United Nations and wanted to see it strengthened, I was portrayed as re- sponsible for America's lack of faith in the United Nations and Congress's unwillingness to pay the huge American financial debt to the United Nations. In reality, the Congress's turn against the United Nations and refusal to pay what the United States owed the United Nations dated back to the 1980s, well before I had arrived at the United Nations. I was even unpopular with some friends of the United Nations and some for- mer employees, who seemed to prefer that the United Nations remain as it had been in the cold war years: morally superior and generally passive. To them, the new secretary-general had taken the world organization down a dangerously activist path.

Along with mounting criticism in the press came speculation about candidates to replace me: Sadako Ogata, the UN high commissioner for refugees; Gro Harlem Brundtland, prime minister of Norway; Mary Robinson, president of Ireland, who was being relentlessly pressed upon the Clinton administration, it was said, by Senator Edward Kennedy. All those named were queried by reporters, and all replied in classical politi- cal style that they loved their present jobs but did so in a way that en- couraged their supporters. After Shimon Peres was defeated in the Israeli election for prime minister, his name, too, was advanced. Instantly the press reported "American officials" as saying that if Peres were a candi- date, he would have U.S. support. I received a telephone call from Jean Friedman, a millionaire French supporter of the Peace Now movement in Israel and a longtime political backer of Peres. He had an idea: let there be two secretaries-general; I would be one and Peres the other. "Impossible," I said. "The Charter would have to be rewritten, and any ship with two captains would sink."

In Stamboul on June 5 I was visited by the Holy See's man at the United Nations, Archbishop Martini. The Holy See was very pleased with the work I had done as secretary-general, the archbishop said, and very much favored my reelection.

The next day, my staff in New York learned that Secretary Christopher would try to telephone me. The U.S. Mission in New York had asked when I would be returning to New York and had been told on July 10, after my attendance at two important upcoming conferences: the summit of the Group of Seven (G-7) in Lyons and the annual summit of the Organization of African Unity in Yaoundé, Cameroon. Christopher, I speculated, would want me to announce my intention not to seek a second term before those meetings. There was also an Arab summit scheduled to take place in Cairo on July 21. The United States wanted me to drop out of the running before the Africans and Arabs might pass a resolution in my favor.

My chief of staff, Jean-Claude Aimé, telephoned Ambassador Albright on June 6 to ask for a "heads-up," the diplomatic courtesy of alerting someone to the purpose of a proposed telephone call. Albright's manner was harsh. "It's not a topic he needs to be briefed on," she said and hung up.

The call that reached me that day in Turkey was not from Christopher but from Cy Vance. "Good news!" Cy exclaimed. "Christopher has obtained a compromise—one additional year for you. So you will have another year and a half to go on with your UN reforms." No, I said, only twelve months. The next six months belong in my first term of office. "Yes, sure," Cy said, "but you would still have a year and a half more from today. Your term would be extended to run until your seventy-fifth birthday." He urged me to accept. I refused. As for the gift of one additional year, I told Cy, "I don't take baksheesh." Cy advised me to seriously consider the U.S. proposal.

Why did Clinton want me to announce now that I intended to leave office? My staff was convinced that the reason was the American political campaign. Senator Dole was being loudly applauded whenever he declared that, when he became president, American troops would *never* serve under the command of "Bootrus, Bootrus-Ghali." My friend John Whitehead, a leading Republican, formerly deputy secretary of state and chairman of the United Nations Association of the USA, had urged Dole to stop. You knew perfectly well, Whitehead had said to Dole, that American soldiers have not been commanded by Boutros-Ghali and never will be. And, Whitehead added, "Making fun of someone's name is beneath the dignity of a candidate for president of the United States." "I know that," Dole replied, "but you don't understand; this is a surefire line. It always gets me a standing round of applause!"

I was in Geneva on June 7 when Christopher telephoned. He was astonished that I knew the purpose of his call. I told him I had learned of "the compromise" from Cy Vance. "We should talk about this in person," I said, "not on an international telephone line." "Why?" he asked. "Because I cannot simply speak for myself and give you a yes or no. My country is Egypt. President Mubarak proposed me to become secretary-general. I represent Africa. I cannot make a decision on my own without informing or consulting them." "But you are now an international civil servant," Christopher said. "You are supposed to be independent." "Yes," I replied, "but I also have a responsibility to those who have asked me to serve a second term."

"Surely you cannot just dismiss the secretary-general of the United Nations by a unilateral diktat of the United States. What about the rights of the other Security Council members?" Christopher mumbled something inaudible and hung up, deeply displeased. When my staff asked me to brief them on Christopher's call, I said it had had to do with the oil-for-food negotiations with Iraq. I still felt bound by my commitment to Christopher not to reveal what was going on. And keeping quiet was in my interest as well; otherwise I would immediately be rendered ineffective and unable to complete the new round of reforms I had begun with Joseph Connor, an American whom I had appointed to the administration and management job previously held by Thornburgh and Wells. At noon press briefings in New York, reporters were now regularly asking whether I had made up my mind to stand for a second term. "Not yet," was my spokesman's answer. "It will be some months before he decides."

I telephoned President Mubarak in Cairo. "All your predecessors have had a second term," Mubarak said. "Why not you?" Mubarak said he would send a letter to Clinton conveying Egypt's official request that Boutros-Ghali be supported for a full second term. A little later I telephoned President Nelson Mandela of South Africa to discuss human rights problems in Nigeria. When we finished with this topic, I asked for his advice. "You must have a full five-year second term," he said, "and all Africa will support you."

French President Jacques Chirac arrived in Geneva on June 11 to open a session of the International Labor Organization. Protocol placed me next to him at lunch. Chirac said he was opposed to any compromise; I must receive a full second term. He supported me completely and was feeling combative about it, he said.

That same day, two pieces about me appeared in *The Washington Post.* One, on the op-ed page, declared that "typical U.S. blundering" had let this issue get away from the administration. It is now too late to prevent a second Boutros-Ghali term, Jessica Tuchman Matthews wrote, but the

United States cannot rebuild its relations with the United Nations as long as Boutros-Ghali is secretary-general. In the same issue, a columnist widely read for inside stories on the official mood called me "the most reviled man in Washington." The administration opposes a second term, the columnist said, but a deal is in the works either to limit Boutros-Ghali to a one- or two-year term, or to give him a second five-year term under an agreement that he will depart after two years. Some on my staff considered this item to be a signal to me, planted by the administration. I doubted it. Next day came a *Washington Post* editorial. Relations between the Clinton administration and Boutros-Ghali, it said, are so bad that there is no way to improve them, so there must be a new secretary-general. Boutros-Ghali had been more a general than a secretary. If the administration was planting anything in the press, I concluded, this was it.

That evening, in Istanbul, I met with President Ezer Weizman of Israel. Years before, we had worked closely on the Camp David peace process. We sat for a long time on the terrace, looking out at the lights along the Bosphorus. Neither of us said a word about the Qana incident or my reelection. Earlier, Prime Minister Shimon Peres had promised me Israel's full support for a second term, but Peres had lost the election, and my report on the Qana massacre had aroused Israeli feelings against me. I had no personal contact within Israel's new Likud government.

During this time Irish President Mary Robinson was in the United States for a state visit. Stopping in New York, she addressed the Foreign Policy Association. Her text, one UN official noted, "could have been lifted from one of Boutros-Ghali's speeches, but she projects an image of the UN that Americans want to see." *The Irish Times* of June 13 reported that Clinton and Robinson would discuss the future of the United Nations when they met in the Oval Office, but "the sensitive issue of her possible candidature as the next Secretary-General will be avoided." Nonetheless, it was reported, Clinton "has already begun confidential discussions with world leaders" on a replacement for Boutros-Ghali.

Late that afternoon in Geneva, I was at tea at the home of an Egyptian friend, Dr. Aleya Hamad, when a call came from President Chirac. He had discussed matters with President Mubarak, and Chirac's adviser on diplomacy, Jean-David Levitte, had called Secretary Christopher to urge the United States to change its position, but to no avail. Two days later, Chirac telephoned again. He and Mubarak had agreed to coordinate on a common French-Egyptian strategy to win a second term for me as secretary-general, an agreement later confirmed to me personally by President Mubarak.

"Very Well . . . We Will Proceed"

On Saturday, June 15, *The New York Times* carried a story that turned a behind-the-scenes dispute into a public battle. *Times* reporter Barbara Crossette wrote that "taking advantage of the Clinton Administration's indecision over whether to support Boutros-Ghali for a second term as Secretary-General, Congressional Republicans want to force the debate into the open and thus into a Presidential political campaign where Bob Dole has already made bashing the UN a popular sport." This article caused the White House to go public with a campaign against me in fear that the GOP was about to seize the anti–United Nations, anti-Boutros-Ghali issue.

On the evening of Monday, June 17, while I was in Geneva on an official visit, Christopher telephoned me once more. Again I asked him to meet with me in person to discuss the problem. "We can meet just before the G-7 summit at Lyons at the end of June," I suggested. "No," Christopher said, "we want it over before Lyons." But the G-7 leaders had agreed not to discuss the issue at Lyons, I said. "How would you know?" Christopher asked sharply. "I want your answer within twenty-four hours." I repeated that I could not give him an answer because Mubarak had just sent a letter to Clinton requesting a second term for me. I repeatedly asked for a chance to talk in person, but Christopher refused. I was hurt by the way he spoke to me.

Well before my twenty-four hours were up, Christopher called; he wanted my answer. I said I had no choice but to stand for a second term. "Very well," Christopher said, "we withdraw our offer of a one-year extension, and we will proceed." I was not sure what he meant by "proceed" and was reluctant to ask.

From Geneva I went to Bonn, where, on June 19, German Foreign Minister Klaus Kinkel gave me a dinner in a dazzling white dining hall with a view of a forest. In an atmosphere of good cheer he praised my record at the United Nations to an audience of 140 guests. Privately, in response to his question, I said that I would continue to avoid any statement to the press about my future; I intended to remain silent until after the American election.

After dinner I returned to my room in the German guest house, where I found a request from the president of Namibia to meet him that night. As we were talking shortly before midnight, a telephone call came from the UN press office in New York *The New York Times*' United Nations correspondent, Barbara Crossette, was trying to get a "reaction" from me. A *Times* reporter had been called in to the State Department "at the highest level" to be informed that the United States would "veto" any attempt to elect Boutros-Ghali to a second term as secretary-general. This decision was "irrevocable." As soon as I heard this, I decided to announce to the press that I would be a candidate for a second term. "Don't you want to think about it first?" my aide Fayza Abulnaga asked. "You have some time to decide. You can take advantage of the time difference between here and Washington."

"My daughter," I said in Arabic, "my life is behind me, not ahead of me. I have nothing to fear but the violation of my principles. You go right to the telephone and tell them that I have decided to present myself as a candidate for a second term as secretary-general."

Although only a few hours before I had told the German press that I was undecided, I was now freed from my pledge to Christopher. The integrity and independence of the office of the secretary-general were under assault. The accepted procedure of consultation among UN member states had been arrogantly ignored. I had no choice but to declare that I was a candidate for reelection as secretary-general for a full term.

The lead story in *The New York Times* on June 20, 1996, was headed:

U.S. WILL OPPOSE MOVE TO RE-ELECT TOP UN OFFICIAL

HE REFUSES TO BOW OUT

WASHINGTON READY TO USE VETO TO PREVENT

BOUTROS-GHALI FROM WINNING SECOND TERM

According to the *Times* story, Clinton had made this decision on March 25. The *Times* reported, inaccurately, that on June 19 I had declared that I would stand for a second term. Clinton's people must have put this out as a way of justifying their public declaration against me. The BBC and other media picked this up, conveying to the world the false impression that the United States had reacted to my announcement rather than the truth, which was just the opposite. The BBC attributed Clinton's decision to "domestic political considerations," noting that he was facing Dole's anti–United Nations reputation. This was, the media said, another case of Clinton adopting a GOP position for campaign purposes. In New York, the BBC reported, "UN officials say there will be blood on the walls." That evening, on the public television network's *NewsHour with Jim Lehrer,* State Department spokesman Nicholas Burns refined the U.S. position: the Clinton administration was on both sides of the issue; it was in favor of the United Nations in general but against Boutros-Ghali in particular. I thought this was a very clever approach: it could appeal to the more than 70 percent of Americans who had a favorable view of the United Nations, yet at the same time satisfy the small number who, according to polls, believed that the United Nations is a world government flying black helicopters secretly through American airspace.

I was heartened to learn that Yemen's ambassador to the United Nations, Abdalla Saleh al-Ashtal, had staunchly defended me on the Lehrer program. The U.S. decision, he declared, was insulting, unseemly, and inexplicable except in terms of American politics. Stories appeared in the press that Dole was "outraged" that Clinton had stolen his anti-Boutros-Ghali issue.

Still in Bonn, I met with Chancellor Helmut Kohl on June 20. He expressed shock at the U.S. announcement. He would support me, he said, but would have to do so quietly, behind the scenes. He urged me to contact him directly whenever I needed help. From Bonn I returned to Geneva, where, after breakfast on June 24 with President Nazarbayev of Kazakhstan, the president spoke openly and strongly to the press, condemning the American position. "If the U.S. has a veto, so do China and Russia," he declared. This was not what I wanted. I did not want to provoke the United States further, but to find a reasonable compromise. I was relieved when the Kazakhstan president's words were not picked up by the international press.

Those who tried to help me only angered the White House further. In an interview on CNN and again at the United Nations' noon briefing, my deputy press spokesman, Ahmed Fawzi, read out the warm words of praise about me that President Clinton had spoken only months earlier, during the United Nations' fiftieth anniversary year. Fawzi made sure the press heard every word of it all over again, quoting Clinton at excruciating length: "Mr. Secretary-General, you have taken the ideas of peace, help, and security that are at the heart of the UN's mission and worked hard to make them a reality. As the cold war has ended, the world has looked to the UN for ever more assistance and leadership. You have met this challenge by effectively placing the UN at the forefront of international affairs."

But my loyal and well-intentioned spokesman had only exacerbated the situation to my detriment. These on-the-record public statements by the president stood in incomprehensible contrast to his current stance against me. The fact was, however, that ever since the Republican victory in the 1994 congressional elections, the Clinton administration had, step by step, turned against me, as the White House apparently felt a growing need to compete with the GOP over which party was more anti–United Nations. My activism, once encouraged and praised, had become an annoyance to the administration.

With the G-7 in Lyons

It was a strange twist of fate that this year of 1996 marked the first time that I or any other United Nations secretary-general had ever been inscribed on the agenda of the annual G-7 summit. I was asked to discuss UN reform and eagerly looked forward to the opportunity. I had carried out more reform measures at the United Nations than any previous secretary-general. I wanted to tell these world leaders, however, that the truly far-reaching reform they wanted could not be made by a secretary-general but had to come from the most influential member states themselves. I wanted to enlist the G-7 in the cause of such major reforms.

As I made my way toward Lyons, comments pro and con about me appeared in the media. The European press was supportive. In the Arab world, *The New York Times* reported, "There is anger, and a feeling of powerlessness. The fury might not transform itself into a confrontation with the United States, but it will seep in and turn itself into a deep resentment." The Egyptian and Arab press was packed with articles and editorials praising me and attacking Madeleine Albright.

The lead editorial in *The New York Times* on June 23 called for me to go quietly in a dignified way. This was the beginning of a stream of advice from those purporting to be deeply concerned about preserving my "dignity." In fact, it was their own dignity that was at stake; if only I would quit, they could avoid the messy job of eradicating me. Madeleine Albright, testifying before the Congress on the United Nations' financial situation, said, "I've been very clear when I talk to people that we'll veto, and if [Boutros-Ghali] wins, we will withdraw support from the UN." The United Nations' liaison officer in Washington reported that those in the congressional meeting room "were surprised, to put it mildly, by the second part of her statement."

Others came firmly to my defense. A. M. Rosenthal titled his *New York Times* column "Mugging Boutros-Ghali." Rosenthal highlighted the undisguised slurs on my name and background, a pattern of disrespect, Rosenthal noted, that would not be tolerated if used in reference to a Mario Cuomo or Martin Luther King Jr. Senator Paul Simon also stepped forward and in an article in *The Christian Science Monitor* strongly defended my record as secretary-general.

In London, late in the afternoon of June 25, I was received by Prime Minister John Major at 10 Downing Street. Speaking with the utmost diplomatic care, Major said that he appreciated my work and disapproved of the way the American administration was behaving. But he said nothing about Britain's position on my reelection. I was later told, repeatedly, that this was established British practice when it came to the appointment or election of international officials. After meetings in London with the secretary-general of the Commonwealth, Chief Anyoko, on the Nigerian human rights crisis, I returned to Geneva for the eighth round of negotiations between the foreign ministers of Indonesia and Portugal on the problem of East Timor. The three of us talked privately on a balcony overlooking the gardens of the Palais des Nations and Lake Leman. We agreed that our next meeting would be at the United Nations in New York in December. I said with a smile that this might be my last meeting with them if the Americans succeeded in expelling me from the United Nations.

On the evening of June 27 in Geneva came a message from colleagues in New York. They suggested a compromise: If the United States would drop its opposition to me, I would agree to serve for two more years after my present mandate ended on December 31, 1996. This would make a total of seven years in office. Because many member states over the years had expressed dissatisfaction with the tradition of two five-year terms for a secretary-general, my seven-year term would become a precedent-setting model for what would in fact be a major UN reform: from that point forward, all UN secretaries-general would serve just one seven-year term. I telephoned my colleagues. "I have received your paper" was all I would say. I had become convinced that my telephone conversations, both from the secretary-general's residence in New York City and while traveling abroad, were being monitored. But I decided to raise this compromise issue with Presidents Mubarak and Chirac.

Lyons conveyed a mood of lush and lovely relaxation despite the mobs of bureaucrats and reporters that crowded the city for the G-7 summit. I was provided a room in an *auberge* called Hôtel de La Tour Rose, which Leia greatly enjoyed. Press speculation was that improving Franco-American relations "could soon be put to the test over Mr. Clinton's decision to oppose the re-election of Boutros Boutros-Ghali as United Nations secretary-general when his term expires at the end of this year. Mr. Chirac supports Mr. Boutros-Ghali and told Mr. Clinton so" (*The New York Times*). Because of this, President Chirac wisely let it be known that this issue would not be allowed to come up during the Lyons summit, as I had predicted to Warren Christopher.

That evening, I attended the dinner given for all the foreign ministers of the G-7 countries. Christopher and I had a pleasant chat, largely about UN reform. I called him "Chris"; he called me "Boutros." It was as though nothing stood between us. Afterward, as we watched fireworks, President Chirac came over to me. After criticizing the poor quality of the fireworks, he said, "We will support you to the end." Then I found myself near Prime Minister Jean Chrétien of Canada, who whispered that he would support my reelection "despite the opposition of our neighbor to the south."

The next morning, June 29, I met formally with the G-7 leaders and read out a paper explaining how the World Bank, the International Monetary Fund, the World Trade Organization, and the United Nations were working cooperatively on the problems of the poorest countries. President Clinton listened with apparent interest. At the lunch that followed I described for the leaders how, before the Oslo peace accords in 1993, I had decided to move the United Nations Relief and Works Agency for Palestinian Refugees in the Middle East (UNRWA) from Vienna to Gaza, despite the strong objections of the UN staff. Afterward President Clinton made a point of saying to me, "Thank you for doing this. It helps Arafat." As the Lyons summit ended, the U.S. spokesman said that the atmosphere in the G-7 toward "the beleaguered Mr. Boutros-Ghali" had been "correct and dignified." Reuters reported that "French president Jacques Chirac and German chancellor Helmut Kohl both dropped heavy hints that they thought Boutros-Ghali deserved a second term." Chirac declared that everyone knew the esteem in which he and the European community held me. Kohl told reporters that "every UN secretary-general has had a second term." Canadian Prime Minister Chrétien said at his final press conference, "We are of the view that Mr. Boutros Boutros-Ghali has done a very good job under difficult circumstances and we would be happy to have him reelected."

The Lyons summit concluded with a statement of support for UN reform. The G-7 communiqué, one observer said, amounted to an A-minus grade for Boutros-Ghali as secretary-general. As a former professor, I was quite happy to be awarded an A-minus. A Japanese delegate who, as a "Sherpa," had been part of the G-7 staff that, over the preceding twelve months, had drafted this communiqué, told an Egyptian diplomat in Tokyo that the text had originally contained many compliments for me, but at the last minute the United States had insisted that all such language be taken out.

Backing and Backlash

From New York reports reached me that Albright was putting all-out pressure on African countries to repudiate me at the Yaoundé summit, which was about to take place. One African ambassador to the United Nations told my chief of staff that he was receiving "endless" messages from the U.S. Mission. Madeleine Albright had even telephoned him in person. "Before this, she didn't even know my name," he said with amazement.

My UN colleague Lansana Kouyate, who had gone to Yaoundé ahead of me, reported that the Americans were on the scene in force, urging the Africans to turn against me.

From my vantage point in Europe, I could see the world press closely following this story, while the American media seemed almost oblivious to it. A friend who was visiting the University of California at Berkeley told me that at a Fourth of July faculty picnic, not one of the many sophisticated and usually well-informed guests was even aware of the Clinton administration's campaign against me. When told about it, the general reaction was surprise: "I thought Boutros-Ghali was okay," one professor said. Despite the general lack of American press coverage, an article by Barbara Crossette, US CRITICS OF UN REFORM DRAW RETORT, pointed out the substantial record of reform brought about by me as "the instigator" and Under Secretary-General for Management Joseph Connor as "the implementor."

Another *Times* story, headed THE US AND THE UN: NOW WHO NEEDS WHOM MORE? asserted that Clinton's effort to oust Boutros-Ghali "has turned into a public embarrassment, if not yet a fiasco." The article accused the United States of using the United Nations as a "fig leaf," making it "easier to affix the blame anywhere but on President Clinton and the White House."

The Yaoundé Summit

After a late-Saturday-night arrival in early July in Yaoundé, the capital of Cameroon and the host city for the OAU summit, I began to seek support among the delegates early Sunday morning. Although warned that the Americans were on the scene in force, I was shocked to find such a high-powered U.S. team of officials working so intensely to discredit me. There, in the hotel lobby, I realized for the first time the full meaning of the American term "lobbying." Countless young American diplomats seemed to be constantly rushing from one part of the hotel to another. Every time I stepped into an elevator, I would encounter a sweating American Foreign Service officer on his or her way to meetings with African leaders.

Assistant Secretary of State for African Affairs George Moose was there. With him was the man who had held that same job during the Bush administration, Herman "Hank" Cohen, now director of a foundation dealing with Africa. I knew both men, because we had often worked together on African issues. Strangest of all to me was the presence of Ahmedou Ould Abdallah, a Mauritanian I had appointed as my special representative for Burundi. Ould Abdallah had slipped into the American camp like an eel, perhaps because he had suddenly left the United Nations to become the new head of Cohen's foundation. My aide Fayza Abulnaga cornered Ould Abdallah with feline fury in a hotel corridor and denounced him as a despicable turncoat.

Assistant Secretary Moose appeared on Cameroon television. The United States, he said, would support *any* African for UN secretary-general so long as it was not Boutros-Ghali. In my long career in diplomacy I had never witnessed such a massive, vituperative propaganda effort. It was hard for me to believe that I was the target of this huge effort by the world's only superpower. Moose's declaration proved counterproductive, as African leaders were as shocked as I was by the threatening tone of the American effort. Only those who have held prominent public office can understand what it is like to be the subject of constant political slander. No matter how thick your skin, it is devastating. I stood up to it because I felt sure that it was being done only for domestic political reasons and that once the U.S. election was over, the administration would cease its assault on me.

Over the course of twenty-four hours I saw so many African heads of state or government that in the pressure of the moment I lost count. The president of Mozambique was positive, the president of Togo even more so. The president of Zambia said he "very much favored" my reelection. The president of Algeria said he would strongly back me and thanked me for sending UN observers for the Algerian referendum over the resistance of many UN "apparatchiks." The president of the Congo said that "emotionally, practically and politically," he was all for me, "but realism dictates that if the only superpower opposes you, it is useless to resist." I said that I had no choice but to resist—for the independence of the United Nations and for Africa's image and integrity.

At midnight I was getting into bed when the telephone rang. Yasser Arafat was on his way to see me. I hurriedly dressed just in time to welcome the PLO chairman and his huge entourage. I told them that at the end of the day I was a bit pessimistic about whether the OAU would be able to resist the powerful American campaign. Arafat became dramatically angry: "Never say this! You will succeed! We are behind you! Your presence at the UN is essential!" I thanked the chairman for his support and attempted to escort him back to his quarters. He objected out of politeness. I insisted as a matter of protocol. We conducted ourselves as "Alphonse and Gaston" in a flowery Arabic colloquy in the doorway before he prevailed and made his departure.

I was up early on Monday to start further contacts. The vote would come soon. The president of Eritrea reacted bitterly to my request for support. He opposed me, he said, because my country, Egypt, had "concluded a secret alliance with Sudan against Eritrea." "That is not true," I said. "I have proof," the president insisted. "Egypt only mildly supported the last UN resolution directed against Sudan." "Forget about my country," I said. "Haven't I done a lot to support your country? My good offices in Eritrea's dispute with Yemen were successful. The accord is being produced at this very moment." The Eritrean president calmed down. "I may support you," he said, "but not your country." I did not understand this ambiguous declaration, but at Yaoundé he did not openly oppose my re-election.

I gave President Abdou Diouf of Senegal a message from President Mubarak asking Diouf to represent Mubarak in presenting my candidacy to the OAU. For tactical reasons I hoped that the African leaders would vote on the resolution naming their choice for UN secretary-general before they opened their formal summit session.

The only persons allowed in the Grand Salon who were not heads of state or government were myself and Salim Ahmed Salim, the secretary-general of the OAU. The heads of state moved into another chamber to hold informal consultations. I could barely endure awaiting the verdict alone in this great hall. The wait seemed endless, reminding me of my student days when I had awaited the results of an examination.

Suddenly Fayza burst into the room: "We won the resolution! By consensus!" President Nelson Mandela came out to hug me and invite me to escort him into the summit session. He had come to Yaoundé for two hours only, specifically for the vote.

Chairman Arafat was one of the first to speak at the formal summit session, a privilege granted under the OAU Charter to the PLO as the last remaining liberation movement. At the conclusion of his speech Arafat noted that the Arab world had decided to support Boutros-Ghali for reelection and congratulated me for the support that Africa had just given me. This was the first official public reference to the fact that the OAU had just passed a resolution in my favor. I received a standing ovation, not so much for me personally but for Africa, which had just defied the American superpower. Fayza was at that time sitting behind the U.S. delegation. One American diplomat turned to another: "What did Arafat say? Does he know what he is talking about?" Fayza leaned over to tell the Americans, "It happened ten minutes ago. The OAU voted by consensus to recommend a second term for Boutros-Ghali." The American turned pale, in amusing contrast to the all-black setting of the auditorium. One of the Americans jumped up and left the hall, saying, "We've got to inform State right away!"

The text of the resolution was released:

DECLARATION OF THE YAOUNDÉ SUMMIT ON
AFRICAN CANDIDATURE FOR A SECOND TERM AS
SECRETARY-GENERAL OF THE UN

The Assembly of Heads of State and Government of the Organization of African Unity, meeting in its Thirty-Second Session in Yaoundé, Cameroon from 8 to 10 July 1996.

Recalling Resolution AHG/Res. 243 (XXXI)1995 by which the Assembly of Heads of State and Government expressed its appreciation to Boutros Boutros-Ghali for his initiatives at the helm of the United Nations Organization:

1. REAFFIRMS the historic importance of the election of an African as Secretary-General of the United Nations, thus enabling Africa to significantly contribute to the attainment of the principles enshrined in the UN Charter and promote multilateralism;
2. WISHES to underscore Dr. Boutros Boutros-Ghali's action at the head of the UN General Secretariat since his election in 1991;
3. RECALLS the tradition and the practice at the UN, which consists in re-electing the Incumbent Secretary-General for a second term;
4. In this regard, RECOMMENDS that the necessary steps be taken by the Current Chairman with all the partners, members of the UN, to give Africa a second mandate, for the next five years, and RECOMMENDS the candidature of Dr. Boutros Boutros-Ghali for a second term as Secretary-General of the UN.

Later, in individual calls I made on leaders to thank them, everyone was warm and optimistic. But one warned me, "This is a humiliating diplomatic defeat for the U.S.; it will make them all the more vicious in their efforts to get rid of you. They will be like a bulldozer."

I traveled by car to Douala on the coast of Cameroon, because the Yaoundé airport was reserved for the OAU heads of state. In the VIP room of Douala International Airport I encountered the entire American delegation. I chatted politely with Assistant Secretary Moose, and all the Americans were pleasant despite the bitter battle we had just fought in Yaoundé.

I arrived at Charles de Gaulle Airport outside Paris at dawn. A French journalist who met me said that every head of state or government at Yaoundé had been telephoned by either Secretary Christopher or National Security Adviser Anthony Lake, and that an American delegation had visited every African country in the weeks before the Yaoundé summit, all in a massive effort against me. "If only such tremendous American energy could have been applied to African development," I said.

Disinformation

The State Department, mainly through its spokesman, Nicholas Burns, tried to turn its defeat at Yaoundé into a victory. Africa's support for me had been only perfunctory and lukewarm, the United States asserted. In response, OAU Secretary-General Salim Ahmed Salim corrected this mischaracterization. The Declaration, he declared, "was taken by overwhelming consensus." Boutros-Ghali was Africa's candidate, and "the decision was taken in full knowledge of the concern expressed by one member of the Security Council [i.e., the United States]." Still the disinformation continued; it was alleged that only a few African heads of state had been present. Again Salim Ahmed Salim set the record straight, declaring that twenty-nine heads of state had been present when the decision in favor of Boutros-Ghali had been made.

But disinformation sometimes outperforms genuine information. The American media, taking the State Department's lead, took little notice of the OAU decision or dismissed it as halfhearted. The African and European press, on the other hand, reported the story as a major rebuff to the U.S. campaign against me.

Another major U.S. theme was that I had "demoralized" the UN staff. But when I arrived back in New York and entered the UN building, a large staff gathering met me with cheers and applause. I had a reputation, undoubtedly deserved, of being hard on them. But they knew they had my deep respect and affection. And, clearly, U.S. opposition to me had only aroused their loyalty and support. As CNN cameras covered the scene, hundreds pressed forward to reach out and shake my hand. In their eyes the U.S. attack on me was an attack on them all and on the United Nations itself. I was nearly moved to tears by the warmth I felt from these friends and colleagues.

The *Washington Times* called it a "hero's welcome," adding:

The Egyptian diplomat and scholar who will be 74 when his current term expires, has done nearly all the U.S. wanted—even if he squawked about it. He has initiated reforms in the Secretariat, implemented Security Council mandates in Bosnia he knew would fail, and tried to cobble together a mission on Rwanda out of the scraps thrown to him by member states. And he has shepherded the United Nations through its role as scapegoat for problems member nations don't want to deal with. Whatever the truth of his rocky tenure, it is lost in the spins of U.S. politicians who have found in Mr. Boutros-Ghali a handy villain to flog in an election year.

The United States then began a very effective effort to silence my supporters at the United Nations. Anyone connected with the United Nations who rose to my defense was attacked by the U.S. Mission spokesman for waging a "political campaign" from an official UN position, which was "paid for by American taxpayer dollars." Reporters were called into James Rubin's office at the U.S. Mission to the United Nations to hear him denounce as "scandalous" the UN press office's alleged involvement in Boutros-Ghali's "campaign." "We will not forget this!" Rubin said. The result was a wholly one-sided contest. My side was silenced while they spoke against me at will.

Washington did not seem to know or care about the implications of the assault on me for the integrity of the United Nations. By threatening to "veto" me, the United States had touched a nerve, for after the demise of the cold war, the veto had virtually disappeared. Many member states believed that it should be confined to questions of international peace and security. Washington's continued reiteration of its veto threat carried the issue beyond that of the independence of the secretary-general to a question of the proper functioning of the Security Council.

I asked a colleague to try to raise some of these concerns at an appropriate level in the State Department in Washington. The response came back: "No second thoughts. We are ploughing ahead. We want to get Boutros-Ghali out of the way ASAP [as soon as possible] and go forward from there. We view the OAU resolution as peculiar and, indeed, as a sign that we have made some headway. The Africans blinked." The mood among Washington's foreign policy people was one of near invincibility, stemming in large part from the total confidence in the White House about Clinton's reelection. What foreign government would want to get off on the wrong foot with the president as he started his second term? In Poland Madeleine Albright put it directly: "Who would you rather have as your friend, Bill Clinton or Boutros-Ghali?"

Ironically, the Clinton administration was doing more to get rid of me than to get rid of Radovan Karadžić, the Serb leader indicted as a war criminal, for by this time it was clear that the U.S.-led NATO force in

Bosnia was going out of its way to avoid encountering Karadžić and other major figures charged with war crimes.

Beijing and Moscow Speak with One Voice

On July 1, 1996, the Chinese government issued a declaration:

> China appreciates the positive role played by Mr. Boutros-Ghali as Secretary-General in strengthening the role of the United Nations. China understands and supports the OAU Declaration on the candidature of the Secretary-General of the United Nations and is convinced that the aspiration and position of the OAU enjoys wide sympathy and support from the international community.

The Chinese statement, timed to come in the context of a visit to Beijing by Clinton's national security adviser, Anthony Lake, was regarded in diplomatic circles as a deliberate slap at the United States' handling of this issue.

Russia followed with an even more pointed jab at the United States. During Vice President Gore's visit to Moscow to congratulate President Yeltsin after his reelection, the Russian Foreign Ministry declared:

> As is known, the OAU Summit has firmly pronounced itself in favor of giving a second mandate of the Secretary-General to Africa and recommended a re-election to this post of the incumbent Secretary-General, Dr. Boutros Boutros-Ghali. We note the importance of this authoritative forum's decision. It reaffirms that—whether someone wants it or not—Dr. Boutros Boutros-Ghali enjoys wide sympathy and support on the part of the world community. Russia highly appreciates Dr. Boutros Boutros-Ghali's role as Secretary-General of the United Nations.

On July 16 I briefed the Security Council on a range of current diplomatic issues from Liberia and Cyprus to Western Sahara and East Timor. All the Council members addressed questions to me except the U.S. representative, who sat tight-lipped, apparently to demonstrate Washington's disapproval of me. Because of the Chinese and Russian declarations, reporters rushed up to me with questions about my reelection. I welcomed the chance to make my position clear: "I am overloaded by daily problems. I will not be able to tackle those problems if I pay attention to reelection. This is in the hands of the Member States. They will have to decide it. It is no longer my problem."

At this time the press noted that James Rubin would be leaving the U.S. Mission to the United Nations to join the Clinton campaign. Privately, reporters speculated that Rubin had agreed to this move because he had concluded that Madeleine Albright was unlikely to become secretary of state. There was a general sense among the press corps that the effort she was leading against me was failing and had diminished her standing with the White House.

But in July and August the American people were busy watching the Olympic Games in Atlanta and the nominating conventions of the two major political parties. So in the United States little attention was given to the remarkable series of diplomatic embarrassments to the Clinton administration delivered in Yaoundé, Beijing, and Moscow.

My colleagues stayed in touch with their counterparts in the administration, if only to get a feel for how they saw the situation. "Look," one State Department official said on July 17, "we offered BB-G a seventy-fifth birthday deal. One more year and a big fête with praises from Clinton. When Boutros turned it down, it was war." Clinton, the official said, "wins only by vetoing. It's his best tool in American politics. And we're getting no blowback. The American press and people don't care. We feel no heat. It's good domestic politics." "Anyway," another U.S. contact said, "Clinton has no flexibility. After saying that his decision was irrevocable, he could never change it; Dole would clobber him."

But what about the Chinese and Russian statements of support? we asked. "Forget it," came the reply. "There are Foreign Ministry statements, and there is real-world diplomacy. You can rack up all the Foreign Ministry statements you want, but they don't count. The Russians are telling us that their statement wasn't authorized by Yeltsin."

I was also getting intelligence reports from my friends in the diplomatic corps. On July 20 a Latin American ambassador passed word that the White House had decided to "advance the process." The United States wanted to get it over with—meaning get a Security Council vote against me—by early September. That way President Clinton would not risk embarrassment when he came to address the opening of the UN General Assembly, as American presidents have always done.

New Threats

Then the United States put forward a new threat aimed to break the resolve of the African nations that had voted to support me. On July 22, 1996, the United States Information Agency (USIA) correspondent at the United Nations quoted a U.S. official's statement that if Africans remained steadfast behind Boutros-Ghali, they "would destroy the chances of Africa to retain the secretary-general post for a second term." In other words, the Africans should follow the Clinton administration's instructions quickly, or the United States would pick my successor from somewhere other than the continent of Africa. This only strengthened my determination to insist upon Africa's right to hold the post for two full terms, as had been the case with secretaries-general from Europe, Asia, and Latin America. The USIA article shocked my friend and consultant John Hughes, a former director of that agency: "This is straight propaganda and an improper use of the United States Information Agency." American law prohibited the use of USIA in this way, he said.

In contrast, the press outside the United States was favorable. *The Economist* issue of July 20–28, 1996, described the situation in what I, however immodestly, considered to be accurate terms. I had been, *The Economist*'s editors said, one of the happier choices as secretary-general and the right man for the time. I was described as "a principled and independent-minded intellectual [who] responded with spirit, struggling with the ill-defined mandates handed down to him from the Security Council." For Americans, the magazine said, "the interventionist adventure swiftly turned sour, and they trained their frustration on the UN and its less-than-tactful boss, a man who does not often suffer fools." *The Economist* floated a compromise: "Boutros-Ghali is open to the idea, promoted by the European Union, of a slightly longer extension. This might be a way of avoiding battle in the Council but probably only after, and if, Mr. Clinton wins America's election in November." This was a version of the compromise I had raised with Presidents Mubarak and Chirac around the time of the G-7 summit at Lyons. Word had reached me through Arab friends in Washington that the French were trying to convince the United States to take this course, but I had no direct knowledge that this was, in fact, taking place.

On July 22 a *New York Times* reporter telephoned my colleague John

Hughes: "The U.S. has just made this extraordinary threat! Jamie Rubin. At USUN. On the record. He said that anyone at the United Nations who is working for the reelection of Boutros Boutros-Ghali will be investigated by the U.S.!" Rubin had ominously declared, "They know who they are!" What made this so shocking, the reporter said, was the Clinton administration's own incessant politicking against Boutros-Ghali. "The White House paid the airfares of those who would go to Yaoundé to trash Boutros-Ghali before the OAU vote," the reporter said, such as the Rwandan officials who were angry with my charges about the genocide there.

The next morning, July 23, *The New York Times* reported the U.S. threat to UN officials, noting that the administration was "in a frenzy" over my refusal to cooperate with its efforts to get rid of me. The article mentioned the names of those at the United Nations whom Rubin had apparently targeted for investigation, including Ahmed Fawzi, the United Nations' deputy spokesman, who amusingly had read to the press corps the fulsome praise given me by President Clinton less than a year earlier. Also mentioned were the American citizens I had appointed in consultation with the Clinton administration to work in important UN jobs: Sylvana Foa, my spokeswoman; James Gustave Speth, the director of the UN Development Program; and Joseph Connor, under secretary-general for administration and management. Speth and Connor were politically close to the Clinton administration, yet both were shocked at this assault.

At the noon UN press briefing my spokeswoman, Sylvana Foa, did not back away. This was disgraceful, she said, calling Rubin's threats "bully tactics" that smacked of McCarthyism. Maybe, one reporter joked, referring to the current Washington scandal, in which some nine hundred FBI files had been acquired by Clinton's political aides, the White House had gotten hold of the FBI files on Americans working at the United Nations.

A *Washington Post* headline read:

UN CONTROVERSY OVER BOUTROS-GHALI HEATS UP
OTHER MEMBERS ATTACK U.S. FOR ITS OPPOSITION TO
REELECTION OF THE SECRETARY-GENERAL

So far all indications were that Madeleine Albright and the small, secret "task force" remained in charge of eliminating me. President Clinton and the White House, preoccupied with the presidential campaign and the conventions, appeared understandably oblivious to it all. But as soon as the press began to take an interest in the matter, it became at least visible at higher levels. A distinguished Democratic Party business-man-philanthropist and strong supporter of Clinton told me he was "ap-palled" at what the administration was doing. Following a fund-raising dinner for Clinton in San Francisco on July 24, he sent a note to the president saying that the efforts against me had gotten out of control and needed to be looked at carefully.

On the Republican side, Joseph Verner Reed, a longtime friend of George Bush, briefed the former president, who was then at Kenne-bunkport, Maine. Bush, a close observer of UN affairs ever since he had served as head of the U.S. Mission to the United Nations, was horrified at the clumsiness of the U.S. effort. "I'm pro-Boutros," he said. He would try to help by talking to the Republican presidential candidate, Senator Dole. All this only reinforced my determination to continue to seek reelection. But the Clinton campaign had hit upon a watertight strategy: the United Nations and I were being blamed for the failures of Clinton's foreign pol-icy. The Republicans, who found United Nations bashing a surefire suc-cess in their political campaigning, would never allow themselves to seem soft on the United Nations, even as a means of attacking Clinton's foreign policy. Underlying this was the fact that in this election year, the Ameri-can public was simply not interested in foreign affairs. The latest *Wall Street Journal*/NBC poll put "foreign policy" dead last in a list of sixteen issues that would affect the American public's vote for president.

The Congressional Black Caucus Takes a Stand

The first positive sign I had from Washington came in a letter dated July 16, 1996, from the Congressional Black Caucus. The chairman, Repre-sentative Donald Payne, invited me to meet caucus members in Wash-ington. "Thank you for your outstanding strides in reforming the United Nations and your leadership to bring light to the dark places of the world," their letter stated. "The members of the Congressional Black Caucus, which represents 40 outspoken members of Congress, support your tenure for another five years."

The Black Caucus understood and appreciated the work that I had done, not only as secretary-general but throughout my entire career, on behalf of development in Africa. As if in reply, *The Wall Street Journal's* editorial page ran a long article, WHY AFRICA NEEDS A NEW UN SECRETARY-GENERAL, blaming me for virtually every act of violence, oppression, and corruption in Africa in recent decades.

Mubarak Goes to Washington

A more immediate Washington opportunity came with the visit of my president, Hosni Mubarak of Egypt. I knew Mubarak would ask Clinton to withdraw his opposition to my reelection when he met with him in the Oval Office on July 31. As the date for the meeting approached, *The New York Times* (July 29, 1996) stated that the U.S. decision to oust me after only one term was being taken as a "personal affront" by Egypt. More than this, press and public opinion all across the Arab world was deeply offended by the U.S. stance on this matter.

On Wednesday, July 31, I flew down to Washington to meet with Mubarak in a bright-colored salon in Blair House after his session with Clinton. Mubarak hugged me in his huge embrace and then held me back to look me over. "You're too thin," he said. "Well," I replied, "I've been through thick and thin."

It was President Clinton who first raised the matter, Mubarak told me. "What are we going to do about Boutros?" Clinton asked as the two of them strolled on the White House grounds. Mubarak replied by saying that Boutros-Ghali was very popular in the Arab world with Muslims and Christians alike. The U.S. effort to deny a UN secretary-general from Egypt a second term presented a political problem for Mubarak. The issue involved Egypt's national honor. All other secretaries-general had been given two terms. Why not Boutros-Ghali? "We must find a compromise," Mubarak said to Clinton. Clinton was silent. Then he said to Mubarak, "Boutros-Ghali is a good secretary-general but too independent." Mubarak had said nothing more on the subject but had the impression, he told me, that Clinton was not really opposed to me. "President Clinton is okay," he told me. "The opposition comes from the State Department." This further reinforced my belief that my nightmare would end once the American election was over. "You must know," Mubarak told me, "that I support you to the end. I have given clear instructions."

Soon after, Warren Christopher, during testimony before the House International Affairs Committee, put forward what would become the sole American justification for its campaign against me. Before this, the administration had shifted from one explanation to another. Now Christopher declared that only when I was gone would the American people believe that the United Nations was being reformed and only then could the Congress be expected to pay the U.S. debt to the United Nations. "The president and I," Christopher said, "have made it clear that tangible reform is essential to sustain the support of the Congress and the American people for the United Nations, and we've insisted on the need for a new secretary-general."

The subsequent exchange between Christopher and Congressman Lee Hamilton seemed to have been prearranged to get this new formulation into the public record:

HAMILTON: You probably know that in this body, in this Congress, and I think probably in the world—there's a lot of doubt about the American position with regard to the Secretary-General, whether we're irrevocably committed to that position or not.

CHRISTOPHER: The President felt that we could not mobilize American support for the United Nations, which he very much wants to support, without a new Secretary-General. . . .

HAMILTON: I agree with your position. Congress won't allow payments without a new Secretary-General.

The European press saw it differently. A view expressed in the German press was that America's friends, allies, and enemies were surprised by its "unilateral arrogance." Clinton was blocking Boutros-Ghali not because he had been incompetent or unwilling to reform but because Clinton wanted to take an issue away from Dole. Boutros-Ghali was increasingly seen as a "tiresome rival" or "stubborn counterweight" by the White House. A revealing comment was provided by Albright's deputy, Edward "Skip" Gnehm in answer to a direct question by my chief of staff: "Tell me truthfully, Skip, what does the U.S. have against Boutros-Ghali?" Gnehm hesitated for many seconds and then replied, "He would not do what we wanted him to do as quickly as we wanted him to do it."

Despite the public hard line, there were signs that Madeleine Albright was worried. Her attacks seemed only to increase support for me in the world outside the United States. As the Sunday *Times* of London put it on July 28, 1996, "All the Clinton Administration's efforts to paint [Boutros-Ghali] as arrogant, corrupt and ineffective have started to backfire." But if the administration does not succeed, it said, "nothing could make the U.S. look more impotent."

Overseas, the string of open embarrassments to visiting U.S. officials continued. In Canberra, the Australian foreign minister, at a joint press conference with Christopher, told reporters that Australia was "not standing in the way of Boutros-Ghali's candidacy." Commentary elsewhere was scathing. In China the *People's Daily* noted that "most countries have expressed that what the U.S. is doing . . . is an act of hegemony." The United States, it continued, is "trying to manipulate the choice of UN Secretary-General to achieve its goal of controlling the UN."

August, as always, would be a time of diplomatic inactivity, and all the more so because of the American political campaign. I rented a house in the woods in Katonah, New York, and resolved to lie low. We felt that the virulence of the U.S. Mission's attack on me might subside somewhat with the departure of Madeleine Albright's spokesman, James Rubin, for the Clinton campaign. My spokeswoman, Sylvana Foa, had a little fun at her noon briefing. She said farewell to "our own Jamie Rubin" by passing out to reporters little bottles produced in South Africa labeled "Boutros Boutros-Garlic," a reference to the legendary powers of garlic to repel vampires.

In early August, as I worked by telephone from Katonah on the unending Cyprus dispute, the human rights situation in Nigeria, and the confrontation between Yemen and Eritrea, other leaders urged me to act on my own behalf. Queen Fabiola of Belgium called to say that she was praying for me. Two days later, I had a long and heartening talk with Nelson Mandela of South Africa. When I telephoned President Glafcos Clerides to discuss the latest problems in Cyprus, he told me that he had talked to Clinton and was "not pessimistic." Clinton seemed ready to accept a two-year extension as a compromise, "but his collaborators are more negative," Clerides reported.

Watching the Republican National Convention

At the house in Katonah on August 15 I watched Senator Dole deliver his acceptance speech after his nomination as the Republican presidential candidate. Leia had gone to bed, but I stayed up, waiting to see whether Dole would once again use his "Bootrus-Bootrus" line. He did. When he became president, Dole said, "our armed forces will know that the presi-

dent is their commander in chief—not Boutros Boutros-Ghali or any
other UN secretary general." I found this morbidly fascinating. The Republican candidate for president had decided that it was more effective
politically to declare that Clinton had given me control of American foreign policy than to attack Clinton's foreign policy directly. How, I
thought, could Clinton ever change course with this accusation hanging
over him? The underlying logic of Dole's line was that Clinton had to get
rid of me in order to reclaim his presidential authority. But, I thought,
looking at it from another angle, Dole had mentioned only two names in
his speech: mine and Abraham Lincoln's. I had entered American history.
Later I was told that Dole's original text had included no mention of me.
At the last minute, however, he could not resist inserting his "surefire"
applause line.

The next day, Sylvana Foa got me into more trouble. Commenting at
the noon briefing on the Republican platform and convention, she declared, "What's being said in San Diego is obviously said for political reasons." It's worrying, she said, "that a party seeking to lead America can be
so ill informed about how the United Nations actually functions. The Republicans are just pandering to the paranoid."

I tended to agree, but Foa had gone too far. UN officials should avoid
commenting on a political party in a sovereign state. Her words provided
fuel for those who wanted to burn me at the stake. But I had chosen her
because I wanted someone who would stand up to slanderous attacks
against the United Nations, so I merely asked her to count to ten the next
time.

Albright continued to insist that the Security Council act immediately
to choose the next secretary-general. She wanted to get it over with fast
so that Clinton would not appear at the United Nations with her campaign against me still unsuccessful. As the president of the Council was
holding informal consultations to ascertain the wishes of the members,
Albright told reporters that the members were "irresponsible" in not
being more active in the search for my replacement. Council members
considered her public statement to be improper at a time when private
discussions were still under way. One ambassador was quoted in the
press as saying he had "never seen a bigger diplomatic mess than that
created by Madeleine Albright."

By this time Chirac had telephoned Clinton many times about my
case. France, rather than Egypt, was taking the lead in arguing for me,
because of Egypt's fear that any direct effort by it on my behalf might

have a negative impact on U.S. relations with Egypt, which received some $3 billion in American aid each year. This fear preoccupied me constantly; it was essential that Egypt remain in the background and let Chirac and Mandela take up my case with the Clinton administration.

On Sunday, August 18, 1996, *The New York Times* carried an article headlined:

U.S. EFFORT TO OUST UN CHIEF
GOES NOWHERE

Suddenly there was a surge of media attention. That same weekend, CNN telecast a forum on foreign policy featuring former Secretaries of State Henry Kissinger, Alexander Haig, George Shultz, and Lawrence Eagleburger. Shultz said he thought I had done "a lousy job," blaming me for preventing U.S. air strikes against the Serbs. Eagleburger, as always, strongly defended me. But all the former secretaries of state agreed that the Clinton campaign against me had been badly handled and was self-defeating.

On August 20 A. M. Rosenthal wrote in his *New York Times* column that "the UN does not exist as Mr. Dole and the platform committee wanted Americans to see it: a strange foreign apparition floating out there whose chief bureaucrat can tell the U.S. what to do." No nation, Rosenthal said, "has more often or more successfully used the UN to get international support for military operations than the U.S." And elsewhere in the same day's paper John Whitehead was quoted as saying, "I have never seen international resentment towards the U.S. as high as it is today over the UN issues. . . . There are indications that our country's negative attitude towards the UN, our refusal to pay dues, our rather brutal discarding of the Secretary-General have all created animosity around the world and resentment as to how it can be that a country that doesn't pay its dues and doesn't support an organization can expect to have any influence."

Friends inside the Washington Beltway told me that the Clinton administration responded only to "heat" or "pain" inflicted by media coverage. If so, my chances might be getting better. I even saw something positive in Senate Foreign Relations Committee Chairman Jesse Helms's article in *The Wall Street Journal* headlined AN ULTIMATUM TO THE UN: REFORM OR DIE. The "reforms" Helms demanded were so radical as to render ridiculous the Clinton administration's claim that my defeat would result in Congress's agreement to pay the U.S. debt. If his demands were not met, Helms wrote, "then the UN is not worth saving, and I will be leading the charge for U.S. withdrawal."

A few days later came a ringing editorial in the *San Francisco Chronicle* that summed up the situation perfectly: "The Clinton Administration's clumsy, election-inspired campaign to deny United Nations Secretary-General Boutros Boutros-Ghali's second term has not only seriously damaged the cause of U.S. leadership at the United Nations, but it has helped undermine important U.S. international interests on a broad range of issues, from foreign trade to terrorism. To cap it off, the campaign appears headed for a politically embarrassing flop. . . . Boutros Boutros-Ghali is, in fact, a global diplomat of the first order, and he is privately recognized as such by most knowledgeable Americans, including those, like Dole, who are reflexively critical of the United Nations."

On August 26 the Security Council president, having concluded his informal consultations, informed journalists that the consensus in the Council was not to raise the question of the secretary-general's election "before the ministerial work of the General Assembly." That meant late October at the earliest, effectively killing Albright's effort to get a vote against me in the first days of September. This was more than a rebuff to Albright; it was an indication that the Security Council wanted to go over her head in determining the outcome of this issue.

Albright continued to try to drum up opposition to me. She invited herself to a summit of Latin leaders in Rio and was not well received. Most embarrassing was her visit to Chile. Albright emerged from her meeting with Chilean leaders to tell the press that "I believe that we have support in the process of getting a new secretary-general." ALBRIGHT ENLISTS CHILE AGAINST BOUTROS-GHALI was the *Washington Times'* headline. But then came a communiqué issued by the Chilean Foreign Ministry: "Chile understands the U.S. position, but remains steadfast in its support for a second term for Boutros-Ghali." Albright's stop in Bolivia was another setback. "She broke the crockery," our sources reported; "really offended the Bolivians."

Iraqi Forces Move North

As September began, Saddam Hussein sent a large military force into northern Iraq to aid one of the warring Kurdish factions. This part of Iraq had been a no-fly zone since the end of the Gulf War in 1991; it was no longer fully under Iraq's control, as the international community had moved in with military support to provide humanitarian relief to the population there.

Because of this military move, I ordered a halt to implementation of the "Oil for Food" resolution. On Monday, September 2, Ambassador Edward Gnehm, the U.S. Mission's second-ranking official, asked urgently to see me at Sutton Place. He embraced me effusively, which was unusual, as he had always been reserved. Speaking in Arabic (he had served as American ambassador to Kuwait), he said that Washington had instructed him to inform me of the U.S. position on renewed conflict with Iraq: Baghdad had launched an attack on the Kurdish city of Erbil in the north of the country, using thousands of troops, including Saddam's Republican Guard units. There were reports of executions, detentions, and house-to-house searches by the Iraqi secret police. These actions by Iraq constituted a clear violation of Resolution 688 of 1991.

"The United States will probably intervene by launching missiles," Gnehm said. The goal of Gnehm's visit was to gain my assurance not to make any statements incompatible with the coercive measures that the United States would apply to Iraq. I explained to him that I needed U.S. support to put "Oil for Food" into effect and that I would avoid any statement that would risk delaying humanitarian aid. Gnehm assured me that it was not Washington's intention to suspend "Oil for Food," even if the current hostilities delayed it. He left satisfied and apparently relieved by our exchange.

In a bizarre attack conducted hundreds of miles away from Saddam Hussein's operation in the north, the United States struck air defenses in the south of Iraq with cruise missiles launched from U.S. Navy vessels in the Persian Gulf and from B-52s based on Guam.

The United States asserted that a previously passed resolution, 688, provided authorization for these attacks. But U.S. reliance on Resolution 688 was not well founded. Unlike the all-purpose Resolution 987, Resolution 688 had not been adopted under Chapter VII, the enforcement part of the UN Charter. Nor was the incursion by the Iraqi land forces a violation of the no-fly zone, which had been subsequently imposed unilaterally by the United States and its allies in what they described as an effort to enforce Resolution 688. And the no-fly zone had never been endorsed by the Security Council. The United States would have faced insuperable obstacles if it had tried to get the Security Council to bless its use of force against Iraq. While Iraq's military move into the north was deplorable, it was, after all, an Iraqi government operation within the sovereign territory of Iraq.

Many at the United Nations thought that the administration had taken this opportunity to impress American voters with the president's decisiveness at a time when his electoral campaign was in full swing. The fact that the U.S. military reaction did not deal with the Iraqi Army's activities against the Kurds but was confined to hitting air defense targets hundreds of miles away only deepened suspicions that the White House wanted to appear courageous while carefully avoiding any extended new military engagement with Iraq's armed forces.

Saddam Hussein had inflicted a defeat upon the United States by wiping out its extensive intelligence operation and infrastructure in the north of Iraq and killing or scattering its many agents. This reality was largely ignored by the American press, which instead depicted Clinton's use of cruise missiles as a firm and decisive response to another challenge from Saddam Hussein. Britain sought to support the United States by proposing a resolution condemning Iraq for its move into the north but gave up when Russia threatened to veto unless the resolution also denounced the U.S. cruise missile attacks. Many governments criticized the U.S. reaction, and some said that the coalition the United States had formed in 1990–1991 against Saddam Hussein began to fall apart at this point.

When the United States made it known that it was prepared to launch further rounds of cruise missiles against Iraq, Russia declared such action to be totally unacceptable unless authorized by the Security Council. Speaker of the House Newt Gingrich said that the Clinton administration had managed to make the United States look arrogant and impotent at the same time. The reality was that Saddam Hussein had gained ground and the U.S. military actions appeared ineffectual and irrelevant. But politically the Clinton administration was successful, and other nations fell into line. The United States disregarded the Security Council and got away with it.

As the United Nations was about to begin its yearly cycle of official activity with the convening of the fifty-first General Assembly, I gave up the country house in Katonah and returned to my office in the UN Secretariat full-time. By this time talk about other candidates for the job of secretary-general had subsided. Most of those discussed back in June had taken themselves out of the picture or were now considered not to

298 · *Boutros Boutros-Ghali*

have a realistic chance. Congressman Christopher Smith, for example, declared Mary Robinson and Gro Harlem Brundtland unacceptable because of their pro-abortion views. All the focus was on me, Boutros-Ghali, pro or con, with the United States almost alone on the "con" side. The Clinton administration mentioned no one, apparently fearing that its choice would be regarded as America's handpicked puppet. Inside the United Nations, however, everyone knew that the United States' candidate was Kofi Annan of Ghana, who had served for years in the United Nations' personnel and budget offices. In 1993 I had promoted him from assistant secretary-general to under secretary-general for peacekeeping operations, hoping to strengthen Africa's presence in the higher echelons of the United Nations. Annan was well aware that he was seen as Washington's choice to replace me, for he had come to my office to declare that he would never present himself as a candidate for secretary-general.

Throughout early September I continued to receive professions of support. Democratic party elder Robert Strauss said he would help. Leonard Marks, a prominent Washington attorney, was on my side. I had positive contacts with Congressman Charles Rangel. Senator Paul Simon was an outspoken advocate for my case. After lunch with the king and queen of Sweden at Sutton Place, the Swedish ambassador said, "This means that Sweden will support you for reelection." But the backing of some others raised problems. Despite his earlier unhappiness with me, Colonel Qaddafi of Libya sent an emissary to tell me that "the colonel" was "annoyed" by the U.S. decision to veto me. What did I want him to do? I replied, as diplomatically as possible, "The less, the better."

On September 13 I went to Washington to accept the Congressional Black Caucus's invitation and enjoyed hearing myself warmly praised by Chairman Donald Payne. The head of the United Nations Information Center in Washington, Joe Sills, who had been gloomy throughout this episode, reported that "the mood here in Washington has turned. This anti-Boutros-Ghali campaign is now seen as an embarrassment for Clinton. Even rabid anti-UN types are calling it 'bungled.'"

The Cardinal's Blessing

Every year at this time the secretary-general always began the UN season by appearing at the Church of the Holy Family in midtown Manhattan, where the new General Assembly would be blessed. On September 16, as

I sat in the front pew of the church, John Cardinal O'Connor led the service. A man of great distinction, he was also a man of the people and a force in American public affairs. Suddenly I heard Cardinal O'Connor declare that he would depart from his usual remarks on this occasion to say something about me. I was stunned. Always, in years past, the cardinal had thanked the United Nations, but he had never singled anyone out.

"I want to say something," the cardinal announced, "that, coming from someone else, could be construed as political, but coming from someone committed to the moral and spiritual should not be construed as such. I want to express personal gratitude to a man whom I consider to be profoundly sensitive to the moral and spiritual issues of world affairs. He is a man with whom I have personally spoken, a man who has impressed me with a decency, with an integrity, with a true concern for the human person, not simply for ideas in the abstract, not simply for the general concept of preventing wars or trying to bring peace, not even for the even more general concepts of trying to feed the hungry and house the homeless and so on. He is explicitly and concretely interested in the human person as made in the image and likeness of God. I am pleased, I am proud, I feel privileged that Mr. Boutros Boutros-Ghali is the secretary-general of the United Nations. It is my personal hope, Mr. Boutros Boutros-Ghali, that I will have the privilege of serving you for a long time ahead. I thank you for what you have done."

The church resounded with applause. Tears stood in my eyes. Afterward I could only stammer a few words of thanks. "I will continue to help you," Cardinal O'Connor said, "because I believe in your work."

Two days later, at the annual UN correspondents' luncheon, I was in a playful mood. "I'm happy to be back," I said. "Frankly, I got bored on vacation. It's much more fun to be back here blocking reform, flying my black helicopters, imposing global taxes, and demoralizing my staff."

This little effort to poke fun at my enemies by mocking the list of charges they were making against me got more media coverage throughout the world than anything I had said before. The new United Nations session opened on this lighthearted note.

Clinton in New York

At 9:20 in the morning of September 29, 1996, I met President Clinton at the entrance to the United Nations. It seemed as though a thousand photographers were present to capture the looks on our faces. I escorted the president to GA 200, the holding room just off the General Assembly chamber. Albright's aides had carried on elaborate negotiations with my staff over who was to be present during the brief time that Clinton and I would be together. She was particularly fearful that the press might get in and photograph or televise Clinton and me together. My staff agreed to the United States' demand for no press coverage, but, not surprisingly, cameramen burst into the little room and began to film Clinton and me sitting stony-faced, side by side, like two ancient Egyptian statues. I leaned over to Clinton and whispered, "Smile!" Clinton came alive and smiled, and the press speculated about what joke I must have told him.

I then tried to talk substantively about Africa, terrorism, and the comprehensive test ban treaty Clinton had come to sign, but soon it was time for the president to enter the big General Assembly chamber. He stood up, shook my hand, squeezed my shoulder with his other hand, looked deeply and feelingly into my eyes, and said in his warm, husky voice, "It's been good talking to you." Then he added, "I'm going to talk about disarmament." I took this to mean that he would not mention U.S. opposition to my reelection.

If I had had any strategy for my own continuance in office, it had been merely to survive until after the American presidential election. Albright's failure to get any Security Council action meant that I had succeeded in attaining this minor objective. Under the *Washington Post* headline MANY COUNTRIES AT ODDS WITH U.S. DESIRE FOR NEW SECRETARY-GENERAL John Goshko wrote that American officials were acknowledging "that since so many countries are unwilling to accept that [Boutros-Ghali must go] and to begin discussing other candidates for the Secretary-General's post, the United States now intends to give its campaign a rest until after American voters go to the polls on November 5."

To this extent I had won the battle so far. Albright had suffered a series of humiliating defeats. Clinton seemed to have become aware of this only recently, through private approaches and through the press, which was openly saying, as Murray Kempton did in a scathing article, that the whole anti-Boutros-Ghali campaign had been created out of fear that Dole would take the issue. Some observers saw it in a sinister light. *Le Nouvel Observateur* of Paris, referring to the Iranian death sentence against Salman Rushdie, called it called it "an American *fatwa* against Boutros-Ghali."

Madeleine Albright, appearing chastened for the first time, told the

Overseas Writers' Association in Washington on October 3 that "despite the fact that we have believed that it was important to take this process up further earlier, I think we—if people don't want to take it up before the election, we can't make that happen."

Najibullah's Horrible End

The U.S. campaign then slipped into neutral, and dramatic events caused me to focus my attention elsewhere. In Afghanistan the Taliban Islamic fundamentalist fighters were about to seize the capital city of Kabul. There, in the UN compound, the former president of Afghanistan, Mohammed Najibullah, had taken refuge following the overthrow of his regime in 1993. Knowing that his life was in danger, I had repeatedly tried to obtain his release and safe passage out of the country, but to no avail. I had, however, obtained promises from President Burhanuddin Rabbani of Afghanistan that his life would be spared; from Pakistan that his transit would be facilitated; and from India that he would be accepted into exile, his wife already having been accepted as a refugee in New Delhi. As the Taliban closed in on the city, I sent Under Secretary-General Marrack Goulding to Kabul to see what could be done. Goulding met with Najibullah, who declined to leave Kabul unless he could do so with dignity. He had no fear of the Taliban, he said; his only enemy was Ahmed Shah Masood, the famed guerrilla who had fought the Soviets with success. Goulding then went on to the Taliban leadership in Kandahar. Disconcertingly, Goulding discovered that the Talibani had never heard of the United Nations, and nothing he could do would make them understand what the United Nations was or what he was doing there. He gave them a copy of the UN Charter in Arabic and drew their attention to the passage in Article 1 about human rights being respected "without distinction as to race, sex, language, or religion." The Talibani passed the text around, discussing it animatedly; it was clear that they had not known of the document before. But Goulding's statement that, as a founding member of the United Nations, Afghanistan was bound to respect those commitments, whoever its rulers were, fell on deaf ears.

When the fundamentalist forces reached the outskirts of the city, I ordered UN personnel to evacuate. We urged Najibullah to leave with them, but he refused, fearing that he would be killed on the road to the airport. The Taliban then seized Kabul, stormed the UN compound, and tortured, castrated, and hanged Najibullah. I felt responsible for Najibullah's security for as long as he was on UN premises. I had never met him, but he had taken shelter under a UN roof, and I owed him protection and immunity. I took his murder as a personal defeat that hurt all the more when I received a sad letter from his wife.

Finally, some good news came. The *New York Times* headline on October 5, 1996, was U.S. TO PAY $660 MILLION OWED TO THE UN, thus "bringing its 1996 dues up to date and making a dent in the debt for peacekeeping ventures." Could this be true? Maybe my "badgering" had worked after all. Just after Louis Farrakhan's Million Man March on Washington in 1995, I had gone to Washington in what I told the press was my "One Point Three Billion–Man March," jokingly referring to the total sum the United States owed the United Nations. The Clinton administration had insisted that Congress would not pay as long as I was secretary-general. Today's news seemed to expose that charge as false.

I wanted to talk to Madeleine Albright alone. I mentioned to my closest colleagues at the United Nations that I was considering inviting her for a tête-à-tête dinner. They were horrified and insisted that I do no such thing. Albright would take it as a sign of weakness on my part. My advisers were convinced that Albright and her task force were not reporting fully or accurately to the White House about the extent of the foreign opposition her campaign against me had created. President Clinton, they felt, was just beginning to awaken to this reality. But if I reached out to her, Albright could use it as proof that I was on the verge of surrender. She would report that I had "blinked," they said, and Christopher would use this to undermine African support for me.

So, without informing my colleagues further, I invited Madeleine to dinner on Sunday, October 6. She replied that she wanted to watch the Clinton-Dole debate on television, so we agreed to meet on Monday night. I awaited her in the library. When she arrived at seven o'clock, I showed her the new arrangement of my collection of bronze and silver penholders, worn at the belt by the intellectual class of officials in the time of the Ottoman Empire. They were the scribes' version of the sword scabbards of Ottoman janissaries. I had first displayed my collection to her in the early days of our UN association. Later, as a guest in her Waldorf-Astoria suite, I saw that she had started her own collection of these items with some reproductions from Turkey.

As we sat down to dinner, I said I had asked her to come so I could tell her directly that I held no hard feelings against her, or Clinton, despite the terrible words she and her spokesman had been hurling at me. Madeleine replied that she had been embarrassed and outraged by the way the White House and the State Department had harshly announced the decision to remove me. She had been riding in her limousine in southern California when she had gotten the news by a telephone call. She said she had "gone ballistic."

"How do you see the end of this?" she asked me. "It is for the member states to decide," I replied. "It is no more my problem." I would continue to be faithful to my commitments to work constructively with the United States, I said, because I shared the ideals and principles that America stands for. "I have paid a political price for this in the past," I said. "After the Suez Canal was nationalized by Nasser I was labeled 'pro-American' and not permitted to travel abroad." Yes, she said, she knew about that.

"Why not just step down with dignity?" she suddenly asked. "How can I?" I replied. "How can I go against my own country, Egypt, which is supporting my reelection?" To this Madeleine replied that she hoped that her current campaign to remove me from office would not harm her relations with the Arab world.

Leia joined us. "Why are you trying to destroy my husband?" she asked. Madeleine replied to this challenge with the standard State Department line, asserting that President Clinton really had no choice; it was a demand of Congress. The dining room was overheated, our conversation lagged, and shortly thereafter the evening ended.

Madeleine Albright and I seemed to have a love-hate relationship. At her request we had agreed to dine together tête-à-tête regularly once a month, and Leia had agreed not to join us on these occasions. Madeleine had been very open in her conversation, often telling me of her personal problems. Until coming to the United States she had been a professor and a Democratic political adviser of no particular prominence. Her first encounter with high international politics had come with her job as head of the U.S. Mission to the United Nations. She loved the scene and thrived on its drama and privileges.

Her uncivil tongue had won praise in Washington from both political parties. Thus her worst characteristic, when it came to diplomacy, was reinforced by her domestic American audience. The more she spoke rudely to other countries' representatives, the more political approbation she received from her own countrymen. As I reflected on all this, I realized that I was the stupid one. I had foolishly disregarded her increasing political influence in Washington. She must also have believed that I did not appreciate her as an intellectual or diplomatic equal. She had said nothing, but she had laid her plans well. Long before this election year of 1996 Joseph Verner Reed had heard her say, "I will make Boutros think I am his friend; then I will break his legs!" When this was reported to me, I brushed it aside as ridiculous. When she insisted that I accept her as my only real contact with the Clinton administration and the Congress, I tried to acquiesce in her demands because I did not want problems between us and because she was overbearing in her efforts to keep me from developing any effective personal relationships in Washington. I was a good boy, but I was naive. Fortune is a woman, Machiavelli said, and should be treated roughly, but in this case it was the woman who was rough, and fortune favored her.

The next morning Fayza Abulnaga rushed into my office to say that under severe pressure from the U.S. Mission to the United Nations, the foreign minister of Djibouti had agreed at the last minute to change the text of his speech to the General Assembly to state that his country was withdrawing its support for my election. I sent Fayza to see him at once with a message from me: "I have a letter from your President pledging support for me. I will distribute this letter unless you return to your original text." The United States, I was told, had contacted all members of the United Nations urging them not to mention or praise me in any way in their annual addresses before the General Assembly. If so, many members failed to follow U.S. directions.

But it seemed that Albright's star had dimmed. A *New York Times* reporter passed us "the inside word" from Washington: "Albright is really on the outs. She's been cut out of Christopher's Africa trip." Referring to a just-passed Security Council resolution on Israel's opening of a tunnel in Jerusalem along the west side of what Arabs call the Haram al-Sharif and the Jews call the Temple Mount, the reporter said, "Albright took a political beating on the Israeli tunnel resolution for letting it get through without criticizing the Palestinians as well as the Israelis. And she's been cut out of Christopher's Africa trip. She now knows she won't be secretary of state."

Christopher's First Safari

Listening to the radio early one morning, I had heard it announced that Secretary of State Warren Christopher would travel to sub-Saharan

Africa in October. This would be his first safari to black Africa since becoming secretary of state. I found it amazing that the chief American foreign policy figure had never taken time to visit the world's poorest continent. In the cold war years the African countries had been objects of intense competition between the United States and the USSR. "Development" was an important concept, and significant consequences for the cold war superpower contest were thought to hinge upon whether Africa followed the communist or the capitalist model. Christopher's neglect of Africa revealed how much had changed. The gap between the rich and poor parts of the world no longer generated much interest or concern among the wealthy.

But now here was Christopher planning to tour Africa only a few weeks before the end of his four-year term of office. Another aspect of this suspiciously sudden surge of interest had been pointed out to me only a few days earlier: a contact in the Department of State's Bureau of African Affairs had noted that after four frustrating years of pleading that a reception be held for all African ambassadors assigned to Washington, Christopher had suddenly agreed to host such an event in the waning weeks of the first Clinton administration. It would not be going too far, I thought, to suspect that this had something to do with the United States' campaign against me. Christopher would tell the Africans that their choice was clear: go on insisting that I be reappointed, or face reality and look forward to five—and maybe ten—more years of *another* African as secretary-general. And during the past several weeks the Clinton administration had continued to say that *any* African would be all right with the United States, just as long as it was not Boutros-Ghali.

But going to Africa for the sole purpose of opposing my reelection would be too blatant an insult. So the announced purpose of the Christopher trip was to discuss "peacekeeping" in Africa. More conflicts were under way in Africa than in all the rest of the world combined. Africa was the scene of by far the greatest number of UN peacekeeping operations. The United States, however, burned by its badly bungled peacekeeping experience in Somalia in 1993, had piled up preconditions to its ever getting involved in African peacekeeping again.

To get out of this predicament, the United States had come up with a bizarre idea. During the summer a CIA official had informally contacted one of my staff to say that National Security Adviser Anthony Lake had been working with African specialists in the Clinton administration on an idea for an all-African peacekeeping force-in-being of 17,000 to

25,000 troops. The United States would provide logistical support but did not otherwise want to be involved. The planning, code-named "Carlisle," was well along, under the immediate supervision of NSC staff member Nancy Sodeberg. But the Pentagon was "dragging its feet." To satisfy the Defense Department, the CIA official said, the mission of the force would be "to stop the dying but not the killing"—in other words, to succor the afflicted but not to deal with the sources of the fighting. The force would need "a lead country" to provide the command structure and many, if not most, of the troops for such a force. It should be an African nation, one with an effective military establishment: for example, my country, Egypt, The CIA official suggested that I might be able to help.

The idea was preposterous and yet another insult to Africa. The United States was in effect saying that Africa was so marginalized and so troublesome that it could not expect to benefit from UN peacekeeping missions in the future; it should prepare to be the only continent asked to handle its conflicts on its own. Whenever I heard such talk, I tried to explain that the idea of regionalizing peacekeeping is dangerous. A German defense minister told me that he wanted German troops deployed only in Europe. In Tokyo I heard something similar: Japanese troops should be used only in Asia. No, I replied, security is best served by international solidarity. The United Nations wants Asian troops in Europe and European troops in Asia. We must not return to regionalism at the expense of internationalism.

This U.S. initiative was soon declared publicly to be the reason for Secretary Christopher's October 1996 trip to Africa. He was going in order to "sell" Africans on the idea. Perhaps Christopher took this seriously; no one else familiar with either Africa or peacekeeping could do so. The African press knew why he was coming. *Fraternité Matin* of Ivory Coast bitterly criticized the United States for threatening to veto me, accusing Washington of "assassinating the law of the majority" of the OAU. But at the same time the newspaper offered the name of Amara Essy, the foreign minister of Ivory Coast, as a candidate to replace me. Rumors were spreading that the United States might take retribution against Africa for supporting me. Christopher's job, it appeared, was to deepen Africans' apprehensions on this score.

The secretary of state's first stop was Bamako, the capital of Mali. I was amazed that he would go directly to a Francophone country closely allied with France to seek support for positions France opposed: removing Boutros-Ghali and forming an African-only peacekeeping force under American tutelage.

On his aircraft before landing at Bamako, Christopher told reporters, according to Reuters news agency, "Everywhere I go, I'm going to be talking about the importance of Africa coming forward with good candidates for the secretary-generalship. . . . We think African candidates deserve special consideration, but unless some are offered up, we're going to be left without some to consider." In other words, if Africa wanted to keep the secretary-general post, it had better retract its support for Boutros-Ghali and come up with other names quickly.

The New York Times, dateline Bamako, reported on October 10, 1996, CHRISTOPHER DROPS IN, BUT AFRICA IS UNMOVED. President Alpha Oumar Konaré telephoned to tell me what had happened. Christopher said that rumors that the United States would drop its opposition to Boutros-Ghali after Clinton's reelection were unfounded. The U.S. position was irrevocable. President Konaré had replied that Africa had made a commitment in the OAU resolution at Yaoundé. And perhaps the United States did not realize, Konaré added, that Mali had very close relations with Egypt. The only way to get Mali to change its position of support for Boutros-Ghali would be to get President Mubarak to drop his support for him.

Christopher's foray into Francophone Africa was clearly irritating to France, and French-American antagonism was rising. This would not do my cause any good. A French cabinet minister declared on television that "France could use its veto in the Security Council to block any U.S. attempt to impose its candidate for the post of UN Secretary-General. The right of veto does not belong only to the Americans. France also has the right." The European media seemed to take delight in the string of embarrassing failures that Christopher was experiencing in Africa. Christopher's trip ended with yet another publicly embarrassing rebuke to a visiting American official, the latest in the series from Beijing to Moscow to Santiago and now Pretoria. Emerging before television cameras at a joint press conference, Nelson Mandela, with Warren Christopher at his side, declared that he "would not support the U.S. effort to unseat Boutros-Ghali as UN Secretary-General." Mandela said to Christopher, "Boutros is my adopted son."

As for Christopher's African peace force idea, it was received poorly. AFRICA HEARS INDIFFERENCE IN A U.S. OFFER TO HELP was one African newspaper's headline. Africans had shed their blood as members of UN peacekeeping operations in the Middle East and other parts of the world. Now they were being told that they would be denied UN peacekeeping assistance for their own conflicts. "There is a nasty double standard operating here" was the press commentary. "Given recent history, [Africans] are left with the strong suspicion that Mr. Christopher's proposal could result in the further writing off of the continent with a grand-sounding plan for which no real funding or interest would follow."

Christopher returned to the United States to declare in a television interview that his trip had been a success. It was evident that Christopher's interviewer, Jim Lehrer, had not been following the issues involved. Their exchange featured the fact that Christopher, with this African trip, had broken the record for most miles traveled by a secretary of state. State Department spokesman Nicholas Burns similarly declared Christopher's mission a success, without challenge from reporters. It was a demonstration of the American media's lack of interest and expertise in world affairs in the post–cold war period. Only Senator Paul Simon offered a different view. In an October 16, 1996, press release, he attacked Clinton's "inept" policy toward Africa.

Christopher's involvement in this farfetched excursion suggested to me that the United States was becoming unnerved by its failure to get rid of me. Madeleine Albright had been virtually silent in public since her failed effort to get the Security Council to take action on me in early September. Her tactics had so clearly backfired that it was assumed she had been told to stand down while Warren Christopher took the lead in the campaign against me. Albright's effort at this point seemed confined to answering questions about me, to which she would invariably reply, "We want a secretary-general who wakes up every morning thinking only about UN reform."

In mid-October I was in Europe. The Egyptian ambassador in Paris informed me of American Ambassador Pamela Harriman's remark that President Clinton "went along" with the pressure by Albright and Christopher to oust me. Harriman had indicated that this mess wasn't Clinton's idea; his two foreign policy advisers had talked him into it and had lost standing as a result of the fiasco that had ensued. But, Harriman added, Clinton could not at this point do anything but allow the effort to continue, because any U-turn on Boutros-Ghali before the election would be seized upon by the Republicans.

President Jacques Chirac said he was willing to go to Washington to see President Clinton on my behalf and to urge a two-year extension compromise. In Germany to inaugurate the International Law of the Sea Tribunal, I received cheers and standing ovations. In Lübeck I had lunch in an old *Bierstube* and then walked through the streets of the ancient port district, looking for the house of the great novelist Thomas Mann. People recognized me and put out their hands with their thumbs up.

I could scarcely believe the incredibly warm welcome I received in Germany. At the conference in Lübeck I received a standing ovation; in Hamburg, Foreign Minister Klaus Kinkel said, "We're with you all the way." And the British journal *The Economist,* in a review of a book on UN reform, came out with the formulation that I had hoped to see in public: "The dotty American view of Mr. Boutros-Ghali—that he seeks world government—makes it electorally convenient for President Clinton to oppose him, despite the views of other governments. An obvious compromise is to allow him two more years, or seven in all, letting everyone off the hook with a term the authors of this sensible study recommended in the first place."

Farrakhan at the United Nations

A strange event then occurred that did me no good. Representatives of Louis Farrakhan's Nation of Islam, an American sect, informed us that Farrakhan intended to mark the first anniversary of his Million Man March on Washington with a "day of atonement" at the United Nations. Groups of all kinds of political and religious persuasions demonstrate in the UN Plaza and have the right to do so. As an added factor in this case, the United Nations Correspondents Association (UNCA) had agreed that Farrakhan could hold a press conference in the association's pressroom located inside the UN Secretariat. This recalled the bitter controversy two years earlier, when UNCA had invited Shen Tong, a Chinese dissident, to hold a press conference, and the People's Republic of China had protested strongly to me.

I decided that the Clinton administration should be made aware of what was about to take place, not least because I might be strongly criticized in Washington for allowing UN space to be used as a platform for Farrakhan. Thus the United Nations informed the State Department of Farrakhan's plans. "Are you suggesting that the U.S. protest, like the Chinese did?" was the reaction from the State Department official. No, we assured him, we are just informing you so there will be no surprises.

"Well, anyway," the State Department official said, "this won't be a problem for the Clinton administration; whatever criticism comes will be directed at Boutros-Ghali."

When the day came, plans changed, and again the United Nations informed the United States. When UNCA learned that Farrakhan would be accompanied by a large entourage of "Fruit of Islam" bodyguards, it declared that the small size of its premises in the Secretariat could not accommodate such numbers. As a result, the representative of Libya at the United Nations invited Farrakhan to hold his press conference in one of the official conference halls of the General Assembly building. The event thus came to be sponsored by a member state of the United Nations, a state under UN sanctions, regarded by the United States as a sponsor of terrorism and an enemy of the state of Israel.

When Farrakhan's "day of atonement" arrived, there were more New York police around the United Nations than had been mobilized for the visit of the pope. Cross streets were blocked off or patrolled over to Second Avenue. Twelve ambulances were arrayed on the UN Plaza across from the Secretariat. Farrakhan addressed an audience that covered First Avenue from Forty-second Street to Forty-fourth and beyond. Then he entered the UN headquarters and held his press conference. When it was over, as Farrakhan was leaving the UN Building, a reporter shouted, "If you met Boutros-Ghali, what would you say to him?" Farrakhan shouted back, "I'd say, just because America is opposed to you, you should stay for another five years. And I hope you get stronger and stronger."

Soon after my return from Germany, a former UN official who had been an American political appointee, Pedro San Juan, was given space on *The Wall Street Journal*'s editorial page for an article stating that I had persuaded Farrakhan to stage his demonstration and press conference at the United Nations and that Farrakhan had rewarded me by making pro-Boutros-Ghali and anti-Israel remarks. I had shamelessly lobbied the Congressional Black Caucus for support, San Juan wrote. That someone I had never met would write such nonsense and that the *Journal* would publish it so prominently could be explained only, I thought, if the article had been stimulated and placed by the "task force" dedicated to my destruction.

Because of the San Juan article and because of Farrakhan's statements about Jews, I asked to meet with the president of the Council of Presidents of American Jewish Organizations, the umbrella group for all Jewish groups in the United States. Malcolm Hoenlein, the president, gathered a delegation from around the country and came to see me on October 31, the very day after my request. I explained the situation in detail to the delegation, whose members expressed appreciation for my sensitivity in reaching out to them and telling them what had happened.

Amazingly, while there had been extensive media coverage of Farrakhan's demonstration outside the United Nations, there had been no coverage whatever of what he had done inside the UN Building. As a result, Washington officials were unaware of what had taken place on UN premises—that is, until Hoenlein's delegation asked to see Deputy Secretary Strobe Talbott to ask him why the Clinton administration had not protested Farrakhan's appearance inside the United Nations in the same way that the Chinese had protested in the Shen Tong case. The story ended without repercussions, but an impression remained that I had invited Farrakhan to the United Nations and had attempted to shift the onus to the United States.

A Senator's Help

After my return from Germany to New York, I found a totally different atmosphere. Europeans had been upbeat and encouraging; I seemed to be admired there. In the United States the media was indifferent at best, hostile at worst.

With this oppressive mood around me, I was pleased when Senator Paul Simon telephoned me to say he planned to hold a press conference to call for my reelection. The senator asked me to make calls to some members of Congress whom I knew to see if they would be willing to join him at this event. I telephoned Senator Olympia Snowe and Representative Lee Hamilton. They were cool about the idea but said that they would check with the State Department. As soon as the State Department learned of my approach, it instructed the U.S. Mission to the United Nations to lodge a protest with the Egyptian Embassy in Washington. Madeleine Albright called in the press to declare that my telephone calls to members of Congress had been an act of "gross interference in domestic politics and the normal functioning of American foreign policy." It was another overreaction designed to prevent any advocacy of my case.

But the administration could not silence Senator Simon, who held his press conference on November 5, the day of the presidential election. He declared that there was still time to reverse a great mistake, that of forcing out of office UN Secretary-General Boutros Boutros-Ghali. "The community of nations is virtually unanimous in responding negatively to our blunder."

The United States was prepared to veto Boutros-Ghali, he said, "either because of domestic political reasons or because he has on rare occasions shown independence from U.S. wishes. Either reason is not worthy of a great power. Greatness suggests something more than a crude use of power. Our position is wrong in substance and wrong in how it has been handled. A sensible compromise should be worked out." Senator Simon took on the White House's arguments directly. The Clinton administration had said that I had originally stated that I would serve only one term; Senator Simon pointed out that when Clinton had run for governor of Arkansas in 1990, he had said he would not run for president in two years. The United States had approved a second five-year term for Kurt Waldheim, Simon said; for it now to oppose Boutros-Ghali is an "action that offends so many nations when they are clearly right and we are wrong" and an embarrassment for the United States. "I hope," Senator Simon said, that "with our election over, rational thinking will return to our handling of this situation."

Senator Simon's blunt but kindly manner, his deep sense of propriety and honor, his bow ties, and his strong, flat midwestern voice—all these made him in my eyes a true representative of America's heartland. I telephoned him to thank him for taking his lonely stand in such a hostile Washington environment.

Another staunch supporter, from the other branch of Congress, symbolized for me an equally great American style and spirit: Representative Charles Rangel, Democratic congressman from New York. Charlie Rangel's raspy, streetwise accent and defiant rectitude stood for America's urban black people. On October 22 Charlie wrote to Cardinal O'Connor. The cardinal's statement at the Church of the Holy Spirit, Rangel said, "clearly reflects the humanitarian concerns of the poor developing nations, where the Secretary-General is especially beloved. You would provide an immense service to those who wish to see his work continued by convincing like-minded religious leaders of this nation to carry their mission to President Clinton. The spiritual and moral basis of your sentiments toward the Secretary-General would raise the issue above national or international politics."

On November 5, 1996, President Clinton easily won reelection. I sent him a letter of congratulation, saying it had been an inspiration for me to observe the marvelous workings of the great American democracy in action. Next morning came the surprising news that Warren Christopher would resign as secretary of state. Staff-to-staff telephone calls between the United Nations and the State Department suggested that the news may have surprised Christopher as well. I wrote him a warm letter, praising his dedicated service to peace. Somehow my letters to Christopher never conveyed the tone I wanted. For one thing, I had been trained to address those of his rank as "Excellency" and did so in letters to other foreign ministers. But Christopher had written to me as "Boutros," so my staff, back in 1993, had insisted that I address him as "Chris." This seemed presumptuous of me, so instead I wrote, "Dear Warren." This threw my aides into an uproar: "Nobody calls him Warren!" they bellowed. So in this final letter I wrote "Dear Mr. Secretary." Christopher replied in a brief note saying that my kind words on the occasion of his departure were surprising in view of all that had happened.

Over the last few months, I had convinced myself that once elected, Clinton would allow the U.S. assault on me to fade away. Many member-state representatives at the United Nations also felt that with the presidential campaign over, the pressure to oust me would stop, and they encouraged me to keep going. The effort led by Madeleine Albright against me had been such a failure and so irrational, they felt, that it made sense only in American domestic political terms.

This was the key moment. Would Clinton change his policy now that he had won reelection? Or had I become the first foreign policy challenge to his second administration, a challenge he could not afford to lose? Until now my "strategy" had been simply to survive. Now, on November 7, 1996, that survival stage was over. What should I do next?

Gaining Church Support

The Catholic Bishops of America had agreed to try to put together a bloc of support for me. They asked me to invite representatives from all Christian faiths to Sutton Place. At that meeting, on October 26, the delegates told me they would make their views clear to the president. Copies of their letters to Clinton were later provided to me. It was a profound expression of support by American civil society.

The National Council of the Churches of Christ in the USA, stating that it represented "Thirty-three communions with a combined total of 53 million church-goers," expressed its support for me and urged the president "to prayerfully examine [Boutros-Ghali's] record of service." For five years, the letter stated, "Secretary-General Boutros-Ghali has been a constant and strong supporter of key U.S. initiatives at the United Nations." The letter was signed by fifteen church leaders, from the African Methodist Episcopal Zion Church to the American Friends Service Committee to the Armenian Church in the USA.

A similarly powerful letter was sent to Clinton from the Anglican Communion's observer at the United Nations, the Right Reverend James H. Ottley, the representative of the Archbishop of Canterbury and of Anglican churches in 164 countries.

The presiding bishop and primate of the Episcopal Church, Edmond L. Browning, added his voice in a letter stressing that I had "opened up the United Nations to allow non-governmental organizations, including the religious community, to have a voice in the organization."

The president of the National Conference of Catholic Bishops, the Most Reverend Anthony M. Pilla, the bishop of Cleveland, wrote that the U.S. administration's public campaign against me was "unnecessarily unilateral and divisive at a time when consensus-building is so important. . . . Boutros Boutros-Ghali has been profoundly sensitive to the moral and spiritual dimensions of world affairs."

The sheikh of Al-Azhar, the spiritual leader of the most venerable Muslim institution of learning, declared his support for me in the Arab press. And the Coptic Orthodox Church, speaking as "the most ancient African church in the world" and citing the contribution of "the ten world conferences and summits convened by Doctor Boutros from 1992–1996" to development in the poorest countries, requested "Your Hon. President Clinton and the American government to stand on the side of the re-election of Doctor Boutros Boutros-Ghali and the poor, needy and marginalized in the world and in Africa."

I could only hope that this remarkable support, conveyed privately, nonconfrontationally, and in an obviously heartfelt manner, would lead President Clinton to drop his campaign against me.

Moving from the spiritual to the political, I knew I had to keep the support of Africa and the willingness of China and France to "veto the U.S. veto." I would also have to get my views to the president himself on a compromise way out. Media coverage remained unbalanced, with the world press following the ins and outs closely, while the American press coverage was sporadic and superficial. Still, a few hard-hitting items began to appear. A *New York Times* columnist, Clyde Haberman, wrote that "a prominent foreign resident was mugged on the east side of Manhattan. The mugging, you should know, was political in nature. The victim: Boutros Boutros-Ghali, Secretary-General of the United Nations. Months ago, the Clinton Administration let it be known that it would rather walk barefoot over hot coals than allow him to continue working in Turtle Bay. . . . Many foreign diplomats and commentators . . . see no good reason to give the boot to Mr. Boutros-Ghali. These people are convinced that the Administration beat up on him only to outflank the Republicans among voters ready to blame the big building on the East Side for everything that ails us, including fallen arches." The columnist pointed out that the United Nations generates an estimated $3.3 billion and more than 15,000 jobs for New York City, and that the Clinton administration "might keep that in mind, especially should the number shrink, however slightly, because of the perceived mugging in Turtle Bay."

In a stunning setback, at least to close observers of the United Nations, the United States was voted off the United Nations' main budget committee, the Advisory Committee on Administrative and Budgetary Questions (ACABQ). The United States had demanded that the UN budget be brought under control. I had done my best and had just achieved, for the first time in UN history, a zero-growth budget. When the voting results were announced, the committee members burst into applause. This insult was the direct consequence of Washington's failure to honor its financial obligations to the United Nations at the same time it was insisting that UN members follow Washington's wishes regarding me and other issues at hand. In reaction the American political commentator Daniel Schorr urged the Clinton administration to compromise, saying that the U.S. campaign against me had created "an unseemly mess."

In the *Times* A. M. Rosenthal called for a two-year extension for me that would "ease the anger of the UN majority. . . . Agreement by Mr. Clinton would show that the U.S. had not taken leave of common sense, self-interest or a decent respect of the rights and opinions of friends."

On November 12, 1996, at an informal Security Council lunch at the restaurant La Grenouille, Madeleine Albright was quiet and apparently downcast. She had learned that Egypt's ambassador to the United Nations, Nabil Elaraby, under instructions from President Mubarak, would introduce a resolution to the Security Council calling for my reelection to a full five-year term. Egypt had the support of the two other

African members of the Security Council at this time, Botswana and Guinea-Bissau. Botswana's ambassador, Legwaile Joseph Legwaila, told the press that Boutros-Ghali "is the choice of the African continent for Secretary-General. The U.S. is almost alone in opposing Mr. Boutros-Ghali."

As the Security Council lunch ended, Albright said to French Ambassador Alain Dejammet that "compromise may be possible." It was the first time anyone had heard her resolve weaken.

A source highly placed in the State Department telephoned on Friday, November 15, "to give you a sense of how it is going at the end of the week" before the Security Council vote. Clinton had been moving toward a compromise, we were told, but now there was a drift back toward a veto. "The President's advisers are all telling him that this is his PATCO." (This was explained to me as a reference to President Reagan's first challenge in office, an air traffic controllers' strike.) "And as long as Madeleine Albright is being considered for secretary of state, it is impossible to do anything but veto, because she is now totally identified with getting Boutros-Ghali."

The Washington Post that Friday morning reported that "A coalition of 60 women's groups, saying that female voters delivered for President Clinton in last week's election, yesterday asked the Administration to reward them with jobs." White House officials acknowledged that women's groups had complained "after an unnamed Clinton advisor described Madeleine K. Albright, the U.S. Ambassador to the United Nations, as in the 'second tier' of candidates under consideration to replace Secretary of State Warren Christopher." Clinton owed his election to the women's vote; the politically powerful women's organizations, an American friend told me, would not let him drop Albright despite her bungled campaign against me. The next morning's headline announced that President Clinton had decided to reverse his promise to withdraw American forces from Bosnia by the end of 1996. Now it was inconceivable, I was told, that Clinton would follow this by reversing his "irrevocable" decision to veto me. I learned from Paris that President Chirac had contacted Clinton to urge compromise but had received a negative reply. Prime Minister Chrétien of Canada telephoned Clinton and talked at length about the need to compromise; Chrétien too was turned down.

Still the pointed rebukes to the United States continued. Even as Secretary Christopher was on his final trip, to Beijing, the New China News

Agency declared that "China appraises positively the important work by Mr. Boutros-Ghali to strengthen the role of the United Nations. . . . China backs the stance of the OAU on Boutros-Ghali's candidacy and will support it." Chinese state media accused the United States of "flaunting high-handedness" and trying to dominate the United Nations by attempting to block my reelection. I was touched most of all by a letter of support sent to Clinton by the president of Honduras, Carlos Roberto Reina Idiaquez, who had been my student in Paris in 1968. I was impressed that such a small country so close to the United States would be willing to say no to the administration.

During these middle days of November I had been in Rome at the World Conference on Food, trying to get support for a relief mission to the refugees in eastern Zaire. Shortly after my return, on Sunday evening, November 17, Madeleine Albright asked if she could come to my residence to talk. I of course agreed. We sat together for an hour as she tried to tempt me to give up. The United States would create a foundation just for me. I would be its director. It could be set up in Geneva. She noted that I had given a speech on international terrorism not long before; perhaps I would like it to be a foundation on counterterrorism. Besides this, she said, the administration would see to it that I had a title. I would become "Secretary-General of the United Nations Emeritus." Later I learned that President Clinton had conveyed this same offer on the telephone to President Chirac. I just laughed. These Americans, I thought, must consider me incredibly naive. They cannot grasp that I have to defend a principle: the integrity of the United Nations and the independence of the secretary-general. But I said nothing. She left without making a sale.

Fourteen in Favor, One Opposed

The next morning, the fifteen members of the United Nations Security Council convened to vote on me. It was immediately clear for the first time that fourteen of the fifteen would vote for me. This came as a shock to the Americans, who had not expected to be totally isolated. The defection of Britain hit the United States hard. The vote was postponed for twenty-four hours, during which the United States applied massive pressure to change the count. But the next day the situation was unchanged.

Albright telephoned Christopher to confirm her instructions; Christopher did so. Fourteen votes were cast in favor of a full second term for me. The vote was 14 in favor, 1 opposed; the United States cast its veto.

As it happened, I was scheduled to attend a Security Council lunch that day at which Madeleine Albright would be present. On two occasions during the meal Madeleine looked at me and winked. I asked a colleague what these winks meant, but he found them utterly inexplicable.

At a reception the following evening at the Plaza Hotel, I ran into Henry Kissinger. "Whatever happens to you," he said, "you have entered history." I don't regard that as much consolation, I replied.

The Washington Post editorialized that the United States had "failed miserably" in not checking to see where the other 185 UN members wanted to go. "It turned out that they were united in readiness to have the secretary-general take that second term. . . . The resulting mess won't be easy to clean up, but the outlines of a resolution are clear enough. And we would bet it will yet come about. Mr. Boutros-Ghali will in a not-so-long time have to go. As we guess, that won't be right away, but in a year or so."

And my friend Charlie Rangel weighed in again with "An Open Letter to Secretary of State Christopher on the U.S. Veto of UN Secretary-General Boutros-Ghali" on November 22, 1996. "As a senior member of Congress," Rangel said, "I feel a deep responsibility to defend my country's actions in anything affecting the national security or well-being, such as the recent controversy over the leadership of the United Nations." But the U.S. veto cast against Boutros-Ghali, Rangel said, gave him no basis of understanding from which he could defend his country's policy. To the world, the administration's action seemed to be nothing but a political attempt to appeal to isolationists in Congress. "The way out of this quandary," Rangel told Christopher, "is to drop our opposition to Boutros-Ghali."

An Agenda for Democratization

The U.S. veto was a rejection of democracy. That America would argue for democracy within every state but reject it in the world's organization of states was a theme heard over and over in the Arab and third-world press. It seemed strange to me too, because the key theme of my term as secretary-general was democratization. The fact that a single vote—that of the United States—could dictate the outcome at the United Nations threatened hopes for increasing democratization on the international scene.

Over the past four years I had devoted many hours to an agenda for democratization. In 1992, in response to the Security Council summit, I had submitted *An Agenda for Peace,* and a year later, in response to the General Assembly, I had produced a report on *An Agenda for Development.* But I had no mandate for proceeding with a third "agenda" beyond one or two minor reports on what the United Nations had been doing in response to requests from countries wanting help in holding elections. Moreover, democracy, which, at the end of the cold war, had been widely hailed as the wave of the future, had become, with each passing year since then, the object of increasing criticism. Outside the West, democracy was being called socially disruptive and an impediment to economic development. Regimes with no patience for democracy called it a tool of American hegemony.

Producing a report may seem a harmless and unexceptionable exercise. But within the United Nations, whose Charter requires the secretary-general to submit an annual report to the General Assembly and to report to the Security Council on threats to international peace and security, I was presumed to have no authority whatsoever to report beyond these two cases unless specifically requested to do so by either the General Assembly or the Security Council.

Nonetheless, early in my term of office, my conviction had deepened that democracy—especially the process of democratization that may lead to it—is crucial for the betterment of peoples in every sphere of life. Within a year of taking office I was stating publicly my conviction that there was a critical linkage between peace, development, and democracy. Without peace there could be no development. Without both peace and development, democracy could not take root. But democracy was the key link in the chain: without democracy neither peace nor development could be expected to last long. A people deprived of democratic expression would eventually turn to confrontation and conflict. And development that did not benefit from the freedoms of thought, assembly, and expression that democracy provides would slowly fall behind those societies and economies that benefited from democratic creativity.

The word "democracy" does not appear in the UN Charter. To pursue my intention to report on the United Nations and democratization was, therefore, a risky business within the context of the culture and politics inside the UN system.

I first attempted to put forward my "agenda" in the form of an introduction to a report that the General Assembly had requested on UN electoral operations in the field and that would be submitted in August 1995. But when the UN bureaucracy got wind of what I intended to do, its counterblast against this idea was of hurricane force.

My senior political adviser, Rosario Green, an impressive Mexican woman with whom I had worked closely, sent me a memo declaring my draft to be "pontificating and paternalistic" and urging me to reconsider. Other senior UN officials lectured me that my case for democratization of the international system was "weak and inchoate." The United Nations had no authority to do anything in the field of democratization beyond what member states requested it to do. Some had asked for electoral assistance; none had asked for anything like what I had written in my report, so "the idea for an Agenda for Democratization should not be encouraged."

So I simply ceased to mention my project and went back to improving the draft. Without telling my staff, I sent my text for review to several distinguished scholars of democracy: Professors Robert Dahl and Bruce Russett of Yale University, Professor Alfred Stepan at the Central European University, and Larry Diamond, Senior Fellow at the Hoover Institution at Stanford University. All sent me positive, encouraging, and constructive comments, as did Cyrus Vance and Dr. David Hamburg of the Carnegie Corporation.

My "agenda" entered very controversial territory, for I argued for democratization *among* nations. Today decisions concerning global matters carry with them far-reaching domestic consequences and can run counter to democratization within a state and undermine a people's commitment to it. How can we ask nations to accept democratic practices within their borders if they see no hope for democracy among nations?

UNvanquished

The 14–1 vote brought the UN election process to a halt. In the Secretariat building someone put up a small poster in the elevator quoting Madeleine Albright's spokesman:

"THE UN CAN ONLY DO WHAT THE U.S. LETS IT DO."
—*Jamie Rubin, Democratic National Convention, August 1996*

Support for me was holding firm. The African representatives to the United Nations met on November 21 to reaffirm that I was the only African candidate. The French reported that the Africans were getting psychological support from the Europeans, "who are happy to inflict continued pain on the United States." The Russians, I was told, were "ready to veto anything that moves." It looked as though the standoff would continue until December, when the presidency of the Security Council would be assumed by Ambassador Francesco Paulo Fulci of Italy.

RESISTING U.S., AFRICANS BACK ANOTHER TERM FOR UN CHIEF reported the November 21, 1996, *New York Times:* "A prolonged standoff at the United Nations has allowed limited support for the Secretary-General to develop in Washington, where there is also growing criticism of the Administration's handling of the case." At home late that evening, I received a telephone call from a longtime friend, the television personality Barbara Walters. She talked for nearly an hour, saying that she was calling on behalf of "a very senior person in the administration," by which I took her to mean the president. Barbara said I would receive a "title" and "perks" if only I would give up the fight. It was the same proposition that Madeleine Albright had made to me earlier but delivered far more persuasively and by someone genuinely friendly to me. I thanked Barbara but said that I had no choice; the nondemocratic character of the U.S. effort against me simply required me to stand against it. The integrity of the office of secretary-general and of the United Nations itself was involved. A few days later a warm and deeply apologetic note arrived. Barbara was embarrassed and ashamed to have been put into this role. "Dear Boutros," she wrote, "I hope you understand that in my telephone call I was only a messenger. I want for you only what *you* feel is best. Whatever that is, is the right thing."

On November 22, before a large audience attending a UN conference dealing with the international impact of television, Ted Turner, the media magnate, suddenly launched into an impassioned speech in praise of me. The audience burst into applause. Turner said that he was revolted by Washington's refusal to pay what it owed the United Nations and that he was considering "buying up" the U.S. debt. Ted Turner had long been an enthusiastic supporter of mine. He told me that he had asked the CNN staff to convey "a positive image of Boutros-Ghali" but that they wouldn't listen to him. And rightly so, I felt.

The Security Council met late in the day on November 25. No one spoke but the African members. There was no need for another vote, they said. Boutros-Ghali is the only African candidate. When the meeting ended, a reporter asked, "When will there be another vote?" Ambassador Legwaila of Botswana answered, "When we have fifteen votes for Boutros-Ghali!" But the Africans were in a painful position. The Clinton administration was not only threatening to deprive Africa of a second secretary-general term but also saying that continued support for me was sending a message to the world that no black African was qualified to be secretary-general. I wondered how long Africa could stand this.

Instructions had gone out to all American ambassadors to press foreign governments to oppose me. In a press conference on November 28, 1996, the Greek foreign minister revealed that the United States wanted Greece to drop its support for me. Greece does not take orders from any foreign power, the foreign minister said and denounced U.S. "intervention, suzerainty, and instructions."

As December began, the African position began to waver. Even as the United States continued to profess a willingness to see any African other than me as secretary-general, it encouraged Ghana to begin openly to promote the U.S. choice, Kofi Annan. Propaganda-like materials attacking me suddenly appeared in the corridors of the United Nations. The president of Cameroon, Paul Biya, then serving as president of the OAU, sent a letter to all African leaders reconfirming that the OAU summit at Yaoundé had recommended me as its candidate for a second five-year mandate for Africa in the secretary-generalship of the United Nations. But, the letter stated, "These steps could not bear fruit because of the veto of one of the Permanent Members of the Security Council." Thus the letter invited "African States who so wish it, [to] present other qualified candidacies, in addition to the candidacy of Dr. Boutros Boutros-Ghali." From my point of view, if the OAU could agree on another African, that was fine; if it could not, attention might return to an extension of my term as a sensible compromise.

But Biya's letter was trumpeted by the U.S. Mission as the sign of a turnaround.

AFRICAN OFFICIALS END UNITY
ON UN TOP JOB

was the *New York Times* page-one headline on December 3, 1996. Then came a wire service story (Reuters, December 3, 1996) datelined Tunis. President Mubarak was quoted as saying that he had done all that he could for me: "The issue is now over, and if Boutros-Ghali wants to maintain his candidacy, it is up to him." *The New York Times* replayed the Reuters story under the headline EGYPT ENDING ITS EFFORTS ON UN CHIEF'S BEHALF.

I telephoned President Mubarak, who firmly declared that Egypt would continue to support me. I asked if I could publicly say I continued to have his support. "Yes," he said, "I was misquoted."

Still the Africans did not break. "African envoys rallied behind Boutros-Ghali" *The Wall Street Journal* reported on December 4, 1996. A spokesman for the Africans on the Security Council said that they "have no intention of naming alternatives to the Egyptian's candidacy." Ambassador Fulci, speaking as president of the Security Council, told reporters that not one additional name had come forward.

Madeleine Albright was now openly attacking me with every weapon from hints of scandal to slurs. "He can't even pronounce 'United Nations,'" she told Barbara Crossette. (In truth, I sometimes drop the "s.") In a more sinister vein, Albright began to tell people that the United States "has something on him," trying to fuel speculation that it had uncovered some wrongdoing in my past. This smear led Congressman Rangel to write to Secretary Christopher, "I have discussed this matter with many senior officials, and I understand that the Secretary-General had never done anything to undermine the national security of the United States. Nor has he been accused of any deficiencies of character or malfeasance of any kind. And no one can deny that he has done more than any previous Secretary-General to streamline operations at the United Nations."

Madeleine Albright's behavior made it all the more important that I continue my candidacy until the end, no matter what happened. But at the same time, I began to gather my thoughts for what I would say in my "farewell address."

Then, at a moment when my guard was down, the situation became fatefully confused. On Wednesday, December 4, Ambassador Fulci telephoned me to convey his view that the Security Council should discuss whatever other African names might come forward. Our conversation was conducted in French. Yes, I said, of course, that is only proper.

After we hung up, Fulci, at a noon press conference, declared that I had "suspended" my candidacy. In French and also in English the word means a provisional hiatus, or interruption. But the American media immediately took it to mean that I had dropped out or removed my name from consideration. The evening television news opened with the statement, unelaborated, that "Secretary-General Boutros Boutros-Ghali has suspended his candidacy for a second term," and commentary indicated that I had withdrawn entirely. I telephoned Fulci at once. What he had intended to convey, he said, was that there would not be another vote for Boutros-Ghali for the time being; that no other African names had come forward; and that the Security Council would meet again on Friday to consider any such names that might be advanced.

The media were portraying this as Boutros-Ghali's capitulation. "Have you resigned?" was the question asked me in a barrage of telephone calls.

Madeleine Albright immediately got to the press to declare that this was the "breakthrough" the United States had sought. U.S. officials were "dancing on air," my press spokeswoman told me. "Fulci did this deliberately," she said. I disagreed. I drafted a press statement: "Press reports that I have suspended my candidacy are incorrect. I remain a candidate, recommended by the Organization of African Unity, for a second term as Secretary-General of the United Nations. The President of the Security Council joins me in this clarification." But the truth is that once a mischaracterization is out, the facts never catch up if the media are not on your side.

I wanted to give my statement to the UN press office so that it could get it out to the media that night. But when the French ambassador, Dejammet, heard of this, he urged that I do nothing more. To issue a statement would be "overkill," he said. President Chirac had seen Vice President Gore in Lisbon and urged in the strongest terms that the United States change course. I let myself be talked out of trying to clarify the matter. But the damage was done. Other names now would flow forward.

The next morning, December 5, 1996, *The New York Times* headlined on page one:

UN LEADER HALTS BID FOR NEW TERM

BUT DOES NOT QUIT

A U.S. OFFER IS SPURNED

BOUTROS-GHALI STAYS AVAILABLE BUT MAKES

HIS FIRST MOVE TOWARD A WITHDRAWAL

"Reports began to emerge of a strange last-minute, face-saving effort by the Clinton Administration to lure him into leaving office by offering to make him head of an international foundation, and give him a title of Secretary-General Emeritus. Diplomats familiar with the overture said Mr. Boutros-Ghali rejected it," and aides to the secretary-general called the U.S. deal "ludicrous."

"An American official remarked," the *Times* reported, that "hostility toward the United States has never been so palpable, as diplomats around the world watched the Clinton Administration attack Mr. Boutros-Ghali's record with dwindling credibility. . . . Until Mr. Boutros-Ghali was judged a potential political liability in an American election year, Administration officials had no serious complaints about his relations with Washington."

That same day, *The Wall Street Journal* noted, "Africans stayed loyal to the Egyptian even after they were released from a pledge to support him, threatening a standoff as a decision deadline looms." But the corridors were abuzz with names, most prominently those of Kofi Annan of Ghana, Hamid Algabid of Niger, Amara Essy of Côte d'Ivoire, and Ahmedou Ould Abdallah, my former special representative to Burundi who had appeared at Yaoundé to lobby against me.

Also on that day, President Clinton named Madeleine Albright his new secretary of state. I received a telephone call from Egyptian Foreign Minister Amr Moussa in Cairo: "This means it is over," he said. I agreed. Albright could not be secretary of state and fail to defeat me. "What is Boutros-Ghali's reaction?" my press spokeswoman was asked. "He is delighted for his dear friend Madeleine Albright, with whom he has always had warm and cordial relations" was the reply.

Last-Ditch Try

I had three options. I could do nothing and thereby simply await my "execution" by the Security Council. I could "commit suicide" by announcing at once that I was finished. Or I could continue to fight and thereby force the Council to "assassinate" me. I decided on the third option.

Albright's nomination was the banner headline in the newspapers the next morning. Barbara Crossette wrote that at the United Nations we had seen two Madeleine Albrights. The first was passionate for "assertive multilateralism," wanted to bomb Bosnia, arrest war criminals, and stop genocidal wars. Then, after the Republican victory in the 1994 midterm election, Albright had seemed to pull back. "She led a campaign to ditch Secretary-General Boutros Boutros-Ghali who, in 1994, she had said she could 'really admire.'" Before the United States "got bogged down in a less-than-diplomatic campaign to force Secretary-General Boutros-Ghali out of office and feelings ran strongly against Washington for its handling of the affair, Ms. Albright seemed to enjoy her job immensely."

The Egyptian ambassador to the United Nations, Nabil Elaraby, came to me to report that the Security Council was "in awe" of Albright now that she had been elevated by Clinton. He and many others now strongly urged me to "step down with dignity" before the Security Council's next meeting. It will all be over in a few days, Elaraby said.

The U.S. drive against me had compiled a record of insults to Africa: the effort to dictate the OAU resolution; the refusal to accept that resolution; the claim that any African was acceptable while the United States had, long before, chosen Kofi Annan; Christopher's eleventh-hour trip to Africa; the threats that unless the Africans accepted the U.S. decision, they would be punished by the loss of the secretary-generalship; and, most recently, the ugly comments that Africa's backing for me suggested that no black African was qualified for the job. This last argument was being particularly pushed by British diplomats in a kind of division of labor between the United States and the United Kingdom at the United Nations.

All this led Sir Brian Urquhart, the distinguished former UN official, to write in *The Washington Post* an op-ed piece arguing that the election had been so poorly conducted that more time should be given so that Africa could be allowed to produce its candidate in a rational process.

Madeleine Albright returned to New York in triumph. A December 7 *New York Times* photograph showed her arrival at the U.S. Mission, rushing to embrace her deputy, Edward Gnehm. "You have to give her credit for uniting the world—185 members against the United States" was the quote from an African diplomat in the accompanying article. Yet the American media were impressed by her success. A panelist on a CNN weekend program said in admiration, "You don't mess with her—as Boutros Boutros-Ghali found out!"

Kofi Annan's name now rose to the top of the list of five Africans. The president of Ghana, Jerry Rawlings, circulated a letter, obviously coordinated with Washington, stating that Annan's selection "would be well-received by the United States." Amazingly, some major foreign leaders still backed me and tried to reach President Clinton by telephone to urge him to change course. President Nelson Mandela of South Africa told me he had tried repeatedly to get through but that Clinton would not accept his calls.

"Oil for Food" Once More

On Monday, December 9, 1996, I informed the Security Council that, in accordance with paragraph 3 of Resolution 986, the "Oil for Food" formula would take effect at one minute past midnight, New York time. Saddam Hussein would celebrate a victory, as Iraqi oil would once again flow in the pipelines. Washington was relaxed; the American election was over. An expert at probing the ambiguities, Saddam had, with his military operation against the Kurds in northern Iraq, found precisely the point that would create differences of opinion within the international community. His move was just outside the coverage of the Security Council resolutions but just inside the line where the United States would have to react or lose face. What had happened was that Clinton had both reacted and lost face in the context of world politics, if not in what mattered more to him, American domestic politics. For Saddam it was a "good crime" and well worth the effort. He had strengthened his position in Iraq's northern provinces, and he had fractured the U.S.-led coalition that had held together since 1991. The southern air defenses hit by the U.S. cruise missiles would be easy to rebuild. The next test would be whether he could turn "Oil for Food" to his benefit or whether the United Nations would be able to ensure that it truly served the suffering people of Iraq. I prayed that the latter would be the case, but I fully expected Saddam Hussein to undermine the "Oil for Food" effort because he felt it might impair his major goal of getting sanctions lifted altogether.

Voting—But Not on Boutros-Ghali

The Security Council met on Tuesday, December 10, to vote on the African candidates. I was still a candidate, but my name would not be considered. The point was to see whether anyone other than Boutros-Ghali could win such a vote.

Fulci announced the results: Hamid Algabid, 5 for, 4 against (including two permanent members); Kofi Annan, 10 for, 4 against (including one permanent member); Amara Essy, 7 for, 4 against (including two permanent members); Ahmedou Ould Abdallah, 3 for, 7 against (including two permanent members). Only Annan had secured the nine positive votes required for a resolution to be adopted, but it could not be adopted because of the veto of a permanent member. This was a semisecret ballot. How each member voted was not known, but the permanent members' ballots were a different color, so if one or more of them voted no, it would be clear to all that the resolution had been vetoed. "Perhaps the time has come to return to the Secretary-General as a compromise," the Russian representative said. "I am in a better position today than before to tell you that won't happen," Albright replied, referring to her new status as secretary of state. This should have given her an aura of invincibility, but still there was uncertainty in the Council, so I persisted.

The release of Security Council balloting infuriated both the French and the Africans, because it revealed that the United States and Britain had agreed to "double-veto" all Africans except Kofi Annan. This was taken as a wholly unnecessary insult to Africa. It also isolated the French as the only power ready to veto Annan. It asserted to the world that the only acceptable African was America's and Britain's African. The United States quickly dominated the media battlefield, telling reporters that the French had vetoed "out of pique" and that France should be embarrassed to stand in the way of a candidate (Kofi Annan) "who clearly has majority support." Observers noted that the United States had revealed no such deference to majority rule when I had had 14 votes to the United States' single veto.

When this session was over, a heated discussion arose among African representatives. The three Africans on the Security Council—from Guinea-Bissau, Botswana, and Egypt—were put under enormous pressure. Boutros-Ghali had no chance, they were told; the United States will never give up. So Egypt should change its position. Egypt owed it to Africa not to lose the secretary-generalship. If Egypt did not relent, the United States would deny the top post to any African.

On December 11 the Council deadlocked again. There were four straw polls, each exactly like the one the day before. The Egyptian ambassador, Nabil Elaraby, told me that Egypt was still holding firm.

French-U.S. antagonism was at a peak. The press reported that at a NATO farewell luncheon for Secretary of State Warren Christopher,

French Foreign Minister Hervé de Charrette had walked out rather than join in the toast to Christopher. U.S. officials called it "an incredible display of petulant behavior"; a French spokesman replied that the story was "an ill-intentioned lie" intended to embarrass France. De Charrette had never walked out; the United States had manipulated the media.

On Thursday, December 12, the straw poll was 14 for Kofi Annan and 1 against, with France casting the veto. That evening our contacts in the State Department said the White House was frustrated. Albright had not yet made the kill. She should now be in Washington, making her calls on Capitol Hill and studying for her confirmation hearings. Instead, there she was at the United Nations, still fixated on the issue that had dominated her life for months: my elimination. Concern was mounting that Albright might be held hostage at the United Nations by this business.

I felt that if the line could be held in the Security Council on Friday and the matter carried over to the next week, the U.S. juggernaut might come to a halt, because the next Tuesday, December 17, was the date set for the end of the General Assembly session. If I could get through Friday, time might start to work in my favor.

Early the next morning, a rainy Friday the thirteenth, all reports were that the French would hold firm. At 12:30 the Security Council met and held another straw poll. Egypt again voted for all the African candidates. But this was only a straw poll; there would have to be a formal vote. The scene in the Council at that point was bizarre. China wanted to hold the formal vote over until Monday. The prospect of losing more time agitated the United States and Britain greatly. To lock in the straw vote count, the British ambassador, John Weston, grinning and breathless, rushed out to convey it to the press. Ambassador Fulci was furious at this affront to his presidential role.

Dejammet telephoned me. France would lift its veto. Chirac, in Dublin, had communicated his decision. France could not continue to stand alone. Dejammet urged that I draft a concession statement before the next official vote, which would take place in a few hours. I would perhaps want to say, Dejammet advised me, that in the interests of the Security Council and the organization as a whole, I hoped that the vote (for Kofi Annan) would be unanimous.

I sat at my desk and listened while my staff argued vigorously about whether I should issue such a statement. "It is the right thing to do, for your own reputation and dignity," one said. "It would be an elegant bow to the inevitable." "No," said the other, "You have been fighting all along against a superpower-imposed choice for secretary-general, and you must not give in now. The Security Council members know that they have surrendered to an American demand; they hope that you will lift their burden of guilt by asking them to vote for the U.S. candidate. Don't give them that pleasure."

I had already decided to force them to "assassinate" me, and I would stay with this course of action. Before the final, formal vote, Madeleine Albright made a statement to the press. She was delighted with the outcome, she said. As for Boutros-Ghali, he is "a renowned international statesman and he has earned his place in history."

After the vote I asked my spokeswoman to put out the following statement:

> The Secretary-General warmly congratulates Kofi Annan of Ghana on receiving the recommendation of the Security Council to become the next Secretary-General of the United Nations. The Secretary-General is gratified that the decision was unanimous and is especially gratified that Africa has been able to maintain the office of Secretary-General for a second five-year term, the objective which the Secretary-General has sought throughout these recent months. The Secretary-General has worked closely with Mr. Annan through these past five years and wishes him every success. The Secretary-General expresses his deepest thanks for the strong support and encouragement given him throughout the past five years by the Member States and peoples of the United Nations.

Later that day, when one of my closest colleagues was leaving work, he overheard two women staff members in the elevator:

> "Are you happy?"
> "Oh, yes, it's wonderful."
> "Don't you think it's the best result?"
> "Yes, but it will be hard for [Kofi Annan]; the Americans will put so much pressure on him."
> "Yes, but it's really good."

Many among the UN staff did indeed favor this outcome. They could look forward to quieter, less controversial times. Others saw an increasingly marginalized United Nations either ignored by, or operating almost entirely under the instructions of, Washington. As *The Economist* put it, the Clinton administration "has cravenly pandered to the numberless demagogues and lunatics among its electorate who say the United Nations is responsible for every ill that affects the planet—and since many of them also believe in aliens, probably for every ill that affects the solar system. In America Mr. Boutros-Ghali has become a hate figure for nutters and right-wingers." With my departure, then, the United Nations would be less of a target and less of a scapegoat for the United States. But I feared that it also was likely to become less in every regard. A perhaps not unintentional indicator came in *The New York Times* under the headline CAST OF CHARACTERS IS SET FOR CLINTON'S SECOND TERM. At the end of the roster of Clinton's personal choices, Kofi Annan was listed as "another key appointment" of the administration, as though he would be joining the president's cabinet. *The Wall Street Journal* followed up with an editorial instructing Kofi Annan to take his lead from Senator Jesse Helms.

All that remained now was the pro forma approval of the General Assembly for what the Security Council had done. Later on December 13 the Security Council and the General Assembly both adopted by acclamation resolutions paying tribute to me. The actual appointment of the new secretary-general took place on the last day of the General Assembly session. My farewell remarks focused on three themes: First, the United Nations had been tested in the crucible of post–cold war confrontations. Second, there was no justification for the failure of the United States to pay its debt: "now that a new Secretary-General is being appointed, all arrears should be paid at once, as has been promised so often in the past few months." And third, I spoke of the integrity and independence that are so vital to the role of the secretary-general. "If one word is to characterize the role of the secretary-general, it is independence," I said. And now that the United States has vetoed me, I said, there remains no excuse for it not to pay its dues to the United Nations fully and immediately, as it promised.

The New York Times reported that "the General Assembly hailed the outgoing leader with a standing ovation, then formally appointed Kofi Annan of the West African country of Ghana as his successor."

Dinner with Madeleine

Madeleine Albright accepted my invitation to dine together a final time the day after my farewell to the General Assembly. She arrived precisely at eight o'clock, wearing an elegant blue dress and carrying a wrapped parcel containing one of those State Department souvenirs for foreign dignitaries.

I received her in the library, the Great Room being full of crates of books and documents bound for Cairo. The library was empty, almost embarrassingly naked. The beautiful Moroccan-period Matisse had been returned to the museum, and my collections of antique birds and pen cases were already in boxes.

"Look how thin I've become because of the fight I've been in during the last six months," I said to Madeleine.

"Me as well, I lost kilos," said Madeleine Albright, straightening up to display her figure. José, the majordomo, interrupted to ask what we would like to drink.

Madeleine did not mince words: "Your speech yesterday was nasty."

"Nasty? I received a standing ovation that lasted for minutes. And I didn't even mention the United States!"

She contented herself with repeating, "The speech was nasty."

I changed the subject. "Now that you occupy the post of secretary of state and you have succeeded in eliminating me and in having your candidate elected in my place, tell me, as a friend, what was the real reason the U.S. waged war against me?"

She gave me a friendly smile. "I have not been confirmed by the Senate, and I am very superstitious. Nothing is definite yet."

"In any event, explain to me why your administration was so hysterically opposed to my reelection."

"You didn't ask at the outset for more than a single mandate," she said, referring to the five-year term of office of the UN secretary-general. "The United States voted for you on that basis."

"You are misinformed," I said. "The United States did not vote in favor of my election in 1991. The U.S. abstained. It was never a question of one or two mandates. Ask Ambassador Pickering, who was your predecessor as U.S. representative to the UN."

"You symbolize the United Nations, and the American Congress is hostile to the United Nations. You are also blamed for trying to control American military power. You used the 'dual key' to oppose NATO air strikes against the Serbs. Your stance was very badly perceived by military circles in Washington."

"But you know very well the decisions were made by the French and British generals who were there in the field, officers from your own NATO allies. The United Nations did nothing more than respect their recommendations. They were the experts. They were responsible for the lives of their troops."

"I know, and I defended you to the Congress, but the perception was that you wanted to control the American military."

"There were personal reasons for your decision?"

"No. It was an irrevocable decision made by the president."

It was useless to pursue the subject. She had no intention of telling me the truth behind Washington's decision. I changed the subject again.

"Madeleine, if I am the 'ugly Egyptian' for Washington, you are the 'ugly American' for the Arab world. There is a shocking article in *Al-Ahram*, which denounces you for leading the campaign to deny a second term to an Arab secretary-general, the only region to be treated this way in UN history. The newspaper claims that the new Clinton administration is dominated by Jews. There is a mood of anti-Semitism in the Arab world that reminds me, unfortunately, of the time of Sadat's visit to Jerusalem."

"I am not Jewish, Boutros. I am a born Catholic."

"You know very well, Madeleine, that for me one's religion doesn't matter. But the opinions of the Arab world have to concern you, because you will be dealing with Middle East issues in your new job."

"I count on you, Boutros, to help me. You come from the Arab world, you know it well, and you will be able to advise me. I will always have need of your good advice."

I suddenly remembered the formula one invariably uses upon the retirement of a diplomatic colleague: "I will always have need of your advice." It seemed that this was a universal style of dismissal . . . "I will always have need of your advice."

Our discussion was interrupted by the entrance of Leia to say that dinner was served. I went to look for the issue of *Al-Ahram* so as to show the future secretary of state the amount of space given in the paper to the anti-Semitic article. The three of us shared a pleasant dinner. Madeleine evoked the art of being a grandmother, helped herself cautiously to the fish, and barely sipped the excellent 1993 Château Margaux Pavillon blanc that I had opened in her honor.

After dinner she seemed eager to leave us. She had accomplished her diplomatic mission with skill. She had carried out her campaign with determination, letting pass no opportunity to demolish my authority and tarnish my image, all the while showing a serene face, wearing a friendly smile, and repeating expressions of friendship and admiration. I recalled what a Hindu scholar once said to me: there is no difference between diplomacy and deception.

Closing Out

As the end of my days at the United Nations drew near, I hastened to finish my Agenda for Democratization in as polished a form as possible. Again I consulted my staff. They remained divided between those adamantly declaring I had no authorization to produce such a report and those who tried to use their bureaucratic wiles to get me to rewrite the text entirely, something I had neither the time nor the inclination to do. Privately I sent a draft to the financier and philanthropist George Soros, who had been promoting democratization in the former Communist-bloc countries of Central Europe. Soros replied that my draft was of no value because the United Nations has no role in democratization and is not itself a democratic institution. I determined to proceed nonetheless. I would barely have time to get my report into the UN system before the General Assembly session closed down. On the final day I sent a letter to Razali Ismail of Malaysia, the president of the General Assembly, detailing the chain of authority that in my view justified my production of such a report. "I should be grateful if you could circulate this text as a document of the fifty-first General Assembly," I wrote, and my report, to which I had given only the title "Supplement," was so distributed. I then asked the UN Department of Public Information to print it in a blue booklet format, just like *An Agenda for Peace,* and to call it *An Agenda for Democratization.*

With my departure from the United Nations, this, my swan song, disappeared from sight. Soon all copies were gone. As a scholarly book on the United Nations later noted, "In December 1996, with barely any mandate, Boutros-Ghali issued 'An Agenda for Democratization' as a supplement to two previous—and minor—reports on operational activities in democratization. This last agenda is by far the most comprehensive and controversial of the three, yet, issued at the close of Boutros-Ghali's term, it has received little attention." *

I left New York early on New Year's Day, January 1, 1997. At the airport to see me off were my chief of staff, Jean-Claude Aimé, and his wife, Lisa Buttenheim, a UN official. There too were Joseph Verner Reed; Benon Sevan, assistant secretary-general; and Ambassador Fulci and his wife. I said to Fulci, "It is now January; your presidency of the Security Council came to an end yesterday; you therefore have no protocol duties to perform today. Why are you here?" "I am here as a friend," he said. As the plane climbed to cruising altitude, Leia said that the past six months had been an exciting nightmare. I was barely listening. With my UN service over, my scholar's habits had already resumed, and I was analyzing for myself the meaning of the past five years.

* Sydney D. Bailey and Sam Daws, *The Procedure of the United Nations Security Council*, 3d ed. (New York: Oxford University Press, 1997).

Afterword

This book has been about the loss of an opportunity to construct an agreed-upon post–cold war structure for international peace and security.

The end of every major conflict in modern times has presented the world's nations with the task of reconstructing a system of relations that offers stability, cooperation, and the possibility of progress.

In the past the job of constructing a postwar system of revitalized international relations generally was completed within five to seven years. The Congress of Vienna, which followed the Napoleonic wars, led to a hundred years of relief from major conflict in Europe. The Treaty of Versailles and the creation of the League of Nations after the First World War were so flawed that they engendered another world conflict within the space of a generation.

After the Second World War, the American-led attempt to devise a stable, just, and cooperative international order centered on the creation, in San Francisco in 1945, of the United Nations. As a young man I watched that moment with awe and admiration, and I have passionately believed in the United Nations ever since. The United Nations offered an opportunity to achieve what humanity has sought since civilization began: a means for all people to reason together, to search for common ways to maintain security, and to act together to deliver mercy, defend freedom, and pursue justice and progress for a better life ahead. But the period of enthusiasm and hope that followed the United Nations' creation in 1945 ended with the opening of the cold war.

Following the end of the cold war, it was the fate of the United Nations—and mine as secretary-general—to be deeply involved in the effort to create a post–cold war structure and to do so with the United

States, the sole remaining superpower of the conflict. But instead of producing a new international partnership to face the twenty-first century, the United Nations emerged from these years seriously damaged, despite some success. A post–cold war international system remains unbuilt, and the post–cold war period has passed, bracketed at start and finish by dramatic events of significance to relations between the United Nations and the United States. The U.S.-led coalition that forced the Iraqi Army out of Kuwait was formed under the authorization of the Security Council, and an unprecedented series of UN resolutions subsequently shaped the world's approach to issues created by that war. At the other end of this period, in late 1995, the U.S.-led negotiations at Dayton, Ohio, on an agreement aimed at achieving a unified, multicommunal state for Bosnia pointedly excluded the United Nations.

During these years a pattern was repeated on major issues involving key member states and the secretary-general. They would call on me to carry out reforms, knowing that I lacked the authority to do so, just as they would call on the United Nations to bring conflict to an end but fail to provide the forces and mandates required. They expected the United Nations to carry out vastly enlarged responsibilities while they allowed the financial crisis to deepen.

Throughout the first half of the decade, many critical international challenges required the closest interaction between the United Nations and the United States. When the United Nations was allowed to do its job without substantial U.S. involvement, as in Mozambique, the operation succeeded. When the United States felt a political need for the United Nations, as in Haiti, the operation also fulfilled its main objective. But when the United States wanted to appear actively involved while in reality avoiding hard decisions, as in Bosnia, Somalia, and Rwanda, the United Nations was misused, abused, or blamed by the United States, and the operations failed, tragically and horribly.

It was said during my UN years that I was "pro–third world," and this was often taken to mean "anti-West." I am of the third world, without doubt, but I am also pro-West; my education, my publications, my official positions over the decades should demonstrate this clearly. But I continue to believe that any secretary-general, from whatever region of the world, must advocate the cause of the developing countries. In a world of many big and wealthy powers, it is the United Nations' job to look out for those marginalized because of ethnicity, gender, religion, age, health, poverty, or whatever other reason. And this duty extends to neglected or ignored situations of warfare, such as in Africa, where violence often exceeds levels experienced in conflicts receiving major attention from the international community and the media, such as in the Balkans and the Middle East. Throughout the United Nations' half century of existence, the great majority of the problems it has tackled have been third world–related. For as far ahead as we can see, the United Nations must continue to be the main voice for the weakest and least regarded peoples, to defend them from the detrimental effects of globalization, and to help them find ways to succeed in a global economy.

Single-superpower hegemony is a transitory phenomenon, but globalization is an irreversible force on a scale heretofore unseen. There are many different globalizations: in capital flows, business, technology, information, environmental changes, drug trafficking, crime, terrorism. Each globalization has its own rhythm and pace and presents its own problems. In many ways, the only truly global mechanism for addressing them is the United Nations.

The dream of the founders of the United Nations was not only that the organization be used as it was envisioned in San Francisco in 1945 but also that it prove capable of transforming itself to engage effectively a world that must and will change in unforeseen ways. I believe that such a transformation is still possible and will succeed—if the United States allows it to do so.

Index

China, People's Republic of:
internal issues vs. international
concerns and, 25
Iraq sanctions as viewed by, 210, 260
political dissidents from, 141,
168–69, 309
secretary-general election and, 222,
285, 286, 314, 316–17, 329
Tibetan claims of, 25, 170–71
U.S. relations with, 285, 292
women's conference in, 175
Chirac, Jacques, 178–79
Boutros-Ghali's reelection promoted
by, 270, 271–72, 277, 287,
293–94, 308–9, 316, 317, 324,
329
Chrétien, Jean, 277, 278, 316
Christopher, Warren, 67, 169, 231
African nations visited by, 304–8,
326
Arab-Israeli conflicts and, 195–96,
197–98, 263
on Bosnian policy, 69–71, 85, 88–90,
91, 142, 145, 215, 245, 247–48
congressional relations with, 99,
121–22
diplomatic style of, 68, 119, 120,
122, 125, 137, 277, 313
on Haiti policies, 119, 151
on multilateral responses, 115
retirement of, 305, 313, 328–29
on secretary-general election, 5–7,
261, 264, 266, 268–73, 282,
290–91, 292, 302, 305–8, 318,
323, 326
on Somalia, 99–102, 103, 105, 110,
116, 118–20, 123
successor to, 216, 304, 316
on UN funds, 98–99
CIA, 110, 119, 305–6
CIS (Commonwealth of Independent
States), 264–65
Claes, Willy, 237, 240–41, 246
Clerides, Glafcos, 292
Clinton, Bill, 174, 232
Boutros-Ghali's meetings with,
71–72, 102, 125, 137–38, 231,
253–54, 277, 299–300

media criticism of, 117, 118
in presidential elections, 28–29, 220,
267, 273–74, 275, 284, 286,
288–89, 291, 293–95, 300, 302,
308, 312–13, 316
UN funding and, 249, 302
on UN troop deployment, 28–29,
114–15, 124, 134, 135
Clinton, Hillary Rodham, 172
Clinton administration:
Africa initiatives of, 179, 304–8, 326
on Arab-Israeli concerns, 193,
194–99, 203–4, 205, 261–64, 277
Bosnia policies of, 68–78, 84–85,
87–92, 114, 115, 142, 143–45,
214–17, 234, 235, 240, 241,
244–45, 247, 256–57, 268,
284–85, 316
on Haiti, 119, 149, 150–56, 218,
219
Iraq sanctions and, 260, 267, 297,
327
on North Korean nuclear power, 129
Russian relations with, 265–66
Somalia policies of, 92–107, 114,
118–24
UN appointments and, 66, 67,
137–38, 227–31, 288
on UN leadership, 5–7, 254, 261,
264, 266–95, 297–334
CNN, 321
Cohen, Elliott, 142
Cohen, Herman (Hank), 279
Collor de Mello, Fernando, 164, 165
Commonwealth of Independent States
(CIS), 264–65
Congress, U.S.:
Boutros-Ghali's relations with, 4,
120, 121–22, 169, 255–56,
311–12, 318
UN policies of, 21, 99, 102, 229,
232, 249, 268, 275–76, 290–91,
294–95, 302, 332–33
Congressional Black Caucus, 150,
289–90, 298, 310
Connor, Joseph, 137, 270, 278, 288
Coptic Orthodox Church, 314
Corell, Hans, 225, 259, 266, 267

BOUTROS BOUTROS-GHALI was secretary-general of the United Nations from 1991 to 1996. As Egypt's minister of state for foreign affairs, he was a chief participant at the meetings that culminated in the Camp David accords between Egypt and Israel. Dr. Boutros-Ghali received his doctorate from the University of Paris. A distinguished academic, active in many international associations, he has written a number of books on Egyptian and international politics and has contributed to many journals. He has been a member of the Faculty of Political Science at Cairo University and of the Parliament of Egypt. He now serves as secretary-general of the International Organization of the Francophonie, an association of fifty-two countries sharing a political, social, and cultural solidarity around the French language.

ABOUT THE TYPE

This book was set in Fairfield, the first typeface from the hand of the distinguished American artist and engraver Rudolph Ruzicka (1883–1978). Rudolph Ruzicka was born in Bohemia and came to America in 1894. He set up his own shop, devoted to wood engraving and printing, in New York in 1913 after a varied career working as a wood engraver, in photoengraving and banknote printing plants, and as an art director and freelance artist. He designed and illustrated many books, and was the creator of a considerable list of individual prints—wood engravings, line engravings on copper, and aquatints.